D0501846

Scandinavia since 1500

Scandinavia since 1500

Byron J. Nordstrom

 University of Minnesota Press ~~~ Minneapolis ~~~ London

Published by the University of Minnesota Press
111 Third Avenue South, Suite 290
Minneapolis, MN 55401-2520
http://www.upress.umn.edu

Printed in the United States of America on acid-free paper

The University of Minnesota is an equal-opportunity educator and employer.

Library of Congress Cataloging-in-Publication Data
Nordstrom, Byron J.
　　Scandinavia since 1500 / Byron J. Nordstrom.
　　　　p.　cm.
　　Includes bibliographical references and index.
　　ISBN 0-8166-2098-9 (acid-free paper)—ISBN 0-8166-2099-7 (pbk : acid-free paper)
　　1. Scandinavia—History.　2. Finland—History.　I. Title.
DL46.N7 2000
　　948—dc21　　　　　　　　　　　　　　　　99-089029

11　10　09　08　07　06　05　04　03　02　01　00
10　9　8　7　6　5　4　3　2　1

In memory of Stewart P. Oakley, 1931–1995

Contents

Maps

Preface

I n many ways this is a very traditional history. I accept the idea that we can talk and write about a conceptual region called Scandinavia that includes Denmark, the Faeroe Islands, Iceland, Norway, Sweden, and Finland. I believe there is sufficient commonality in languages (except for Finnish and Sami), cultures, and shared pasts on which to base a history that is not simply manufactured to satisfy some personal or political agenda. (One can, of course, with equal legitimacy, also approach each unit within this region as unique and separate.) The chronology, in which the long "modern" period from 1500 is subdivided into the Renaissance, early modern, modern, and contemporary, follows a well-established European model. This periodization works reasonably well in terms of political history. It is less useful if other approaches are emphasized, such as social history, for which there might be only two periods (medieval and modern), or women's history, for which one might argue there is one long period extending from the Middle Ages or before down to the nineteenth century, at which point sufficient changes began to take place to justify demarking a new era. The structure is built around the states/nations of the region; and politics and international relations receive considerable attention. At the same time, I have tried to include economic, social, and cultural developments; to provide some degree of gender balance; to introduce some of the interpretive debates; and to avoid making heroes of individuals or perfect little worlds of the Nordic countries.

In terms of explaining why things happened, I prefer a multicausal approach. Large factors like geography, resources bases, and climate provide the fundamental environment. Internal and external factors including individuals, social groups, economic conditions, ideas, technologies, and accidents are just some of the determiners of events. I am also not a determinist; I believe the history of Scandinavia and of the

～～～～～～～～～～～～～～～～～～～～～～～～～～～～

Norden

Several words are used as labels for the region that today includes Denmark, the Faeroe Islands, Finland, Iceland, Norway, and Sweden. The one most often used outside the area, *Scandinavia,* derives from the Roman geographer Pliny the Elder (A.D. 23–79), who in his *Naturalis historia* described an area in the north he referred to as *scadinauia.* Exactly what part of the region he was describing is unclear, but his Scandinavia was based on secondhand information and probably did not extend beyond Denmark and southern Sweden. The label *Scadinauia* may have been of Germanic origins or a garbled latinization of Skåne. One interpretation is that the first *n* in Scandinavia was the result of a medieval copying error.

From a number of perspectives, *Scandinavia* is a restrictive expression. Geologically, Denmark is part of the northern German plain; Norway, Sweden, and Finland form the Fenno-Scandian Shield. Iceland lies astride the mid-Atlantic rift. Linguistically, all the languages of the region are related except Finnish and Sami. Culturally, there are similarities (and differences) across the area. The state histories may be written separately or as a unit.

Norden, the north, is more inclusive and is used more often by the peoples of the region. Today it is embodied in the names of organizations such as the Nordic Council or in *Projektet Nordens Historia, 1397–1997* (Nordic history project), a multinational effort to describe and define inter-Nordic historical developments.

～～～～～～～～～～～～～～～～～～～～～～～～～～～～

individual states in the region could have taken very different courses—courses impossible to affirm but always interesting to contemplate.

There are several themes, many of which are not unique to Scandinavian history, that I have tried to address at various points throughout this text. One is the frequency with which historical accounts of events or personalities become canon, fundamental and unquestioned pieces of a personal, cultural, or national identity. For example, uncritical assessments of individuals such as Gustav II Adolf (Gustavus Adolphus) of Sweden, Christian IV of Denmark, or Christian Frederik, the

Danish prince who played a central role in the attempts to establish Norway's independence in 1814, have been incorporated into the national historical mythologies of Sweden, Denmark, and Norway, respectively; and establishing the truth of their roles and importance has often been difficult. Similar problems exist in the treatments of topics like the resistance movements in World War II or the Scandinavian welfare states. Conversely, there is the problem of what has been played down or ignored in many histories. Although the Nordic countries are today among the most affluent, just, humane, and democratic in the world, there are dark sides to their histories and to contemporary conditions. For example, early modern governments and nobilities exploited the lower classes; women were long regarded as nonpersons, often denigrated and abused; the region had its share of witch-hunts; legal punishments were cruel and inhumane; Denmark participated in the slave trade; alcoholism has long been a serious social problem; a few got very rich during World War I from profiteering; Swedish church and government officials knew about the Holocaust long before they did anything; and violent crime, racism, and drug abuse are not just American problems—they are Nordic problems in the late twentieth century. From an ethical perspective, there are numerous cases in Nordic history when expediency was more important than "doing the right thing."

Other themes are the importance of external factors in the shaping of Scandinavian history, the importance of internal factors in that history, and the interaction between external and internal factors. It is not difficult to catalog what has come to Norden from abroad. A list must include religions (Christianity, Lutheranism, a long list of Protestant denominations, and, in the late twentieth century, virtually all of the world's religions), political ideas and ideologies (absolutism, liberalism, socialism), economic ideas and practices (commercial capitalism, mercantilism, industrial capitalism, state capitalism), intellectual movements (the scientific revolution, the Enlightenment, romanticism), technologies (weapons, ship designs, iron- and steel-making methods, energy sources and exploitation techniques), fashions, tastes, art styles, and literary genre. Nor is it difficult to identify the carriers of these influences. On the one hand, Norden has been a receiver of peoples—of all kinds of immigrants—throughout its history. Major chapters could be written on the roles of the Dutch, English, French, Germans, and Russians. Merchants, entrepreneurs, artisans, religious reformers, government officials, mercenaries, and intellectuals from outside the region are just some of the categories of in-migrants that have brought (and continue to bring) influences into the region. At the same time, travelers, students, and astute seekers of the new and the useful from Scandinavia brought back much that affected the area's history. It is easy, however, to overemphasize the foreign influences at the expense of seeing the unique ways in which the peoples of Norden adapted what was imported. In-migrants were absorbed into the societies. Ideas, techniques, technologies, and the like were modified. Nordic individuals and groups contributed to new developments and to the integration of the imports. Gustav II Adolf's military reforms, Danish absolutism, the constitutions of the nineteenth and twentieth centuries, Ibsen's and Strindberg's plays, Scandinavian modern design, management techniques and shopfloor production strategies, and the welfare states are just a few examples of aspects of Nordic history that are amalgams of the external, internal, and genuine originality.

I hope this work will be a useful contribution to the understanding of Nordic history and to the ongoing conversation that is history.

There are many people to thank for their help and encouragement. First and foremost is Odd Lovoll, King Olav V Professor of Scandinavian-American Studies at St. Olaf College. In the early stages this book was to be a collaborative effort with Professor Lovoll, and I am particularly indebted to him for his work on chapter 8. Brian Magnusson contributed significantly to the chapter on prehistory. I would also like to thank my teaching colleagues in this and related fields, including H. Arnold Barton, Oddvar Hoidal, Steven Koblik, Terje Leiren, Roger McKnight, Michael Metcalf, Lee Sather, Marvin Slind, and Roland Thorstensson; my early mentors, Stewart P. Oakley, J. Kim Munholland, David Kieft, Gudmund Stang, and Kristian Hvidt; all those whose works in Nordic history have been indispensable to me; my colleagues, students, and the administration at Gustavus Adolphus College; for illustrations, Brian Magnusson, Denmark's National Historical Museum at Frederiksborg, the Royal Library in Copenhagen, the Bergen Museum, the National Gallery in Oslo, the Museum of Science and Technology at Trondheim University, the Stenersen Museum in Oslo, Sweden's State Museums of Art, and Uppsala University; the University of Minnesota Press; and my wife, Janet, my most perceptive and demanding editor.

1

~~~~~~

Scandinavia before the Modern Era

The intentions of this introductory chapter are to provide a thematic overview of Scandinavian history from the earliest evidence of human settlement down to about 1500 and to supply the reader with some background and sense of context before beginning the more thorough examination of the modern period.

The record of human activity in Scandinavia spans about 11,000 years. By far the greatest share of this, about 10,000 years (from the earliest evidence of human presence to the Viking Age), belongs to prehistory, to the past at its most obscure. Evidence for these times is fragmentary, scattered, and often subject to conflicting interpretations. Entire societies and the nature of human lives are defined by archaeologists analyzing a rich but still limited and silent base of prehistoric remains including tools, household articles, building foundations, and human and animal skeletal remains generally found in settlement, burial, or sacrificial places. Some of these sites have revealed quite spectacular items, objects made of precious materials whose workmanship demonstrates the remarkable skills of prehistoric artisans. The oldest written accounts about Scandinavia appear in *Historia naturalis,* by the Roman scholar Pliny the Elder (A.D. 23–79), but these are vague and based on uncertain secondary sources. In general, the Roman and early medieval periods are largely silent, and it is only with the ninth century and the increasing contacts between Norse peoples and others both outside and inside Scandinavia that more references to the area appear. Among these sources are *The Anglo-Saxon Chronicle,* the travel accounts of the Persian Ibn Fadlan, and early Church literature such as Rimbert's *Vita Ansgarii* (Life of St. Ansgar) or Adam of Bremen's history of the archbishopric of Hamburg-Bremen. The earliest written sources from Scandinavia, which date to the pre-Viking and Viking periods, are inscriptions in runic characters—an alphabet of twenty-four (later sixteen) rectilinear letters adapted from the Roman. Most often these sources were brief descriptions carved on stone about the deeds of an individual or an event, but a few surviving wood pieces from late in the period indicate the runic alphabet was used to keep account records as well. In either case, these inscriptions make for a thin history indeed. The first histories written in Scandinavia come only after the conversion to Christianity. These include *Ælnoths Krönike* (Ælnoth's chronicle) from around 1120, and from the early thirteenth century Saxo Grammaticus's sixteen-volume *Gesta Danorum* (Deeds of the Danes) and Snorri Sturluson's *Heimskringla,* a saga history of Norse kings. It is only since then that there are both written histories and written sources about Scandinavia, from Scandinavia.

The oldest archeological evidence of human presence in the Nordic region dates to before the last glaciation and includes a recent find from a cave in Kristinestad, Finland, which points to a Neanderthal occupation of the site over 100,000 years old. However, the last glaciers and altered land masses and sea levels have erased most remains. As a result, Nordic prehistory deals primarily with the peoples who have lived in the area for about the last 12,000 years. The earliest humans in this period migrated in, probably from both the south and the north. This in-migration occurred as the great glaciers that had completely covered the area and at one time were up to 3,000 meters thick slowly melted and laid bare a gradually expanding area of arctic and subarctic tundra. During a period spanning almost 20,000 years, the geographic outline of contemporary Scandinavia took shape. This process was determined by the glaciers and the waters produced by their melting, the slow rebounding of the land as the weight of the glaciers was removed, the changing ocean levels, and significant climatic variations. At first a Scandinavia entirely unrecognizable compared with today's appeared. It was composed of a thin belt of land along the coasts of western and northern Norway, a piece of northern Finland connected with Russia, and an extension of the north German plain that reached into south central Sweden and also extended westward to the British Isles. Around 8000 B.C. the huge freshwater lake formed by the glacial melting on the east side of the region broke through to the North Sea and became a saltwater bay. Half a millennium later this state was reversed, and a new freshwater lake developed—only to be reversed again, as erosion and sea level changes slowly made the lake into the Baltic Sea. By 2000 B.C. a

Scandinavian History Periodization

Old Stone Age/Paleolithic	11,000–9000/8000 B.C.
Middle Stone Age/Mesolithic	8000–4500 B.C.
New Stone Age/Neolithic	4500/4200–1800 B.C.
Bronze Age	1800–500 B.C.
Iron Age	500 B.C.–A.D. 800
(Celtic Iron Age)	500/400 B.C.–0
(Roman Iron Age)	0–A.D. 400
(Migration Period)	400–550
(Vendel Period)	550–800
Viking Age	800–1100
Medieval	1100–1500
Early Modern	1500–1800
Modern	1800–

This periodization is one of many possible for Scandinavian history. It is based on a pattern used in general Western and European history. The dates are all approximate, and some are adapted to specifically Scandinavian developments.

geography recognizable as Scandinavia had evolved. During this same period the region also underwent profound climatic changes. Subarctic at first, the climate gradually grew more temperate, and Norden actually enjoyed an era when it was warmer than today (from c. 5000 to 700 B.C.). Taken together, the geological and climatic changes determined the animal and plant life patterns of the region as well as the topography; all of which, in turn, shaped the nature of the human cultures that developed there.

The oldest artifactual evidence, which includes flint tools of Old Stone Age peoples in Norden, dates to about 9500–9000 B.C., was discovered at Bromme in Denmark, and parallels similar finds in nearby northern Germany. (There are some much older finds from Hollerup in Denmark that contain indications of human activity in the region during the Inter-Glacial Period, c. 90,000–50,000 B.C.) Evidence nearly as old has also been found in northern Norway. Over the ensuing several thousand years people slowly spread into Sweden and the coastal regions of Norway. The range of human habitation was surprisingly wide, as evidenced by discoveries reaching from Galta in southwest Norway to Sarnes in the far north. In general, the archaeological record indicates the presence of nomadic, hunting-gathering-fishing cultures across Norden that were entirely dependent on and shaped by variations in the natural environment. The climate, animals, and vegetation determined their lifestyles and diets as well as their material and spiritual cultures. Tools were made of bone, wood, stone, and flint. Amber, as well as flint, appears to have been used in religious activities. Clothing was probably made most often of hides, which may also have been used in housing, along with wood and grass.

The Stone Age archaeological record paints a surprisingly complex picture. The living and geological resources of differing regions produced specialization such as coastal fishing and inland game-hunting groups. Tool materials varied by area, and tool-making abilities became strikingly sophisticated. An extensive trade in flint developed that reached far into northern Sweden, as evidenced by finds at Bjurselet on the coast of Västerbotten. Artifacts of bone or amber and petroglyphs and pictographs, such as those at Alta in Norway or the somewhat later ones at Nämforsen in northern Sweden, depict reindeer, moose, bear, birds, fish, whales, and humans. These depictions indicate the presence of animist religious beliefs from very ancient times.

The break between the Old and New (or "peasant") Stone Ages falls sometime around 4200 B.C. and is defined by several important transitions that occurred first in the southern areas of Scandinavia and then gradually spread northward into central Sweden and eastern Norway, and finally reached up the Norwegian west coast. Among these transitions are the development of fired pottery, the systematic cultivation of crops and domestication of animals, the increased permanence of settlement sites, and growing cultural and trade contacts with other parts of what we now call Europe. All of them are evidenced in the increasingly varied and often monumental archaeological finds from southern Scandinavia such as those at Sarup on the Danish island of Fyn or Barkaer in Jutland.

The Neolithic also appears to have meant new religious beliefs and practices in parts of the region, particularly with regard to death and an afterlife. Hundreds of megalithic graves, including dolmens and passage or chamber graves, survive, principally in Denmark but also into southern Sweden, dating to between 3300 and 2000 B.C. The style seems to have had its origins in the Mediterranean world and spread across

Neolithic dolmen grave at Porskær, Jyland, Denmark. Photograph courtesy of Brian F. Magnusson.

western Europe and the British Isles into Norden. These monumental graves were made of large, vertically placed stones capped by a lintel stone and then covered with turf. The dolmens were smaller than what are generally regarded as the later styles, and they appear to have usually been used as individual graves. The more complicated passage graves, such as those at Falbygden, Sweden, were elaborate structures whose chambers appear to have been used by successive generations as burial sites: the earlier remains were unceremoniously removed. Two things are particularly important about these graves. First, their construction must have required the efforts of many people, and this suggests some kind of social or religious hierarchy. Second, although we know nothing about the actual practices and ideas connected to these graves, their presence and long-term use certainly point to the existence of strongly held and long-lasting beliefs and burial customs.

Between 2500 and 2000 B.C., Scandinavia was invaded by a new ethnolinguistic group, the so-called boat axe, battle axe, or single-grave people, named for their beautifully shaped and crafted stone weapons or their simple graves. They were Indo-European nomads from the eastern Urals who spread across much of northern Europe and probably established cultural dominance over the earlier peoples of southern and central Scandinavia. Although opinions differ about their importance, one of their legacies to Scandinavia appears to have been the tall, long-skulled physical type so often cited as characteristic of the region. In addition, their simple graves (normally containing the remains of the dead person facing east and one or more weapons) replaced the passage graves and support the contention that they brought a new religion. Finally, through their contacts with other groups further south, they appear to have contributed to a significant increase in trade and cultural interaction between late Neolithic Scandinavia and the European continent.

One of the richest periods in the early prehistory of Norden, at least for the southern areas of the region, was the Bronze Age. During this era, Norden was geologically and topographically very similar to today, but its climate was warmer and more comfortable. Although most people probably had an easier time eking out an existence from simple farming, hunting, fishing, and gathering, it is clear that early in the period a chieftain-trader class, whose roots may have extended back to the battle axe people, enjoyed both prominence and affluence based on herding, exploitation of local resources, and control of trade with areas as far off as the Middle East. Rich in amber, furs, honey, wax, and (probably) slaves, an elite in southern Bronze Age Scandinavia appears to have exchanged these goods for copper, tin, bronze, and gold. Three important types of archaeological finds bear witness to this: the petroglyphs (*hällristningar*) of southern Sweden and Norway, the grave goods from several large burial mounds, and an array of remarkable offering finds from what appear to have been sacrificial sites.

Generally situated on low-lying outcroppings of stone and on the stones of burial chambers, the Bronze Age petroglyphs are found primarily in southern and central Sweden and in southeastern Norway. Among the most striking are those at Tanum in Sweden. Although they show some local variations, they are thematically similar, with their simple outline images of hunters, farmers, herdsmen, oarsmen, women, domestic and wild animals, boats, wheels, weapons, suns, footprints, and geometric shapes. They are believed to represent the common activities of a complex, socially stratified society in which hunting, farming, and trade were important. They also suggest that religion was based on either a panoply of gods or a single sun god who looked

Bronze Age rock scribbing at Tanum, Sweden. Photograph from the author's collection.

after the essential aspects of life. (These dual interpretations indicate the difficulty of determining the real meaning of many sources from these periods.)

Burial mounds were common to much of the Bronze Age, and even today there are literally hundreds scattered throughout Denmark, southern Sweden, and southeastern Norway. Most were located at prominent spots in the landscape and were probably meant to be seen from the sea or other waterway. A few were of monumental scale, including the one at Egtved in southern Jutland and another near Uppsala in Sweden. The Egtved mound is estimated to have been about 90 feet in diameter and 13 feet high. This structure, whose construction was complex and involved the labor of untold many, was a grave for a young woman buried in the summer of 1370 b.c. At its core was a well-preserved oak casket that contained an animal-hide robe, a young woman's remains and clothing, a woolen rug, several small containers with everyday articles, and the remains of a child. The clothing was especially interesting. The body was buried in a revealingly short, braided wool skirt and woven woolen top. Experts suggest that this costume was intended to announce the girl's maturity and to attract young men. This clothing also tells us much about the textile skills of the people of this period. Clearly, spinning, dyeing, and weaving were parts of this culture, perhaps as aspects of women's work. The Håga mound southwest of Uppsala measured about 150 feet in diameter and was between 18 and 25 feet tall. Several hundred years more recent, it contained a cremation burial, and excavations have yielded a magnificent bronze sword and gilt brooch. (In addition to the mounds, the people of Bronze Age Norden also constructed ship settings. These stone monuments were arranged in the shape of a vessel and usually were placed close to a waterway. They appear to have been used as burial sites or to commemorate someone who had died elsewhere—and reinforce the argument that travel and trade were important aspects of the era.)

The individual artifact record of the Bronze Age is also striking. In part it is made up of weapons—swords, daggers, and spearheads—some of which are elaborately decorated. In addition, there is a wealth of gold and bronze jewelry, including circular belt buckles, bracelets, and armbands. There are also lures—beautifully curved musical instruments—some of which are still playable. One particularly striking artifact is the Trundholm wagon, a small, wheeled bronze cart carrying a golden sun disk and drawn by a cast bronze horse, which gives added credence to the argument that the sun was the center of Bronze Age religion for a time. Like many other important pieces from this period, the wagon was probably left as an offering in what was then a small body of water and is now a bog.

The richness of the Bronze Age, as well as the richness of the archaeological record, ended around 700–500 B.C. The climate turned colder and wetter. The growing season shortened, and livestock had to be sheltered in the winter. Trade was interrupted, in part because of the dominance of Celtic peoples, whose influence reached from central Europe to the British Isles. At the same time, iron replaced bronze. Although at first an imported material, iron was found in Norden as small, unrefined globs in bogs or marshes and processed in simple kilns. Overall, life in southern Norden appears to have become poorer, harsher, and more violent, and the simple cremation graves from the period are seen as evidence of these trends. In the northern reaches the semi-nomadic hunting and the more settled coastal cultures continued to develop, largely independently and virtually with their own chronologies.

The spread of the Roman Empire, which ended the dominance of the Celts, brought renewed trade and new cultural influences to Scandinavia. Evidence of contacts may be seen in archaeological finds throughout southern Norden that include glassware from the Rhine, metalwork such as the silver Hoby cups found in Denmark with their depictions of scenes from the *Iliad,* and thousands of Roman coins, many of which were turned into items of jewelry. A large number of these items were deposited in graves as objects probably intended to accompany the deceased on the journey into the afterlife.

There is also an amazing group of human remains unearthed (usually quite by chance) in Denmark that date from the early years of the new millennium. These remains are of the so-called bog people and include Tollund man, discovered in a bog in central Jutland in 1950. This corpse, along with others, is almost perfectly preserved, tanned in the special chemistry of the evolving peat bog in which it was found. Hair, skin, skeleton, stomach contents, and facial expression have survived. What these finds appear to reveal is the presence of a religion devoted to fertility, in which humans were sacrificed in order to ensure an abundant harvest. This is hardly surprising, given the environment and the central importance of agriculture to the people of this area.

Collectively, these finds point to a time in southern Scandinavia when farming was the occupation of the many, and trade in luxury items was the domain of the few. It is also clear that small numbers of people became specialists in iron making, smithing, weapon making, and silver and gold work. The discovery of buried treasure hoards, as

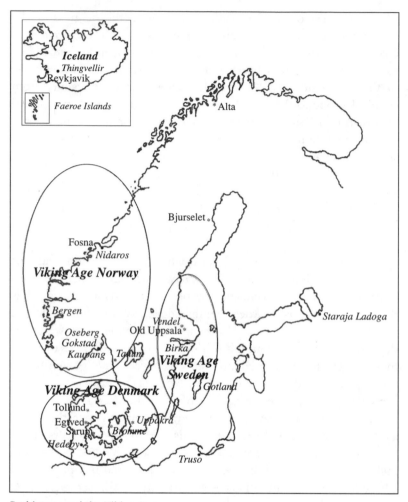

Prehistory and the Viking Age.

well as refuge forts and fortified villages, indicates that violence was also very much part of life in this period. The Baltic islands of Öland and Gotland became important trade centers. Low and with few natural barriers, these islands were open to attacks. Consequently, more than ninety fortified sites were constructed, including Eketorp on Öland and Torsbugen on Gotland.

Beginning in the late fourth century, the peoples of what we now call Europe became involved in one of history's great migration phases. Pressure from the nomadic Huns, the constant need for new (or better) farming land, and the growing troubles in the Roman Empire all served to feed this process. The Ostrogoths and Visigoths, whose distant origins lay in Sweden, were bumped out of what are now central Europe and the Ukraine around A.D. 375 and moved into western Europe—eventually into the Italian peninsula and Spain, respectively. The Angles, whose home was in Slesvig, crossed into England, as did the Saxons and Jutes. For the people of Scandinavia this movement appears to have involved more turmoil and cultural interaction than actual tribal migrations. The archaeological history of the period contains evidence of continuing high levels of violence in the literally hundreds of refuge forts that were constructed, weapon finds in graves, and innumerable treasure hoards. Although the years between 400 and 600 are usually referred to as the Migration Period, they are also known as the "Period of Gold"—a time when, with the collapse of the Roman Empire in the West, huge amounts of this precious metal reached Scandinavia in the form of coins, ornaments, and bullion. This influx served as the basis for both wealth accumulation and artistic development, and some art historians argue that Scandinavia's first truly indigenous art style developed in this era. (Others prefer to see the Scandinavians as borrowers of external design traditions.) The several mound burials at Vendel in Sweden testify to all these aspects of the period, including an apparent link between central Sweden and what is now East Anglia in England. These ties may be seen in a comparison of the contents of the Swedish "boat graves" at Vendel and Valsgärde with those at Sutton Hoo in England.

At the close of his 1962 work on the Vikings, Peter Sawyer reminded readers that every historical period is "the subjective creation of observers." This was especially true of the Viking Age, which emerges in many ways imperceptibly from the Migration Period. As Sawyer pointed out, for contemporaries "it began when the men of the West first became aware of the strangers of the North who came in search of land, wealth and glory. It ended when they were no longer strangers." Subsequent generations, especially in Norden or in areas where significant numbers of Nordic immigrants or their descendants can be found, have repeatedly revisited, reinvented, or amplified the achievements of this period. Unquestionably, the years between about 800 and 1100 form an important unit in Norden's history. It is the prehistoric period that is the best known and the most written about. Both accurate and fanciful accounts abound and are parts of the national canon of Nordic history. Exaggeration aside, this period does stand out as one of the most important extended moments in all of Scandinavian history—at least from the Nordic perspective. (Most general European histories devote very little space to the Vikings and usually treat them as nuisances and not real contributors to Europe's development.) Spanning nearly three centuries, the Viking Age was, in many ways, the final phase in the Migration Period and the time when Scandinavia made some lasting contributions to the general history of Europe in the Middle Ages. It was then that people from the region moved out to settle unoccupied places (including Iceland and the Faeroe Islands in the ninth century, and Greenland at the close of the tenth century), to trade, attack, plunder, intermingle with, and rule over peoples in already settled areas (especially in parts of the British Isles from 793), and to create and maintain a commercial world that reached from Greenland to Asia.

Although the scale of their impacts and the long-term or lasting importance of the Vikings in European history are debatable, the vitality and richness of this period from the Nordic perspective are not. The abilities and achievements of relatively small groups of people are truly remarkable—seen through the prism of either their external or their internal activities. People from what is now east-central Sweden established trade and production centers on the island of Helgö and at Birka (on Björkö) in Lake Mälar, at several sites on Gotland and along the south Baltic shores, and in western Russia. At the same time, people from what is now Denmark and Norway maintained similar centers at Hedeby (near the present-day town of Slesvig in northwest Germany), Kaupang near Oslo, and probably near the present-day south Swedish community of Uppåkra. These thriving towns served as commercial and production centers in a trade world that reached east down the Volga and Dnieper rivers, crossed northern Europe, and extended west to Greenland and beyond. Along this arc flowed goods from Asia, the Byzantine Empire, the Islamic Mideast, the Baltic, Europe and the British Isles, the Atlantic islands, and even North America. Simultaneously, Norse peoples from what were emerging as Denmark and Norway raided the British Isles and the Frankish kingdom, conquered and established dominance over part of England (the Danelaw), discovered and settled the islands of the north Atlantic, and reached at least as far west as today's L'Anse-aux-Meadows on the tip of northern Newfoundland. In Scandinavia the same period witnessed the continued coalescence of the early Danish, Norwegian, and Swedish monarchies from the cauldrons of tribal localisms, as well as the founding of the Icelandic, Faeroese, and Greenland republics. At the same time a variety of ancient local and regional legal systems and representative institutions remained vital. It was also an era of achievement in artistic and craft production (be it original, copied, or a blending of the two) in wood, metal, textiles, and boat construction that rivaled or surpassed the rest of Europe.

All these developments were possible and occurred because of a combination of Nordic and European factors. Among the former were the boat building and maritime skills of the Scandinavians, which gave them a temporary advantage over their neighbors; a polytheistic religion that emphasized conflict, daring, and reputation; population growth that put pressure on the existing land bases in some areas; and discontent with the developing political centralization Among the European factors were the relative weakness or complete absence of political organization and defenses in areas where the Vikings were most successful, commercial opportunities, the availability of trade resources (often in the form of the riches of the Church), and the attractiveness of land for settlement.

Contemporary and later written sources on the Viking Age are important to our understanding of what life was like in late–Iron Age Scandinavia. But these sources tell only part of the story, and they should be seen alongside the rich archaeological inventories from the period. The material record that has survived from the Viking Age is exceptionally rich. The great ship burials from Oseberg and Gokstad (Norway), along with the several ships found at Skuldelev in Denmark, demonstrate the shipbuilding skills of these people. In addition, the Oseberg's wagons, sledges, beds, chairs, tapestries, weapons, and other everyday articles, with their lavish decorations, have helped define "Viking art" and in many ways epitomize what people today see as the true character of Viking culture. But these finds, along with countless axes, swords, shields, brooches, harness fittings, bracelets, rings, silver caches, and the like, tell only part of the story of this period. In addition, there are the monumental and structurally sophisticated fortifications at Aggersborg, Fyrkat, Nonnebakken, and Trelleborg in Denmark or the likely site of the pagan temple at Old Uppsala, adjacent to three immense Iron Age burial mounds and described in grisly detail by Adam of Bremen.

The apparent magic that the Viking Age holds for the people of Norden and for many of Scandinavian descent is hardly surprising. As art historian Brian Magnusson has written, to understand its enduring character, "one need only walk along a country lane in Denmark, Norway, or Sweden to experience physical testimony to Viking culture. Stately mounds, ship-settings, communal grave fields with their stone monuments and runestones, refuge sites, and occasional house foundations are all observable and, though mute and alien in our modern world, evoke an immediacy which tantalizes the imagination."

By the end of the eleventh century, Scandinavia had become part of western Christendom, and the history of the region over the next four hundred years is increasingly a history tied to events, institutions, and patterns of development in Europe. Politically, the area came to be dominated by three medieval, monarchist states: Denmark, Norway, and Sweden. The Faeroe Islands, Greenland, and Iceland lost their independence in the mid–thirteenth century. What is now Finland was a sparsely settled field for conversion and exploitation by the Swedes. Internal politics were characterized by almost constant civil strife, wherein wars were triggered by succession struggles; by conflicts between kings who wanted to rule and great men who wanted weak kings and extensive personal powers; and by a powerful Church that jealously guarded its authority and prerogatives. In international affairs, Scandinavia lay outside the sphere of most continental events. However, competition among the Nordic kingdoms became increasingly important and was characterized by struggles for territory or over autonomy versus control of the region by a single power. In religion, the polytheism of the Vikings was gradually replaced by Christianity and the Church of Rome, although conversion was slow and many old beliefs and practices were retained for centuries. Lund, Nidaros/Trondheim, and Uppsala were established as archbishoprics in 1104, 1152, and 1164 respectively, and the division of the countries into bishoprics and parishes was put in place. Schools and monastic orders followed within a century. Although many of the old motifs survived in the folk arts of Norden, high culture was almost entirely the domain of the Church. In economic life, the Viking-dominated trade system collapsed, and many of the old centers of commerce disappeared. Germans gradually took control of almost all international commerce in the North, as well as much internal Nordic trade. Bergen, Stockholm, Visby, and Copenhagen slowly developed as economic centers. The Middle Ages also witnessed the continued evolution of male-dominated hierarchical societies in which social groups were set apart by function, birth, and wealth in land.

In many respects, life in medieval Scandinavia was little different from a millennium or even two millenniums earlier. The overwhelming majority of the people in the southern areas of the region were engaged in subsistence agriculture, often supplemented by hunting and fishing, and played out their lives in worlds no larger than they were able to traverse in a day. In the far north the Sami were largely untouched by the events taking place to their south, except by the increasingly frequent incursions of the kings' tax collectors. They continued to follow their semi-nomadic, pastoral patterns of living. Throughout the region people worked with simple tools of ancient design, lived in dwellings of similarly ancient styles, and used methods that went unchanged from the prehistoric periods to the eighteenth century. The common folk were far removed from and little interested in state politics or high church affairs. With a few notable exceptions, such as Bergen, Nidaros/Trondheim, Copenhagen, Ribe, Lund, Uppsala, and Stockholm, towns were small and relatively insignificant.

The label *Dark Ages,* so often applied to the medieval period, is, however, as inappropriate to use in Norden as elsewhere in Europe. Intellectual life went on, largely in the monastic houses and church schools of the bishop towns. A university was established at Uppsala in 1477 and at Copenhagen in 1479. Travel, trade, and contacts with the Continent and the British Isles did not end. The clergy were often educated abroad. Art and architecture, in the sense of high culture, centered on the Church, and the centuries between 1100 and 1500 yielded some significant treasures in the history of art in the North including the cathedrals of Lund, Nidaros, and Uppsala; the hundreds of parish churches, many of which survive; and the stone, glass, wood, metal, and textile interior decorations that adorned those churches. In terms of the folk arts there is continuity from the earlier periods right down to the present. Woodworking and wood carving, metal work, and textile production remained important and formed the bases of modern folk art traditions.

One of the most important aspects of intellectual activity in the late medieval period was in a new medium for Norden: written literature. Many of the fundamental treasures and crucial primary sources of medieval Nordic history were produced or written down from older oral sources in this period. These included the histories mentioned earlier, the Icelandic sagas, skaldic poetry, ballads, myths, law codes, and a variety of church literature such as the revelations of St. Birgitta.

All the essential elements for the history of modern Scandinavia are in place by the close of the medieval period including the political units (and their internal problems and rivalries), social hierarchies, rural and urban economies, religious base, cultural heritages, international connections, and patterns of everyday life. What follows is intended to be a more detailed picture of what has happened since the emergence of these foundations.

Part I

The Early Modern, 1500–1800

2

~~~~~~

An Age of Transformations

In the traditional chronology of European history, 1500 is seen as the beginning of the early modern period. In Scandinavian history, the Renaissance is often merged with this moment, and the two periods are seen to have coincided. Proof that a new age had been entered was found in the "revolutions," most of them actually quite gradual, which help define and organize the history of the sixteenth century. Among them were the geographic revolution marked by a "doubling" of the globe and the beginning of the age of European predominance; the commercial revolution defined by the creation of a European-centered global commercial economy; the intellectual revolution based on increased interest in the classics, inquisitiveness, and confidence in humankind's capacity to understand the physical world; the religious revolution marked by the disintegration of Christian unity and the development of a pluralistic "Christian" Europe; the political revolution characterized by the emergence of increasingly centralized dynastic (sometimes called tax or warfare) states led by monarchs and elites intent on increasing their power through the centralization and professionalization of government; a military revolution centered on the growing predominance of gunpowder weapons and the resultant changes in the composition of armies and the nature of warfare; an urban revolution marked by the rapid growth of urban centers with economic and political functions, especially in Western Europe; and a set of social revolutions including the expansion of the middle class and the transition of the medieval nobilities into service nobilities.

The peoples of Scandinavia experienced all these developments to varying degrees. Although somewhat isolated and sheltered by distance, Scandinavia had been part of what was called Christendom for much of the medieval period and was part of what after 1500 was

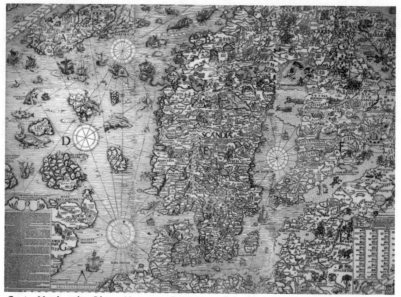

Carta Marina, by Olaus Magnus. Courtesy of the University of Uppsala Library, Uppsala, Sweden.

increasingly coming to be called Europe, whose events, ideas, and developments constantly influenced Norden. As in earlier periods, the developments in Scandinavia during the sixteenth century reflected the merging of external factors—such as German and Italian political ideas, German and Low Country intellectual and religious ideas, German architectural styles, and Spanish fashions—with internal factors.

Political Development

Politically, the sixteenth century is defined throughout Europe by the attempts of many rulers and their supporting elites to alter the constitutional nature of their states; to strengthen the power of the crown; to increase their fiscal resources; to weaken the decentralizing tendencies of the nobility and to convert that nobility to a class of loyal servants of the state or to reduce it to powerlessness; and to create new bases of power in state assemblies, the growing middle class, national military establishments, and national churches. It was a century of turmoil—of plots and civil wars, of violence, murder, and deception. In large part these efforts involved a fundamental political struggle between monarchy and what is often called aristocratic

Monarchs

Denmark	Sweden
Hans I: 1481–1513	Hans I: 1497–1501
	Sten Sture the Elder: 1501–3 (Regent)
	Svante Nilsson Sture: 1504–11 (Regent)
	Sten Sture the Younger: 1511–20 (Regent)
Christian II: 1513–23	Christian II: 1520–23
Frederik I: 1523–33	Gustav I Vasa: 1523–60
Christian III: 1534–59	
Frederik II: 1559–88	Erik XIV: 1560–68
	Johan III: 1568–92
Christian IV: 1588–1648	Sigismund I: 1592–99
	Karl IX: 1599/1607–11

Dates are of reigns.

---

constitutionalism or council constitutionalism—between a modern concept of the state ruled by a king (or queen) with the help of a loyal nobility and a medieval concept of a state ruled by a king (or queen) in concert with a nobility that regarded the monarch as little more than a first among equals. Rarely was the outcome of any of these attempts clear, and in many respects the century ended as it began. For Scandinavia, as we shall see, the political struggles in Denmark and Sweden followed different paths to quite similar outcomes.

In Scandinavia the new century began in the 103d year of the Kalmar Union. The medieval kingdoms of Denmark, Norway, and Sweden were united, and Hans I of the Oldenburg dynasty was the recognized ruler of the entire North. One hundred years later the union was gone. Sweden (with Finland and the beginnings of a Baltic empire) and Denmark (with Norway, Iceland, the Faeroe Islands, and a collection of north German territories) stood as independent dynastic states. Between these points lay a set of civil and dynastic-state wars and political developments that gave rise to the new geopolitical division in Scandinavia.

The Hanse

The Hanse, or Hanseatic League, was a federation of over seventy north European trading towns that developed from the early thirteenth century and was dominated by Germans. Lübeck was from around 1280 a kind of capital for the organization. During the thirteenth and fourteenth centuries Nordic trade fell increasingly under Hanse control exercised through offices in the principal towns, including Bergen, Copenhagen, and Stockholm. In addition to its economic power, the league was a political, military, and cultural force. It made and unmade governments and carried on wars. It also affected the languages, arts, and architecture of urban Scandinavia. The federation declined slowly from the late fifteenth century, faced with trade competition from the Dutch and the English and the growing political and military strength of the developing early modern states. The last Hanse federation meeting occurred in 1669. It is important to keep in mind that the Hanse functioned for nearly four hundred years as an alternative to the state as a form of economic and political organization.

The Kalmar Union (1397–1523) was the result of the convergence of several factors. Two were external: a growing concern over the economic influence of the Hanse (Hanseatic League); and a perceived threat of German political domination. Both arose because of the weakened condition of the Nordic region that resulted from the loss of life during the Black Death and the recurrent episodes of civil strife. In addition, the native dynastic lines in each country converged as a result of a web of royal marriages and accidents. The marriage of Margrethe (1353–1412), the oldest daughter of Denmark's Valdemar IV, and Norway's Haakon VI, a son of the deposed king of Sweden, Magnus Eriksson (d. 1374), and a grandson of Norway's Haakon V, linked all three Nordic dynasties. Valdemar's death without a male heir, the Swedish civil wars against Magnus and then against his successor, Albrekt of Mecklenburg, and the premature deaths of Haakon VI and his son, Olav IV, provided the immediate situations from which the union grew. From 1380 to 1387, Olav was king of Denmark and Norway. Following his death in 1387, the succession fell to Erik of

Scandinavia in 1500.

Pomerania, Margrethe's nephew. By 1396 he was recognized as king of all three Nordic countries, but real power remained with Margrethe. In 1397 this convergence was given more substantive form through the conclusion of agreements among the regent and the leading men of Denmark, Norway, and Sweden, which formed the bases of the Kalmar Union. The merger of the Scandinavian kingdoms was recognized, although whether this was a unitary state under a single crown, as Margrethe envisioned, or a federation, as the magnates preferred to think, was unclear. Following Margrethe's death in 1412, the union faced one crisis after another. From the mid-1430s its history

SIC·REX·GVSTAW·   VVLTV·QVE·HVME·
ROSONE·   FEREBAT·
FOELIX·IMPERIO   SVECIA·MAGNATVO
1542

Gustav I Vasa of Sweden (c. 1494–1560), by Jacob Binck. Courtesy of the University of Uppsala Library, Uppsala, Sweden.

was marred by almost constant civil wars fought in the name of constitutional principles or national ideals but generally controlled by self-interested men seeking to serve individual or social group ends rather than state ends and often encouraged by the merchants of the Hanseatic League to perpetuate Nordic disorder and weakness.

The final collapse of the union (although Norway remained tied to Denmark until 1814) was the result of yet another civil war in

Early Modern Nationalism

Many have argued that a kind of nationalism emerged, at least in Sweden and Denmark, during these struggles. It is difficult, however, to see the events of the period in anything approaching a modern nationalistic context. Most people were neither aware of nor thought in terms of nationality as we know it, and many historians have distorted the history of this period by attempting to make the union conflicts into wars of national liberation.

Christian II's mistakes in Sweden, Gustav Vasa's leadership, and some early form of nationalism were not the only causes of the union's collapse. Other important factors include the unrest Christian created by his actions at home in Denmark; the willingness of Lübeck to loan money, soldiers, and ships to Gustav, certainly hoping to reap economic gains as a result; and the weakened state of the Swedish class of magnates, which allowed Gustav to play a leading role in events.

It is also misleading to argue that the collapse of the Kalmar Union was inevitable because the forces of nationalism had to triumph and Scandinavia as we know it was predestined. Such is simply not true. In the early 1520s a wiser ruler with greater political talents and more personal balance might have been able to hold the union together, and the union option might have prevailed over narrower identities, including some form of early Swedish nationalism. Furthermore, it should be kept in mind that the hopes for a united Scandinavia did not die in 1523. For more than a century Denmark's leaders held to the idea of restoring the union, and several of Sweden's kings (Karl X Gustav, Gustav III, and Karl XV among them) had similar ideas. In addition, the concept has reappeared in various forms down to the present, including the Scandinavianism of the nineteenth century and today's Nordic Council.

which Danish pro-union forces were pitted against anti-union Swedes led by one of the heroes of modern Swedish history, Gustav Eriksson Vasa (c.1494–1560), and aided by foreign mercenaries and naval forces supplied and paid for by the Hanse. The conflict was triggered by the foolish and vengeful actions of the union king,

Christian II (1481–1559). In 1520 the armies of Christian won a round in the union conflicts, and in September the young king went to Stockholm to receive the Swedes' recognition as hereditary monarch. While there he sanctioned, probably on the advice of Gustav Trolle (c. 1488–1535), archbishop of Uppsala, the arrest and execution of eighty-two Swedish men, including many members of the magnate class who were potential threats to Christian's authority, in what has come to be known as "The Stockholm Bloodbath" (November 1520). In addition, Christian left a trail of similar cruelties along the path of his return to Denmark in late 1520.

According to a traditional interpretation that is at least partially accurate, Gustav Eriksson Vasa, the twenty-four-year-old son of one of Christian's victims, made skillful use of domestic and foreign anger toward Christian to arouse patriotic fervor, defeat the Danes, and make himself king in Sweden. Gustav was a master of propaganda, a compelling speaker, and a clever politician, who played well the favorable hand dealt him. He won the support of commoners and many of the surviving magnate families and gained financial and military assistance from the Hanseatic city of Lübeck. In August 1521 at Vadstena, a national assembly of leading men declared Gustav "Captain of the Realm." In June 1523 another national assembly convened at Strängnäs to recognize him as king. When Stockholm fell to his forces that fall, the union's collapse, so far as Sweden was concerned, was sealed.

Denmark

As the union dissolved around Christian II, so too did his hold on the throne in Denmark. Christian dreamed of forging a more modern state in Scandinavia, one in which he would rule as hereditary monarch, in which the church and nobility were under his control, and in which a native merchant class would end the influence of the Hanse. Events would not match dreams, however. Christian was a man with modern ideas but little political skill, and he alienated potential supporters among the leading men, clergy, burghers, and commoners by his actions and policies. He antagonized the magnates by violating the promises made in his accession charter to guarantee their prerogatives, which included their right to advise the crown and enjoy a virtual monopoly on government appointments. Instead, he awarded power to favorites, especially to Sigbrit Willums, the mother of an early mistress, Dyveke. (Dyveke died mysteriously in 1517, possibly

Christian II

Christian II of Denmark (1481–1559), artist unknown. Courtesy of Det Nationalhistoriske Museum på Frederiksborg, Denmark.

Christian II (1481–1559) is a figure surrounded by controversy. He is seen by some as a tragic figure, a man with modern ideas ruined by a lack of sensitivity to the realities of sixteenth-century political life, or by the medieval forces working against him. Others view him as a Machiavellian "tyrant"—violent, vengeful, and mentally unstable. He dreamed of a united Scandinavia and of himself as a strong king. Deposed in 1523, he spent eight years in exile searching for support for a return to Denmark, especially from his brother-in-law, Emperor Charles V. In 1531 he attempted to recover his throne through Norway, went to Denmark on a promise of safe passage, was betrayed, and spent the rest of his life in prison, first in Sønderborg and later in Kalundborg. In many ways he was like his contemporaries, Gustav I Vasa, Henry VIII of England, and Francis I of France, with whom he shared goals and personality traits.

poisoned by enemies at court.) His support of the Lutheran reform movement turned the clergy against him. His attacks on the Hanse damaged trade and alienated urban groups; his taxes on the commons turned them against him. Unrest turned to open revolt in 1522, and by early the following year he had been deposed, forced into exile, and replaced by his aging uncle, Frederik (I) (1471–1533).

Frederik's brief reign (1523–33) was, at least on the surface, politically peaceful. Old, cautious, and relatively passive, Frederik worked with the nobles who had put him on the throne and restored the traditional crown-noble constitutional relationship reflected in his accession charter, by which he promised to honor the privileges of the nobles, including their exemption from taxation and claim to government positions and to rule with the council of state (Rigsråd). His most significant and lasting contributions to Danish history came through the support he gave to the Reformation.

Far more important in shaping Denmark's sixteenth-century political history was Christian III (1503–1559), who established his place as king as a result of the Count's War (1534–36) (Grevens fejde). This complicated, confusing, and bloody civil war revealed many of the factions and fissures within Danish society in the period: advocates of strong central government versus advocates of weak and decentralized government, noble versus peasant, merchant versus urban commoner, Catholic versus Lutheran, Danish noble versus German noble, etc. On one side were ranged the forces of Christian (Frederik I's elder son), the Jutland nobility, and Sweden. On the other stood those of Christian's younger brother, Hans (1521–80), the deposed Christian II, Count Christoffer of Oldenburg (c.1504–66), elements of the peasantry, and the burghers of Lübeck, Copenhagen, and Malmö. This was the last Danish civil war, and it left legacies of bitterness, the finances of the Danish state in disorder, and potential opponents of the monarchy discredited. However, it also directed Denmark down a road of political development somewhat different from that taken by Sweden. The alliance between crown and nobility that formed the basis of power in the state and lasted into the mid–nineteenth century in Denmark was confirmed, and the country remained an elective monarchy for over another century. Government in Denmark was to be founded on the king working in concert with a reformed/secular council of state controlled by the upper nobility. Day-to-day administration was to be in the hands of the king and his chancellor. Although the opportunity was there for Christian to destroy the elements of the nobility that had opposed him in the Count's War, he did not take it. In his accession charter he guaranteed the secular nobility its privileges, took his revenge only on the Church, and perpetuated an essentially medieval constitutional order. Once in power Christian III showed little interest in the day-to-day affairs of the state, preferring to pursue his passions for theology and cartography. However, he was committed to reforming the administration and improving state finances, and he surrounded himself with able men who shared these goals and who successfully used the desire for peace and order in Denmark following the Count's War to build a relatively efficient government based on expertise, more effective exploitation of crown properties and other resources for income, creation of a state Lutheran Church, and a peaceful foreign policy.

Foremost among his advisers, and one of the most remarkable public officials of the century, was Johan Friis (1494–1570), who served as chancellor for the entire twenty-five years of Christian's reign. According to most historians of the period, it was Friis who directed the affairs of Denmark, not the king. Administration was divided between the German Chancery, which handled foreign affairs, and the Danish Chancery, which dealt with domestic matters and relations with Sweden. Friis focused on the development of the latter, which came to be staffed by younger nobles, many of whom had been educated at Continental universities or had become familiar with the new political ideas and practices through European travels. Coupled with the development of a provincial administration based on royally appointed county governors and their sheriffs, the Christian III–Johan Friis period witnessed the beginning of the transition of Denmark's nobility from a medieval, military nobility to an early modern government service nobility.

Friis's most important reforms involved state finances. The principal resources of the crown included income (in cash or kind) from crown lands and fiefs, direct taxes, customs, the Sound Tolls (fees collected on ships passing through the Øresund since 1429), and church tithes. Implementation of the Reformation revolutionized land ownership in Denmark. Through the appropriation of Church properties, the crown tripled its holdings—thereby acquiring nearly 50 percent of all the country's land. These properties were productive for the crown in three ways: some were managed directly by royal agents; some were donated as fiefs (*len*) to members of the nobility in return for payments; and some were awarded to nobles as fiefs in return for service without pay. A serious problem with the latter two options, which long plagued Denmark's kings, was that fiefs granted to individuals for payment or service tended to become the permanent property of nobles, income from them dwindled, and they were lost from the pool of royal lands. No less serious was the fact that many crown fiefs were pawned in times of crises and then never recovered. Friis tried to solve these problems by fixing the term for which a fief was granted, ensuring the payment of rents, and putting an end to the practice of pawning. Although the systems he established were by no means perfect, crown income rose, and, coupled with Christian III's thriftiness and cautious foreign policies, the government's financial situation improved.

When Christian died in 1559, he left his impetuous son, Frederik II (1534–88), a well-governed realm in sound financial condition and at peace at home and abroad. Frederik, however, quickly squandered his inheritance. Even before his father's death, he led an attack on Ditmarsken, a tiny peasant republic located to the north of the mouth of the Elbe River and surrounded by territories belonging to the Duchy of Holstein. The successful campaign erased the 1500 defeat at Hemmingstedt and resulted in the incorporation of the area into the duchy. Apparently, this victory whetted the king's appetite for further campaigns. Convinced that Denmark deserved preeminent status in the North and that the union should be restored under his leadership, he went to war with Sweden in 1563.

The Northern Seven Years' War (1563–70) nearly undid the reforming efforts of Johan Friis and altered the constitutional balance in the kingdom. Frederik was forced to recall Peder Oxe (1520–75), whose ruthlessness and greed had alienated the crown and led to his being forced into exile in the late 1550s. Oxe became treasurer and quickly managed to restore financial order by imposing new taxes on the peasants, extracting donations from the nobility, and altering the bases on which the Sound Tolls were collected. In the last instance, by charging tolls on the value of cargoes rather than on each ship, Oxe tripled the income of the Sound Tolls. From 1570 to 1575, Oxe was, in effect, the ruler of Denmark, and his successors, Niels Kås (Kaas) (1534–94) and Christoffer Valkendorf (1525–1601), played similar roles while the king withdrew to pursue the pleasures of hunting and eating.

The parts played by Friis, Oxe, and other members of the high nobility increased the influence of that group in the constitutional order of Denmark. When Frederik died suddenly in 1588, his heir, Christian IV (1577–1648), was only eleven, and a regency of nobles ruled the country for the next eight years. To a degree, the country became an aristocratic republic dominated by a small number of nobles in a constitutional situation recognized but later rejected by Christian IV in his accession charter. This reversal of the pendulum of political power is typical of the period, and it reflects the tenuousness of the development of centralized monarchy.

Sweden

In Sweden during the sixteenth century a succession of rulers also worked to create a more centralized, more modern state at the expense of centrifugal or medieval forces. These efforts involved fiscal and administrative reforms, the import of new political ideas and experts to implement them, efforts to convert the magnates' estate into a service nobility, and exploitation of the Reformation. The developments in Sweden were unique in several respects, especially in terms of the development of a parliament (Riksdag) into an important component of the system, the weakening of the council of state (Riksråd) at the expense of high nobility, and the acceptance of hereditary monarchy. Of course, there was considerable resistance to these efforts, as there was throughout Europe, and they met with only a limited degree of success. It would be an exaggeration to say that Sweden or any other European state became an efficiently governed, centralized monarchy in the sixteenth century.

Sweden's post–Kalmar Union political history begins with Gustav I Vasa, who, according to a widely accepted version of the story, inscribed on Sweden's history a record of achievements similar in importance, if not in form, to those of Christian III and who deserves to be considered the father of modern Sweden. A man of stark contrasts, Gustav could be charming, witty, generous, and eloquent, or miserly, cold, and violent. He was, above all else, a king who wished to rule, and he was willing to use any means at his disposal to establish the power of the crown over the Church, the nobles, the commons, and foreign influences. By advocating his own version of the Reformation, he broke the power of the Catholic Church in Sweden, acquired its land resources for his own use, and then built a church loyal to and an important agent of the monarchy. By threat, action, and bribery he secured at least the passive consent of the nobles.

In contrast to events in Denmark, the council of state, traditionally dominated by a few powerful families, lost influence. A man of enormous energy and talent, Gustav ran Sweden as if it were his personal estate. He relied on experts, including the Germans Conrad von Pyhy (?–1553) and Georg Norman (c.1490–1553), for advice and to oversee the day-to-day operations of the emerging government. Surprisingly, he generated relatively little opposition among the magnates to what were clear violations of Sweden's medieval constitution. In part this was because many of his potential opponents had

Riksdag

Each of the Nordic countries had representative assemblies in their histories, and the origins of these bodies long predate the early modern period. Generally, these assemblies had functioned at the local and provincial levels. However, there were instances in the Middle Ages of meetings of national assemblies, most notably Iceland's Althing. From the 1430s in Sweden, more and more frequent use was made of national meetings to sanction the election of a union monarch or a Protector of the Realm. Who attended those meetings varied, but the broadest of them included representatives of the four principal estates (ständer): clergy, nobles, burghers, and commoners. During the early sixteenth century, Gustav I Vasa was recognized as Protector of the Realm by an assembly gathered at Vadstena in August 1521 and as king at Strängnäs in June 1523. His moves to effect the Reformation were sanctioned by what some believe was the first modern parliament meeting at Västerås in 1527, and his decision to make Sweden a hereditary monarchy was approved in 1544 at a similar gathering. Gradually, these meetings came to represent all or some of four recognized estates. The name Riksdag was first used in 1561. Gradually, this parliament became a third factor along with the crown and the nobles in the council in the political system, and it acquired the bases in precedents to claim a voice in constitutional, legal, tax, and diplomatic decisions. In contrast to these developments, the assemblies in Denmark and Norway lost influence. The Norwegians' assembly vanished after 1536; the Danes' Rigsdag, or Herredag, after 1660.

---

been conveniently eliminated in the Stockholm Bloodbath. Furthermore, he drew on the magnates at the central and provincial levels to fill administrative and legal positions. This assured them of power and incomes from the fiefs attached to their government posts. No less important was the fact that Gustav created a standing army that could be (and was) used to intimidate and quell domestic unrest and in which the nobles found careers. As in Denmark, Gustav skillfully provided an environment in which Sweden's leading men moved toward becoming service nobility. His successors, however, found that the medieval constitutional prerogatives of the nobles were not forgotten. By similar means and manipulation of the emerging parliament, he won the support of the commons. Overall, his efforts resulted in more rational government, sounder state finances, economic growth and an accompanying decline of Hanseatic influence, an improved international position, and, despite a series of nasty peasant uprisings, general peace at home.

When Gustav died in 1560, his eldest son, Erik XIV (1533–77), succeeded to the throne. Unstable and unrealistic, he quickly undid many of his father's achievements. Three problems proved to be Erik's undoing. The first involved the question of how to deal with his three half brothers in a hereditary monarchy. Gustav had attempted to address this in his will, by which Erik was to become king and Johan (1537–92), Magnus (c.1542–95), and Karl (1550–1611) were to receive large pieces of the realm as semi-autonomous dukedoms. This solution bore within it the danger of destroying all that Gustav had labored to achieve. First Johan and later Karl ignored whoever was the king and behaved like independent rulers in their shares of the kingdom. Erik recognized the threats and attempted to negate the will through the Articles of Arboga (1561), which was designed to place the brothers under his control. Johan, as duke of Finland, paid little heed to these constraints. His marriage to Katarina Jagellonica (1526–83), sister of Poland's king Sigismund August, and his independent foreign policy in the Baltic led to his arrest and imprisonment in 1562.

Second, Erik alienated the leading men of the realm. Although he sought to secure their support through the introduction of new noble titles (counts and barons), appointments to government posts, and donations of land, he was frequently disdainful, mistrustful, and violent toward them. His use of commoner favorites like Göran Persson (c. 1530–68) and his marriage to Karin Månsdotter (1550–1612), a peasant farmer's daughter, were particularly objectionable. Finally, there was the matter of the king's sanity. In May 1567, in a moment of madness, he participated in the murder of five nobles, including Svante Sture (1517–67) and his sons, Nils and Erik, who were being held on trumped–up charges of treason. For several months following these murders, Erik was incapable of governing. His credibility was severely weakened, and open revolt under Johan's leadership erupted in the summer of 1568. In January 1569 Erik's deposition and Johan's succession were recognized by the parliament. Erik spent the remaining eight years of his life in prison and may have been slowly poisoned to death by his brother.

Johan III was a more cautious ruler. He supported the development of the nobility and strengthened his ties with them in 1583, when he took as his second wife a daughter of one of Sweden's leading families, Gunilla Bielke. His policies in this regard were designed largely to reduce the influence of his brother Duke Karl and did little to enhance the authority of the crown. Continuing Erik's practice of alienating crown lands through donations to the nobility, he also weakened the crown's financial base and increased the landholding position of the nobles. Although an intelligent and cultured person, these and several other problems, including his Polish marriage and religious views, have marred his historical reputation.

Sigismund I (1566–1632), already king of Poland (as Sigismund III), succeeded his father in 1592. Determined to rule in both his countries and to bring Sweden back into the Catholic fold, Sigismund generated opposition from the outset. Secular and Church leaders met at Uppsala in early 1593 to discuss the situation. From the meeting came an affirmation of Sweden's commitment to the Lutheran faith. The political situation was more complicated. Initially, Sigismund attempted to establish a compromise under which Duke Karl and the high nobles would govern when the king was in Poland—and Sigismund hoped the nobles would be able to keep his uncle in line. In fact, however, this was no solution. Karl was not to be contained. He alienated members of the council, drove some members into the arms of Sigismund, and forced the king to return to Sweden with an army to crush the troublesome uncle and his supporters. But Sigismund failed. In 1598 he was checked at Stångebro and retreated to Poland. Not until 1660, however, did the Polish Vasas renounce their claim to the throne in Sweden, and that claim remained a cause of conflict in the relations between the two countries until then.

Following Sigismund's defeat Duke Karl, the last of Gustav Vasa's sons, could finally play king. Cautious about claiming a throne to which he had only a weak claim, he acted as regent until 1604 and was not crowned until 1607. Only after carefully consolidating his power and eliminating a number of opponents did he feel strong enough to take the title of king. Politically, he was much like his father, as he sought to focus authority in himself. In 1600 at Linköping he orchestrated revenge on disloyal nobles when the parliament, acting as a high court, condemned four of his opponents. Karl's style created many enemies, especially among the nobles, and his sudden and unexpected death in 1611 created an opportunity for them to restore greater crown-noble balance.

International Relations

The history of international relations in Norden in the sixteenth century may be conveniently divided into three periods. During the first (c. 1500–23), the leaders of Denmark and Sweden were engaged in an almost constant civil war over the union question. This conflict, as we have seen, ended with Gustav Vasa's successful break with the union—although the idea did not die and remained an element in Denmark's foreign policy for much of the century. Foreign involvement in the Dano-Swedish conflicts came mainly from Lübeck. This Hanse city sided variously with Denmark and Sweden, as its leaders tried to perpetuate political weakness and foster their own economic interests in the North.

During most of the second period (c. 1523–60), Danish and Swedish leaders sought to maintain peace between their two countries and occasionally even cooperated. The former policy was embodied in the 1541 Treaty of Brömsebro. The latter was reflected by Sweden's support of Christian III during the Count's War. In the same period, the Nordic monarchs also tried to avoid conflict with other powers in the region, especially between Sweden and Russia.

The final period began around 1563 and lasted until 1721. During it Denmark and Sweden became ensnared in the question of the fate of Livonia (Estonia and Latvia), as German influence there declined, and in the larger issue of control in the strategically and economically important Baltic. This so-called Baltic Question remained at the center of north European international affairs for over a century and involved Denmark, Sweden, Poland, and Russia, as well as more distant European powers including England, the Netherlands, and France. The reasons for this involvement are widely debated and include issues of territorial expansion, economics, noble power and influence, image in a highly competitive European environment, personalities, and security. Although suffering several losses, Danish leaders successfully maintained a primary position in the area until the 1620s. Thereafter, Sweden came to play the leading role in the region during much of the seventeenth century. This role was lost to Russia in the Great Northern War (1700–1721), and no Nordic state has controlled Baltic affairs since then—although the region contin-ued to be and remains an area of foremost concern and interest.

Denmark, Sweden, Poland-Lithuania, and Russia entered the tan-gled power struggle in the eastern Baltic in the late 1550s brought on by the secularization of the Livonia Order/Knights of the Sword (a branch of the Order of Teutonic Knights) and the search by the for-mer knights and the burghers of the region for security. In 1559 first Christian III and then Frederik II were involved in eventually success-ful negotiations to "purchase" the bishopric of Ösel (with its accom-panying mainland territories) for Frederik II's brother, Magnus. At about the same time, Johan secured several fiefs from his brother-in-law, Sigismund August, when he married the Polish king's sister, Kata-rina; and Erik XIV secured the vital port city of Reval and initiated an aggressive policy of adding territories in Livonia.

These moves, coupled with the designs of Poland-Lithuania and Lübeck and Danish-Swedish rivalries symbolized in Frederik II's dreams of restoring the Kalmar Union and his continued claim to the right to use the three-crowns symbol in his coat of arms, quickly led to the Northern Seven Years' War. In it Sweden faced the imposing but internally fragmented alliance of Denmark, Lübeck, and Poland. Principally, the war was over primacy in Norden and was the first in the series of Dano-Swedish conflicts that ended in 1720–21. At sea Sweden's navy, under the command of Klas Fleming, won some im-pressive victories but failed to gain firm control of the Baltic. Erik's land campaigns in Livonia led to almost total Swedish control of the area. On the other hand, campaigns in southern Sweden, around Älvsborg (Sweden's "window" on the west coast), and in Norway caused great local suffering and had mixed results. None of the par-ticipants could afford the enormous costs (direct and indirect) of a pro-longed struggle, and the war ended in a virtual draw by the Treaty of Stettin in 1570. Denmark gained temporary possession of Älvsborg —until such time as a crippling ransom was paid—and Sweden agreed to turn over its Livonia possessions in return for payments from the Holy Roman Emperor Maximilian II.

In 1575 the long and often renegotiated truce between Sweden and Russia was broken by Ivan IV's attack on Livonia. The countryside quickly fell to the Russians, and the Swedes were hard-pressed to retain Reval. Johan III launched a counteroffensive in 1578 with Poland as his ally, and the Russians were driven back and Narva was captured. Renewed fighting in 1590 followed a 1583 truce, and this round of the Swedish-Russian struggles ended with the Treaty of Teusina (1595). Under this agreement the eastern border of Finland was redrawn to Sweden's advantage, and Sweden and Poland were left in possession of the principal eastern Baltic ports and hinterlands.

Overall, Sweden was the victor in the conflicts of the second half of the sixteenth century. Älvsborg was recovered. The Livonian territories were, for the most part, in Swedish hands because the Imperial payments were never made, Denmark renounced its claims in 1575 and the Holy Roman Empire followed suit in 1579, and the creation of a situation aimed at the formation of a joint Polish-Swedish monarchy through the election of Sigismund, son of Johan III and Katarina, to the Polish throne in 1587 temporarily ended the Polish threat to Swedish interests. The Russians were, for the moment, defeated and turned their attention to channeling trade through the new port city of Archangel in the Arctic. But the Baltic Question was by no means settled, and for more than another century it remained central to the history of international relations in Scandinavia.

The Reformation

Throughout Europe, the changes occurring in the political, economic, social, and intellectual spheres during the sixteenth century were inseparably bound up with the Protestant Reformation. The religious revolution developed on several levels. It was, on the one hand, profoundly personal and involved gradual and fundamental changes of belief and practice for individuals across Europe. On the other hand, the Reformation was a group of structural and institutional changes imposed from above. The personal reformation frequently took much of the century; the structural changes often occurred in little more than a decade.

In 1500 all of Scandinavia was Catholic. The Church owned significant percentages of the land in each country, and its leaders were powerful in political, economic, social, and cultural affairs. There was, however, little criticism of the Church and, outside of a few towns, almost no desire among the peoples of the region to abandon the old faith. Two decades later the Roman Church was under attack throughout Scandinavia. By the mid-1530s official shifts toward Lutheranism had been made throughout the North; by 1600 all of Scandinavia was Lutheran in structure and practice. The landed property of the Church and its wealth had passed to the states, its political power and focus changed, and the clergy became financially dependent agents of those states.

Denmark

Lutheran ideas reached Denmark early, and the strength of popular interest in the Reformation was stronger there than in the rest of Scandinavia, largely because of the proximity to the centers of the new thinking, the extent of German influence in the kingdom, and the more urban nature of the population. Young reformers who had studied at Wittenberg or other German universities carried the ideas of Luther and the humanists into Denmark. The reformers found their earliest field for preaching in Duke Christian's (the future Christian III) territories: Slesvig-Holstein and especially in Haderslev-Tönning. There, Wittenberg-trained evangelists such as Hermann Tast (1490–1551) were tolerated as early as 1522. Within the kingdom, the Jutland towns of Viborg and Ribe became active Lutheran centers. Hans Tausen (1494–1561), for example, became a popular evangelical preacher in Viborg in the mid-1520s. When he became Frederik I's chaplain and moved to Copenhagen in 1529, he was succeeded by Jörgen Salodin. Similarly, Klaus Mortensen developed a strong following in Malmö. The new ideas also reached beyond the urban setting and influenced the nobility and the rural commons.

The theological teachings of Luther and his followers in creating an environment for their acceptance were joined in importance by the social ideas some found in those teachings. For example, many commoners were attracted to what they saw as releases from the social, fiscal, and ceremonial impositions of the Church. Implicit, of course, was the revolutionary idea (a misconception) that the evangelical ideas included rejection of the existing secular social and political order, too.

Without the acceptance or, at very least, the toleration of the state, the Reformation would have made little progress anywhere in Europe. Christian II, Frederik I, and Christian III were all friends (to varying degrees) of Lutheranism. For a time Christian II saw the new ideas as useful in his campaign to break the power of the nobility (secular and Church) and as a tool of political reform. His position was, however, complicated by his ties through marriage with the Hapsburgs, and he returned to the Catholic faith around 1530. Like many of his contemporaries, Frederik I tried to take a middle course between the Lutherans and Catholics. Doctrinally he preferred toleration; structurally he preferred a church subservient to state interests. At a national meeting in 1526 he broke the ties with Rome by ending the practices of securing papal approval of episcopal appointments and sending payments to Rome. The following year, he authorized the preaching of the evangelical ideas and supported the confiscation of some Church properties.

Unfortunately, a middle way was impossible in the sixteenth century, and Frederik's decisions satisfied few. Efforts in 1530 to reach a negotiated settlement between Catholics and Reformers came to naught. Christian II's plans to recover his throne through an invasion that began in Norway and his subsequent arrest only complicated an already volatile situation. When Frederik suddenly died in April 1533, the country was on the verge of a civil-religious war. The reformers were well entrenched in Viborg, Malmö, Copenhagen, and other merchant towns; the Catholic bishops were determined to preserve a Catholic national church and a constitutional situation in which they played a central role. To some extent the sides as they developed in the Count's War reflected the religious divisions in Denmark. Christian III and his supporters were Lutheran; Count Christoffer's allies were, for the most part, Catholic.

Christian III's victory in the Count's War gave him the opportunity to affect the structural aspects of the Reformation. In August 1536 Denmark's seven bishops were arrested and deprived of their authority and properties. (Five were released within a year. Bishop Joakim Rønnow of Roskilde died in prison, and Bishop Stygge Krumpen of Børglum was released in 1542.) A new Church and School Ordinance, the work of the Wittenberg theologian Johannes Bugenhagen (c. 1485–1558) and a group of Danish reformers, was promulgated in Latin in 1537 and in Danish in 1539. The king became the head of a national church. The bishops were replaced and, for a time, were called superintendents. They were dependent on the crown for appointment and were excluded from the council of state. Their principal functions were to ensure the spread of the new faith and to supervise the work of the clergy in their districts—tasks that, as in the case of Peder Palladius in Roskilde, they pursued with remarkable energy. Parish priests were to be chosen by each parish and were, to a degree, agents of the secular state.

Theologically, the new church was largely Lutheran, but with significant Zwinglian overtones. Catholic practices gradually disappeared. The remaining properties of the Church were confiscated, and the houses of the religious orders were gradually closed and converted to crown uses. Several catechisms and church manuals appeared in Danish. The Christian III Bible, largely the work of Christiern Pedersen, was published in 1550. Additionally, several psalm books in Danish were published, including Klaus Mortensen's *Tøndebinders* from 1534 and Hans Thomesen's from 1569. Along with other works from the period, these books were important in the development of a formal, written Danish.

Norway

Structurally, the Reformation in Norway occurred quickly. Christian's actions in 1536 set the process in motion, and the new Church ordinance was imposed on Norway, where there was very little criticism of the existing Church and few reformers had found support. Resistance, headed by Archbishop Olav Engelbriktsson, developed but was quickly crushed. The old Church aristocracy was effectively eliminated. Lands and properties were confiscated, and the religious orders' houses closed. Episcopal fortresses were destroyed or taken over by secular authorities. New bishops were appointed for Oslo, Stavanger, Bergen, and Nidaros/Trondheim. All of them were Catholic in background, but were obligated to support the reforms. By the 1560s a new generation, thoroughly Lutheran, had replaced them, and the Reformation could be pursued more earnestly.

It was, however, impossible to effect a genuine change of faith overnight. Beyond Bergen there were few Lutheran preachers in the country before the 1530s. After 1537 an essentially Catholic clergy remained in the parishes, and it took a several generations for a reformed clergy to replace them. Lutheran practices only gradually displaced Catholic.

In contrast to developments in Denmark or Sweden, the Reformation did not aid the development of a literary language in Norway. The new church was Danish. Danish was the language of the literature and the services. The Bible, in Danish translation, was introduced in the 1550s. At the same time, church interiors were gradually "purified." They were stripped of their saints' images and the other artifacts of the Catholic faith, and pews and pulpits were installed.

Iceland

The Reformation in Iceland followed a pattern similar to that in Norway. The official transformation was imposed from Copenhagen, and the actual adoption of Lutheranism took much of the rest of the century. It is also clear that initial resistance was among the strongest in all of Scandinavia. The Church in Iceland was the subject of little criticism, and it was intimately woven into the social, political, and economic fabric of this poor and sparsely populated country. Iceland had no archbishop and only two bishops at the time: Ogmundur Palsson at Skálholt and Jón Arason at Holar. Both opposed the introduction of Lutheranism. However, Palsson was forced to retire, taken to Denmark in 1540, and replaced by a Lutheran, Gizur Einarsson. The following year, the Icelandic Althing adopted the Danish Church ordinance. These changes, however, did not effect reform, and the two bishops were in clear opposition. When Einarsson died in 1548, Arason considered taking over the Skálholt bishopric, but worked instead to have a Catholic candidate appointed there. A meeting of the clergy resulted in the election of two bishops, one Catholic and one Lutheran—the latter being recognized by Christian III. Arason kidnapped the Lutheran candidate in an act of open revolt. Declared an outlaw by the crown, he and his two sons were captured and executed in 1550. Arason's resistance to Danish control made him a national folk hero in later literature. The leadership of the Church in Iceland now became firmly Lutheran and set out to carry through the spiritual transformation by carefully monitoring the activities of the clergy and educational efforts. Overall, the Reformation and the accompanying increase in control of Iceland from Copenhagen was another aspect in the long period of exploitation, decline, and hardship for Iceland.

As in the rest of Scandinavia, the Reformation in Iceland was a significant moment in the cultural-linguistic history of the country. In 1584 an Icelandic translation of the Bible, largely the work of Gudbrandur Thorlaksson, was published. A hymnal appeared in 1589 and a worship manual in 1594.

Sweden

The history of Sweden's Reformation is more complicated and more drawn out, chiefly because royal leadership did not provide a consistent doctrinal course, and for long periods there was little popular support for a change of faith. Gustav Vasa was little interested in the theological side of the Reformation, although during his long reign Lutheranism made significant progress. Driven by political and economic factors, Gustav gave support to Lutheran preachers and effected the break with Rome, the confiscation of Church properties, and the building of a state church. At Västerås in 1527, the parliament sanctioned steps that initiated this process. Some Church properties were confiscated, noble land donations made to the Church since 1454 were recovered, and the bishops were deprived of their private armies and most of their governmental functions.

Aiding the early progress of the Reformation were the close relations that developed between the crown and the first generation of evangelical reformers, including the brothers Olaus (1493–1552) and Laurentius Petri (1499–1573). Olaus served as Gustav's chancellor for nearly three years, for example. These ties also had their dangers, however, especially when religious and state goals clashed. In 1533 Olaus and Gustav disagreed over how much control the king should have of Church affairs, and the chancellor was dismissed. A few years later, Gustav had his former ally condemned on charges of treason and then commuted the sentence to a large fine.

Olaus Petri was most active as a preacher, especially in Stockholm, and he provided much of the essential literature of the new faith to Sweden. He was central in the publication of a Swedish translation of the New Testament in 1526. (The full Gustav Vasa Bible was published in 1541.) His Protestant manual appeared in 1529, a Swedish hymnbook in 1530, and a Swedish mass in 1531. Laurentius Petri became archbishop in 1531 and held that office for forty-one years. His Church Ordinance of 1571 was a statement of the progress of Lutheran development in Sweden, but it was not without a certain element of vagueness.

Confusion developed in religious matters following the accession of Johan III in 1569. Johan's wife, until her death in 1583, was the Polish princess Katarina Jagellonica. She was a Catholic, and the court became a center for Counter or Catholic Reformation activity. She was permitted to have her own priests there, and for several years in the late 1570s, the Norwegian-born Jesuit Laurentius Nicolai ("Klosterlasse") and the Papal ambassador Antonio Possevino were active in efforts to convert the king and bring the Catholic Reformation to Sweden. Nicolai was even permitted to open a college of theology in Stockholm. Johan sought a middle way, and this was reflected in his so-called *Red Book* (1576), a new liturgical manual with both Lutheran and Catholic elements that satisfied no one in the religious struggle. Anti-Catholic demonstrations took place in the capital in 1579, and Johan was compelled to expel Possevino and Nicolai. The queen's death quieted some of the turmoil, but the fact that Sigismund (b. 1566), heir to the throne, was baptized a Catholic further

complicated the situation. All these developments did much to desta-
bilize the religious environment in Sweden and undermined Johan's
political position as well. His younger brother Karl appears to have
delighted in Johan's travails.

Following Johan's death in 1592, Sigismund succeeded to the
throne. Already the king of Poland, Sigismund presented an unequiv-
ocal threat to Lutheranism. The critical situation led to the calling of
the Uppsala Assembly, a gathering of about three hundred Church
leaders in the spring of 1593. At this meeting a clear affirmation of
Sweden's Lutheran position was taken. The religious question was,
however, inseparable from the political. Sigismund was compelled to
spend most of his time in Poland, and government in his absence fell
to Duke Karl and the council. A rebellion in 1597, led by Karl, ended
in Sigismund's deposition, and this, in effect, put an end to the religious question. Although Karl may have had Calvinist preferences,
and although he continued to debate Church organizational and theological matters, Sweden was irreversibly Lutheran.

Finland

The Reformation in Finland parallels that in Sweden. Several German-
educated preachers, including Peder Särhilahti, Mikael Agricola (c. 1508–
57), and Paaveli Juusten (c. 1516–76), began to spread Lutheran ideas
in the 1520s. The terms of the Edict of Västerås (1527) applied to Finland, and this led to the confiscation of Church properties, the recla-
mation of noble donations, the transfer of the tithe and other payments to Gustav's coffers, and the creation of a "state"-controlled
clergy. The first Reformation bishop of Åbo/Turku, Martin Skytte,
pursued a middle course in effecting the actual transformation, and
many Catholic practices continued. When Gustav split church administration in Finland by creating the new bishopric of Viborg/Viipuri
in 1554, the two new bishops (Agricola in Åbo/Turku and Juusten in
Viborg/Viipuri) pursued a more aggressive course. Still, the vagaries
of events for the remainder of the sixteenth century meant that Finnish religious practices remained a changing mixture of the old and
new, and it was only after 1593 that a purer form of Lutheranism took
hold in the country.

More than anywhere else in Scandinavia, the Reformation played
a role in the development of the vernacular language. Although
some Finnish was used in church services and a few religious texts
were translated into Finnish before the Reformation, the religious

revolution rapidly accelerated this trend and was vitally important to the development of Finnish as a written language. Mikael Agricola's Finnish language primer from 1542 and his translation of the New Testament (published in 1548) are central in this context.

Overall, the Reformation resulted in a significant increase in the wealth of the state and the authority of the crown, a landownership revolution, the transformation of the clergy into a crown-dependent social class with continuing importance in local affairs, the spread of the vernacular languages and the development of modern literatures, and the slow transformation of actual religious practices. Negatively, the Reformation also resulted in the loss of a cultural richness previously fostered by the Church, the decline of educational institutions and welfare networks, and the move from an independent Church to one easily manipulated and corrupted for State purposes. It also narrowed the options for women by closing the convents.

Social, Economic, and Cultural Developments

Although there were considerable regional differences, the societies of sixteenth-century Scandinavia shared several common elements. In general, they were all hierarchical, male-dominated, and overwhelmingly rural. Each kingdom had its nobility (untitled until the 1560s in Sweden and until the mid–seventeenth century in Denmark), clergy, town dwellers, and rural commoners. Each group had its own internal and oftentimes highly complex hierarchy. Ninety percent or more of the population lived in rural settings and made their living farming. Towns, based mainly on medieval church organization, ancient commercial or trade foundations, or royal prerogative, were few; and even the emerging capitals of Copenhagen and Stockholm were small, crowded, filthy, and miserable places for most of their inhabitants.

Land was the principal measure of wealth, and a person's relationship to land a determiner of social status. Ownership was divided to differing degrees among the Church, crown, nobles, and freehold peasants. In Norway, Iceland, and the Faeroes, most land was held by independent small landowners, and only small percentages were in the hands of either the Church or the nobility. Although each country began the century with a similar pattern of landownership, vastly different landownership revolutions occurred during the century in Denmark and Sweden. In the early sixteenth century in Sweden over half of all farmland was owned by peasant farmers (*bönder*), while the Church and nobility each held about 20 percent, and the crown claimed only about 5 percent. In Denmark the Church was the primary landowner, followed by the crown, smallholders, and the nobility. The Reformation and subsequent developments altered these situations. The crown and nobles were the chief benefactors of the redistribution of former Church properties. In Sweden, for example, after the Reformation the crown held 27 percent of the land, and in Denmark it held nearly 50 percent. Another striking difference in ownership came in the freehold farmer group. In Sweden the figure of around 50 percent remained relatively constant through the century, which indicated the continued viability of a class of independent farmers. In Denmark, however, the number of smallholders dropped. War (especially the Count's War), tax burdens, price fluctuations, the feudal social-economic model of the German parts of the kingdom, and the crown-noble alliance worked to erode the position of the smallholders. It was in the sixteenth century that Denmark's early modern exploitative landlord-laborer rural society was molded.

Subsistence farming was the occupation of most people, and their lives were regulated by the particular forms of agriculture practiced in a given area, by the crops and animals they raised, and by calendars of work and recreation centuries old. Tilling, planting, harvesting, preserving, and storing consumed endless hours. Tools and implements were simple and made mostly of wood. Although the moldboard plow had been introduced to Scandinavia in the Middle Ages, it was little used. The hoe and spade remained the most common implements of tillage. The principal crops included grains such as oats, rye, and barley along with some legumes such as peas. Typically, half of the cropland was left fallow each year, and crop yields were small (about three or four seeds returned for each planted). Scandinavia was also a region of livestock raising, but specific patterns varied. South Denmark was a major producer of cattle for export to Germany and the Low Countries. In the far north, stock raising was difficult largely because of fodder shortages during the long winters. In Norway, Iceland, and northern Sweden, animals were usually pastured away from the main farms for the summer months. Throughout Scandinavia the stock were much smaller than the animals of today—an average Nordic hog, for example, weighed only about 100 pounds. Dairy products were important throughout the area, and butter became a major export of Sweden. The diets of most people were determined by the marginality of agricultural practices and were dreary and repetitive, composed of flat breads; dried, smoked, or salted meat and fish; and milk and other dairy products from cows, sheep, and goats. Most foods were heavily salted and were washed down with large amounts of beer. In this marginal system, any natural disaster could (and often did) lead to great human suffering.

The organization of farming varied. In Iceland, the Faeroes, Norway, Finland, and parts of Denmark and Sweden single- or extended-family farmsteads predominated. Village farming was important in parts of Sweden and much of Denmark. In the latter cases, the village constituted a kind of commune that regulated virtually every aspect of life.

In addition to farming, the rural populations in many areas pursued supplementary economic activities. Peasants in coastal areas throughout Scandinavia engaged in fishing. The forests of the interiors of Norway, Sweden, and Finland became increasingly important during the century. Silver, copper, and iron mining were important in Sweden. The ancient copper mine at Falun grew during the century, and Gustav Vasa recruited German experts to expand iron production in the Bergslagen region of central Sweden. By the end of the century, iron was Sweden's leading export. Gustav also encouraged the development of a cannon industry.

Although towns, even the capitals, were generally small in size and the percentage of the population living in them tiny, they grew in number and size. Denmark had some eighty chartered towns in the early sixteenth century, including Ribe, Odense, Roskilde, Helsingør, Lund, and Malmö; Norway had just over a dozen, including Bergen, Hamar, Nidaros/Trondheim, and Oslo. Sweden's towns numbered about thirty-five, among them Uppsala, Sigtuna, Växjö, Kalmar, and Älvsborg. In Finland there were only about ten, the largest being Åbo/Turku.

Town development was both a barometer and an engine of the growth and the overall prosperity of the period. Towns were centers for internal and international commerce, production of goods, and governmental business. Although death rates in them were generally higher than in rural areas, they attracted an almost constant flow of immigrants. Each town had its commercial and political elite, its craftsmen (often organized in guilds), and its underclasses. Most of Scandinavia's early modern towns were largely unplanned, their churches, shops, and houses located at random and their streets

Dorothea of Sachsen-Lauenberg

Christian III's wife, Dorothea of Sachsen-Lauenberg (1511–71), illustrates the roles played by upper-class women in this period. A woman of strong opinion and, at times, influence, her letters clearly reflect her intellectual abilities, opinions, and interest in the affairs of the state. German in background, culture, and political ideas, she never spoke Danish well and favored Germans at court. In 1536 she urged her husband to take revenge on the nobles who had opposed his succession, but he opted for a more conciliatory course. In 1544 she helped negotiate the Treaty of Speyer between Denmark and the Holy Roman Empire. Following Christian's death, she repeatedly criticized Frederik II after his succession and plotted to arrange a marriage between Frederik's younger brother Magnus and Erik XIV's sister. As a widow, she maintained court at Koldinghus, from where she also demonstrated her abilities as the manager of her estate.

a maze grown up within medieval walls. Although Christian III and Johan III undertook extensive remodeling projects on Copenhagen Castle and Three Crowns Castle, respectively, these royal residences remained rough and unappealing by later standards.

Housing, rural and urban, was crude by modern measures. For all social groups, varying forms of wooden construction prevailed in styles of ancient origin—dominated by log or timber construction in the north and daub and wattle in the south. Until midcentury even the nobility lived in conditions little better than those of the commoners, and noble houses often resembled American frontier forts and reflected the relative poverty of the region. The second half of the century, however, witnessed generally improved economic conditions and the development of a new high nobility, especially in Denmark. A mark of these developments was the building of some seventy brick manor houses there before the end of the century. Concurrently, the wealthy burghers of merchant centers like Helsingør, Ribe, Copenhagen, and Stockholm began similar projects.

For women the sixteenth century was a period of continued inferiority in status and even of worsening in the conditions of their lives. Their mental and physical capacities were regarded as inferior, and women themselves were thought of as sexually licentious and even dangerous to men. The Reformation did nothing to change these attitudes and removed the option of a life within the Church for women. Women were most important for their labor, their reproductive capacities, and their usefulness in forging extended family connections or elevating a family's status through carefully arranged marriages. Despite the restrictive conventions and attitudes, women made vital contributions at all social levels. Although "noble" women rarely played direct roles in political affairs, their indirect influence could be great, and they did much to help shape the emerging life of the courts. At the level of the commoners, their contributions to the life of a farming community or an artisan's business were indispensable and highly valued. On farms, for example, women were essential in caring for livestock, planting and harvesting, preserving and preparing most food, producing the textiles and the clothing of the family, and raising the children.

One can in all fairness ask, what did the men do? They were responsible for the heavier work, including plowing, timber cutting (for lumber and fuel) and building construction, and they did most of the carpentry and toolmaking on a farm. Many were also, as noted, engaged in secondary trades. On the other hand, men, especially among the lower classes, had more leisure time than women—and they often spent that time drinking alcoholic beverages in excess.

Culturally, Norden began the sixteenth century far behind Italy, France, or the Low Countries, and the Renaissance had thus far had little impact on the region. Art, reflected in the portraits of monarchs and nobles of the period, was primitive. Native artists were almost nonexistent, and there were few resources to spend on importing talent from the south. Books were few. The Reformation produced a large number of publications in the Nordic languages. The body of secular literature also grew during the century. Examples include Johannes Magnus's chronicle of Sweden's kings; Olaus Magnus's *Historia de gentibus septentrionalis,* the text and illustrations of which offer a marvelous, though skewed, view of mid–sixteenth century Norden; and Arild Huitfeldt's history of the Danish kingdom.

The religious turmoil of the century had largely negative impacts on education. The schools of the Catholic religious orders vanished, and the contributions to learning made by them ceased. The old Latin (Cathedral) schools of the bishop towns generally survived, but their resources were reduced, and they served only a tiny number of students seeking to prepare themselves for university studies. Scandinavia's two universities, Uppsala (founded in 1477) and Copenhagen (founded in 1479) were small, poor, often neglected, frequently caught up in the doctrinal disputes of the period, and at the mercy of the monarchs. In the ideal, each was to have faculties of theology, law, medicine, and the liberal arts. Students began with studies in the liberal arts (grammar, logic, rhetoric, mathematics, physics, astronomy, and music), and most then moved into one of the other three areas, usually theology. Professors were poorly paid and often had to supplement their incomes by tutoring and renting out rooms to students. The students were usually from the lower classes (most aspired to become clergy), and their numbers were very small—ranging from a few dozen early in the century to perhaps 150 by 1600 at each university.

For higher education in Norden, the Reformation meant the conversion of the universities into state institutions existing at the will of the monarch and subject to every political and political-religious conflict of the period. For example, Copenhagen University ceased operation during the Count's War and was refounded by Christian III in 1537. Uppsala University went through two periods of crisis. In the 1540s and 1550s Gustav I allowed the university to languish, preferring to support Swedish students studying practical subjects abroad. Erik XIV restored it, and Uppsala began to flourish under Johan III. However, Johan's drift toward Catholicism led to controversy with the faculty, and the king "closed" the university in 1580. It was reopened in 1593 with the support of Duke Karl (Karl IX), but remained subject to the political turmoil. Only in the seventeenth century did these universities enjoy more consistent support from the crown and become important centers of intellectual activities.

Although this picture of Nordic culture has been painted in largely negative terms, it must be remembered that change was afoot. Education and, especially, the universities survived the shocks of the Reformation and were poised to enter a period of important growth and development. At the same time, more and more sons of noble families studied at foreign universities and gained practical political experience through visits to foreign courts, and this pattern indicates the gradual transformation taking place within an important segment of the Nordic nobilities. The courts of kings also increasingly became centers of high culture—in part because the kings understood the importance of splendor in the making of monarchy. The kings and

Tyge Brahe

Tyge (Tycho) Brahe (1546–1601), Danish astrologer/astronomer, artist unknown. Courtesy of Det National-historiske Museum på Frederiksborg, Denmark.

Tyge (Tycho) Brahe (1546–1601), the son of a Skåne noble, was one of the extraordinary figures of this period—for reasons more important than his abrasive personality and his silver nose. Rejecting his family's desire that he pursue a political career, Brahe became the foremost mapper of the heavens of the century and was a key figure in the scientific revolution of the period. He studied astronomy at several European universities, and by the time he was twenty-four he was recognized as a superb scientific instrument builder and observer of the heavens. Granted the island of (H)ven between Denmark and Sweden in 1576 by Frederik II, he constructed Uraniborg, which became the base from which he taught and for twenty years collected precise information on the location of the stars and planets. In 1597, out of favor at court and hated by the island's peasants, he left Hven and eventually settled in Prague, where he worked with Johannes Kepler. Brahe's accounts of his observation of a new star in 1572 (probably a supernova) helped undermine the idea that the universe was unchanging, and his records helped Kepler establish his laws of planetary motion and also contributed to the acceptance of a heliocentric view of the solar system.

their courts encouraged the arts, including painting, sculpture, and jewelry making; and they worked to provide themselves with more kingly and comfortable residences. Erik XIV and Johan III added to the royal castles in Stockholm, Gripsholm, and Kalmar. Frederik II outdid them when he began the construction of Kronborg on the site of the medieval fort at Helsingør. The fashions of court came more and more to resemble those found in the south and west of Europe. The monarchs also founded court orchestras and patronized scholars —though usually with a purpose. Frederik II, for example, supported the work of Tyge Brahe at Uraniborg on the island of (H)ven in the sound between Helsingør and Helsingborg because of his superstitious nature and the importance of astrology.

At the same time that a new cultural level and intellectual awareness were creeping into the upper classes, the new churches took up the tasks of attacking superstition, folk religious practices, witchcraft, and chronic abuse of alcohol among the commoners.

3

Absolutism and Empire

Throughout Europe, the seventeenth century was a period of stark contrasts: of prolonged civil and international wars and unprecedented devastation opposed by periods of peace in individual countries and remarkable accomplishments; of government by so-called absolutists (such as France's Louis XIV) and oligarchies (such as the Polish nobility or the Dutch burghers); of economic decline and economic prosperity, of great wealth for a few and poverty for the many; of superstition and ignorance illustrated by the hysterical persecution of "witches" and opposed by increased educational opportunities, intellectual achievements, and a "scientific revolution."

In Scandinavia two main themes have dominated the written histories of the period: the constitutional swings in Denmark and Sweden between the extremes of aristocracy and monarchy, between aristocratic republic and royal "absolutism," and the rise and decline of Sweden as the central power in the Baltic (and the parallel decline of Denmark). There are, however, many other equally important aspects of the century, including the development of government service–oriented nobilities; the expansion of towns; the growth of increasingly complex preindustrial economies; the influence of foreign ideas, capital, and individuals; the growth of the middle class; the founding of overseas colonies; the increased degree to which Scandinavia was part of Europe in terms of politics, economics, diplomacy, and culture; and the continuing sameness of everyday life for the vast majority of people.

Political Developments

Several general themes help define the political history of Norden in the seventeenth century. First, the struggles in Denmark-Norway and

~~~~~~

Monarchs

Denmark	Sweden
Christian IV: 1588/1596–1648	Karl IX: 1599–1611
Regency: 1588–96	Gustav II Adolf: 1611–32
Ruled: 1596–1648	Kristina: 1632/1644–54
	Regency: 1632–44
	Ruled: 1644–54
Frederik III: 1648–70	Karl X Gustav: 1654–60
	Karl XI: 1660–97
	Regency: 1660–72
	Ruled: 1672–97
Christian V: 1670–99	Karl XII: 1697–1718
Frederik IV: 1699–1730	

Dates are for reigns.

~~~~~~

Sweden-Finland over the "constitutional options" of government by a noble oligarchy, a blend of noble and crown authority, or a single "absolute" monarch continued, culminating during the second half of the century in the triumph of the royal option. Second, the growth of the scope and power of the state in terms of resources, roles, and administrative complexities characterized the period. Third, many of the developments that occurred were triggered by the abuses of power by individuals or social groups. Fourth, monarchs wishing to concentrate sovereign power in their hands used the discontents of the lower social orders to aid them in determining the outcomes of the constitutional conflicts. Finally, the political and economic power of factions within the nobilities declined and new factions rose, but the essentially privileged place of this estate remained intact.

Denmark

When the century began, Christian IV (1577–1648)—an intelligent, cultured, hardworking man with high aspirations but often less-than-adequate abilities or means to achieve them—was king in Denmark. Constitutionally, a tenuous balance between the authority of the crown and that of the high nobles in the council, with whom Christian was committed to share power, prevailed. Denmark was the predominant

~~~~~~

Christian IV

Traditionally, Christian's reign is divided into two periods: 1596–1625 and 1625–48. The first was prosperous; the second, deeply troubled. A contemporary of James I and Charles I in England and Louis XIII in France, much about his reign illustrates the constitutional conflicts of the century and the lives of monarchs. In politics he was often at odds with his nobility, especially in the latter period of his reign, and he was ultimately the loser in this conflict. His personal life was no less troubled. His first wife, Anna Katarina of Brandenburg, died in 1612. A succession of mistresses followed, including Kirsten Munk, whom he married in 1615. He fathered twenty-three children, ten of whom outlived him. His lasting contributions were in culture, the arts, architecture, education, and military development.

~~~~~~

Nordic power. Internal and international trade were vital. Copenhagen and other older towns flourished. New towns such as Kristiania, Kristianstad, and Kristianopel were founded. New economic enterprises were encouraged. Attempts were even made to establish regular trade between Copenhagen and India (Tranquebar). The king's building projects, including the Copenhagen Exchange (Borsen), the university's Round Tower, Rosenborg palace, and a new Frederiksborg, were designed to reflect the grandeur of the crown and the prosperity of the state.

Until the mid-1620s all seemed to go well for the young king. Christian's character was, however, flawed by an arrogance that led him to discount the advice of others and to undertake adventures that cost Denmark dearly. His troubles began in 1625, when, against the advice of the council, he took Denmark into the Thirty Years' War. In this venture he was able to act independently because his possessions in Germany made him a prince of the Holy Roman Empire, and he could draw on his personal wealth for funds. He believed he could defeat the Catholic-Imperial forces and secure Denmark's position in northern Europe against both the Hapsburg Empire and Sweden. However, at Lutter am Bärenberg (17 August 1626) his troops were routed. Subsequently, Jutland was occupied and pillaged by Imperial mercenaries, and Christian was compelled to accept the Treaty of

Slesvig and Holstein

Denmark's history has been frequently tied with persons and events in several relatively small territories in northwest Germany. When Christian I was elected king of Denmark in 1448, he brought the family duchy of Oldenburg as well as Stormarm and Delmenhorst with him. Far more important and more complicated, however, has been the long history of involvement in Slesvig and Holstein. Both entered the country's history in the twelfth century, Slesvig as a sparsely settled border region and Holstein as an attractive territory on the fringes of the troubled German empire. Danish influence spread slowly and rarely without challenges. At Ribe, in 1460, Christian I was recognized as duke in each region, but this arrangement proved unstable and temporary, and provided the bases for constitutional and succession questions four hundred years later. Over the following century a mixed situation developed in which the Danish crown claimed sovereignty over parts of the duchies while the Gottorp family in Holstein claimed sovereignty over other areas. Although Frederik III was compelled to accept this dualism in 1658 as part of the peace settlement with Karl X Gustav, it remained a cause of trouble and a complicating factor in international relations until 1773, when the Gottorp lands in the duchies were exchanged for Oldenburg and Delmenhorst. This settlement did nothing to solve old fears on the part of Holstein nobles of Danish influence, and relations between Copenhagen and the duchy's elite were repeatedly strained. History and the forces of change provided the basis for the nationality struggles of the nineteenth century. (See chapter 9.)

Lübeck. Luckily, Denmark lost no territory in this misadventure. But the costs to Christian in personal resources and to the people of Jutland were enormous. The favorable crown-council relationship was gradually destroyed during the 1630s and 1640s and culminated in his efforts to build a faction of support in the group of young men married to several of his daughters by Kirsten Munk, the so-called sons-in-law party. Christian faced criticism from every quarter for much of the remainder of his reign and was blamed for every trouble that

Corfitz Ulfeldt (1606–64), son-in-law and close adviser of Christian IV of Denmark. He fell from favor with the accession of Frederik III and died in exile. His wife, Leonora Christine, was imprisoned for twenty-two years in the Blue Tower in Copenhagen. Painting by Sebastien Bourdon. Courtesy of Det Nationalhistoriske Museum på Frederiksborg, Denmark.

beset Denmark in the last twenty years of his reign, including high taxes, inflation, social tensions, and Sweden's invasion in 1643.

In 1648 the constitutional pendulum appeared to swing in favor of the power of the high nobility. Denmark was still an elective monarchy, and when Christian IV's eldest son (Christian) died in 1647, the aging king was forced to accede to noble demands in order to secure the succession of his younger son, Frederik III (1609–70). The new king was also compelled to accept one of the most restrictive accession charters in Danish history. It appeared as though the council, expanded to twenty-three members, would govern Denmark. Frederik, however, although less interested by disposition and ill-prepared to be king, did not take the passive role expected of him and proved far more politically astute than many expected. Drawing from his experience as archbishop of Bremen-Werden, encouraged by his wife, Sophie Amalie of Braunschweig-Lüneburg (1628–85), and a clique of German military and political cronies, and capitalizing on fractures within the council, he effectively negated the accession charter. The council became largely his creature, stacked with loyal or weak members. The two powerful members of the "sons-in-law party," Corfitz Ulfeldt (1606–64) and Hannibal Sehested (1609–66), were ruined by their enemies with the king's compliance.

For nearly a decade Frederik did little of consequence with his powers. At the close of the 1650s, however, events presented him with a new opportunity to redefine government in Denmark. The decade was not a bright one, as the country experienced economic stagnation, plague, and two wars with Sweden that brought Denmark to the verge of disaster. Although not entirely justified, blame for the troubles was focused on the nobility. In September 1660 "the estates" (nobles and representatives of the clergy and burghers) met in Copenhagen. The lower estates demanded an end to the nobles' exemption from regular taxes. The latter balked, and a crisis followed. Exactly what Frederik's role was in the subsequent events is unclear. Certainly, he did not stand in the way of a coup organized largely by a few nobles in the king's favor, including (a rejuvenated) Sehested and Christoffer Gabel (1617–73), Hans Nansen (1598–1667) (mayor of Copenhagen), and Hans Svane (1606–68) (Bishop of Roskilde), that resulted in Denmark becoming a hereditary monarchy. In January 1661 an "act of absolute succession" was issued, and the completion of the Kongelov (King's law) in 1665 gave Denmark's absolutism its written form. (This document, kept largely secret and not published until 1709, served as Denmark's "constitution" until 1848.) A remarkable and peaceful revolution had occurred, and for the next 187 years, sovereign power in Denmark lay solely with its monarch, who ruled by divine right and on whom only three limitations were placed: the sovereign could not dispose of the territories of the kingdom, allow any reductions of his powers, or depart from the Lutheran faith.

In practice, Danish government throughout the absolutist period

Peder Schumacher

The life of Peder Schumacher (Count Griffenfeld) (1635–99) epit-
omizes in many ways the nature of politics in seventeenth-century
Denmark. The brilliant son of a Copenhagen wine merchant, university student at twelve, accomplished scholar of theology and
politics, European traveler, linguist, and poet, Schumacher entered
government service in 1663 and rose to become chancellor and
closest adviser of Christian V in 1674. For two years he thought
he could act as virtual ruler of the country. Then ambition, mistakes, arrogance, and a host of enemies helped bring about
his ruin in 1676. His conduct of foreign policy was attacked, and
a search of his personal papers revealed insulting comments
about the king. Condemned for treason, his execution was commuted to life imprisonment at the last moment. Schumacher's
career reflects the social mobility achieved by a few, the benefits
to be gained from having the right friends and marriages, the
power an individual close to a king could acquire, and the dangers accompanying that power.

(1661–1848) was typically dependent on the qualities of individual monarchs and usually defined by various crown-favorite combinations
working through different administrative structures or systems. One
such system developed during Frederik III and Christian V's reigns.
Guided by Hannibal Sehested, Christoffer Gabel, and Peder Schumacher (Count Griffenfeld), administration came to be based on five
"colleges" (Danish chancery, German chancery, war, admiralty, and
justice) in a pattern similar to that in Sweden. The old council disappeared and was replaced by a small "privy council" of close advisers
to the crown. At the same time, local government was revised. The
old royal fiefs were eliminated, and the country was divided into counties (*amter*), each headed by a government-appointed, salaried official
(*amtmand*) who was usually a local noble and oversaw the activities of
the local authorities but who had no independent military or tax powers. Sheriffs (*fogder*) were responsible for maintaining order and collecting taxes. Local magistrates (*sörenskriver*) handled judicial matters.
Reorganization of the militia elements of the army led to the station-
ing of small units in the districts, which could be used to maintain

The Royal Law of 1665

The Royal Law was largely the work of Peder Schumacher. It opens with a paragraph explaining and justifying the "constitutional" change, followed by forty paragraphs of specifics on powers, rights, and obligations. The following text illustrates some of those powers:

> Part B, Paragraph II: The absolute hereditary king of Denmark and Norway shall hereafter be, and by all subjects be held and honoured as, the greatest and highest head on earth, above all human laws and knowing no other head or judge above him, either in spiritual or secular matters, except God alone.
>
> Part B, Paragraph III: Therefore, the king shall possess supreme power and authority to make laws and ordinances according to his own good will and pleasure . . .
>
> Part B, Paragraph IV: The king alone shall . . . appoint and dismiss all officials, high and low. . . .
>
> Part B, Paragraph V: The king alone shall have control over the armed forces . . . the right to wage war, to conclude and dissolve alliances . . . and to impose duties and levies. . . .
>
> Part B, Paragraph VI: The king alone shall also have supreme power over the clergy. . . .

See Ernest Ekman, "The Danish Royal Law of 1665," *Journal of Modern History* (1957): 102−7.

order. The clergy also played an important role in the development of the new absolutist state by serving as the ears and the mouthpiece of the crown at the local level.

In late-seventeenth-century terms, Denmark became reasonably well governed. State revenues, based on income from crown lands, the Sound Tolls, customs, and a basic land tax, became more stable and predictable—though rarely adequate. Even the nobles were subject to some taxes. The old practice of parceling out crown lands (*len*) to compensate officials was ended and replaced with salaries. The organization of the army and navy were improved. Economic growth and trade were encouraged. Under Christian V, a uniform law code for all of Denmark was completed in 1683, which replaced the collection of regional and local codes.

Sweden

In many respects Sweden ended the seventeenth century with a system similar to that in Denmark. However, the steps along the way were vastly different. The century began with the arbitrary (some would say despotic) Karl IX on the throne. When he died in 1611 his heir, Gustav II Adolf (1594–1632), was only sixteen, and the high nobles, led by Axel Oxenstierna (1583–1654), seized the opportunity to redress the constitutional balance, that is, to restore power to the nobility. Gustav Adolf agreed to an accession charter that guaranteed the nobles' prerogatives and privileges and reestablished a system of shared sovereignty involving crown, nobles, and parliament. Over the following two decades a highly effective system of government evolved. The king ruled with the advice of his council, which was composed of the five great officers of the realm (chancellor, steward, master of taxes, marshal, admiral) and about twenty other officials. This body evolved into a kind of cabinet responsible for governing with the king when he was present and able to act independently in the king's absence. The council was controlled by an elite faction of the nobility. The Riksdag was assured a place in the system through the Riksdag Act of 1617, which affirmed its right to be consulted in important matters and more clearly defined its estate structure. Not surprisingly, the nobles were the greatest gainers in these changes. The noble estate (divided into three ranks) dominated the parliament; most government and officer appointments were open only to members of nobility, and they were exempt from regular taxes.

In addition, several important other reforms were introduced. Administratively, five "colleges," roughly equal to modern government departments (chancery, war, admiralty, treasury, and justice), developed. Local administration was revised based on a new division of the realm into twenty-three counties (*län*), each headed by a governor (*landshövding*). A new high court was created.

Many of these changes were embodied in the Form of Government of 1634. This sixty-five paragraph document was a fundamental statement of council constitutionalism, the political option that prevailed after the death of Karl IX and under which factions of the nobility enjoyed great power. It was probably the work of Oxenstierna and may have had the approval of Gustav Adolf before his death. Although never formally adopted by the Riksdag as a constitutional document, it functioned as such until the shift to absolutism in the 1680s.

Further reforms were implemented that aimed at underpinning the new constitutional order and the more extensive state that was emerging. For example, recognizing the need for an educated elite from which state officials could be drawn, a new system of university preparatory schools (*gymnasia*) was established. (Västerås, Strängnäs, Linköping, Åbo/Turku, and Reval were among the first of these schools.) In addition, the university at Uppsala was financially stabilized through royal donations. Economic development was encouraged by state policies and investment. The army and navy were improved by recruitment, training, and funding reforms.

Overall, Sweden became, in the context of the period, one of the best-governed and most internally peaceful states of Europe. The system was not, however, without its flaws. There was never enough money in the state's treasury. Abuses of power by some nobles were common. The workability of the system depended on numerous internal and external factors. Sweden was not immune to domestic unrest, and several crises, especially around 1650 and again in the 1670s, developed. The first of these threatened, and the second undid, the constitutional balance.

A swing of the pendulum away from the constitutional balance established under Gustav II began following the king's death in 1632. His only heir, Kristina (1626–89), was just six years old. For the next twelve years the council, acting as a regency, ruled; and Axel Oxenstierna (and his family) acquired even more power and wealth. After reaching the age of majority in 1644, Kristina showed mixed interest in state affairs. Although the council remained central, for several years Kristina stacked it with her favorites at the expense of the old council nobles. At the same time, the queen's generous elevation of favorites to the nobility, which grew from about 230 families in 1632 to over 600 in 1654, and the accompanying donations of royal property, significantly changed landownership patterns in the kingdom, inflated the self-image and the vanity of high nobility, weakened the crown's financial position, and generated smoldering social unrest.

Had Karl X Gustav (1622–60), Kristina's cousin and successor following her abdication in 1654, been less interested in and preoccupied with foreign affairs, Sweden's political history might have taken

Gustav II Adolf

Gustav II Adolf portrayed as a Roman emperor. Painting by D. K. Ehrenstrahl. Courtesy of Statens Konstmuseer, Stockholm, Sweden.

Gustav II Adolf (Gustavus Adolphus) (1594–1632) is often viewed as one of the primary architects of the early modern Swedish state, and in many older sources he is treated as a national hero. Both reputations are at least partially deserved. He was a man of extraordinary intelligence, education, abilities, and energy. At home he contributed to the achievement of a stable constitutional balance between the crown and nobility, development of the structures of a reasonably efficient administrative system, definition of the parliament's organization and functions, judicial reform, regional government reform, education encouragement and reform, and the foundation of a postal system. In military history he is usually credited with improving the fighting capacities of the Swedish army and contributing to fundamental changes in the nature and tactics of seventeenth-century armies. Among his achievements were recruitment reforms intended to reduce the number of mercenary troops in the army, abandonment of the cumbersome Spanish *tercio* formations for more mobile lines, improved training, rigorous discipline enforcement, adoption of lighter and more mobile artillery pieces, and encouragement of arms production. How much credit for any of this he deserves is unclear. He was frequently out of the country, and Axel Oxenstierna and other talented aides were important in the changes at home; few of his military innovations were original, although the total package may have been. After his death the parliament voted to call him Gustav Adolf the Great, and a mythology in stories and images was consciously cultivated.

Kristina

Kristina (1626–89) is one of the most fascinating personalities of the seventeenth century, and her biography is quite exceptional among the few women to rule during the early modern period. For the ten years she was queen, she contributed to the development of a vibrant social, culture, and intellectual court; stimulated the renewal of Stockholm; and presided over the continued development of Sweden as an imperial power. Then, in 1650, she announced her intention never to marry and manipulated growing social tensions to secure the succession of her cousin, Karl (X) Gustav. Four years later she abdicated, left Sweden, and converted to Catholicism. These actions naturally gave rise to questions, rumors, and often bizarre explanations. To this day the real Kristina remains a mystery.

a different turn. However, Karl spent almost all of his reign away from Stockholm, and, although he tended to rely on personal favorites, the council nobility's role in state affairs remained central. When the king suddenly died in 1660, the old elite secured control of the regency for Karl XI. Led by Magnus De la Gardie (1622–86), this group worked to protect its political and economic positions against the growing opposition of the lower nobles and the other estates. Although the regents were probably less self-serving and careless with the country's affairs than history has generally recounted, they did much to create an environment ripe for change.

From the late sixteenth century a gradual landownership revolution took place in Sweden, a revolution created by the practice of alienating crown lands. In theory this meant assigning crown properties and their accompanying incomes for fixed periods of time to members of the nobility as compensation for services. In practice some lands were given as outright gifts to royal favorites, or the time limits were ignored and the alienation was regarded as permanent. This process was accelerated by the generosity of Gustav II Adolf and, especially, Kristina. A partial effort by Karl X Gustav to reverse the trend slowed the process. Still, in the 1660s, the nobility owned over three-fifths of all the land in Sweden, and a small elite within that nobility had become fabulously wealthy. At the same time, the number of independent farmers in Sweden, the country's principal taxpayers, declined because of the increased burdens placed on them. Some feared the freehold farmer class would vanish entirely and that Sweden would become a Nordic Poland with its dominant nobility and enserfed rural laboring class.

Karl XI (1655–97) was fully aware of the problems the alienations had created. At the same time, he was well versed in the absolutist theories of the day and in tune with developments beyond Sweden. Declared of age in 1672 and crowned in 1675, this somber, hardworking, bureaucratically minded young man cultivated his own group of loyal advisers and bided his time. When his popularity rose and that of the high nobles' fell even further as a result of the war with Denmark (1675–79), he took the opportunity to change the constitutional order. Now the pendulum swung fully to the opposite side. Supported by members of the lower nobility and the three commoner estates in the Riksdag, Karl asked for and received sanction for legal action against the regents, the recovery of crown donations to the nobility going back to the sixteenth century (called the *reduktion*), and the establishment of royal absolutism. The old council of state was replaced by a king's council and much of the old council aristocracy ruined. The nobility lost approximately half its former lands—to the benefit of the crown. (By 1700 landownership in Sweden was divided approximately into thirds: crown, nobles, freehold farmers.) The Riksdag became little more than a consultative body. The business of government was taken over more and more by salaried bureaucrats. The Church was brought under greater central control as an agent of government propaganda and keeper of population statistics. The monarch was the sole source of sovereignty.

Karl XI was not, however, an arbitrary or capricious user of the powers allotted to him. Careful and methodical, he understood the competitive world in which Sweden lived and the weaknesses that plagued the country in its overextended position as a Baltic power. During his years as king he worked hard to avoid war and to prepare Sweden for war. Perhaps most important among his accomplishments was the reform, based largely on earlier foundations, of the way in which Sweden's army of nearly 60,000 was recruited and paid for. Sweden's standing army was based on a local militia of infantry, cavalry, and officers. During times of peace the foot soldiers and cavalry lived as farmers on lands provided by each recruitment district. Officers lived on farms carved from the crown's estates. Direct government costs were limited to equipment and wages during wars. Although far from perfect, the fact that the system was retained until the early twentieth century speaks of its effectiveness.

When Karl XI died in 1697, he left his young heir, Karl XII (1682–1718), a well-ordered and peaceful realm. He squandered that inheritance. Government under Karl XII drifted from bad to worse. The king left Sweden in 1700 to direct the conduct of the new war with Sweden's Baltic enemies and did not return for fifteen years. Decisions were made in the field and were expected to be carried out by an unquestioning administration back in Stockholm. During Karl XII's rule, the Baltic empire and Sweden's preeminence were lost, the domestic and state economies thrown into chaos, and the absolutist option discredited. It is hardly surprising that a new chapter in Sweden's political history began with the king's death in 1718.

As a whole, the political systems that developed in the seventeenth century in Norden were far from being pervasive, absolutist, or (even) very effective in contemporary terms. No government in Europe possessed the means to control a state to the degree implied by the term *absolutism*. Furthermore, greed, incompetence, and corruption could be found at all levels. Communications were so poor that central governments knew only partially what was going on at the local level. Ultimately, the effectiveness of Denmark's and Sweden's governments hinged on the abilities of the rulers and those in their favor. Intelligence, diligence, recognition of the limits of the state's resources, and an understanding of matters (be they economic, political, social, or diplomatic) in their larger contexts were essential to success and rare.

International Relations

The primary themes in Nordic diplomatic history in the seventeenth century include the struggle for primacy in the Baltic, the struggle for primacy in Norden, the rise of Sweden, and the decline of Denmark. These themes must be seen in both Nordic and European contexts. The continuing religious conflicts of the first half of the century, continental and regional balance of power struggles, economic competition, dynastic aspirations, and the rise of new players influenced Nordic policies and actions. Also, although the diplomatic history of this century reveals considerable initiative by Scandinavian players, events made clear the growing links between Scandinavia and the rest of Europe.

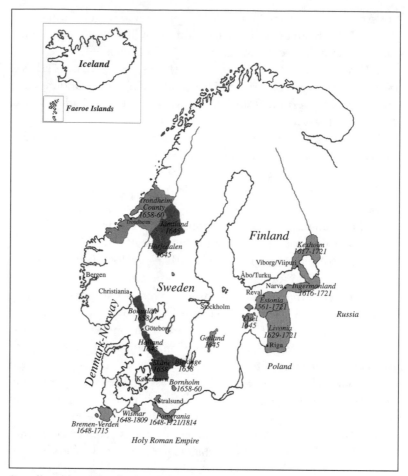

Scandinavia and Sweden's empire, 1561–1721.

The events of the first two decades of the century established a pattern of conflict that continued throughout the century. Denmark, with one notable exception, consistently faced Sweden as its single adversary and was sometimes supported by England or the Netherlands. Sweden, on the other hand, faced various opponents, sometimes singly and sometimes in alliance, including Denmark, Russia, Poland (and Saxony), the Hapsburg Empire, and Brandenburg-Prussia. Manipulating the balance through a changing maze of alliances were France, England, and the Netherlands, each seeking to preserve its interests, economic and strategic, in the North.

The wars were typical of the period in form and conduct. On land, sieges were preferred over set-piece battles. Armies moved incredibly slowly and usually only during favorable times of the year. Cooperation and coordination among allies were difficult to achieve. As the century progressed, the percentage of mercenaries making up the troops declined in relationship to native recruits. The use of gunpowder weapons increased, and tactics changed to accommodate these weapons. Of particular importance was the gradual adoption of linear formations. At sea the relatively small Nordic navies were used to control shipping and effect blockades. Only occasionally did great sea battles take place. War was enormously expensive, and no country could afford long conflicts. The direct costs of troops and matériel could quickly bankrupt an early modern state. The costs to civilians who stood in the path of seventeenth century armies were also horrific. Plundering and pillaging were common. An army with its baggage train and retainers could pick a countryside clean of food, live stock, and riches. For obvious reasons, no government wanted to fight on home territory. Rarely was there a clear winner in these conflicts, and wars tended to end either from the exhaustion of the belligerents or under pressure from outside powers.

Although it is easy to find a trend toward Swedish predominance in northern affairs in the late sixteenth century, Denmark was the primary power in Norden when the seventeenth century began. The Danish kingdom stretched from the North Sea to Ösel in the eastern Baltic. Several territories in what is today Germany were under Danish control or linked to the kingdom through the royal family, including Slesvig, Holstein, Delmenhorst, Bremen, and Verden. The modern-day Swedish provinces of Blekinge, Halland, and Skåne and the island of Gotland were Danish, as was a Norway that included the present-day Swedish provinces of Bohuslän, Jämtland, and Härjedalen. Denmark controlled the accesses to the Baltic. Sweden's territories, including Finland, Reval, and Narva, were extensive and its human and material resources potentially imposing, but the country was not yet ready to challenge successfully Denmark's position.

In 1600 a new round in the century-long conflict between Sweden and Poland over territory and Poland's claim to the Swedish throne began. This continued on and off until an extended "truce" was reached in 1629. Simultaneously, Sweden's leaders attempted to extend the realm's territories at the expense of Russia and to influence the outcome of the succession crises there. This struggle lasted until 1617,

Dano-Swedish Wars of the Seventeenth Century

1611–13	Kalmar War	Treaty of Knäred
1643–45	Torstensson's War	Treaty of Brömsebro
1657–58	Karl X's First War	Treaty of Roskilde
1658–60	Karl X's Second War	Treaty of Copenhagen
1675–79	Skanian War	Treaty of Lund
1700	Great Northern War (I)	Treaty of Traventhal
1709–20	Great Northern War (II)	Treaty of Frederiksborg

when, by the Treaty of Stolbova, Sweden acquired Kexholmslän and Ingermanland/Ingria and thereby cemented its control of the Gulf of Finland.

Christian IV could not resist the opportunity Sweden's troubles presented, nor could he endure what he considered direct challenges to Danish interests in Sweden's expansionist polices in the far north and in the founding of Göteborg. He also wanted to strengthen his constitutional position and dreamed of restoring the Kalmar Union. Going against the advice of his council, Christian declared war in early 1611. In the following year his forces captured Göteborg and established predominance at sea, but failed to destroy the Swedish fleet at Vaxholm. The war ended in Denmark's favor in 1613. Sweden suffered no territorial losses, but agreed to abandon its Finnmark expansion and was saddled with a million-riksdaler ransom for the return of Göteborg. At best, Christian expected Sweden would default on this, and the city would stay with Denmark. At the least he expected the ransom would overburden Sweden's economy and render the country powerless. Perhaps a more serious result of the war was Christian's newly inflated sense of his abilities as a shaper of foreign policy and a military commander.

The exceptional period in the history of Nordic diplomacy in this century came between 1618 and 1648. The actions shifted from the Dano-Swedish and Swedish–Eastern Baltic patterns to the direct involvement by the Nordic states in Germany. This shift illustrated how external events could affect Scandinavian policies and actions.

In 1618 began what now is called the Thirty Years' War, one of the longest and most destructive wars in early modern history. Initially, it was a religious and constitutional struggle in Bohemia between

Protestant nobles and the Catholic Hapsburgs. However, in the charged environment of the Holy Roman Empire, it became a general conflict fought in the German states and involving almost every country in Europe, including Denmark, Sweden, Spain, France, England, and the Netherlands. For each of the Nordic states developments in the war contributed much to the shaping their histories in this period.

Almost from the outset, both Nordic states were approached to join the war on the side of the Protestant forces. It was, however, Christian IV, acting as a prince of the Empire in his capacity as Duke of Holstein and against the advice of his council, who entered the fray first. In 1625 he joined forces with other Protestant princes alarmed at the successes of the Catholic Hapsburg armies and fearful of the triumph of the Catholic Reformation in Germany and an imposed revision of the German "constitution." Christian also saw intervention as a chance to strengthen the monarchy in Denmark and assert Danish supremacy in Norden. Performance did not, however, match aspirations. Christian was overconfident, and the troops under his command were ill prepared to fight against the mercenaries of the emperor Ferdinand II led by the brilliant Jan Tserclaes, Count of Tilly. At Lutter am Bärenberg (August 1626) Christian's army was defeated, and the next year Jutland was invaded and ravaged. At Lübeck, in 1629, Christian signed a treaty with the Empire that cost him mostly pride and promises to stay out of German affairs. His failure opened the door to new Imperial successes. Most of northern Germany fell, and Protestant resistance collapsed. The Hapsburgs appeared poised to dictate both the religious and the political situations in the German states, to create a more centralized and largely Catholic Germany, and to put a fleet in the Baltic.

Although religious and economic considerations as well as issues of Sweden's credibility as a great power and the king's legitimacy as ruler were important, it was the upset in the Baltic balance of power that triggered Gustav II Adolf's entry into the war. A disunited and fractious Germany was little threat to Sweden's interests. A united Germany was another matter; the Catholic victory over Denmark, the presence of an Imperial army in northern Germany, and the threat of an Imperial fleet in the Baltic made that threat appear very real indeed to Sweden's leaders. The decision to intervene was made and a truce with Poland concluded (with French assistance). Swedish forces landed in northern Germany in summer 1630.

Initially, Gustav II Adolf had trouble finding support for continuing the struggle, and for months he sat in Peenemünde. Gradually, however, a coalition formed, and military successes like the Swedish victory at Breitenfeld on 7 September 1631, where his well-trained and mobile lines of infantry, aggressive cavalry, and lighter and more mobile artillery temporarily established an impression of Swedish invincibility, added to his ranks. To help finance his campaigns, Gustav concluded a subsidy agreement with France in January 1631 and extracted tribute from German cities.

Not surprisingly, success enlarged Gustav Adolf's confidence and his war aims. Some have argued he dreamed of deposing Ferdinand II and making himself Holy Roman Emperor. More credible are the claims that he hoped to create an expanded northern kingdom by adding parts of north Germany, Denmark, and Norway to the realm. But the total victory to attain either of these goals eluded him. As was so typical in the wars of the period, victories were only partial, enemy armies that one day seemed to have been destroyed reappeared, allies proved unreliable. Efforts to subdue Bavaria failed, and Gustav Adolf had to turn his troops back into Saxony in response to a new Imperial campaign led by Albrecht von Wallenstein, who threatened his supply lines to the north. On 6 November 1632 the two armies, each numbering about 19,000, met at Lützen near Leipzig. The battle lasted much of the day, and both sides suffered horrible casualties. In the end the Imperial forces abandoned the field, and the outcome is usually seen as a Swedish victory. However, Gustav Adolf was killed, and hopes for an overall Swedish/Protestant triumph in the war dashed.

After Gustav Adolf's death the nature of Sweden's involvement changed. Under Axel Oxenstierna's leadership, the country's direct participation diminished. Swedish armies became increasingly foreign mercenary armies under Swedish command. Yet for another sixteen years the fighting continued without clear results and at great cost. Back in Sweden the struggle became increasingly unpopular and contributed to growing social unrest.

During the last phase of the German war, Sweden also fought the second Dano-Swedish War (1643–45) of the period. It was precipitated by Christian's continued desire to establish Denmark's primacy in the Baltic and his consequent attempts to find allies for a war against Sweden. (In this search he approached Russia, Poland, and the Hapsburgs.) Sweden's leaders tired of Christian's plottings. Troops under Lennart Torstensson easily occupied Jutland, and much of Skåne fell to Swedish forces. Around the Danish islands Swedish naval units tried to strangle Denmark with a blockade. Christian played military hero admirably and even lost an eye while commanding his fleets in the naval battle of Kolberger Heide in July 1645. But the king's heroism could not win the war. At Brömsebro Denmark handed over Halland for thirty years and ceded the Baltic islands of Ösel and Gotland and the Norwegian provinces of Jämtland and Härjedalen to Sweden. Only French and Dutch support of Denmark prevented even worse losses.

It took almost six years of negotiation to conclude the Treaty of Westphalia, which ended the Thirty Years' War. The treaty's terms appeared to justify Sweden's involvement. For its troubles, Sweden acquired the bishoprics of Bremen and Verden, the port of Wismar, western Pomerania, and "membership" in Imperial Germany. Germany remained a hodgepodge of states, weak and disunited, and the survival of Lutheranism (and Calvinism) in Germany was ensured. Overall, Sweden's security appeared strengthened and an influential position in the European state system established.

At midcentury Sweden's Baltic predominance was clear and its empire almost at its peak. Karl X Gustav, who succeeded Kristina in 1654, was, perhaps more than any other Swedish monarch of the sixteenth and seventeenth centuries, committed to the idea of empire and to actual Swedish control of the Baltic. His campaigns against Poland, Russia, Brandenburg, and Denmark were aimed at cementing Sweden's position. With the traditional enemies in the east, he achieved no lasting successes. In the west, however, he came close to eliminating Denmark entirely as an independent state.

In 1657 Frederik III, believing Sweden was too deeply involved in the eastern Baltic to be a serious threat, smarting from the losses of 1645 and the gains Sweden had made through the Treaty of Westphalia, and searching for diplomatic triumphs that might strengthen the crown's hand, declared war on Sweden. Again, a Danish leader miscalculated, and the country proved unprepared for war. Karl marched his troops across northern Germany, secured control of south Jutland, and then managed to get much of his army across the ice of the Little and Big Belts and on to Sjaelland by early February 1658. Unprepared to meet the Swedish challenge, the Danish government agreed to humiliating peace terms at Roskilde. Halland (turned over in 1645 for thirty years but not ceded) was awarded to Sweden along with Skåne, Blekinge, and the islands of Hven and Bornholm. In

Sweden's Empire: Growth and Decline

Additions

1561	Reval
1581	Narva
1595	Österbotten
1617	Kexholmslän and Ingermanland
1629	Livonia, and five cities in Prussia, including Elbing
1638	New Sweden
1645	Jämtland, Härjedalen, Gotland, Ösel, and Halland
1648	Pomerania, Stettin, Wismar, Bremen, and Verden
1658	Skåne, Blekinge, Trondheims län, Bohuslän, and Bornholm
1814	Norway

Losses

1655	New Sweden
1660	Trondheims län and Bornholm
1721	Baltic provinces, Kexholm, Bremen, Verden, part of Pomerania
1743	Parts of eastern Finland
1803	Wismar
1809	Finland
1814	Swedish Pomerania
1905	Norway

addition, the Norwegian province of Bohuslän and the district around Trondheim (Trondheims län) became Swedish.

The maximum extent of Sweden's northern empire had been reached. Yet by late summer 1658 Karl was again at war with Denmark, this time probably intent on the country's demise. In this effort he was not successful, and for reasons that illustrate the complexities of Nordic diplomacy in the period. Karl sought too much within the European state system. Swedish primacy in the Baltic was acceptable; Swedish supremacy was not. The latter threatened the interests of the maritime powers (England and the Dutch Netherlands) and France, as well as those of Russia, Poland, the emerging Brandenburg-Prussia, and the Hapsburg Empire. Instead of facing an isolated Denmark, two coalitions took the field against Karl: Denmark and the Dutch Netherlands in the west and Poland, Brandenburg, and the Empire in the east. The former neutralized the Swedish fleet; the latter attacked Swedish forces in Denmark from the south. At the same time, Karl's attack on Copenhagen was bravely repelled, and a horrible siege followed. Overall, a stalemate developed that was broken only by the Swedish king's sudden death in January 1660. Peace then came quickly with Denmark, and Sweden returned Bornholm and Trondheims län but retained all its other territorial gains. In the east, Poland finally renounced its claim to the Swedish throne and to Livonia. Brandenburg gained East Prussia at the expense of Poland and considerable prestige. The Russians settled at Kardis for recognition of the prewar status quo.

The Baltic wars of the 1650s well illustrate the tenuousness of Sweden's position. Although empire was good for prestige, business, and as a source of potential state revenues and places to fight, its potential was never realized, and it imposed impossible burdens on the country. It turned potential allies into enemies, as Denmark, Poland, Russia, and Brandenburg became implacable foes of Sweden. It demanded of Sweden the commitment of resources that might have been turned to other uses. It drained the state's treasury, siphoned off human resources, and generated internal unrest. At the same time, the wars showed the willingness of the west European powers to protect their own interests, the weaknesses of so-called alliances, and the indecisiveness of military campaigns.

In the last forty years of the century Denmark and Sweden's leaders generally sought to avoid war while they prepared for it with military reforms and constant diplomacy aimed at achieving superiority through alliances and securing subsidies to help pay for their military forces. With the exception of the years 1674–79 there was peace in the region, although that peace was repeatedly threatened by war scares (1683, 1689, and 1695).

The 1674–79 Dano-Swedish War grew out of Louis XIV's "Dutch War" (1672–78) and Sweden's commitments to Louis. When Brandenburg entered the war on the side of the Dutch, Sweden grudgingly met its subsidy agreement obligations with France and attacked Brandenburg. Initially, the action went well, but it soon soured, and at Fehrbellin in 1675 the Swedes were defeated. With this defeat Denmark and the Hapsburgs joined in against Sweden. The war in Germany became the fifth Dano-Swedish War of the century, and everything seemed to go badly for the Swedes. The Danish navy established control in the Baltic, Gotland was occupied, and a Danish attack (supported by local sympathizers) was mounted in Skåne. But victory eluded the Danes. At Lund in December 1675 the Swedes, now led by Karl XI, defeated them. A new Danish campaign in 1677 failed as well. When peace came in 1679, it was based on the status quo.

For both Denmark and Sweden the war made clear the dangers of the international situation and their internal weaknesses. Although little occurred in Denmark to correct these problems (other than helping bring down Peder Schumacher), the war helped catalyze political and social unrest in Sweden and usher in two decades of reforms including the *reduktion,* the introduction of absolutism, rationalization of the army recruitment system, and improvement of naval facilities, including the founding of Karlskrona in southern Sweden. Although there were even moments when Dano-Swedish relations improved, the overall situation in the North was fraught with instability. So long as Denmark's leaders remained unreconciled to the country's reduced status and territorial losses, and so long as Polish, Prussian, and Russian leaders remained dissatisfied with the status quo in the eastern Baltic and believed they had the means to change that status quo, the instability and threats to Sweden would remain.

At the end of the 1690s a new Danish-Polish-Russian anti-Swedish coalition formed. (Eventually Brandenburg-Prussia and Hanover joined.) The reasons for this were familiar. An expanding Russia under Peter I sought to replace Sweden in the eastern Baltic. Poland's king, Augustus of Saxony, hoped to gain territory at Sweden's expense and to use a successful war policy to weaken the contentious Polish nobility. In Denmark, the ill-prepared but hardworking Frederik IV hoped both to win the lands of the Duke of Holstein-Gottorp (an ally of Sweden) and thereby eliminate a threat on his southern borders and to regain the lost provinces in southern Sweden.

The combined resources of the allies were imposing indeed. Russia alone could field an army of 130,000—twice the size of Sweden's native forces. Had the allies been able and willing to fight a unified campaign, Sweden would most certainly have been quickly defeated. As usual, however, such was not the case, and Sweden could concentrate its efforts on one opponent at a time.

Denmark was the first to declare war in 1700 and the first to be forced to sue for peace. Although Frederik's forces easily occupied the lands of Holstein-Gottorp, the Swedes were able to counter this with an invasion of Sjaelland, supported by Dutch and English naval forces, and a peace agreement soon followed. The bulk of the Swedish troops were then transferred east, where successes against Augustus led to his temporary withdrawal from the conflict. At Narva, in November 1700, the numerically superior Russian forces were routed in a snowstorm. It looked as if the war would soon be over, but this was not to be the case.

Karl XII, although only eighteen, was now in command and insisted on Augustus' abdication in Poland. The Polish king refused, and Karl became ensnared in six years of campaigns and political intrigues. Not until 1706 did Augustus step down and the Polish front appear secure. In the interim Peter I improved his army, seized control of the eastern Gulf of Finland, founded a new capital, and established a naval presence in the Baltic. When Karl turned against the Russians in 1707, he faced a far better-prepared foe whom he unwisely chose to fight on its home territory. Everything went wrong with Karl's campaign in Russia. Reinforcement units and supplies were lost. The winter of 1708–9 was exceptionally severe. In early summer 1709 Karl was in the Ukraine, with a much-weakened army of 25,000 at the end of a broken supply line. He chose to fight the Russians at their entrenched camp at Poltava (June 1709) and was defeated. The remnants of his army, numbering 16,000, surrendered and were taken into captivity. Karl managed to escape into the Ottoman Empire with a small contingent. He established a camp at Bender in present-day Romania, where he stayed until the sultan had had enough of him and his conspiring. After an incredible fight against the Ottoman forces, he was taken under arrest to Demotika and forced to remain there until 1714.

While Karl attempted to conduct the war from his camp at Bender, the alliance re-formed, and new vultures joined in the feast. Denmark invaded southern Sweden but was forced to evacuate after the Battle of Helsingborg in February 1710. Denmark, Prussia, and Hanover seized most of Sweden's German territories. Russia occupied the Baltic provinces and Finland. The military situation seemed hopeless for Sweden. At home the costs of the war and natural disasters bore heavily on the people. Karl, a prisoner of history and his own character, would not yield. While his diplomats attempted to divide the allies, he demanded new armies for new campaigns. In November 1718, while observing the siege of Frederikshald on the Swedish-Norwegian frontier, Karl was killed, perhaps by a very lucky shot from the fortress,

Questions Surrounding Sweden's Empire

Many questions are asked about Sweden's imperial period, including why was the empire acquired, what made its acquisition possible, what was the empire like, what held it together, and why was it lost? None of them is easily answered, and historians continue to debate the answers.

In response to the first question, some historians argue that the empire was acquired for reasons of security. Sweden needed an empire for resources, additional state income to meet the costs of defense, and places to fight rather than at home. For a time the empire provided these. Others believe that the empire was built to secure control and reap the benefits of the Baltic's vital commercial economy. Still others argue for the role of power-hungry individuals, the selfishness of the nobility, the importance of prestige in the international community, a kind of historical inevitability in which Sweden's leaders responded to situations in ways any European statesman would have in the period, the conscious development of a new identity by Sweden's leaders, or a kind of chain reaction in which the addition of one territory triggered circumstances that called for the addition of more.

In response to the question of how, most argue for the convergence of numerous favorable circumstances including good leadership, sound government, a well-ordered population, a well-trained army with a high proportion of native troops, iron and copper exports, weak competitors, and helpful allies.

To define the empire is difficult because it was so heterogeneous. It was a hodgepodge of disparate parts separated by language, culture, history, economics, and politics. The added territories contained three distinct elements: Baltic, German, and Danish. In all but the last, the differences were greater than the similarities. Except for the old Danish provinces, efforts were rarely made to establish strong central control or to create uniformity.

The end of the empire appears to be more easily explained. Simply put, the favorable circumstances were lost. Leadership failed; domestic advantages and economic resources were not enough; weak competitors became strong; and old friends turned elsewhere. Overall, Europe had changed, particularly northern Europe, and Sweden's place in the North shifted with these developments.

Scandinavia and the Baltic in the eighteenth century.

perhaps by one of his officers. Whichever the case, serious negotiations now began. Agreements were quickly reached with Prussia, Hanover, and Denmark. Sweden surrendered Bremen and Verden, Wollin, Usedom, part of Pomerania, Stettin, the earlier exemption from the Sound Tolls, and a 600,000-riksdaler payment to Denmark. The Duke of Holstein-Gottorp lost his claims in Slesvig. Peace with Russia came more slowly, and even while negotiations were going on the Russians twice invaded Sweden. Finally, in November 1721, the Treaty of Nystad/Uusikaupunki was signed. Sweden ceded Livonia, Estonia, Ingria, and south Kexsholms län to the Russians, and the Great Northern War came to an end.

All that remained of Sweden's Baltic empire was Sweden proper, Finland, and Swedish Pomerania. Its age of greatness was over, and

Sweden now joined Denmark as a minor player or pawn in Baltic and European affairs.

The process of Norden moving closer to and becoming more involved in the affairs and the cultures of Europe accelerated in the seventeenth century. In politics, the ongoing conflict between royal versus aristocratic power was won by the crown (temporarily, at least) in both Nordic "tax" or "warfare" states. At the same time, the resources of those states were consciously nurtured and increasingly put to the service of the one activity that seemed to take precedence over all others: the conduct of aggressive foreign policies. In this area, Denmark grew less competitive while Sweden enjoyed nearly a century of predominance in the Baltic region and was, for a time, a player in a wider European context.

4

Early Modern Societies

The Nordic societies of the seventeenth century remained "estate" based, stratified into broad groups, each with further internal sub-divisions. However, there was considerable change and development in all social groups, and several general themes help describe the social history of the period, including modest growth in population, the ascendancy and then decline of the old high nobilities, the growth of the noble estates accompanied by their conversion to salaried service nobilities, the expansion of the old urban merchant and productive groups and the addition of new entrepreneurial and manufacturing ranks, increases in the landless sectors of the rural populations and a general decline in the status of the rural laboring classes (especially in Denmark), and the immigration of people with special knowledge, skills, and capital from Europe.

In terms of economic development, this was a century of contrasts, of new affluence and continued poverty, boom and bust, innovation and tradition. It was a century in which Norden became, more than ever before, part of the European economic system and even a participant in the "European world economic system." For 80–90 percent of the people agriculture remained central and rooted in traditional practices. But in areas such as state involvement in economic life, internal and international commerce, mining and metals production, and manufacturing, new ideas and practices appeared. Overall, Norden's economies became more complex, and certain sectors enjoyed phenomenal growth.

In general, social and economic developments were driven by several factors including the increasing size, complexity, and cost of government; the constitutional conflicts between crown and nobility and the ultimate triumph of absolutism in Denmark and Sweden; and the tensions and conflicts within and between social groups.

Early Modern Population

	1600	1700	1800
Denmark	700,000	800,000	1 million
Finland	300,000	400,000	1 million
Iceland	—	50,000	47,000
Norway	200,000	450,000	880,000
Sweden	900,000	1.15 million	2.1 million

Knowledge of Nordic population trends, social group size, and land ownership improved significantly in the seventeenth century, largely because the developing "tax states" needed better information in order to make tax collection more efficient. General population information was kept by the parish pastors in local church books, and special land censuses, such as one for Norway collected in 1665–69 and one for Denmark from 1688, contributed additional information. The reliability of the data from these sources is, however, subject to debate.

Other important factors were Nordic and European wars, increased affluence of a few, and enlarged tastes for the luxuries of the period.

Social Developments

Amounting to about 1 percent of the population, the Nordic nobilities were small and highly heterogeneous groups at the top of the social pyramids of Denmark and Sweden. (There was almost no "native" nobility left in Norway, and a Swedish elite made up the nobility in Finland.) Their place in these societies was defined largely by privileges that included virtual monopolies on government and officer corps appointments, exemption from most regular taxes, and varying degrees of authority over those who worked for them. Within each of the noble estates there was, of course, a wide range of wealth and power, and each had its dominating elite or aristocracy.

The Nordic nobilities of Denmark and Sweden grew and underwent a functional transformation during the century. (In Sweden nearly 1,000 families were added to the noble estate during the seventeenth century.) Much of the growth came from the ennoblement of members of the merchant class or from abroad, especially Scotland,

Hörningsholm on Mörkön in Södermanland, a sixteenth-century palace destroyed by the Russians in 1719. This is one of many drawings by Erik Dahlberg (1625–1703), who served as a quartermaster officer under Karl X, Karl XI, and Karl XII and was important in the design of Sweden's defenses. Courtesy of Brian F. Magnusson.

France, the Low Countries, and Germany. (The names Schumacher/ Griffenfeld, Reventlow, De la Gardie, De Geer, Douglas et al. illustrate this continuing Europeanization of the Scandinavian nobilities.) Functionally, the nobles increasingly became salaried bureaucrats or professional military officers. At least four factors contributed to these developments, including the states' need for officials and officers, the conscious policy of monarchs to displace the "feudal" nobility from power and to replace it with a nobility dependent on and loyal to the crown, the conscious policy of monarchs to use the lower estates and especially the middle class to bolster their positions, and the increased availability of educated and supportive bourgeois and immigrants. These changes were important, but not revolutionary. Although there were shifts in the traditional power elites, they did not upset the estate order of societies that remained fundamentally "feudal."

The first sixty years of the century marked the heyday of the old nobility of Denmark; in Sweden the nobles enjoyed their greatest prestige during the years 1611–80. In both countries the estate enjoyed increased opportunities, power, and wealth, and the high nobility partook of the fruits more than others. In each country the council played a central role in government affairs. In Denmark the council nobles won their struggle with Christian IV in the 1630s and 1640s and claimed a central place in the political system until 1660. In Sweden Gustav II and his chancellor, Axel Oxenstierna, established a cooperative crown-noble relationship that worked smoothly while the king lived. After Lützen a handful of great nobles, most of them related to the chancellor, governed Sweden during Kristina's minority. During her ten-year reign, Kristina ruled with an elite of favorites. Karl X may have had other ideas, but the brevity of his rule and his frequent absences from Sweden left the high nobility in firm control, and this continued during the regency period for Karl XI (1660–72). Even after absolutism was established in both countries, however, noble favorites continued to enjoy influence and all the privileges that came with such power.

This golden age of the Nordic nobilities was defined by more than political influence, however. It was also evident in the economic gains and in the tastes and luxuries many of its more affluent members enjoyed. Their country estates and capital city palaces, filled with imported luxuries and, in some cases, the booty of wars, were monuments to their success. In their consumption, the nobility also played vital parts in the growth of the Nordic commercial and production economies and in bringing high European culture to Scandinavia. Central Stockholm today contains at least nineteen palaces of the high nobles dating from this period, including those of Axel Oxenstierna, Carl Gustav Wrangel, Nicodemus Tessin, Gustav Horn, and Louis De Geer. The rural palaces of the high nobles, such as Ulrich Frederik Gyldenlöve's Charlottenborg, Wrangel's Skokloster, or Magnus De la Gardie's Läckö, rivaled the royal residences in splendor.

Historically, the old nobility's wealth was based on land and the incomes extracted from it in the form of rents, fees, taxes, and the sale of products. In theory, the nobles served the state, and in return received "donations" of land as compensation. In practice, many nobles sought to minimize the former and maximize the latter, and a few became fabulously rich. Overall, the system bore poor results. Economically and politically, the crown was impoverished through its donations while some of the nobility became rich. Socially, the loss of crown incomes led to increased regular taxes that fell most heavily on the landed peasants. These burdens, in turn, led to bankruptcies, the sale of peasant lands to noble or bourgeois buyers, the social degradation of freeholders, social tensions, and frequent complaints by peasants to the crown. If this way of paying for government had continued, the Nordic countries might have taken vastly different roads of political and social development—in all likelihood becoming "aristocratic republics," like Poland, in which the formerly free peasants became serfs.

In Sweden the *reduktion* (the recovery of donated crown lands begun in 1680) reversed the process, and the nobility lost half its lands. (The demands for the *reduktion* came from peasants, lower noble government employees, and the bourgeois merchants, all of whom saw their interests hurt by the growing power of a few.) Some of the recovered estates were then used to finance part of the military through the allotment system (*indelningsverket*). At the same time, the council of state became the king's council, a body with much reduced powers and staffed by a new clique of favorites. In Denmark, crown domains were sold for cash, principally to the nobility, which helped foster the decreased independence of Denmark's peasantry. In both countries the financial bases of the state shifted away from the royal domain to taxes—regular land taxes, tariffs on internal and international trade, fees, extraordinary taxes, and foreign subsidies. The taxes increasingly were collected by salaried administrators, many of whom were newly ennobled individuals, and enforced by state-controlled armies. Denmark-Norway and Sweden-Finland became "tax states" instead of "domain states," and their economies became strong enough to sustain the shift, so long as state expenditures were carefully controlled.

The development of the middle class, a group that included extremely wealthy merchants and entrepreneurs at the top and poor artisans and shopkeepers at the bottom, was important in the context of the region's economic growth and essential to the social-political changes outlined above. Three trends in this period include the overall growth of the middle class, the increased wealth and the greater political importance of the merchant/entrepreneur elite within the estate, and the increasingly central role of foreigners in these changes. In general, development occurred as a result of the overall expansion and increased complexity of the commercial and protocapitalist economies of Scandinavia and Europe. They were also developments that were furthered by state interests, external demands, and new technologies.

The seventeenth century was hard for the rural commoners of Scandinavia. Fluctuating agricultural prices, higher taxes, increased noble demands and intrusion into their lives, war, and natural disasters were some of the problems they faced. Although there may have been modest improvements in the standards of living for some landowning farmers, overall the century ended with the vast majority of Norden's people no better off than when it began—and some were far worse off.

In contrast to the general rise of agricultural prices during much of the 1500s, prices varied unpredictably during the seventeenth century. The variability was driven by internal factors including modest population growth, increased management of production on crown and noble estates, and bad harvests, as well as by external factors such as new competition from Baltic producers and foreign demand. War acted as both an internal and external determiner of prices.

In Denmark an agrarian landownership revolution occurred in parts of the kingdom. Much of the royal domain was sold off to members of the nobility or upper bourgeoisie, and by 1700 as much as 20 percent of the country's land was owned by the middle class and only about 1 percent by freehold peasants. The crown peasants who had worked the domain became peasants on noble manors or peasants under managers for bourgeois owners. As taxes rose in an essentially inflexible or worsening price situation, the capacity of the peasant freeholders to pay their taxes declined. Some were forced to sell, and in many cases the buyers were noble or bourgeois. At the same time the crown was busy either selling or alienating (donating) its lands. In general, most peasants became landless agricultural tenants bound to the land by rental contracts. Mobility was lost. The landlord determined rents, labor demands, and production techniques. Gradually, a kind of serfdom gripped Denmark's rural working class, a serfdom that helped support the increasingly costly lifestyles and tastes of the nobility.

In this changing context, profits from farming became increasingly important. As a result, efforts were made to raise production and cut costs. These efforts included the shift to large-scale agriculture (*stordrift*) and specialization on many noble and bourgeois estates. Some estates, for example, were given over entirely to dairy operations, based on the expertise of Dutch immigrants in milk, cheese, and butter production. These changes contrasted starkly with the traditional agriculture of the peasantry, altering not only what they did but how they did it. Although there was great variety in the impacts of these developments, overall the lives of Denmark's peasants changed for the worse, as their freedoms dwindled and their labor became their only asset.

Sweden and Finland's peasants avoided this degradation, but the threat existed until the 1680s, driven by the wholesale donations of crown lands, especially under Kristina, and the ever-higher taxes demanded because of the wars. Outbreaks of peasant unrest, which took the forms of protest and petition at the meetings of the Riksdag and rural violence, were common from the late 1640s to the 1680s. Demands for a general recovery of donated lands by the crown (*reduktion*) and tax decreases were voiced by the farmers at every meeting of the parliament in this period. Only Karl XI's reforms and the long period of peace after 1679 quieted the protests and eliminated the threat.

War had largely negative impacts on the lives of the rural people of Norden. Denmark was invaded five times during the century. Sweden, which was at war for fifty-two years of the century, felt the scourge of invasion at least four times. Finland was a battleground in the early decades of the eighteenth century. Although Norway was invaded in 1643–45, 1675–79 and 1718, the impacts were less noticeable. In addition to the direct costs of invasion on the domestic population, there were the costs of recruitment. Although mercenaries continued to serve in Nordic armies, most of the regular soldiers came from the rural poor, especially in Sweden. (Denmark's army numbered around 30,000 in the late seventeenth century; Sweden's, around 60,000. The size of the navies varied greatly during the period, but they, too, drained the populations of young men.) The human losses may appear minor compared with those in the European wars of twentieth century, but in proportion to the populations of the Nordic countries in the seventeenth century, they were significant. Sweden's wars of the 1620s are estimated to have cost 35,000 lives. Some 6,000 (one-third of the troops engaged) died in the Battle of Lützen, including the king and seven commanders. The human costs in killed, wounded, and captured in Karl XII's 1708–9 Russian campaign were enormous. At the Battle of Poltava 7,000 died, and about 17,500 (more than twice the population of Göteborg at the time) were later captured or surrendered

Leonora Christine Ulfeldt

Leonora Christine (1621–98), daughter of Christian IV and Kirsten Munk, was one of the extraordinary women of the seventeenth century. Betrothed at nine and married at fifteen, she was the mother of ten children. Her husband was Corfitz Ulfeldt, to whom she remained loyal during his stormy political career. When he was condemned in absentia in 1663, she was imprisoned in the "Blue Tower" in Copenhagen Castle and held there for twenty-two years. During that time she began *Jammers-Minde* (Memory of woe), an important work in Danish memoir literature. Long denied almost all comforts, she used a wooden spoon to make part of a small strap loom, pins and a piece of wood for a weaving reed, and a piece of glass for a knife. She wrote on the walls or on sugar sacks with ink made of soot and oil. Released in 1685, she spent her last years at Maribo convent finishing her memoir and writing poetry and even a play.

> I will here describe my prison. It is a chamber, seven of my paces long and six wide. It was freshly whitewashed, which caused a terrible smell. . . . It is eighteen feet high, with a vaulted ceiling, and very high up is a window which is two feet square. (*Memoirs of Leonora Christina*, 150–51)

to the Russians. Very few of them returned to Sweden after 1721. (None of these figures include the losses from diseases such as cholera, which often carried off more soldiers than battles did.)

Adding to the hardships were natural disasters, diseases, and crop failures. Some of these were localized, and some were national or regional; all contributed to high mortality rates and held almost all population growth in check. The plague returned to Norden around midcentury and again in the early 1700s. Crop failures struck Denmark in 1661 and 1682, and Norway in the 1650s, 1670s, and 1690s. Sweden experienced serious agricultural troubles in the 1690s and again in 1708 and 1709. It is estimated Finland lost as much as 30 percent of its rural population as a result of the crop failures and the ensuing famine of 1696 and 1697.

Life for women during the century changed little and may have even worsened for some. As before, noble and middle-class women enjoyed greater comforts and slightly better educational opportunities, although not in schools; a few enjoyed influence and even some economic importance. For the most part, however, they remained marriage assets for social climbing. For women of the commons, life continued to mean endless work in rural or artisan partnerships with men. On the farms they were expected to do everything—to help with the plowing and planting and harvesting, to tend the livestock, to keep the gardens, to maintain the household, to spin and weave and make clothing, and to bear and raise children.

Adding to the burdens of a woman's life in the seventeenth century were the witch-hunts that spanned the century throughout Europe. Norden did not escape these orgies of irrational and ignorant hysteria. It is estimated that about three hundred witches were executed, often by burning or drowning, in Sweden before the hunts abated at the close of the century. Twenty-three were killed in Mora, eight in Stockholm. In Denmark the last witch burning took place in 1693—although accusations and lesser punishments continued for more than a century. In Norway some five hundred trials took place. The victims were often accused of holding "witches' sabbaths" or of carrying children off to the devil. People who practiced folk medicine or so-called white magic within the societies were frequently the targets of the hysteria. (Interestingly, in Iceland most of the accused were men.) Many times, the so-called witches were just the victims of personal animosities and rumor.

There are, however, brighter aspects to these pictures of everyday life. Some things got better, at least for a few. Housing improved. In cities more permanent materials were used and fire protection improved. Glass for windows became more common. Erik Dahlberg's (1625–1703) standard house designs for Sweden's regimental soldiers and officers were models for general rural housing improvement. The better off among the rural populations sought to emulate on a small scale the nobility, which tended to raise the standards of material culture. The furniture, interior ornamentation, housewares, and clothing reflect these modest improvements. The foreign experiences of many young men who fought in the wars of the period also led to a transmission of ideas and practices from the Continent, which helped break down some of the parochialism of rural Scandinavia.

Economic Developments

The development and growth of the Nordic economies of the seventeenth century had several causes. Increasingly, governments played active and vital roles in development by manipulating trade conditions, chartering commercial companies, licensing, subsidizing ventures, and encouraging capital and expertise immigration. These activities followed the mercantilist economic thinking of the century and were believed to serve the state's interests in increasing economic activity and thereby increasing tax revenues. They were not always very wise or successful, but, in general, they did contribute to the overall economic developments of the period. Another important factor was the vitality of economies outside Scandinavia, reflected in the growth of Western European cities, armies, navies, and merchant fleets. These developments called for the raw materials of Norden, including lumber, pitch, tar, iron, and copper. The increased domestic demand for everyday staple goods and luxuries in Europe and Scandinavia was also significant and fed the growth of Nordic international commercial ventures and the development of native raw material, semi-finished, and finished-goods sectors of the Scandinavian economies. Socially, the developments contributed to the growth of a commercial and entrepreneurial elite, an expanded artisan sector, and larger merchant marines.

All of Norden benefited from these developments. New waterdriven saws increased the output of beams and planks. Commercial companies sprang up to exploit the area's raw material resources. Most important were the developments in the copper and iron industries in Sweden (and Norway). Copper, as a building material and a metal for coinage, was Sweden's main export until the mid–seventeenth century. Thereafter, even though export volume declined, it remained important. Iron replaced copper, and the demand for iron grew constantly in Europe from the late sixteenth century. Sweden, previously a major exporter of a medieval product form called *osmund*, a relatively pure and malleable iron, benefited from that increase. In the seventeenth century the iron industry in Sweden underwent two fundamental transformations, as iron exports rose from 8,300 tons in 1601 to over 32,000 tons in 1715—with England as the principal buyer. The first change involved the form in which the iron was exported. Driven by technology and demand, Swedish production for export shifted from osmund and pig iron (*tackjärn*) to bar iron

Louis De Geer

Many foreigners came to Scandinavia during the seventeenth century and contributed to the economic developments of the period. Louis De Geer (1587–1652) was one of the most important. Born in Liege, he later became a merchant (in the broadest sense of the word) in Amsterdam. He first came to Sweden in 1627 and quickly became involved in many facets of the country's economy, including international trade and finance, diplomacy, banking, shipping, iron production, and weapons manufacturing. By some accounts he became the richest person in Sweden. He was ennobled in 1641.

(*stångjärn*). The second major change involved revolutionary technological, structural, and financial changes with broad social implications. The old iron export sector was based on a decentralized and relatively capital-cheap system centered on small-scale production units. Making large quantities of bar iron required far greater organization and capital investment. Production was reorganized and dominated by export merchant entrepreneurs who coordinated the mining of ore, the production of charcoal, the transport of the raw materials, the refining of the ore in new blast furnaces and hammer mills, and the export of the finished iron. This was protocapitalist industry; more centralized, more capital intensive; more factory-like in the organization of labor. Although external demand helped drive these changes, they were made possible by the immigration (with conscious government encouragement) of people, technologies, and capital. French, Walloon, Dutch, and German migrants brought to Sweden the latest blast furnaces and hammer mills, entrepreneurial skills, and capital. Immigrants from these countries were similarly important in Denmark and Norway.

Other goods-producing sectors that grew, largely as a result of domestic demand, included textiles, clothing (especially uniforms), armaments, glass, and paper. In addition, internal demand for the products of the traditional craft guilds grew as well. Some guild restrictions—for example, those on the number of apprentices and on master mobility—were eased to facilitate output growth for products including wigs, lace, gloves, silk, gold and silver work, furniture, and tableware. The domestic production sectors responded to the growing demand for things fed by urban expansion, the additions to the nobility, and the increased importance of luxury.

European trade in staple products and raw materials and international (global) trade in luxuries were important sectors in all early modern economies. A few important merchant houses, often with family connections that were European in scope and built up through migration, marriage, and diplomacy, tended to dominate the European trade sector. Their activities were frequently protected by the governments, and close relationships regularly developed between them and the crown—generally because of their affluence. International commerce was a high-risk but potentially high-profit activity and required the greatest measures of state involvement. Generally, this trade was controlled by companies that were chartered by the crown and enjoyed monopolies in certain commodities or regions. The companies were often joint-capital ventures that drew on the crown and the wealthy for their funding. In many ways, they were the multinational corporations of this period.

Many commercial companies were founded and active in Norden in the seventeenth century. In Denmark these included the first Danish East India Company (1616–50), the second Danish East India Company (1670–1729), and the Danish West Indies and Guinea Company (1671–1754). In Sweden over twenty companies were established, including the Tar Company, the Africa Company (1649–1717), the West Indies Company (1640–1793), the Levant Company (1648–1806), and the New Sweden Company (1637–55). As the names indicate, some of them handled specific commodities while others monopolized trade areas or routes. In the latter case, colonies were often important. The several Danish East India companies were connected with a trading station established at Trankebar on the southeast coast of India in 1620 by Ove Gjedde (1594–1660)—a colony that remained in Danish control until 1845—and a warehouse in Canton. In the Caribbean, Denmark developed a trade in small amounts of tobacco, sugar, and cotton based on St. Thomas, St. Jan/John, and St. Croix. Similarly, the short-lived New Sweden Company was based on a colony established along the shores of the Delaware River near present-day Wilmington to trade in tobacco and furs.

Few of these ventures were successful in the seventeenth century.

Denmark's Caribbean and African Possessions and the Triangle Traffic

Denmark's Caribbean involvement centered on the islands of St. Thomas (annexed in 1660), St. Jan/John (annexed in 1718), and St. Croix (purchased from France in 1733). The main town was Charlotte Amalie. For almost two hundred years a plantation and slave-based economy in sugar and tobacco survived there, and Denmark had its own triangle trade. Ships from Copenhagen brought goods to several Danish posts on the coast of West Africa including Frederiksborg (established in 1649) and Christiansborg (established in 1661) in present-day Ghana. These goods were traded for slaves, who were transported to the Caribbean. Sugar from the islands was shipped back to Copenhagen for refining. About 300,000 slaves were transported by the Danes for use on the islands or sale before the trade ended in 1803. In the early nineteenth century around 34,000 slaves and 4,000 Danes lived on the islands. Liberation of the slaves came after 1848. The African posts were sold to the British in 1849. Today the president of Ghana lives in Christiansborg/Osu castle. The Danish West Indies were sold to the United States in 1917.

International trading ventures were expensive to mount and especially risky. The products of the Danes' trade with the Far East were usually sold to foreigners at auctions in Copenhagen. New Sweden never turned a profit for its investors. Generally, the companies did best when they could take advantage of wars in Europe to make inroads into trade dominated by the English or the Dutch.

Towns

Vital to the economic, social, cultural, and intellectual developments of the century were the growth and development of Copenhagen and Stockholm as capitals; the growth of other old, established towns in the region; and the founding of many new urban centers.

During the century, Copenhagen and Stockholm became capitals, more clearly established as the centers of government and economic life in the two monarchies. Their populations grew by factors of four

New Sweden

Sweden was less successful than Denmark in establishing colonies for international trade. Several small posts in Africa were quickly lost. Best remembered is the New Sweden colony, established under the leadership of Peder Minuit in 1638, along the banks of the Delaware River. The idea of a colony in North America had been suggested in the 1620s, but could not be followed up on. It was hoped a genuine Swedish presence could be established and that investors would earn profits from the tobacco and furs sent back to Sweden. The venture was always marginal, despite the energetic leadership of the colony's governor from 1644 to 1653, Johan Printz. Government support was inconsistent, capital scarce, and willing colonists few. In 1655 the Dutch in the area defeated the Swedes and assumed control. A few years later, the British replaced the Dutch. Many settlers remained in the area, however, and the Swedish congregations there continued to receive support from Sweden until the end of the eighteenth century. Descendants of the early settlers contributed variously to U.S. colonial history.

---

or five, reaching 65,000 and 45,000, respectively, by 1700. Aided by several fires (e.g., Stockholm, in 1625), urban planners in both capitals were given opportunities to recast large sections of the old parts of these cities and to plan development in new areas. Central squares and broad avenues were laid out. Royal and noble residences such as Christian IV's Rosenborg, new government buildings like the Copenhagen's Kancelliet and Stockholm's House of the Nobility or the National Bank, economic centers like Christian IV's great commodity exchange (Borsen), and lavish new merchant houses added to each city's status. Harbor facilities and defenses were also improved, and productive capacities increased during the century. At the same time, relatively uncontrolled growth among the lower ranks of society continued, and behind the sparkling facades of court and commerce lay all the ills of the early modern city: overcrowding, poverty, filth, polluted water, disease, and high mortality rates.

Overall, the number and size of towns increased throughout Norden in the seventeenth century. By the close of the century nearly 20 percent of all Danes lived in towns, compared to about 10 percent for Norway and Sweden, and somewhat less than that for Finland. At least twenty-eight new towns were established in Sweden and Finland in the century, including Göteborg, Karlskrona, Luleå and Vasa/Vaasa; in Denmark, Glückstadt (in Holstein), Kristiansted (in Skåne), and Kristianopel (in Blekinge); and in Norway, Kristiania (immediately next to the medieval town of Oslo), Kristiansand, Røros, and Kongsberg. They served variously as centers of trade or production, administration, and defense.

Intellectual and Cultural Developments

The patterns that dominate the intellectual and cultural aspects of seventeenth-century Nordic history may all be clustered around the increased Europeanization of the region. In almost every aspect, Scandinavia became more and more part of a greater European intellectual and cultural world. Be it art, architecture, music, fashion, court ceremony, science, political philosophy, etc., European modes and ideas were adopted or adapted. These influences were most apparent at the upper levels of society, but they even reached into the commons from the exposure many received to differences as soldiers abroad or contacts at home. In general, there were more books, readers, schools, travelers, and foreigners than ever before. Better roads, inns for travelers, postal systems, and regular newspapers helped spread information. Although Scandinavian contributions to the development of European culture may have been few, there were some notable exceptions.

The achievements in the arts were the monopoly of the upper classes. Almost all the leading artists were foreigners, including J. H. Elbfas (?–1664), David Beck (1621–56), David Klöcker Ehrenstrahl (1628–98), Abraham Wuchters (1610–82), and Karel van Mander (1548–1606), and the styles and subject matter reflected the influence of the Continent. The portraits, still lifes, landscapes, and "naturalistic" scenes of everyday life, commissioned by rulers, nobles, and well-to-do merchants, bear witness to the increased affluence of the period and to the importation of styles. The same may be said about the state, noble, and merchant buildings of the period. Christian IV's Kancilliet was done in Roman Baroque, and Frederiksborg in Dutch Renaissance style. Dutch and French influences can be seen in Sweden's House of the Nobility or in Nicodemus Tessin the Younger's design for the new royal palace in Stockholm following the 1697 fire that destroyed the old Three Crowns Castle.

In education, important steps were taken to improve and systematize. The basic idea behind all efforts was to provide people with the necessary skills to administer the more complex states (bureaucrats), to minister to the people (clergy), and to carry on business. Intellectual liberation or creativity was generally not the goal of seventeenth-century education at any level. Rote learning of established knowledge was the basis of pedagogical method. Still, the three levels of basic schools in Sweden, culminating in the *gymnasia,* or the estate schools of Frederik IV in Denmark, contributed to a small increase in literacy and an inevitable infusion of new ideas.

The universities of Copenhagen and Uppsala remained the primary educational institutions of the period, and both prospered under increased royal support. New universities were also established at Dorpat (1632), Åbo/Turku (1640), and Lund (1667–68). All depended on the crown for support, and their histories reflect the shifting tides of royal interest. Christian IV and Gustav II Adolf were supporters of their universities. During their reigns new buildings like Christian IV's residence hall in Copenhagen and the Gustavianum at Uppsala were added. The land donations of Gustav II Adolf formed an endowment that helped secure the finances of Uppsala and support many student scholarships. The booty of wars helped create a library there of over 20,000 volumes by the end of the century. Although difficult to determine exactly because many so-called students registered but did not attend classes, it appears about 350–400 students were regularly enrolled at Copenhagen during the period. On average about 1,000 students were in attendance at Uppsala, and the faculty there numbered over twenty-five professors. Most of the Copenhagen students were either Danish or Norwegian; Uppsala was more nationally diverse. The social makeup of the student body at Uppsala probably reflects trends elsewhere in Norden. A third or more of the students were the sons of clergy. Sons of burghers and farmers made up as much as a fifth. Some nobles were reluctant to send their sons into the corrupting environment of the universities, but a few did. Special programs in riding, fencing, dancing, and modern languages were developed for them to supplement the usual curriculum, and toward the end of the century they even had their own building. Most students studied with the liberal arts and sciences faculties. Their course of studies included classical languages, aesthetics

Late-Seventeenth-Century Scientists

Ole Römer (1644–1710). Danish astronomer. Argued that light had speed. Developed celestial maps and instruments, a thermometer, weights and measures system, new land survey of Denmark.

Ole Worm (1588–1654). Danish physician, botanist, antiquarian, and early runologist.

Thomas Bartholin (1616–80). Danish physician, anatomist. Discovered the lymphatic system.

Ole Borch (1626–90). Danish chemist, botanist, and philologist. Rejected the "four elements" view of chemical composition and conducted a systematic study of Denmark's flora.

Niels Steensen (Steno) (1638–86). Danish empiricist, anatomist, and physician. Proved the heart is a muscle.

Olof Rudbeck the Elder (1630–1702). Swedish anatomist. Discovered the lymphatic system, developed botanical collections, produced *Atlantica*.

Christopher Polhem (1661–1751). Swedish engineer and inventor. Developed clocks, weapons, and machines for mining, metallurgy, textile making, and agriculture. His workshop at Stjärnsund was a center of experimentation and teaching.

(classical poetry), rhetoric (argumentative and speaking), math, and astronomy. Only a few took master's and doctoral degrees in the other divisions: theology, law, and medicine.

The faculties of these universities were generally rather undistinguished. (The most creative thinkers tended to be outside the academic community.) There were, however, some notable exceptions. Olof Rudbeck the Elder (1630–1702) was a dominating figure at Uppsala for almost half a century. He is credited with being one of the first to discover the lymphatic system—along with Thomas Bartholin (1616–80) in Denmark—for a time was intensely interested in anatomy, developed major botanical collections at Uppsala, and produced *Atlantica* (1679), in which he argued that Sweden was the home

Olof Rudbeck the Elder, a discoverer of the lymphatic system and advocate of Gothicism, which included the idea that the lost city of Atlantis was located off the coast of Sweden and that Swedes were the founders of Western culture. Painting attributed to I. Klopper. Courtesy of Statens Konstmuseer, Stockholm, Sweden.

of human culture and the site of Atlantis. His equal at Copenhagen was probably Ole Römer (1644–1710),who held the chair in astronomy there for nearly thirty years. Among Römer's accomplishments were a convincing argument that light had speed (1676), the development of increasingly accurate celestial maps based on his observations and on instruments of his design, a thermometer very close to Fahrenheit's, a new weights and measures system, and a new land survey of Denmark. (What may strike a twenty-first-century reader as an odd dichotomy between the rational and irrational in Rudbeck's work was typical of the century.)

The universities were also centers for vicious intellectual arguments over the fundamentals of truth and knowledge. By and large they were bastions of orthodoxy, religious and secular, and new ideas had great difficulty penetrating them. Early in the century the faculty at Uppsala was rent by arguments over the validity of Aristotelian teachings. In the last quarter of the century a battle raged over the influx of Cartesian ideas, which had to be settled by the king.

5

Politics and Diplomacy in the Age of the Enlightenment

The eighteenth century's own contemporaries saw this period as different from earlier times, and it is one with which twentieth-century readers are far more comfortable. In terms of its intellectual vocabulary, approaches to and organization of knowledge, social organization, economic activities, politics, and use of technologies it strikes one as familiar and "modern." It is a century often defined by its optimism, faith in the power of human reason to understand humankind and nature, and confidence in the human capacity to create progress, to change society for the better. Europeans made great gains in their understanding of the physical world, and several of the modern sciences were defined in this period. Even history became an ordered discipline with a more defined methodology. An unprecedented population growth began. Societies and economies became more complex as they moved from predominantly agrarian-commercial toward pre- or proto-industrial. In politics, the concept of the state took on new meanings as its functions grew and the old order came under increasing attack from above and below. This was also the century in which technology was increasingly applied to solving everyday, practical problems. Various labels have been attached to this period because of these and other aspects, including the "Enlightenment," "the Age of Reason," and, at least for the last forty years of the century, the "Age of Revolution."

Conversely, however, the eighteenth century was also a period of continued conservatism, resistance to change, and superstition; and contrasts or paradoxes can be seen in many aspects of life. In politics, absolutism and democratic experiments, status quo and revolution from above and below opposed each other. Although the nobility and privilege remained dominant in much of Europe, both were struck down in several countries. Religion came under scathing criticism while Pietism and a variety of new Christian sects flourished. The middle class enjoyed increased economic prosperity, but remained largely closed off from real political influence. In some parts of Europe, the landed peasants enjoyed significant legal and economic gains; in others serfdom remained unchallenged. Although economic change and growth created new opportunities for the laboring classes, these changes rarely led to improved living conditions. A few women played leading roles in the conversations of the Enlightenment and achieved places of importance in many spheres of activity, but women in general were still considered inferior and extensively exploited. These dichotomies sustain an ongoing debate among scholars over whether or not the century was fundamentally modern or medieval, progressive or conservative.

More than ever before, Norden participated fully in European affairs. Its political, social, economic, intellectual, and cultural histories are, more than at any previous time, connected to and microcosms of the larger European experiences. The international exchange of ideas through travel, education, reading, and conversation made Norden more and more a part of Europe. Tourism was an increasingly important activity for the wealthy. The grand tour remained essential to any proper upper-class education. The beginnings of general public education, the founding of new technical schools, the expansion of university programs, and the activities of learned societies helped enlarge and deepen the literacy base in Scandinavia. Newspapers, journals, broadsheets, fiction, encyclopedias, and the like brought the world to the literate. The salons, to some *the* vital aspect in the spreading of the new ideas, were not the monopoly of the French and took root among Norden's polite society.

Political Development

The political history of Denmark and Sweden in the eighteenth century contains all of the elements of diversity mentioned above and clearly reflects the dynamic forces at work during the period. Although each began and ended the century as a state in which the crown claimed varying degrees of absolute authority, the histories of the events in-between are remarkably different. In Denmark the fundamental system went unchallenged, but there were significant changes in who wielded power within that system. The political history of the century revealed the inherent weaknesses of a form of government

Monarchs

Denmark	**Sweden**
Frederik IV: 1699–1730	Karl XII: 1697–1718
	Ulrika Eleonora: 1719–20
Christian VI: 1730–46	Fredrik I: 1720–51
Frederik V: 1746–66	Adolf Fredrik: 1751–71
Christian VII: 1766–1808	Gustav III: 1771–92
	Gustav IV Adolf: 1792–1809

Dates are of reigns.

so dependent on the qualities of the monarch. The biases, incompetence, drunkenness and depravity, mental illness, or simple disinterest of individual rulers affected the political life of the country and allowed individuals and cliques, foreign and Danish, to come to the fore. In contrast, in Sweden abrupt changes of the constitution occurred three times during the century (1719–23, 1772, and 1789). Absolutist until 1719, the country then turned to a system in which parliament was primary until 1772. Thereafter followed a two-stage return to virtual absolutism.

Another feature of the political history that carried over through this period was the changing nature or definition of *the state* for both the rulers and the ruled. No longer dynastic states and more than simply "warfare" or "tax" states, governments in Denmark and Sweden expanded in scale and scope as they became increasingly involved in economics, education, culture, etc.

Denmark

Constitutionally, the records of the eighteenth century form a varied chapter in the 188-year history of absolutism (1660–1848) in Denmark. Although there were no "popular" revolutions or abrupt swings of the constitutional pendulum during this period, there were striking variations in the nature of political life and in the achievements of government determined by the personalities of the rulers, the other actors on the political stage at the time, and a wide variety of other internal and external factors.

The century began with the best king of the period, Frederik IV (1671–1730), on the throne. He is often only remembered for his passion for beautiful women, his taking of his mistress, Anna Sofie Reventlow (1693–1743), for his second wife in 1721 and filling the court with her German relatives ("the Reventlow gang"), his love of travel, or for his pietism and the so-called sabbath laws. However, Frederik is one of Denmark's most popular rulers, and he earned this reputation as a well-meaning, intelligent, and hardworking king who took the drudgery of governing seriously. He filled his working days with attention to the most minute of details, and, although he had around him a changing body of advisers, he never turned the affairs of state over to favorites. Frederik also understood the problems Denmark faced, including a backward and inefficient agriculture, an exploited and downtrodden peasantry, a thin economy based on limited resources, the importance of commerce, the fragility of state finances, and a precarious security position. His record of domestic achievements includes the abolition of the *vornedskab* (a legal practice dating from the medieval period whereby the peasant heirs of a lease-hold on noble lands in Sjaelland and the other islands were bound to remain on the property), the founding of some 240 schools on crown estates, the introduction of a regularized poor relief system, the establishment of a Danish missionary presence in Greenland, and the introduction of a law that made entertainments illegal on church holidays and church attendance on Sundays compulsory.

That the list is not longer may be because of several factors. First, Frederik's strength was in dealing with detail, not in conceiving great plans or programs. Second, for almost two-thirds of his reign, he was preoccupied with war in the Baltic. He took Denmark into and then out of the war with Sweden in 1700, cautiously nurtured the country's economic resources and preserved its army (by leasing troops to Great Britain and the Hapsburgs) and then reentered the war in 1709, when it appeared safe to do so. From then until peace came in 1720, his attentions had to be focused on campaigns, recruitment, and paying for the war. Third, almost all attempts at change ran headlong into the resistance of established factions in the society, most often the Danish nobility—which he came to hate and distrust.

The timid, awkward, unattractive, and singularly unkingly Christian VI (1699–1746), with his equally unattractive wife Sofie Magdalene (1700–70), also worked hard at his calling. His accomplishments, however, unless one counts the number of royal residences he commissioned, were few. The king and queen were private, hated appearing in public, and lived for most of the reign away from Copenhagen.

Under him the pietist-inspired blue laws continued and were extended. Although probably an exaggeration, the common conception is that fun was virtually outlawed. Confirmation became compulsory in 1736, which contributed to an increase in literacy. Although a school ordinance was published in 1739, little was done to make it effective. The lives of the peasants of the kingdom were again controlled through the introduction of *stavnsbaand* (1733), which bound male peasants to their tenancies in order to guarantee a supply of recruits for the militia. This move was designed to ensure the landowners a steady supply of labor during difficult economic times. The measure, along with the existing rights of the landowners to set the conditions of tenancies and administer "justice," increased the "serfdom" the peasants faced. Christian also imposed a grain import ban on Denmark and southern Norway to protect Danish farmers and encouraged international commerce.

Fun, an entertaining court life, and the theater returned to Denmark under the amiable and popular Frederik V (1723–66). However, these gains were offset by the new king's debauched lifestyle, which worsened after the death of his first wife, Louise (1724–51), and culminated in alcoholism. Frederik allowed government responsibility to pass from the crown to a group of able, well-meaning, and effective advisers and bureaucrats, and Denmark became a German aristocratic bureaucracy. In a sense royal absolutism vanished for the remainder of the century, as one group or another dominated political life while the monarchs, either because of inclination or health, remained in the background.

Under Frederik V this group included J. H. E. Bernstorff (1712–72), a Hanoverian noble who directed Danish foreign and commercial policy for over twenty years after 1750, and A. G. Moltke (1710–92), a Mecklenburger in charge of financial matters. Both were men of the Enlightenment: well educated, reform-minded, and inclined to apply reason to the solution of problems. However, although each was able to establish his own estates as models for social and agrarian reform, neither was able to effect far-reaching changes in the kingdom. The best that can be said for their efforts is that Denmark remained at peace and entered a period of economic growth over which they had little control.

Whereas Frederik V was uninterested in participating in the business of government, his son Christian VII (1749–1808) was unable to do so. This handsome young man was mentally ill, probably a schizophrenic, some say as a result of his father's alcoholism or the "degenerate stock" of his mother. In the early years of his reign (1766–71) Christian was occasionally charming and even effective. But he could suddenly become vicious and mean or sullen and withdrawn. Over time the latter traits prevailed, and, although he lived until 1808, he was incapable of governing after 1771. Naturally, the king's condition created an environment open to abuse. Someone or some group had to carry on the affairs of state.

Christian VII's long reign can be divided into five periods: 1768–70, when the young king "ruled" with the help of changing circle of sycophants; 1770–72, when power was wielded by Johan Friedrich Struensee (1737–72); 1772–84, when a clique of conservative Danish nobles headed by Ove Høegh-Guldberg (1731–1808) ruled; 1784–97, when power lay with a small group of reform-minded German nobles and Crown Prince Frederik (later Frederik VI, 1768–1839); and 1797–1808, when the crown prince assumed more independent control. The middle three of these will be considered in greater detail below.

One of the most fascinating episodes in Danish history began in 1768, when Johan Friedrich Struensee, a physician from Halle in north Germany, was appointed to serve as doctor to the king on a grand tour of Europe and Great Britain. For reasons that are unclear, Struensee was able to control the king's mood swings, and when the entourage returned to Denmark, Struensee came along. He lived at court and in a short time became the king's closest adviser and the lover of the queen, Caroline Matilda (1751–75). By September 1770 he was the de facto ruler of the country.

Struensee was an advocate of the Enlightenment. He believed in progress and in the ability of humans to make a better world. Without any clear plan and certainly without a firm base of support beyond the royal court, he set out to make Denmark a "better" place. With the king's compliance Struensee and a small group of friends created a new administrative structure for the central government, abolished serfdom, freed the press of censorship, outlawed torture, reformed the judiciary, freed internal and international trade, changed Copenhagen's government, and created public health programs. In all, over 1,800 so-called cabinet orders were issued between September 1770 and December 1771, touching almost every aspect of

Louise Augusta (1771–1843), daughter of Denmark's Christian VII and Caroline Matilda. (Her father was actually Johan Friedrich Struensee.) Painting by Jens Juel. Courtesy of Det Nationalhistoriske Museum på Frederiksborg, Denmark.

Danish life. Certainly, many of his efforts were well meaning and necessary. That they were imposed suddenly, by a foreigner, a usurper, and a philanderer with little regard for the people they affected made them unacceptable. Struensee alienated almost every group in Danish society, even those he thought he was helping. The scarcely concealed affair between him and the young and lonely Queen Caroline Matilda, and the birth of a daughter (Louise Augusta), made matters worse and handed his enemies a "cause" for his downfall.

A group of opponents coalesced around the king's stepmother, Juliane Marie, and Ove Høegh-Guldberg. In January 1772, with the king's approval, Struensee was arrested. He was quickly tried, condemned for "crimes against the crown," and cruelly executed. Caroline Matilda went into exile in Hanover, where she died in 1775, at the age of twenty-four. Most of Struensee's reforms were withdrawn, and for the next twelve years government was in the hands of Høegh-Guldberg, Juliane Marie, and a clique of well-meaning but conservative nobles firmly committed to the status quo. The most notable achievements of this group lay in the realm of promoting Danishness. A 1776 citizenship law closed public offices to all but Danes, Norwegians, and Holsteiners. Danish again became the language of the court and the command language of the army.

A second and far more lasting period of reform opened in 1784. The king's son, Frederik, with the support of a circle of educated and farsighted nobles, carried out a bloodless coup on 14 April that unseated the old clique. The crown prince now stood at the center of government and was committed to a reformist path. Four individuals played key roles as the architects of change: Christian Ditlev Reventlow (1748–1827), Christian Colbjørnsen (1749–1814), and Ernst Schimmelmann (1747–1831). Reventlow, whose career in government service spanned over forty years, became head of the treasury (*rentekammer*). Schimmelmann, a Dresden-born noble and longtime government servant, became minister of commerce. Norwegian-born Colbjørnsen, a juridical counselor in the Danish chancery, was the primary formulator of laws to ensure peasant rights. The fourth and leading figure was Andreas Peter Bernstorff (1735–97), a Hanover-born nobleman, career diplomat, and nephew of J. H. E. Bernstorff. He was essential for the examples he set and for his successes as foreign minister. Together they led Denmark through "one of the most illustrious periods" in its history. Over the following thirteen years, a set of top-down agrarian, social, and economic reforms were designed and implemented that established the basis for the future and, some have said, set a pattern for peaceful change in Denmark that has prevailed ever since.

The agrarian reforms were largely the work of the Great Agricultural Commission (*den store landbokommissionen*). They included ending serfdom in the kingdom through the phased-in abolition of the *stavnsbaand* (1788) and revision of the recruitment system, ensuring lifetime tenancies for peasants and their wives (1790), fixing labor demands for tenants (1791), protecting tenants from arbitrary landlord "justice," encouraging enclosure, and providing credit to facilitate peasant land purchase. (For the social and economic aspects of these reforms, see below.) The nobility, the principal landowning group and the most fearful of change, was ensured fair compensation for their lands and found a ready source of agricultural labor in the growing rural population.

Social reforms included a system of poor relief based on community responsibility and "contributions" from the wealthy, improvement of the country's road system (1793), a new program of national forests (1805), and the creation of a school commission to work on the issue of public education. (Its recommendations became the basis for the School Law of 1814.) In legal and governmental areas, the judicial process was made more efficient, a police court was established to guarantee citizen rights, county government was revised, greater public participation at the local level was encouraged, Jews were given limited citizen rights (1798), and the slave trade was abolished (1792–1803). (Slavery per se was not abolished in the West Indies possessions until 1848.) Among the economic reforms were the revision of the currency-issuing bank system, abolition of the Iceland and Finnmark trade monopolies (1786 and 1787, respectively), removal of restrictions on the grain trade with Norway (1788), end to the noble monopoly on the cattle trade (1788), end of craft guild monopolies in Copenhagen (1800), and rationalization of the tariff system (1797).

After A. P. Bernstorff's death in 1797 the reforming spirit of the government waned. Although the reformers remained in the government, Frederik took on more and more personal control and listened to new voices. At the same time, events in Europe undermined the economic prosperity on which so much depended and made further reform difficult.

Sweden

The absolutism established by Karl XI prevailed through the Great Northern War, and, despite the fact that Karl XII never returned to his capital after 1700 and throughout the conflict carried on the business of government by royal dispatch, the system worked remarkably well. The king's council functioned as a provisional government, and the bureaucracy remained loyal. But Karl's obsession with the war and his refusal to heed the advice that emanated from Stockholm went far to discredit the system. After the king's return in 1715 he set up a capital in Lund and turned over more and more domestic authority to his favorite, (Baron) Georg H. von Görtz (1668–1719), a Holsteiner whose emergency policies alienated wide sectors of the public from the government.

Karl's death at Fredrikshald in November 1718 may or may not have been a murder. In any case it unleashed events that led to Görtz's arrest and execution, the convening of a Riksdag, the election of Karl's younger sister, Ulrika Eleonora (1688–1741), as queen, and the adoption of a new constitution under which the crown's powers were severely limited and the estates, dominated by the nobles, were predominant—all within about five months. Overall, these changes established the bases for the period in Swedish history called "the era of liberty" (*Frihetstiden*) that lasted until 1772.

The new constitution (including the Form of Government Act of 1719–20, Riksdag Act of 1723, and Accession Oaths of 1719, 1720, 1751, and 1771) was largely the work of nobles eager to reestablish their view of a constitutional balance. Many of the elements in these documents went back to the reign of Gustav II and the 1634 Form of Government. The crown was stripped of its "absolutist" powers and was now to govern only with the advice and consent of a revived council composed of individuals chosen by the crown from lists submitted by the estates. Law, taxation, war and peace-making powers, and the power to nominate candidates for the council and to review the actions of its members and the administration lay with the parliament, which was to meet every three years and continued to be made up of the four estates: nobility, clergy, burghers, and farmers. (In all, this body represented about 7 percent of the population.) Within the estates a complex system of committees was established. The most important of these was the Secret Committee, which dealt with foreign affairs, economic issues, and almost anything else it determined to be important. The nobles had fifty seats on this committee, the clergy and burghers twenty-five each. The farmers were excluded.

Exactly how this new system would evolve was certainly not pre-determined by its creators. Largely the work of the aristocracy, its authors believed it would ensure noble predominance and privilege and prevent the revival of absolutism. No one imagined the fac-tionalism, the development of political parties, the role of foreign influences, or the degree of political involvement by the lower estates that emerged.

The first twenty years under the new order were remarkably tran-quil. Ulrika Eleonora abdicated in favor of her husband, Fredrik of Hesse, in 1720. After 1723 the new king showed little interest in the work of government, preferring instead to pursue his passions for hunting and women. Count Arvid Horn (1664–1742), an experi-enced, conservative, cautious person, served as both chancellor and head of the House of the Nobles until 1738–39 and was the effec-tive ruler of the country. He pursued policies to encourage eco-nomic recovery and avoid costly foreign policy adventures. In both regards he was successful, but he fell under increasing criticism dur-ing the 1730s from younger nobles and veteran officers from the Great Northern War for his caution.

A new phase in Sweden's political history began in the late 1730s. An opposition faction to Horn, referred to as the Hats, gradually developed to secure the election of individuals to parliamentary com-mittees and the council and to work within the Riksdag to effect poli-cies. Derogatorily, Horn's followers were referred to as Caps—or "nightcaps." In 1738 the Hats won control of the council and forced Horn's resignation. This faction ruled Sweden until 1765.

Between 1738 and 1772, and especially in the 1760s, the Hats and Caps developed some aspects of modern political parties, including parliamentary groups and voting discipline, more formal central organ-ization, local clubs, and regular publications. They also developed clearly different outlooks and programs in domestic and foreign pol-icy areas, broadened their social bases beyond the House of the Nobility, campaigned in elections for seats in the estates and on par-liamentary committees and the council, published newspapers and broadsheets, and became entwined in a system of bribes for votes in which Britain, Denmark, France, Prussia, and Russia sought either to obtain favorable decisions or to perpetuate Swedish weaknesses. In general, the Hats' social bases were with bureaucrats, officers, merchants, foundry owners, and manufacturers. The Caps drew their members principally from the upper nobility. In the 1760s, however, the Cap party underwent a nearly complete change in composition and policy. Called "the Younger Caps," this faction now attracted much of its support from the unprivileged estates and advocated increasingly radical reform policies.

The Hat period was defined by ill-considered adventures in foreign policy, friction and crises with the monarchy, "enlightened" intellectual and cultural policies, a conservative and pro-noble social agenda, and mercantilist economic policies. In foreign policy the Hats were more adventuresome than their Cap rivals and favored anti-Russian and renewed great power status lines. These fundamentals resulted in two fruitless conflicts: a short war with Russia in 1741–43 and involvement in the Seven Years' War on the Continent in 1756–63. The Hats favored increased authority for the estates and further limitation of royal powers. Fredrik I had shown little interest in government, and his successor in 1751, Adolf Fredrik (1710–71), was in many ways their pawn. The new king's position was weak. Formerly the prince-bishop of Lübeck and guardian of the Duke of Holstein-Gottorp, he was chosen heir and crown prince in 1743—in part because of pressure from Russia. His wife, Louisa Ulrika (1720–82), sister of Frederick the Great of Prussia, had different views, was more assertive, and urged on her timid husband. In response to a parliamentary statement on the limits of royal power and the creation of a royal signature stamp by the Riksdag to be used in cases when the crown refused to sign legislation, the royal couple supported plans for a coup in 1756. The coup was uncovered and eight conspirators executed; Adolf Fredrik and Louise were publicly admonished and embarrassed. Socially, Hat policies favored the nobles in landownership issues, taxation, and government appointments; their economic policies were designed to foster trade and economic development at home through protective tariffs, monopolies, and subsidies—policies that won them the support of the upper-middle-class burghers.

General economic problems and the fiasco of participation in the war in Germany discredited the Hats and contributed to their defeat in 1765. The new generation of Caps who now assumed power included reform-minded nobles and, increasingly, politically active burghers, clergy, and peasants. Press freedom, liberalization of internal trade, reduction of craft guild restrictions, and the easing of limits on labor migration were among the reforms introduced in the late

1760s. However, when the Caps, and especially their non-noble elements, expressed ideas of depriving the nobles of their privileges or of extending privileges to the other estates, they overstepped the limits of change in the context of the period. In 1772 nobles from both factions, fearing a revolution from below, turned to the new king, Gustav III (1746–92), for insurance against the mob. On 19 August 1772 he carried out a bloodless coup, paid for by France, which brought to an end the parliamentary experiment. The estates were forced to accept a new constitution under which the power of the crown was again central and a limited absolutism imposed.

The Era of Liberty was a remarkable period in Swedish and European political history. At a time when so-called absolute monarchy was dominant in Europe, Sweden's new system and the political life that developed within it were exceptional. Comparisons between Sweden and Great Britain, where similar developments occurred, have often been drawn. The literature on this period, which is particularly extensive, generally falls into two groups: the positivists and the negativists. The former, to varying degrees, see the period as a high point in Swedish history and as a precursor of the country's contemporary democracy. The latter emphasize the factionalism, discord, and foreign meddling of the period and argue Sweden was lucky to escape the fate of Poland. (Poland ceased to exist in 1795.)

Gustav III's new constitution, the Form of Government of 1772, was an intentionally vague document that returned to the crown the power to "govern," appoint members of the council, and call parliament. The king was to rule with the council's advice on judicial, legislative, and diplomatic matters. The estates, which were to meet now only at the king's call, retained authority over taxes and a veto voice in offensive wars. King and estates shared the right to initiate legislation. During his reign, the estates met only four times—1778, 1786, 1789, and 1792.

Gustav III has received mixed treatment from historians. Although most admit his intelligence and often see him as the most complex of Sweden's monarchs, many also accuse him of being a chameleon or an actor without a real personality of his own. Words used to describe him include well educated, cultured, charming, cunning, impulsive, emotional, melancholy, unpredictable, and authoritarian. Initially, his coup and the restoration of order won him wide popularity. That popularity waned over time, however, and he is the only modern Swedish king to have been assassinated.

Familiar with the ideas of the Enlightenment, Gustav was convinced of the need for reforms. Because of his efforts, especially in the first decade of his reign, he is generally listed alongside other so-called enlightened absolutists or enlightened despots such as Joseph II of Austria, Leopold of Tuscany, Frederick II of Prussia, and Catherine II of Russia. All of whom tried, in varying degrees and with varying amounts of success, to revolutionize their countries from above. Gustav introduced a wide range of changes. Torture was abolished (1772), and the number of crimes punishable by death reduced (1778–79). In an effort to stabilize the currency and improve trade, a new silver-based coinage was introduced in January 1777. Although the Caps' freedom of the press law, which had been considered part of the constitution, was abrogated, Gustav believed in at least limited freedom of expression and replaced the older law with his own in 1774. Certain topics were off-limits, such as foreign policy, and a religious censor remained. The focus of possible liability shifted from authors to publishers, who were made accountable for what they put into print. The restrictions on the internal grain trade were removed. A measure of religious freedom for non-Lutherans was introduced in 1781, and limited citizen rights were afforded to Jews in 1782. Gustav also introduced a state lottery to raise funds, cut the number of religious holidays, improved government salaries, and increasingly used talent as a basis for appointment to offices. Admittedly, many of these reforms were liberal in the context of late-eighteenth-century enlightened thinking. They also had other motives, the most important being Gustav's desire to encourage economic development.

As was the case with other so-called enlightened absolutists, Gustav's efforts often earned him the anger of his subjects, not their thanks. For example, in what began as an effort to alleviate food shortages caused by the wholesale use of grain in the home distillation of brandy (*brännvin*) by the peasants, he banned private distillation in 1772 and established a state monopoly three years later. Although some savings in grain were won and per person consumption of brandy fell to about 5 quarts per person per year, the peasants hated the restrictions and openly violated them. The monopoly was lifted in 1787.

More dangerous than peasant animosities, however, was the growing hatred among the nobility that developed in the 1780s. Gustav's strong-monarchy constitutional views ran counter to theirs, which looked back to the early years of the Era of Liberty. Furthermore, the nobles disliked his preference for favorites as advisers, conscious cultivation of the favor of factions within the non-noble estates for support, and reforms that struck at their privileges. Many nobles, perhaps rightly, feared Gustav would effect a social-political revolution from above. The Russo-Swedish War (1788–90) was the last straw. Many believed (correctly) the king had violated the constitution, and an antiwar/antiroyalist conspiracy developed among the noble officers in Finland.

The nobles' actions led only to their further degradation, however. Gustav's propaganda blitz in late 1788 successfully inflamed anti-noble sentiments. When the estates convened in Stockholm in early 1789, the three lower houses were strongly anti-noble. Gustav used the opportunity to carry out another "revolution." In a plenary session on 17 February, the nobles were publicly chastised for their opposition to change and actions in Finland. A few days later, in another plenary session, "The Act of Union and Security" was read and accepted by voice vote by the three lower estates. Over the nobles' objections, the king declared the act passed, despite several violations of constitutional practice.

The Act of Union and Security, a brief and vague document, was fundamentally conservative. First, it specified that the king was to govern, defend the realm, dispense appointments, administer justice, and propose legislation. Second, it stipulated that all were to be equal before the law, and that a new high court (*konungens högsta domstol*) was to be created with equal places for privileged and nonprivileged members. Third, it stated that "a free people ought have equal rights, and therefore each estate shall have the right to own and acquire land." This meant that nonprivileged individuals could purchase crown and noble lands—with certain exceptions. Fourth, except for "the state's highest and most important offices and those in the king's court," all appointments were to be based on ability, merit, and experience. The crown's powers were not wholly unchecked, however. The fifth section assured the people of their right to petition the king. The sixth stipulated that the estates could only discuss those matters presented to it by the crown. In areas untouched by the act, the 1772 constitution remained in effect. So, for example, the estates retained control of taxation and acquired other powers in the management of state finances at the 1792 Riksdag.

Clearly, the Act of Union and Security increased royal power and promised greater economic and legal equality. But it also preserved Sweden's hierarchical "corporate" social order. The principal gainers were Gustav, the freehold farmers, and the middle class. In theory, at least, the principal losers were the nobles. Broadly interpreted land-ownership was thrown open to all, and former noble privileges such as hunting rights on tenancies were denied. The noble monopoly on appointments, which was increasingly fictional anyway, was gone. The act contained no mention of an obligation to fill every vacancy in government or to rule with the council's advice, and Gustav used these omissions to replace the council with administrative commissions that dealt with routine matters.

Most of the nobility only accepted the new constitution in principle a decade later and were irrevocably alienated from Gustav. Anger against the king turned to plots to eliminate him. On 16 March 1792 he was shot and seriously wounded by Jacob Anckarström, a twenty-nine-year-old noble and the pawn of a clique of aristocrats led by Carl Fredrik Pechlin (1720–96). The king died two weeks later. A trail of evidence easily led the police to Anckarström, and eventually some forty nobles were arrested. Fourteen were tried. Five were condemned. Only Anckarström, however, was executed (27 April 1792). The investigation, which clearly revealed the extent of noble involvement, was terminated.

The conspirators' hopes that a new constitutional order could be forced on the young heir came to naught. Under the regency of the dead king's brother, Karl (the future Karl XIII), and during the reign of Gustav IV Adolf, the power of the crown remained central, and the late-eighteenth-century constitutional order continued into the nineteenth.

Historian H. Arnold Barton has written that "by the time the revolution—properly speaking—began in France during the late spring of 1789, Scandinavia had in effect already undergone its revolution." The truth of this statement should be evident from the preceding narrative. But it is important to add certain reminders. First, the Nordic revolutions came from above and reflected the willingness of monarchs and some of the nobility to make limited or controlled changes—perhaps to save themselves and at least some of the old order. Second, there was no mass movement for revolution, no mob, no Bastille, no march on Versailles, no revolutionary war. Third, the Nordic revolutions reflect many of the common elements of the revolutionary era including the intellectual culture of change; a shared vocabulary in words like liberty, equality, natural rights, citizenship, and progress; and similar problems and solutions. Fourth, the revolutions were certainly only partial. Although some measure of economic and legal equality was gained in Denmark and Sweden, social and political equality were not. These revolutions were, perhaps, as thorough as was possible within their contexts. Finally, they were gradualist and peaceful, and these traits may be characteristic of the political environment of Norden.

International Relations, 1721–1800

The eighteenth century is often called the "age of diplomacy"—a title that derives from the growth of diplomatic institutions and forms and the extent and intensity of diplomatic activity. War, of course, remained a central aspect of the European state system, but so too did negotiation, alliances, intrigue, subsidies, and meddling in the internal affairs of states, great and small. The major players of the century were the Hapsburg Empire, Prussia, Russia, Great Britain, and France. For small states, the costs of conflicts continued to escalate beyond their means, and security and freedom of action became increasingly difficult to ensure.

In the North, the central themes of the period included conscious efforts by several European powers to maintain Swedish political weakness through diplomacy, Russian predominance but only occasional preoccupation with Baltic affairs, continued British and French interest in the Baltic and their pursuit of policies designed to prevent any single power from establishing hegemony in the region, moments when Swedish policy became centered on revenge or reestablishment of the country's former power status, Denmark's fifty-year preoccupation with the Holstein-Gottorp lands question, the problem of how to maintain neutrality during great power conflicts, and the fundamental military and economic weaknesses of Denmark and Sweden.

Compared with the previous one hundred years, the eighteenth century was one of remarkable quiet in Scandinavia, and for much of the period the principal actors behaved like satiated players. Although various Russian rulers or their advisers advocated expansionist policies in the Baltic and threatened war several times, they were generally held in check by internal and external restraints. For the first twenty years following the end of the Great Northern War in 1721, Denmark and Sweden's leaders steered cautious and peaceful courses while concentrating on national economic recovery. In the 1740s, under the less cautious leadership of the Hat faction, Sweden became involved in a fruitless war with Russia, out of which it gained nothing and lost both territory in Finland and freedom of action in domestic affairs. The reckless Hats took the country into war again at the close of the 1750s, this time against Prussia. They gained nothing. Following another fifteen years of peace, Gustav III initiated the third Russo-Swedish War of the century, from which he was lucky to emerge with his crown and the realm intact. Throughout the century, Denmark's policymakers pursued a generally peaceful course, which kept their country out of war for nearly seventy years—although there were several changes of alliance partners and numerous war scares over relations with Sweden. Only in 1788 did Denmark go briefly to war, when the government honored its alliance with Russia.

The Great Northern War redrew the Baltic map and established a new power system in the region. Sweden lost virtually all its gains since the mid–sixteenth century, retaining only a slightly smaller Finland and a share of Pomerania. The new constitutional order in Sweden was seen as the basis for weakness there, and the survival of that system became a goal of Russian and Danish foreign policy. Denmark gained an international guarantee of its southern borders, the end to Sweden's exemption from the Sound Tolls, and a 600,000-riksdaler indemnity payment from Sweden. Hanover took Bremen and Verden. Prussia secured part of Pomerania. Russia, the great gainer, kept Livonia, Estonia, Ingria, and southern Kexsholm.

In Denmark, down to the 1740s, Frederik IV and Christian VI shaped their own foreign policies, and both sought to avoid war and preserve "tranquility in the North." Russo-Danish relations were strained over the Holstein-Gottorp lands question, and Frederik tilted toward France or Britain for support. Christian continued this line but also reached a long-term friendship agreement with Sweden in 1734.

Until 1738 Arvid Horn was in charge of Swedish foreign policy, and he wisely attempted to steer Sweden clear of entanglements that might draw the country into a conflict and to resist temptations for avenging the loss of the empire. Although increasingly criticized for his seemingly tired and unassertive policies, which included a Russo-Swedish friendship pact (1724), Horn understood the limits of Sweden's resources and the new situation in the Baltic. Carl Gustav Tessin, as effective leader after Horn's fall, and his colleagues were less willing to accept the status quo and less mindful of their country's weaknesses. In 1741, riding a wave of popular anti-Russian sentiment, expecting a succession crisis in St. Petersburg, assured of French subsidies, and believing the west European powers were preoccupied with the war of the Austrian Succession, the Hats initiated an attack on Russia from Finland. The failure of the Swedes' offensive in November 1741 and the collapse of their forces in Finland condemned the rest of the Swedish policy to failure and opened the door to more foreign meddling in the country's internal affairs. In addition to a piece of eastern Finland, including the city of Fredrikshamn, the Russians demanded a voice in the naming of a successor to the childless Frederik I as the price of peace.

The settlement of the Swedish succession "crisis" illustrates the convoluted nature of eighteenth-century Nordic diplomacy. At first there were two primary candidates. The Russians favored Duke Karl Peter Ulrik of Holstein-Gottorp. Frightened by the possibility of a Russian-Swedish union that would support the duke's claims in Slesvig and Holstein and a dreamer who wished for a new Nordic dynastic union, Christian VI put his son, Frederik, forward. The farmers' estate in Sweden favored the latter, but general agreement was reached in the parliament on Karl Peter. Then Tsarina Elizabeth chose him to be her heir (as Peter III) in Russia. A second choice had to be made, this time between the Danish prince and Adolf Fredrik of Holstein-Gottorp-Eutin, prince-bishop of Lübeck. Despite strong popular support for Frederik and even open rebellion by the peasants of Dalarna (the so-called Stora Daldansen of May–June 1743), the Swedes were compelled to accept Adolf Fredrik.

The year 1743 was a low point for Sweden in the century. Once again Finland had been occupied and nearly lost. The choice of a king was dictated by the Russians. When the Danes threatened war over the choice of an heir, the Swedes had to ask for Russian troops to check a possible invasion. An alliance with Russia was forced on them, and the Russians tried to dictate Adolf Fredrik's choice of a spouse. In the long run, the Russians' bullying met with little success, however. Within a few years the Hats had renewed their ties with France and entered into an alliance with Prussia, and the heir was married to Frederick II of Prussia's sister, Louisa Ulrika. Furthermore, under the direction of J. S. Schulin and then J. H. E. Bernstorff, relations with Denmark were much improved. An agreement to drop Adolf Fredrik's claims to Gottorp lands in Slesvig and Holstein was reached in 1749, a friendship pact concluded, and a marriage contract between Frederik V's daughter Sofia Magdalena (1746–1813) and the future Gustav III arranged in 1751.

The second military-diplomatic folly of the century for Sweden came during the Seven Years' War (1756–63). Believing that the modest military reforms of the 1740s and early 1750s were sufficient, hoping for territorial gains in Germany, and wanting to punish the queen even further for her hand in the planned coup of 1756, the Hat leadership again accepted French subsidy support and, despite considerable internal opposition, joined the continental war against Prussia in September 1757. To justify their actions they argued Sweden was right to intervene under the terms of the Treaty of Westphalia (1648) designed to guarantee the status quo in the German states.

During the summers, when Frederick II of Prussia was preoccupied with major campaigns elsewhere, Swedish armies met with some success and even moved into Prussia. At the close of each campaign season, however, they returned to safer quarters in Pomerania. Five different commanders, each of them inept, led the Swedish troops. Officer discontent was high, and several hundred left the troops to attend the 1760 meeting of the estates. Hunger and disease plagued the soldiers, and the conflict is sometimes called "the potato war" because the men took to eating the previously disdained tubers. At home, where financial resources were exhausted and economic conditions worsened, the conflict was seen as a "Hat war" and not a national conflict. The Hat leadership was attacked from within its own ranks and by the Caps and crown in the longest Riksdag of the century (1760–62). Leadership of the Hats shifted to Axel von Fersen the Elder (1719–94). In early 1762, when Sweden's position was further weakened by events in Russia, the queen agreed to ask her brother for peace talks in exchange for the withdrawal of the 1756 chastisement of the crown (*riksakt*) and more money for the court. As a result, a settlement was reached with Prussia at Hamburg in May 1762 on the basis of no territorial change.

In early 1762 the entire character of the Baltic situation changed because of a flood of events in Russia. In January Tsarina Elizabeth died and was replaced by Karl Peter Ulrik of Holstein-Gottorp as Peter III. A strong admirer of Frederick the Great, he promptly took Russia out of the war against Prussia. In the north attention now turned to Denmark, which was threatened with invasion by Peter over the unsettled family claims of the new tsar to ducal lands in Slesvig and Holstein. However, in July 1762, Peter was overthrown by his wife, Catherine, and murdered. The war threat against Denmark evaporated.

Catherine II favored a settlement with Denmark over the Gottorp lands question, and J. H. E. Bernstorff willingly abandoned his pro-French line for what appeared to be a safer pro-Russian one. A friendship agreement was signed in 1765, and four years later an anti-Swedish defensive alliance was concluded, both of which served as the basis for Danish foreign policy down to the 1790s. The 1767 settlement of the Gottorp lands issue was also important. Under its terms the Danish crown received full title to the former Gottorp claims in Slesvig and Holstein. In compensation, a secondary line of the Gottorps received a cash payment and title to Oldenburg and Delmenhorst. This agreement matched that reached with Sweden earlier and put to rest an issue that plagued Danish leaders for nearly a century.

Although Norden now enjoyed general peace until 1788, there were war scares in 1769, 1772, and 1784. Russian and Danish fears that the factional strife in Sweden was about to give way to increased royal power provoked the first, and Gustav's coup triggered the second. Gustav III's increasingly aggressive foreign policy—a policy arising from his romantic attachment to Sweden's age of greatness, his desires to live up to the likes of Gustav I and II, and his use of foreign-policy adventures to deflect attention from domestic problems or to affect domestic policies—turned to plots for a campaign to acquire Norway and triggered the third crisis. All passed. In general, Denmark's foreign ministers, including J. H. E. Bernstorff (to 1770) and his nephew Andreas Peter Bernstorff (1773–80 and 1784–97), preferred peace; and the Russians were drawn away by Polish and Turkish matters.

Peace in the North was finally broken in the early summer of 1788. During the 1780s Gustav III faced growing complaints at home because of his increasingly autocratic style and economic problems. A successful foreign-policy adventure became a way to deflect this criticism. He also believed he could safely attack a Russia distracted by war with the Ottoman Turks, end Russian meddling in Swedish domestic affairs, and regain lost Finnish territory. But how was he to circumvent the 1772 constitutional restriction on his power to declare offensive war? According to many accounts, he did so with a theatrical ruse. Gustav had a troop of Swedish soldiers dress in Cossack uniforms made in Stockholm and attack a border station at Puumala in Finland on 28 June 1788. The staged attack then justified a defensive response. However, there is another version of the story in which, although the staged attack was planned, a Russian patrol actually fired on the Swedes, thereby creating the necessary incident to justify Gustav's response. The truth will probably never be known. Certainly, Gustav's critics were quick to accept the costume story and brand the war as illegal.

The planned attack, led by the king, against a lightly defended St. Petersburg stalled. The fleet failed to establish control of the Gulf of Finland. An offensive against Fredrikshamn had to be abandoned. In early August a small group of officers sent a note from Liikala to Catherine in which they stressed the war's illegality and their hope for peace. A few days later 112 officers signed a statement at Anjala containing similar sentiments and sent it to the king. To make matters worse, the Danes honored their alliance with Russia and attacked Sweden from Norway in September.

The situation was not as bad as it seemed. The front did not collapse in Finland, and Catherine was suspicious of the Swedish officers' conspiracies. The Danes' attack was halfhearted and the Swedish defenses at Göteborg effective. Gustav maximized the propaganda benefits inherent in both the noble officers' treason and the Danish attack to arouse public support, to call the estates and revise the constitution.

Although the Danes quickly withdrew and concluded an agreement under pressure from Great Britain, the war with Russia dragged on for two years. The army's campaigns in Finland in 1789 and 1790 were indecisive. Only the overwhelming Swedish naval victory at the second battle of Svensksund in July 1790 affected the military balance. This victory, the defection of Austria from the Russian war with the Ottomans, and external diplomatic pressure finally led to peace. The Treaty of Värälä (14 August 1790) involved no territorial changes.

The war was a very costly adventure. As many as 22,000 Swedish sailors and soldiers died, most of them of cholera and other diseases. The estimated material cost was set at 20 million riksdaler. The political gains among the nonprivileged estates were offset by the enmity of the nobility—a hostility that ultimately cost Gustav his life. On the positive side, the Russians recognized the constitutional changes of 1772 and 1789 and yielded their claim to the right of intervention in

Swedish domestic politics. The experience may also have convinced Swedish leaders for at least the next decade of the wisdom of avoiding involvement in war.

The other issue of the peaceful interlude, 1763–88, was the question of neutral shipping rights during great power conflicts. This was especially important after 1776, when Denmark and Sweden took the opportunity to trade with the American colonies during their War of Independence. Russian and Swedish negotiators concluded an armed neutrality pact in 1779. The Danes joined in 1780, although they were also careful to reach a parallel agreement with Great Britain over the definition of contraband. Following the war, Sweden was among the first European countries to recognize the new republic and concluded a treaty of friendship and commerce with the United States in 1783.

The French Revolution raised new questions and problems for the Nordic governments. Where did they stand on the question of the revolution: were they for, against, or neutral? If against, were they willing to intervene? In Denmark, Crown Prince Frederik and A. P. Bernstorff preferred a neutralist position. Gustav III became a passionate opponent of the Revolution and talked of military action. However, his plotting to intervene was cut short by Anckarström's bullet, and his successors followed a more detached course. When the revolutionary wars began in spring 1792, the Nordic governments opted for neutrality. They were, however, again plagued by the problems of how to protect the rights of neutral commerce, and established a new league of armed neutrality in 1794 and introduced convoying four years later. In the early nineteenth century, as the intensity of the conflicts increased, neutrality was rejected by Sweden's king and made impossible for Denmark by Napoleon and Britain.

6

Tradition and Reform:
Societies in Transition

Within the context of unprecedented population growth, the Nordic societies of the eighteenth century remained fundamentally the same as in previous centuries: class or estate organized, hierarchical, and relatively rigid. However, patterns of change that had appeared earlier, such as the conversion of the nobility into a class of civil servants and the expansion and increased complexity of the middle class, continued and in some cases were accelerated. There were also new developments among the lower orders of these societies in both the rural and urban settings as a result of new technologies, new economic ideas, government actions, increasingly rapid population growth, and external factors. At the same time, the "old order" of society and especially the privileges enjoyed by the upper classes were causes for unrest and came increasingly under attack, especially from a growing and articulate middle class.

In economic terms, the Nordic societies generally enjoyed, after the terribly destructive years of the Great Northern War, a century of growth and prosperity. No economic sector escaped the increasingly rapid pace of change, driven by the same factors affecting the social order. In general, the Nordic countries as a group moved away from the old agrarian/commercial economies toward so-called protocapitalist or preindustrial economies.

Culturally and intellectually, Norden continued to be mainly an absorber of European developments, although it made some important contributions during the century. The economic, political, and social ideas of the Enlightenment found their way into Scandinavia and permeated intellectual life and practical politics. Although immensely productive in art, architecture, and fashion, the styles and tastes of the cultivated came from the Continent, especially from France, Rome, and England. In education there were trends toward broadened opportunities and increasing practicality. The major universities also were scenes of important intellectual discussions and home to a number of significant personalities, especially in the natural sciences.

In general, Norden, along with much of the rest of Western Europe, was caught up by the spirit of "the Enlightenment" and experienced a century of material and intellectual developments and change that even contemporaries found remarkable.

Social Developments

Overall, the populations in Scandinavia grew rapidly after 1720, nearly doubling in each country. (See chapter 3.) This growth resulted from the absence of prolonged and destructive wars during the century, coupled with relatively few famine periods, the disappearance of the plague around midcentury, some very modest improvements in sanitation and health-care practices, and a slight improvement in diet. Statistically, birthrates remained high while death rates fell slightly. Life expectancies were short, about forty years for men and slightly less for women. This growth needs to be kept in mind as a contextual element affecting virtually all other aspects of Nordic history in this period.

The nobilities of Denmark and Sweden grew during the century and continued to dominate cultural, social, economic, and political life. Their fashions and tastes were imitated by the lower orders; they continued to be important consumers of luxuries; they played active roles in various sectors of the economies; and they remained central in the political systems at the state and local levels. Small (and occasionally quite vulnerable) cliques controlled Danish state politics. In Sweden the nobles were the primary players during the Era of Liberty, running the Riksdag and its committees and throwing in their lot with the crown when threats to their primacy developed in the 1760s.

However, the new ideas sweeping north from the centers of the European Enlightenment, the increasing economic power of the middle class, and the discontents of factions within the nobilities themselves and within the middle class and peasantry brought the nobles and their privileges under increasing attack. The nobilities jealously attempted to guard those privileges. They claimed a monopoly on the higher civil service and officer corps appointments, continued to assert their rights to tax exemptions, and insisted on special landownership rights and control over their renters and laborers. They were not, however, wholly successful. In a pattern begun in the seventeenth century, many civil service positions came open to talent rather than social rank, and examinations were introduced to ensure competence. By the close of the century noble land could be purchased by non-nobles in both Denmark and Sweden. Rental and labor agreements were subject to more and more governmental controls. The end of the virtual enserfment of the rural workers (*stavnsbaand*) and the gradual creation by government policies and actions of an independent peasantry in Denmark was a culmination of this trend. In Sweden, Gustav III's coup in 1772 was supported by nobles fearing the loss of privileges, and the king was, in part, murdered for his revocation of those privileges twenty years later.

The noble class and its internal hierarchy was, however, by no means laid to rest in Norden in the eighteenth century. For well over another century it retained high importance in social and political realms, and to be ennobled remained a goal of many aspiring bourgeois.

The urban middle class was the class of the future, and its assaults on the monopolies of the nobles in the eighteenth century were just the beginning of a radical transformation of the social order. In the eighteenth century this heterogeneous group continued to grow in numbers and complexity. A merchant aristocracy (the so-called Skeppsbroadeln, or Skeppsbro nobility, in Sweden—named after the quayside area of old Stockholm where many of the houses of this group were located) was also present in Copenhagen, Bergen, Christiania, Gothenburg, Malmö, and other port cities. As in the previous century, members of this group dominated international and regional trade. They also were active as investors in economic enterprises of a wide variety, as bankers, and as entrepreneurs. Merchant meant far more than merely a buyer and seller of goods. Among the richest in Stockholm were the Plomgren, Arfwidson, and Hebbe families.

For much of the century mercantilism remained the theoretical bedrock of state economic policies, policies that favored this merchant elite with monopolies, trade licenses, tariff protection, and subsidies. After midcentury, however, more "liberal" utilitarian policies began to be adopted. For example, Stockholm's monopoly on the staple trade in the Gulf of Bothnia was lifted between 1766 and 1776, allowing for the development of trade-based towns along the coast of the Gulf of Bothnia. In 1787 the Danish trade monopoly with Iceland was removed, as were the grain trade restrictions with Norway in 1788.

Copenhagen lost its import monopoly in 1797, which encouraged town development in Denmark. A rationalized tariff system in Denmark from 1797 helped increase trade. These steps spurred the development of new regional trade centers and the merchant houses in them. A kind of second tier of elite merchant families developed in the provincial towns as a result.

Also experiencing growth, especially in the lesser towns and cities of the North, were the civil servant, artisan, and shopkeeper elements of the middle class. Government simply became larger in terms of sheer numbers. Although artisan-based production remained the most usual form, increased population and wealth meant greater demand. Although the guilds spread to many of the small cities, their absolute hold on craft production lessened over the century. There were attempts to establish factories for the production of some goods, especially textiles, which resulted in the growth of a working class based either in factories or in households.

In the countryside several important social trends characterize this period. In the older settled areas of Norway, Sweden, and Finland, the number of farmsteads reached a maximum that could not be increased without reducing the size of farms—dividing them among heirs. Within the context of growing populations this situation created serious social pressures. The options were few. The number of farmhands was, in some areas, strictly regulated, and need was not very elastic. Some of the new population excess could move away, migrating into unsettled areas of the north or into growing towns and cities. A few might even leave their homelands. For many, however, the new land situation meant social degradation, which might involve years of service as a servant or farmhand or a social move downward into the cottager or squatter classes (*torpare, husmän, bondhjon*). At worst, it could mean becoming an itinerant farm laborer (in Sweden the term *statare* or *statkarl* came into use in this period as a label for people in this group)—landless and without the security of a long-term rental or work agreement.

In Denmark, the most notable rural social change was the beginning of the development of a landowning small-farmer class as a result of the land reforms of the last two decades of the period. Between 1784 and 1814 about 50 percent of Denmark's "peasantry" had become freeholders. However, estate farming did not vanish in Denmark, and the population pressures mentioned above created similar problems there.

Economic Developments

Several main trends help define economic development during this period. One was the continued importance of Norden in European trade. Scandinavia remained a vital source of fish, wood products, iron, copper, dairy products, and livestock. At the same time the area's needs for salt, grains, finished goods, and luxuries remained. England and the Netherlands continued to be central in this trade. From about 1730, Denmark and, to a lesser degree, Sweden developed as relatively prosperous global commerce centers. The second Danish East Indies Company, founded in 1670, was liquidated in 1729 and replaced by a new company in 1732. It enjoyed a golden age between 1772 and 1807. Ships laden with copper and iron goods, some domestically made cloth, and metal currency sailed east. On the return they were loaded with cotton and silk, tea, herbs and spices, porcelains, and other luxuries. Some 350 cargoes, valued at around 135 million rigsdaler, arrived in Copenhagen for auction. As noted in chapter 4, the Danish West India Company carried on a reasonably profitable triangle trade between Copenhagen, the small bases in Africa, and the Danish West Indies.

A Swedish East India Company was founded in 1731 and remained active until it was dissolved in 1813. Most of the early capital was foreign, but by midcentury the company was largely Swedish-owned. In its eighty-two-year history, 132 expeditions, which took anywhere from fourteen to twenty-four months to complete, were dispatched. As with the Danish company, the outgoing cargoes were mainly metal goods and coin currency. Tea, which made up over half of the value of the homebound cargoes, and the usual list of luxury goods filled the returning ships. Although Stockholm played an impotant role in the company's life, Göteborg was its center.

Production of goods for the general market remained largely under the control of the craft guilds, which continued to dominate in the capitals and larger towns of the region. In 1773 in Sweden restrictions were eased that controlled the number of masters in a craft who did not belong to a guild, thus allowing for greater entrepreneurial freedom to establish independent shops. In Denmark the guilds' monopolies were eliminated in 1800. At the same time, two other production trends continued. One was the growth of the domestic production sector (*hemslöjden*) and of output from rural tailors, shoemakers, cabinetmakers, and the like. The second involved

Early modern economies in Scandinavia.

efforts to create, with considerable government encouragement, "man-ufactories," in which at least some of the steps in production could be concentrated. Jonas Ahlström (ennobled Ahlströmer, 1685–1761) developed a "factory" in Alingsås, Sweden, in the 1720s that employed several hundred workers and produced a strange array of goods including cloth, ribbons, stockings, and wallpaper. Such centers were rare, however, and all of Sweden's industries employed only about 1 percent of the population.

In the mining and metal sectors, copper output fell while prices remained solid or rose. In Norway, for example, production declined from 6,000 kg in 1760 to 3,400 kg in 1800. In the same period, the value of this output rose, however, to over 300,000 rigsdaler. Production at the Stora Kopparberg mine at Falun, Sweden, also declined, in part because of difficulties with removing water from the increasingly deep operations. Prices, however, remained high, and outputs rose in the 1780s. Iron mining and the production of bar iron remained central in the Swedish economy. In the 1770s there were over 270 small mills in operation. Annual production of bar iron reached some 620,000 kg by the last quarter of the century, about 90 percent of which was exported. England was the main buyer. Changes in the iron industry were coming, however. Technological developments in England gradually altered the nature of product demand. The adoption of coke and several new techniques in iron and steel production there resulted in a decline in the call for bar iron and an increase in demand for the less profitable export of iron ore.

In certain respects agriculture experienced relatively little change. Modest gains in output of both field crops and livestock were achieved through better soil management, including greater use of two- and three-field rotation systems, more careful gleaning of seeds, improved livestock breeding practices, and the occasional use of new equipment like the seed drill. New crops had difficulty overcoming the inherent conservativeness of this sector. For example, although the potato was introduced in Sweden in the late seventeenth century and experimented with by Jonas Ahlströmer and others, it made little headway. Most important, chiefly in Denmark and Sweden, were conscious and well-intended government policies reflecting the utilitarian and rational ideals of the Enlightenment and adopted after midcentury to change the nature of landholding. In Sweden they took the form of the movement for consolidation, a process by which the government consciously attempted to end the centuries-old village-based agricultural system with its practice of dividing farmland into thin, scattered strips owned by members of the village but worked largely communally. Through a series of *storskifte* (large division) ordinances (1749, 1757, and 1783), conceived by the director of the Land Survey Office, Jakob Faggot (1699–1777), and based on voluntary participation, about one third of Sweden's village-based strip-farms were at least partially consolidated by the end of the century.

The consolidation efforts in Sweden continued during the 1800s, embodied in the *enskifte* (single-division) ordinances of the first decade of the nineteenth century and the *laga skifte* ordinance of 1827. The process was not considered complete until the 1870s, and parts of northern Sweden and Finland were never affected by it.

The private efforts of Skåne landowner Rutger Maclean (1742–1816) served as a primary model for these reforms. Maclean, in the 1780s, forced the breakup of four villages on his estate and the consolidation of holdings into seventy-three farms of about 65 acres each. He also converted the rents of his tenants from kind to cash. Initially, Maclean met with resistance, and some former tenants chose to leave Svaneholm rather than be subjected to these changes. In the long run, however, he was proved correct. Productivity increased, and his tenants' standard of living rose.

In Denmark the focus was on the elimination of the near-serfdom imposed on most of Denmark's rural peasants, as well as on consolidation. The reforms were designed by the Great Agricultural Commission and introduced between 1788 and 1794. Change came quickly. By 1814 over half of all Denmark's small farmers were freeholders, and three-quarters of all the holdings in the islands and about half in Jutland had been consolidated.

Overall, the purposes of these reforms were to free the individual peasants to make independent decisions about what to grow and how to grow it and to remove the individual from the tyranny of the agricultural village or the landlord. Ultimately, it was hoped greater prosperity (and higher tax revenues) would result. Although some of the outcomes did not match the expectations, these reforms did give the landed lower classes greater freedom, and higher agricultural output and prices ensured a modest (if temporary) improvement in their standards of living.

Within the context of the developments outlined above, life for most women changed little during the eighteenth century. They were still considered fundamentally inferior to men and continued to face lives of endless work described earlier. Yet some "progress" was made. The educational reforms discussed elsewhere in this chapter included the intent that girls would acquire a basic literacy along with boys. In addition, several special schools for girls of middle-class families were founded, especially in the capitals. In Copenhagen, for example, there were as many as fifty academies for girls in the late eighteenth century. Most probably focused on providing an education in domesticity—in needlework, conversation, dancing, and etiquette. At least one, Döttreskolan (the daughters' school) from 1791, had a more varied curriculum that included instruction in writing, mathematics, history, and modern languages. It has been argued that this curriculum reflected the desire on the part of the fathers who ran the school to provide an education for their daughters that would serve them well as partners of husbands who would expect them to work in the shop, keep accounts, and prepare correspondence as well as entertain and raise children. The conversations of the Enlightenment in the salons of Scandinavia cannot help but have turned to women and their roles in society. Mary Wollstonecraft's *Vindication of the Rights of Women* was translated into Danish only a year after its publication in 1792. There were also several influential women writers in Scandinavia in this period including Hedvig Nordenflycht and Anna Maria Lenngren. Although there were these modest gains, and a few voices for women were heard, no influential women's rights movement developed until the middle of the next century.

Cultural and Intellectual Developments

In intellectual history, the eighteenth century was "the age of reason," the century of the Enlightenment. It was a period of great intellectual activity and creativity. The rococo, neoclassical, and early romantic styles defined the arts and architecture of the period, and the concepts of reason, natural law, optimism, and utilitarianism shaped many of the philosophical, political, social, and economic views of the times. In the sciences new efforts were made to define and systematize the natural world, and technology became increasingly important in solving practical problems of the period.

As the scope of activity increased, the audiences interested in these activities swelled. The salon was a principal medium for communicating and discussing the ideas and developments of this period, and in every European city a culture of Enlightenment conversation developed, often based on the organizational efforts of noble and bourgeois women. At the same time, books, scientific journals, pamphlets, and newspapers served as communication media for an increasingly literate population. Although far from the centers of enlightened society, Norden shared in all aspects of the intellectual life of this period and contributed to it in many ways.

Education was essential to the vitality of the Enlightenment and received a boost from at least two sources during the century. First, Pietism, a Lutheran reform movement with its roots in Germany, made inroads in Scandinavia, particular in Denmark during the reign of Christian VI. The Pietists' focus on the Scriptures and on compulsory confirmation (from 1726 in Sweden and from 1736 in Denmark) necessitated increased literacy. How, after all, could the devout know the Gospel if they could not read? Second, a reasonable conclusion of the fundamental ideals of the Enlightenment was enhanced education for the general public. Throughout the century reforms were encouraged by intellectuals and Enlightenment-friendly nobles, and there was a drift toward greater educational opportunities for the commons and improved (more practical) curricula at all educational levels.

Both Frederik IV and Christian VI had schools built on crown estates, and by 1740 these numbered some 240. Christian also encouraged other landowners to follow his example, but with little success. In addition, although a 1739 school ordinance for Denmark stipulated that a system of general public education should be established, little developed because it. At the end of the century a royal commission issued a series of recommendations that were followed up in the early nineteenth century.

In Sweden a 1724 law stated that education was the responsibility of parents or the parish, and a 1768 government circular called for the founding of a system of local rural schools. Statements like these did not, however, provide the funds for schools or the infrastructures to support them. In general, rural education took place, without very much uniformity, in peasant homes. Itinerant teachers, who were often retired soldiers, the local parish clerk, or some elderly person, all without any formal training, spent a few weeks each year giving basic instruction in reading and writing.

In the towns basic schools were few, badly funded, and poorly staffed, and the same was true for the so-called Latin, or cathedral, schools. (There were twenty of these in Denmark, four in Norway, one in Iceland, eleven in Sweden, and one in Finland.) The students often came from the poorest families, and a high percentage were orphans. It is hardly surprising that most of the better-off burghers and the nobles avoided these schools, preferring to send their children to one of the many small private schools that developed or to educate them at home using tutors.

The universities continued to be important and were centers for the discussion of new ideas. They were also targets for experimentation by meddling monarchs and government officials. At Copenhagen, Christian VI and his queen, Sofie Magdalene, tried to impose their stifling pietism in a new university charter from 1732. They also called for more thorough studies of the Scriptures and Church history, encouraged frequent religious assemblies, and attempted to gain control of the faculty through manipulation of professorial appointments. Although their efforts set a tone that lasted until midcentury, they were not successful. Intellectual vitality, though subdued, remained, and modest efforts to modernize the curriculum were made. The university also was quickly rebuilt following a disastrous fire in 1728. From the 1750s on Copenhagen University became more and more a center of the Enlightenment's conversation. The empiricism and rationalism advocated by intellectuals of the age and personified in Ludwig Holberg became predominant. During the Struensee period a plan to overhaul the university was developed by the Norwegian-born bishop J. E. Gunnerus (1718–73), which added another element of the Enlightenment—practicality, or social utility. Gunnerus's ideas were taken up after 1784, when the size of the faculty was increased and a new charter adopted that recognized the university's obligation to train clergy and doctors, judges, and the higher civil servants for the good of the society. The new charter also set limits on royal meddling.

In Sweden, Uppsala remained the primary university, and its history also reflects both general European trends and governmental interference. In the 1740s the Hats created an educational commission that recommended turning the country's universities into trade schools for the training of clergy and bureaucrats. They also wanted to change the structure of the faculties and discourage research. The proposals were not adopted, but several new government-service degrees were introduced. At the same time new buildings were added, the faculty grew, and new courses in more modern subjects were introduced. In addition, a debate began over the conventions that the ideal education meant an encyclopedic grounding in the classics and that a general education was superior to a specialized one.

Although the period between 1730 and 1772 is considered to have also been a golden age at Uppsala, especially in the sciences, the last quarter of the century was more somber and bore fewer achievements. To some extent this was because many of the greats who had dominated the earlier period had died. It was also because Gustav III imposed a personal dominance on the university, and his interests in the humanities and his changeable nature showed in faculty and curricular development.

The number of students enrolled remained relatively constant at Copenhagen, but declined at Uppsala from around 1,000 in 1700 to

Sweden's Enlightenment Scientists

Characterized by important achievements in the earth sciences and technologies, Sweden's "golden age" in the natural sciences extended from the early eighteenth century to around 1770.

Torbjörn Bergman (1735–84). Entomologist, astronomer, mathematician, geographer. Credited with developing a precursor of the modern periodic table.

Anders Celsius (1701–44). Physicist and mathematician. Developed a 100-degree thermometer upon which today's "Celsius scale" is based.

Axel Cronstadt (1722–65). Mineralogist and classifier.

Urban Hjärne (1641–1724). Chemist, pharmacist, geologist.

Samuel Klingenstierna (1698–1765). Mathematician, physicist, contributor to studies in optical geometry.

Carl von Linné (Linnaeus) (1707–78). Physician, botanist, and systematizer. Studied plant reproduction, developed a binomial system of plant classification, and studied and classified much of Sweden's flora.

Carl W. Scheele (1742–86). Apothecary and chemist. Credited with having discovered eight elements including oxygen.

Emanuel Swedenborg (1688–1772). Mechanic, mathematician, geologist, mineralogist, and mystic. Established Sweden's first scientific journal.

Johan Wallerius (1709–85). Soil chemist.

Pehr W. Wargentin (1717–83). Astronomer. Studied comets and the moons of Jupiter and established the Swedish Bureau of Statistics in 1754.

---

fewer than 500 at the close of the century. At the same time the composition of the student bodies changed noticeably. Most significant was the decline in the percentage of students who came from clerical families. In Sweden this figure went from 40 percent of the total in

1700 to 25 percent in 1800. There was a parallel development in career choices. Up to midcentury nearly half of all university students studied to become pastors. This proportion fell thereafter and was about 35 percent by 1800. Increasingly, students prepared for careers in government, law, and medicine.

Overall, the century witnessed the decline of theology's dominant position, improved programs in the sciences and especially in medicine, increased use of the vernacular languages in texts and instruction in place of Latin, and the increasingly frequent inclusion of "practical" courses in the curriculum, including modern foreign languages and contemporary politics and history.

Despite the limited nature of most education developments in the eighteenth century, especially in the realm of general education, they should not be dismissed as insignificant. Unquestionably, by 1800 more people in the lower classes were literate, more in the middle and upper classes were better educated, and a greater percentage of women had received some education than a century earlier. Education also meant more than learning a classical curriculum in preparation for a clerical career. New sciences, new history, modern languages, better medicine, and new technologies were being taught and used. Furthermore, there was much more "information" accessible to the public in books, pamphlets, broadsheets, and newspapers. Private libraries grew, and the first lending libraries appeared. All these developments helped encourage the discussion of issues, bring former outsiders into the political processes, and foment change. They were, in other words, vital aspects in the transformations Norden was beginning to undergo in the late eighteenth century.

Other important contributors to the intellectual vitality of the eighteenth century were the so-called academies. These were more than merely societies of distinguished advocates of certain intellectual pursuits. They were also centers for research, publication, discussion, and sponsorship of those pursuits. In Denmark the academies included one for science and letters (1742), art (1754), agriculture (1769), and literature (1780). In Sweden they included science (1739), music (1771/1796), art (1735/1768/1773), language and literature (1786), and letters, history and antiquities (1786). A Norwegian scientific academy was established in 1767. The Aurora Society was founded in Åbo/Turku in 1771 and a Finnish Economic Society in 1797. Even Iceland had its academy.

The arts enjoyed a century of prosperity in eighteenth-century

Newspapers

The first newspaper in Denmark was Anders Bordning's *Den Danske Mercurius*. Printed between 1666 and 1677, it contained mostly poetic praises of the king. The country's oldest paper is *Berlingske Tidende,* which derived from a 1720 publication. Sweden's first paper, *Ordinarii Post Tijdender,* was founded as a weekly in 1645 by Postmaster General Johan Beijer as a source of official news to be sent to postmasters around the kingdom. In the early 1790s it became *Post och Inrikes Tidningar,* was taken over by the Swedish Academy, and became a daily. It remains in publication today. There was not a printing press in Norway until 1644, and the country's first newspaper, *Norske Inteligens Sedeler,* was founded in 1763 in Christiania. It was quickly followed by news publications in Bergen and Trondheim. The circulations of all these papers were small, but the numbers probably do not reflect the size of the readership. Throughout the late eighteenth century the press faced the threat of censorship. Freedom of the press came to Sweden in 1766 via the Caps and to Denmark in 1770 via Struensee. However, Gustav III's 1771 law qualified this freedom and burdened publishers with monitoring what was printed. In Denmark, censorship returned in 1773, was loosened after 1784, and then imposed again in 1790 and 1799. In all cases, the tightening of controls over the press went hand in hand with criticism of the governments and fears of spreading revolutionary ideas.

Scandinavia, based on the traditional demands of court and nobility and on growing bourgeois interests. In contrast to previous centuries, however, the arts (painting and sculpture) drew mainly on native talent, and some significant contributions in portraiture, landscape, miniatures, sculpture, and interior decoration were made. Stylistically, however, Norden remained tied to the major centers of Europe, and many artists studied abroad. Until midcentury Paris was primary, and the rococo style prevailed. Thereafter, Rome became the center and neoclassicism the style. However, neither major style ever went unmodified by artists in Scandinavia, and other foreign influences were also important, including romantic and realist impulses from England. In Sweden, for example, a Gustavian style, which has been described as a blend of rococo, neoclassical, and naive romantic, evolved. Many of these trends among the arts for the upper classes were echoed in the provinces. The folk arts also remained vital, and some, like the wall paintings of Dalarna, combined folk traditions with a rococo primitivism.

A few of the best-known artists from the rococo period include Gustaf Lundberg (1695–1786), Johan Pasch (1706–69), Peter Adolf Hall (1739–93), Cornelius Höyer (1741–1804), Pehr Hilleström (1732–1816), and Carl Gustaf Pilo (1711–93). Among the leading neo-classicists were the sculptors Bertel Thorvaldsen (1770–1844) and Johan Tobias Sergel (1740–1814) and the painters Louis Masreliez (1748–1810), Nicolai Abildgaard (1743–1809), Johannes Wiedewelt (1731–1802), and Peder Als (1726–76). Romantic impulses help define the work of Elias Martin (1739–1818), Carl F. von Breda (1757–1818), and the late work of C.G. Pilo.

In literature, Bergen-born Ludvig Holberg (1684–1754) dominated the first half of the century. Educated at Copenhagen University, he later became professor of metaphysics and then of history there, was for a short time the university's rector, and was a leading personality in shaping the university and maintaining its intellectual integrity against the threats of the Pietists and the interference of the crown. Holberg was a writer of poetry, drama, history, and philosophy. Outside Denmark he is best remembered for his comedies, twenty-five of which he wrote between 1722 and 1725. Each was an insightful, though always exaggerated, view of Danish society. Except for the king, no one was safe from his wit. Foolish, shortsighted, irrational, tradition-bound nobles, burghers, clergy, peasants, and academics were among his victims. Intellectually, he was a European, a man of the Enlightenment, a believer in human reason, the power of education, and natural law. He was also an advocate of absolutism. His other publications include *Introduction til Natur-og Folke-Rettens Kundskap* (1716), the 6,249-line epic *Peder Paars* (1719–20), *Dannemarks Riges Historie* (a three-volume history from 1732–33), and *Nicolai Klimii Iter subterraneum* (a novel in Latin in which he argued for religious toleration, from 1741). After Holberg there was no giant to carry on the brilliance. Still, there were notable literary contributions, including the poetry of Johannes Ewald, and of the Norwegian, Johan Wessel.

Swedes dominated the Nordic literature of the late eighteenth

Bordssällskap i en bondstuga (Around the table in a peasant home), by
Pehr Hilleström (1732–1816). Courtesy of Statens Konstmuseer,
Stockholm, Sweden.

century, and in some measure this reflects the tastes of Gustav III
for the humanities over the arts. Gustav encouraged all the perform-
ing arts, and his court became a center for writers. Among the leading
figures of the period were Olof Dalin (1708–63), Hedvig Nordenflycht (1718–63), Gustaf Philip Creutz (1731–85), Johan Kellgren
(1751–95), and Anna Lenngren (1754–1817). Above them all, however, was Carl Michael Bellman (1740–95)—an unlikely giant. A Stockholm native, minor government official, poet, and balladeer, Bellman
captured "the other" Stockholm, the Stockholm of everyday men and
women, of seven hundred taverns (for 70,000 people), of prostitutes,
minstrels, and beggars.

Finally, it is worth noting that history developed significantly as a
discipline and became an important literary genre in the eighteenth
century. Source criticism, the careful consideration of the authentic-
ity and believability of sources, became more and more important.
At the same time, history was increasingly used as a tool for the creation of national consciousness, along with language and mythology.

The works of Johannes Ewald (1743–81) and P. F. Suhm (1728–98) in Denmark, Gerhard Schöning (1722–80) in Norway, Sven Lagerbring (1707–87) in Sweden, and H. G. Porthan (1739–1804) in Finland illustrate these developments and strike early romantic national chords. All in all, the literature of this period, although rarely original in style, was important in establishing bases in vernacular genres.

7

On the Periphery: Finland, Norway,
the Faeroe Islands, and Iceland

D uring the early modern period, Iceland, the Faeroe Islands,
Norway (which nominally retained its status as a kingdom),
and Finland were integral parts of the central kingdoms of
Denmark or Sweden. The first three had been independent states in
the Middle Ages. The Faeroes became part of Norway's medieval
empire in 1035, and Iceland was absorbed in 1262. Norway (with its
empire) entered a dynastic union with Denmark in 1380 and gradually
lost its autonomy. Although the exact nature of the union changed
over time, it lasted for Norway until 1814 and for Iceland until 1944.
The Faeroes are still part of the Danish kingdom. In contrast, Finland
had no history as an independent state in medieval times. The sparsely
settled region was gradually absorbed into the Swedish realm from the
mid–twelfth century and treated as an integral part of the kingdom.
In 1809 Finland was taken over by Russia and given the status of a
grand duchy. Finnish independence was declared in 1917 and secured
in 1918.

Many of the histories of these parts of Scandinavia in this period
are heavily tainted by nationalist sentiments, and conditions in them
are often described in strongly negative terms. The governments of
Denmark and Sweden are depicted as ruthless exploiters of the periphery's native populations and their resources. We are also led to believe that national consciousness, always present and long repressed
by the Danes or Swedes, burst forth in the late eighteenth century.
Although there are elements of truth in these generalizations, all of
them must be subjected to careful scrutiny, and there are other possible interpretations.

Unquestionably, the peoples and resources of all these areas were
exploited for the benefit of the core governments. Taxes, tariffs, fees,
and rents were collected. Territorial fiefs, economic monopolies, and

Towns

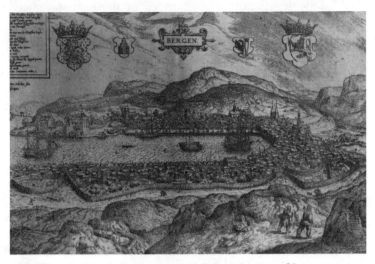

View of Bergen, c. 1580, by Hieronymus Scholeus. Courtesy of Bergen University, Bergen Museum, Norway.

In Norway and Finland the number and size of towns grew in the period. Bergen's population went from about 5,500 in 1500 to about 18,000 in 1800, and Christiania's (Oslo) from about 2,500 to about 9000. Åbo/Turku's population rose from about 3,000 to 11,000. Although tiny by comparison (their populations were about 300 in 1800), Torshavn and Reykjavík eventually became trade and government centers. In the eighteenth century, Denmark became an important carrier of European maritime commerce, and Norwegian ships made up half or more of the kingdom's merchant marine. In Finland some 3,000 new farms were established during Gustav III's reign.

special privileges were created that served the interests of a few. Natural and human resources enriched the economies of the dominant powers. Men from the periphery fought and died in their wars. In most cases, however, this exploitation was no worse than that in Denmark or Sweden; in many instances it was less. In the long run Norway benefited from the relationship with Denmark. Finland probably gained less from its ties with Sweden, and there are few pluses to be seen in the Faeroes' or Iceland's links with Copenhagen. Many factors influenced the negative or positive aspects of these unions, including proximity, strategic importance, and natural resources. What might have happened to any of these areas had they stood alone is impossible to say but interesting to consider.

Overall, several patterns emerged in this period. Centralization prevailed in politics, and the institutions of government increasingly matched those of the core. In terms of political personnel, however, the trend was toward greater peripheral participation. In terms of social classes, general European patterns are present, but with unique regional differences. Gradual growth and increased complexity characterize the economies of these areas. Internal and international commerce, merchant marines, shipbuilding, the extent of land under cultivation, and the size and number of towns show this. Another important element of the period is the growth of knowledge about each area. Studies of history, folklore, geography, and natural science established important bases from which later national identities were built. There also were several instances in which events either challenged the continuation of union with the core states or appeared to do so in the eyes of later observers.

Assigning Finland, the Faeroes, Iceland, and Norway "peripheral" status in the context of a traditional state-approach to the period does not mean they had no histories or that they were unimportant in a local sense or in the larger Nordic and European contexts. Each developed political institutions, societies, economies, and cultures uniquely shaped by external and local forces as they contributed to the histories of the central kingdoms.

Finland

In the mid–twelfth century a small strip of territory along the southwest coast of present-day Finland fell under Swedish control in a religious-political crusade. Over the following two centuries this base was gradually expanded. In the Treaty of Nöteborg/Pähkinäsaari (1323) a border running from the eastern end of the Gulf of Finland to the top of the Gulf of Bothnia was established with Novgorod. (Sweden's medieval Finland was about one-third the size of today's Finland.) Settlement beyond this line proceeded and resulted in frequent border skirmishes in the east. The Treaty of Teusina / Täysinä

(1595), which ended the "Twenty-five Years' War" between Sweden and Russia, redrew the boundary, this time moving it north to the Arctic coast. The settlement reached at Knäred (1613) of the Dano-Swedish "Kalmar War" (1613) closed off expansion into the far north, however. Although there would be many more border changes, the Finland of the early seventeenth century constituted an area roughly equal to the country of today.

The Swedes' conquest was not a victory over any established political unit. The areas they entered were sparsely settled and probably organized along extended family lines. It was the Swedes who founded the first formal organization of the region. Consequently, whereas Finns can claim a unique cultural, social, or economic history, they cannot assert, as the Norwegians, Faeroese, or Icelanders, that a medieval state was taken over by a foreign power and then held in bondage until the triumph of nationalist forces in the nineteenth or twentieth century. For over six hundred years Finland developed as an integral part of the Swedish state.

From a traditional political perspective, Finland's history is the history of Sweden in most respects. The centralizing efforts of Gustav I and the Reformation were carried out there, too. When Gustav II created county-based regional government in the 1620s, Finland was divided into seven counties (*län*). The imposition of absolutism, the factionalism of the Era of Liberty, and other main themes in Nordic and Swedish history had their Finnish aspects. Finnish delegations for each estate attended meetings of the Diet. Finland's laws, religion, and administration were Swedish. So, too, were tax policies, military organization, and security concerns. Ethnically, officials and clergy were usually Swedish. The Swedish kingdom's eastern border was with Russia, not with Finland.

Of course, there were many unique aspects to this region's history. For example, Gustav's son Johan became duke of Finland in 1557 and established a "court" at Åbo/Turku. He treated his duchy as his own petty state. When Johan's brother Erik succeeded to the throne in 1560, conflict broke out. Johan's independence threatened the unity of the realm and the king's authority. Erik was compelled to invade Finland, defeat his brother, and imprison him. Similarly, at the close of the sixteenth century, the nobility in Finland sided with Sigismund in his struggle with Karl (IX) and had to be suppressed. As we will see, other crossroads were reached during the Great Northern War, the early 1740s, and the late 1780s.

Just as the provinces of the west and south in Sweden straddled the line of conflict between Denmark and Sweden, Finland (and especially the southeast) lay on the line of conflict between Russia and Sweden. Almost constant border warfare characterized much of the sixteenth and early seventeenth centuries. Swedish strengths, Russian weaknesses, and a shift of attention to the Baltic provinces, Germany, and Denmark made most of the seventeenth century a more settled one from a Finnish perspective. In the eighteenth century conflict returned, as the Great Northern War and the Russo-Swedish Wars of 1741–43 and 1788–90 aptly illustrate.

The eighteenth century was a crucial period in the development of Finland. Until then, being part of Sweden had not been viewed negatively by the region's noble and officer corps elite. However, wars, two Russian occupations (1713–21 and 1741–43), inconsistent attention to Finnish security, and intellectual developments worked to change this perception.

In 1713 Finland was invaded and, for the first time in its history, occupied by Russian forces. For eight years, a period the Finns call "the great wrath," the region was under Russian control. Eastern Finland was governed by military authorities, the west by Gustaf Otto Douglas (1687–1771), a former member of Karl XII's bodyguard who had been captured and changed sides after Poltava. Although less horribly than some of the exaggerated accounts would have us believe, Finland suffered during the war and occupation. In some areas farms were destroyed, livestock killed, and the people driven into exile or sent to Russia. Most of the officials and clergy fled to Sweden. Helsinki was burned. The economy was shattered. It is estimated that almost an entire generation of young men was lost. Under the terms of the Treaty of Nystad/Uusikaupunki (1721), the Russians took a slice of territory in the southeast and the important city of Viborg/Viipuri.

Twenty years later Sweden was again at war with Russia, and the performance was pathetic. Preparations were inadequate, leadership ineffective, and morale terrible. The occupation (known in Finnish history as "the lesser wrath") that followed the military's collapse was less onerous than the previous one. However, it and the Treaty of Åbo/Turku, which awarded another piece of the southeast to Russia, served as reminders to some people in Finland of how dangerous their position between Sweden and Russia was. The efforts to improve Finland's defenses, including the building of Sveaborg near Helsinki, and the interest Gustav III showed in the region's development, helped ease some of the anxieties. However, for an increasingly vocal elite the ties with Sweden were becoming too costly, and the war in 1788–90 only added to their desire to break with Sweden.

In the late eighteenth century a politically active segment of the nobility in Finland, with an increasing sense of Finnish (variously defined) identity, became convinced the country was too often used as a battleground between Sweden and Russia and that it would be in its best interests to seek autonomy and even a link with Russia. Even before 1788 there were conspiracies. Colonel G. M. Sprengtporten (1740–1819), who had supported Gustav's coup in 1772, fell out with the king and resigned his commission in 1777. During the 1780s he tried to secure Russian support for a separate Finland. He later became an adviser to Catherine II, planned the 1808 Russian invasion of Finland, and became the first governor-general of the Grand Duchy of Finland in 1809.

As we have seen, Gustav's war with Russia triggered the sending of the Liikala Note and the Anjala League's mutiny. Jan Anders Jäger-horn (1757–1825), who advocated self-government for Finland and may have been inspired by the introduction of an Irish parliament in 1782 and the American War of Independence, was behind the note and delivered it to Catherine. Some, but certainly not all, of the 112 signers of the league's protest to Gustav held similar views.

Neither these episodes nor Sprengtporten's plottings were parts of a genuine independence movement or manifestations of popular nationalism. In fact, the peasantry was outraged by the conspiracies and supported Gustav's actions against the officers. Great care must be taken in viewing these events as more than expressions of a small group's perceptions and interests.

The eighteenth century, especially its last few decades, was a period in which various particularistic interests (social, military, economic, and political) developed. At the same time a broader understanding of Finland from a variety of perspectives was nurtured by academics. This discovering and defining of Finland centered on Åbo/Turku Academy. Hundreds of brief studies of Finnish towns, regions, geography, and natural science were written. Some were soundly based, others heavily ladened with myth. Central to this project was Henrik G. Porthan (1739–1804), who published studies on Finnish folk poems, language, dialects, and history. Just how deeply any of these developments reached into Finnish society in general is difficult to assess, but it would certainly be misleading to argue that they demonstrated the growth of a popular nationalism.

Finland's Finnish-Swedish society was unique in the Nordic region. In this period approximately 80–85 percent were Finns in terms of ethnicity or first language. They were predominant in the southeast and central areas. The Swedish-speaking Finns occupied mainly the coastal areas of the southwest and west. Although church and secular officials tended to be Swedish in background, bilingualism was common. Nationality or ethnicity were not serious issues, and such multi-ethnic states were common in Europe.

Social standing was important, and the same estates that defined Swedish society existed in Finland. A small Finnish nobility developed that dominated the bureaucracy and officer corps. This group had strong ties to Sweden, and many owned lands in both areas. The clergy was also small, and the burgher estate was tiny, probably because of the small size of Finland's towns and the restrictions placed on economic enterprise from the seventeenth century. For example, twelve families owned the entire Finnish iron "industry" in the eighteenth century. Rural society contained the familiar distinctions between owners and leaseholders.

The Finnish economy was overwhelmingly agrarian. Rural Finland was dominated by farm villages and strip fields or isolated farmsteads carved from the forests by the slash-and-burn farming techniques so widely practiced by the Finns. The main crops included rye, barley, oats, wheat, peas, hemp, and flax. The potato was introduced in the 1730s but only slowly adopted. A two-field rotation system was most common. Livestock included horses, cattle, sheep, goats, pigs, and chickens. Gardens provided cabbage, turnips, onions, and herbs. Except for some relatively rich areas in the west and southwest, the farming there was among the most marginal in all of Norden. Crop failures appear to have had greater impact there than anywhere else in the region. The worst of these occurred in 1695–97, when it is estimated one-third of the country's population died. As was the case in much of Scandinavia, the rural male population engaged in supplementary economic activities, including hunting, fishing, trapping, and timber cutting, to survive.

During the late sixteenth and late eighteenth centuries extensive areas of the interior (Savo, Tavastland, Satakunta, and Ostrobothnia) were colonized. Often, however, the new lands added little to the long-term viability of the economy. They were opened using one or more slash-and-burn techniques. Typically, settlers moved in, the forests were cut, the stumps and undergrowth burned, and crops planted on the infertile soil for a few years. Soon the land was exhausted, and the settlers forced to move on. (Finnish immigrants using similar methods colonized tracts of Värmland in the sixteenth and New Sweden in the seventeenth century.)

Of the contiguous Nordic countries, Finland was the least economically developed and the least urban. Although there were twenty-two chartered towns by 1800, all of them were small, especially in comparison with Stockholm or Göteborg. The growth of coastal commercial towns in the sixteenth century, generally dominated by Germans, Dutch, English, and Scots engaged in the tar and timber trades, was cut short by the mercantilist policies of the seventeenth century. Stockholm then became the key city in Finland's commerce, and the tar trade was in the hands of a monopoly after 1648. Åbo/Turku was Finland's largest and most important town. Founded in the thirteenth century as a center of the Church in Finland, it became an administrative and educational locus as well. In 1500 the population was about 3,000; in 1800 it was about 11,000. Helsingfors/Helsinki, founded in 1550 by Gustav I as a commercial center intended to dominate the eastern Baltic trade, remained small throughout the period. By 1800 its population was just under 3,000. Viborg/Viipuri was important in the seventeenth century, but was lost to Russia in 1721. Vasa/Vaasa, founded in 1606, and Borgå/Porvoo remained small until the trade restrictions were removed in 1765. Clearly, an argument can be made that Swedish elites exploited Finnish economic resources for their own benefit and to the detriment of Finland's economic development.

Norway

In 1380 Denmark and Norway, as the result of the dying out of the Danish male line and the marriage of Margrethe to Haakon V, entered into a dynastic union that preserved the autonomous nature of each medieval kingdom. Seventeen years later the three continental Nordic states formed the Kalmar Union. The exact nature of this entity was a matter of debate at the time. Some viewed it as a confederation of independent states under a common crown; others saw it as a new unitary state centered in Denmark. After almost a century of "civil wars," Sweden, as we have seen, broke away from this arrangement in

The Sami

Norden's oldest "indigenous people" are the Sami. It is believed they and their culture evolved, without significant influences from in-migrants, from peoples who first came to the region over 10,000 years ago. Although now limited mainly to the far north, in the past the Sami-land extended from the northwest coast of Norway into Sweden as far south as Dalarna and on across much of modern Finland. Historically, the Sami have been either semi-nomadic hunters and herders of reindeer or more settled fishers and traders; and they developed a unique and rich culture with its own forms of social organization, religious beliefs, art, and oral literature. Their language, like Finnish, belongs to the Finno-Ugric group.

Beginning with the Viking period, the autonomy of the Sami was encroached on by the Europeanized Scandinavians from the south. Raids, taxes, settlements, missionary activities, economic ventures, and conscious state policies all worked to erode the native culture. For three hundred years or more the governments of the Nordic states pursued policies intended to turn the Sami into Norwegians, Swedes, and Finns.

Although far from secure in the face of the unavoidable pressures and influences of national and global economic and cultural forces, the culture of Norden's nearly 70,000 Sami appeared less threatened in the late twentieth century. A revival of Sami identity and new state policies and programs helped reverse the assimilationist trend and assured the preservation of at least some aspects of this people's culture. Between 1973 and 1993 Norwegian, Swedish, and Finnish Sami gained their own representative assemblies. Special schools and curricula were designed to preserve the culture; university programs were developed to, among other things, research and write the Sami's history. Yoiking, a traditional form of singing stories, enjoyed a resurgence, and a body of written Sami literature began to emerge. Art and handicraft traditions were nurtured. Cross-border Sami contact and cooperation were encouraged.

1523. Norway did not. In 1536 the newly crowned Danish king, Christian III, executed what amounted to a state coup by which Norway became in theory little more than a province, although its kingdom status remained. Native Norwegian political institutions disappeared. Within a few decades, virtually all high government officials were either Danish or German. Norway's native nobility, weakened by the Black Death and intermarriage, shrank to a few families who could put up little resistance. The Church, another potential source of opposition, was forced into submission, became Lutheran, and fell under Danish control.

Does the period 1536–1814 constitute what some have called "the Danish night"? Was the union entirely one-sided, with Denmark taking and Norway receiving nothing from it? Was Norwegian national identity repressed? For many historians writing in the nineteenth and twentieth centuries, the answer to these and many similar questions was yes. Recent, less-biased studies, however, are revising this outlook.

Overall, the Norwegians were not made into Danes. Norwegian law remained based on the medieval code compiled during the reign of Magnus Lawmender (1257/63–80), and modified under Christian IV (1604) and Christian V (1687). Local representative assemblies continued to meet for much of this period, and even the national estates were called to recognize new monarchs until 1661. The Norwegian economy generally grew during the period, and several sectors enjoyed remarkable prosperity and independence. Although social elites developed with strong ties to Denmark, many elements of Norwegian society and culture survived, including dozens of dialects, a uniquely independent peasantry, and distinct material cultures.

For the government in Copenhagen, Norway was a resource of the realm to be used for the good of the kingdom—to be developed and not squandered. Cultural homogeneity was not a goal—or even an issue. Extraction of economic benefits in the form of taxes, tolls, and profits was. As Denmark moved from being a medieval domain state to being an early modern tax-warfare state, those economic benefits became more and more important—important enough to divert state resources to protect and develop.

Structurally, Norway clearly came under the control of Copenhagen. In the sixteenth and early seventeenth centuries, political organization was built on older territorial units and terminology. The country was divided into four large districts or fiefs (*len/storlen*) and about thirty smaller districts (*smålen*), each headed by an official (*lensmænd*) appointed by the crown. In the 1630s the number of these units was changed, but the essential system remained intact. The introduction of absolutism in 1660 resulted in many changes. The term kingdom (*rige/rike*) reappeared in reference to Norway, the administrative terms and structure throughout the Danish realm changed, and the system became increasingly centralized. The *len* became *amter,* or counties. The four large units, *stiftamter,* were now headed by regional governors, or *stiftamtmænd.* Each of the eight amter was headed by an *amtmand.* These officials were responsible for the implementation of central policy and acted as an interface between Copenhagen and the people. Sheriffs (*fogder*), responsible for the maintenance of order and collection of taxes; local magistrates (*sørenskriver*), responsible for the administration of justice and the execution of other legal matters; the parish priests; and a small contingent of army officers filled out the administrative hierarchy. In all, there were about 1,000 to 1,200 officials in seventeenth-century Norway, and about 1,500 at the end of the union period (1814). Initially, the holders of the secular offices were from Denmark, the German duchies, or other parts of Europe. Over time, however, an official class developed that became increasingly self-recruiting.

Centralization was a key element of the absolutist transformation, and normally the officials reported directly to Copenhagen. Only occasionally was there anything resembling a central administrative apparatus in Norway. From 1572 there might be a *statholder,* or viceroy, to represent the crown and oversee government affairs in Norway, but this office was often left vacant and the influence of individual viceroys varied widely. Oslo, refounded and renamed Christiania by Christian IV following a fire in 1624, only gradually developed as a government center.

Norway was an important source of revenue for the Danish state. Income came from taxes, tolls, fees, and government-sponsored enterprises. The most important tax was on land and was paid primarily by the farmers. The tax rates and the willingness of the commoners to pay them varied. During times of financial trouble, additional taxes were levied on people or necessities. Export tolls on Norwegian commodities such as dried fish and timber were highly productive for the government. Less important were enterprises such as the royal silver mines at Kongsberg. Overall, Norway often contributed as much to the state's coffers as Denmark, excluding the German territories.

However, after the mid–seventeenth century an increasing percentage of tax income from Norway was actually used to pay for government in Norway.

The union with Denmark, of course, meant that Norway would be affected by Copenhagen's foreign policies and wars. In almost every conflict of this period tax demands increased and the economy was disrupted, the government's demands for sailors rose, and the country was either threatened by or experienced invasion. During the Northern Seven Years' War, the Swedes attacked and annexed the Trøndelag. Interestingly, the Trønders apparently cared little about who controlled them and put up minimal resistance against the invading Swedes. There was no Norwegian army, and special contingents had to be recruited to drive out the Swedes. The experience showed there was almost no loyalty to a state and that regular troops were needed in Norway. Both were consciously developed. In the seventeenth century a force based on locally recruited foot soldiers and mostly foreign officers was established. Its effectiveness varied widely. Experiences in the so-called Skåne War (1675–79) revealed great reluctance on the part of Norwegian troops to fight their Swedish neighbors. The opposite was the case during the last years of the Great Northern War, when the Norwegians fiercely resisted Karl XII's campaigns against them.

The early modern Norwegian economy was predominantly rural, subsistence based, and highly localized. Ninety percent of the population was dependent on the country's arable land (4 percent of the total area) for all or part of its living. From 1500 to 1800 the population rose from about 150,000 to over 800,000, and the number of farms grew from around 16,000 to more than 76,000. At the same time the percentage of land owned by the farmers (*bønder*) rose to almost 80 percent. (The small nobility held little land, the Church retained control of about 2 percent, and the crown sold most of its holdings.) Methods, crops, and productivity changed relatively little. There was no extensive enclosure movement, and the experiments of a small number of large landholders had little impact. Cultivation of the potato made some progress in the late eighteenth century. Throughout this time the overall marginality of Norwegian agriculture was revealed in the negative impact bad years had on population.

Few rural Norwegian families were solely dependent on farming for their livelihood. Fishing, shipping, lumber cutting and hauling, providing labor or materials for mining operations, and crafts were essential secondary occupations. The importance of each of these varied from district to district, and they illustrate the diversity of the Norwegian economy.

Fishing centered on the shifting herring grounds of the south and west and the enormous cod resources of the west and north (especially Lofoten). From the late sixteenth to the mid–seventeenth century the fishing sector grew. It then experienced a period of stagnation that lasted into the eighteenth century, followed by a new phase of growth and diversification that continued from the 1740s to the early nineteenth century. It is estimated that Bergen, the center of the cod trade, exported about 400,000 pounds annually in the sixteenth century. In the mid–seventeenth century this figure was about 14 million. By 1800 it had increased to around 28 million. Most of the catch was dried, brought to Bergen by individuals, and then exported by the city's merchants. A system of fish-for-credit between fishermen and merchants developed that dominated the period. The markets for Norwegian fish changed during the period from the Baltic to southern Europe.

Norway's other great natural resource to be exploited in the early modern period was its forests. Growing European demand for beams and lumber, the development of water-driven, reciprocating saws, and the proximity of the forests to sawmills and shipping facilities were essential to the expansion of this sector in the sixteenth century and its continued importance through the period. Initially, lumber production and export was in the hands of the farmers. Getting started was fairly inexpensive. The saws were simple, waterpower accessible, and the forests close at hand. Over time, however, as the coastal forests were cut and transportation costs rose, the control of the industry shifted to urban entrepreneurs. In 1662 lumber export became a burgher monopoly, and a government sawmill ordinance from 1668 strictly controlled the number of mills until 1795. These regulations assured the entrepreneurs their profits by limiting production, but they also guaranteed some farmer suppliers security and established a basis for social conflicts.

The mining, production, and export of silver, copper, and iron formed a third important sector of the Norwegian economy. Its complexity provided employment opportunities for miners, haulers, timber cutters, charcoal makers, furnace builders, smelters, and smiths. Although many of these jobs were filled by local people, as in Sweden immigrants with special expertise were vital to the metal sector's

The Farm at Tofte, from Henrich Willemsen's account of a tour by the royal couple of Denmark in Norway in 1733. Courtesy of the Royal Library, Copenhagen, Denmark.

development. These activities also required large amounts of capital, much of which came from outside Norway.

Silver production, a crown monopoly after 1683, was centered at Kongsberg west of Oslo. The mine's output varied widely, peaking in 1768. It was closed as unprofitable in the early nineteenth century. The copper industry of the south Trøndelag region was developed in the seventeenth century, with the most important works at Røros. In the period 1644–1814, the estimated value of these works' production was 7.2 million rigsdaler. Iron was mined and refined at sites including Moss, Eidsvoll, and Fossum in the south, but never developed to the scale reached in Sweden.

Commerce and shipping also were vital aspects of the Norwegian economy. Coastal trade was and remained largely in the hands of individual operators. When the early modern period began, Bergen was the main port, and the Hanse merchants in the city dominated international trade. Gradually, during the sixteenth and early seventeenth centuries, the Hanse's role declined. One of the most important

From the King's Mine at Kongsberg, by Johannes Flintoe, c. 1830. Courtesy of the National Gallery of Norway, Oslo; copyright Nasjonalgalleriet 1998.

aspects of this period is the growth of a native merchant class in Bergen and throughout Norway. During the first three-quarters of the seventeenth century, shipping was in the hands of foreign carriers, including Germans, Danes, Dutch, and English. The wars of the late seventeenth and eighteenth centuries contributed to economic growth and helped create a Norwegian merchant marine and a shipbuilding industry to support it. The golden age came in the last quarter of the eighteenth century. In the early seventeenth century the Bergen (in effect, the Norwegian) merchant fleet numbered about 60 ships. By the early nineteenth century, the Norwegian fleet had over 1,400—most of which had been built in Norway.

Like all other European societies of the period, Norway's was based on clear and well-understood estates. In the early modern centuries this society developed along several basic lines. First, there was an increasingly clear rural-urban split. Second, the urban and rural components developed new elements within their internal hierarchies. Third, a cultural element was added to geography, occupation, economic position, etc., as a determiner of social position.

Norwegian rural society was unique in Europe for the extent of its freedoms. A large percentage of Norwegian farms had been in the hands of freehold farmers for centuries, and this percentage grew after 1536. The nobility never established a position of control over the peasants, nor did the Church or the crown. Although lease terms may have been less than ideal and exploitation extensive, serfdom never threatened Norway's rural commoners.

Throughout the period the number of farms in Norway rose, driven by profitability and population pressures. But without the adoption of new methods or new crops, there were clear geographic limits to agricultural growth in Norway. For two centuries population increases were absorbed by out-migration, emigration, internal colonization, and farm subdivision. In the eighteenth century, although some migration options remained, expansion lands became increasingly marginal, and the limits of farm subdivision were reached. It was then that the numbers in the landless agricultural groups began to rise. The cotter class (*husmænd*) grew from 11,814 in 1723 to 39,412 in 1801. Similar growth came in the number of servants and day laborers. Formerly homogeneous and remarkably peaceful, rural society in Norway became increasingly split between an elite peasant aristocracy of haves (*odelsbondearistokrati*) and proletariat of have-nots.

Urban society was similarly fractured into three basic groups: a wealthy Norwegian merchant elite; a middle rank of ordinary craftsmen, merchants, and shopkeepers; and a diverse lower class of laborers. The first of these groups was new, a result of the economic growth of the period and the political climate in which that growth occurred. This urban elite was tiny and included only about a dozen families in Christiania and about eight in Trondheim. One family, the Dedekams, controlled the timber trade in Arendal. Their cultural and intellectual outlooks tended to be very cosmopolitan and, in a few cases, quite eccentric. Bernt Anker (1746–1805), for example, was an international merchant in Oslo. In the late eighteenth century he was perhaps the richest man in Norway, and his flamboyant home was the site of a salon dedicated to the arts and conversation. Curiously, although he championed greater autonomy for Norway, he sent his shirts to England to be laundered.

The secular officials and clergy made up another elite element in the society. For much of the early modern period the former were mostly foreign, predominantly Danes or Germans. The clergy tended to be mostly Norwegian in origin. Over time, both groups became increasingly self-recruiting and self-perpetuating. Their distinctions were political and cultural. They spoke Danish, were educated in Denmark, and, for most of the period, identified with the union. Although they interacted with and some were recruited from the other elites, they stood apart from the rural and urban commons.

In the last four decades of the eighteenth century, Norway experienced several outbursts of discontent including strikes by miners at Røros and Kongsberg, protests and strikes in Christiania, localized protests against taxes or officials, and a national religious revival movement. These events had little or nothing to do with nationalism. The issues were similar to those at work across Europe and included unpaid wages, unfair taxes, high prices, anger over social and economic privileges, and the tyranny of local officials. All three elites mentioned above were the targets of criticism and contributing causes to the unrest of the late eighteenth and nineteenth centuries.

One such disturbance was the "Stril War" (Strilekrigen), which amounted to a tax strike by peasants in the rural areas near Bergen. The Dano-Russian war scare of 1762 led to the adoption of costly military reforms in Denmark, which were to be paid for by a special poll tax to be collected throughout the kingdom. For many the tax was a burden that could not be met. Failure to pay in some cases led to exemptions, in others to property confiscations by overzealous bureaucrats. These inconsistent outcomes tended to follow class lines and aggravated the situation. Appeals to the county governor in early 1765 went unanswered, and in April he was pressured by a crowd of over 1,000 to refund some tax payments. The unrest continued, troops were called in to preserve order, and several peasants were imprisoned. The crisis soon passed.

A second example, the Lofthus Rebellion, had many of the same ingredients, including commoner discontent, overzealous or corrupt officials, urban-rural social tensions, and economic policy inequities. Christian Jensen Lofthus (1750–1797) was a successful Sörland farmer who had extended his economic activities into timber cutting, shipping, and trade during the commercial boom of the American Revolutionary period. These activities violated urban privileges and led to prosecution by local authorities. Following a long tradition of seeing the crown as a supporter of the commons, Lofthus turned to Crown Prince Frederik. His trips to Copenhagen in summer 1786 with appeals and evidence of injustices produced no results. The public meetings he organized were declared illegal. Branded as an outlaw and subject to arrest by the authorities, Lofthus was protected by an armed band of followers. The situation grew increasingly tense during the fall. But Lofthus failed to act. The government temporarily defused the situation by setting up an investigative commission, which recommended several reforms. Lofthus's arrest in February 1787 triggered a new phase of unrest, but with the threat to use troops and with time the crisis abated. The cancellation of the hated grain monopoly removed one complaint. A regularization of the system of officials' fees in 1788 removed another. Poor Lofthus spent the last years of his life chained to a rock in Akershus fortress.

The work of Hans Nielsen Hauge (1771–1824) provides a third example of popular discontent. For Hauge the issue was the cold impersonalness of the Church and, more importantly, its arid and officious clergy. Following an intense personal religious awakening in 1796, Hauge began an eight-year period of writing and proselytizing. Through widely circulated publications and small gatherings in rural homes across Norway, he sought to revive religious convictions and trigger a reform of the clergy. The number of his followers, called *readers*, or Haugeans, grew. Quite unintentionally, "the first national movement" in Norwegian history developed. With time the focus of the movement broadened, as Hauge drew attention to rural poverty and the exploitation by the urban burghers of the peasantry. He encouraged independence, religious and economic.

Not surprisingly, Hauge attracted the attention of the clergy and officials, most of whom considered him a threat. He was arrested many times for violations of the Conventicle Act (1741) or on charges of vagrancy. His publications were confiscated and destroyed. From 1804 to 1811 he was imprisoned in Christiania, and when he emerged

View of Trondheim, c. 1674, by Jakob Maschius. Courtesy of Norges teknisk-naturvitenskapelige universitet, Vitenskapsmuseet, Institutt for arkeologi og kulturhistorie (Museum of Science, Trondheim, Norway).

he was a broken man. These efforts, however, did not destroy the movement, and it played a role in several aspects of nineteenth-century Norwegian history.

A growing sense of Norwegianness became evident in the late eighteenth century with the activities of scholars and others who promoted national identity, a national bank, and a separate university for Norway. Geography, natural science, history, and literature were the focuses of scholarship. The Danish-born Erik Pontopiddan (1698–1764), while bishop in Bergen in the 1750s, published a study of Norwegian natural history. Bishop Johan Gunnerus (1718–73) of Trondheim conducted studies of Norwegian flora and was a founder of the Trondheim Society in 1760, which became the Royal Norwegian Scientific Society in 1767. The Norwegian Topographic Correspondence Society, founded in 1791, published thirty-two editions of its journal before 1808. Gerhard Schöning published the first two volumes of his history of the Norwegian kingdom (*Norges Riiges Historie*) in 1771–73. In the 1770s and 1780s Johan Nordahl Brun (1748–1816) wrote nationalistic plays, poetry, and songs. In Copenhagen, the meetings of the Norwegian Literary Society at a coffeehouse (1772–1813) encouraged the development of a national consciousness. The brief moment of press freedom during the Struensee period (1770–71) also allowed for an outburst of pro-Norwegian/anti-Danish pamphlets. In contrast to the relative success of these intellectual activities, the calls for a university and bank in the 1770s and 1790s met with no success.

Just how deeply any of these developments penetrated into the thinking of the general population is difficult to estimate. Although literacy rates had risen significantly since the school ordinance of 1739, which resulted in the development of itinerant schools, books were relatively rare, educational opportunities limited, and a popular press undeveloped.

The Atlantic Islands

Faeroe Islands
The Faeroes, a cluster of seventeen islands about five hundred miles west of Bergen, were settled in the Viking period, and a marginal subsistence agricultural society based on sheep and wool developed. They became a tax region of Norway in 1035 and have been governed by Denmark since 1380, treated either as a royal fief to be allotted to the highest bidder or as a less important and occasionally ignored part of the kingdom. During the early modern period the islands' medieval institutions and law code were absorbed or ignored. For example, the assembly (*lagting*) lost its legislative powers and functioned mainly as a law court until it was disbanded in 1816. Officials included a royal bailiff and tax collector (normally a Dane) and district sheriffs (usually Faeroese). The structural changes that defined the shift to absolutism were delayed in the Faeroes until the early eighteenth century, when the islands came under the jurisdiction of the governor of Iceland.

Life was hard on the Faeroes, and their distance from the continent made matters worse. The growing season was short. Only 7 percent of the land was arable. The people were scattered across the Faeroes in about eighty small agricultural villages. Their houses were made of stone and turf. Outbuildings included small barns and, unique to the Faeroes, special "wind houses" (*hjallur*) for preserving food. Timber was used sparingly and available only as driftwood or through imports. The people's lives were ruled by a calendar of survival: fishing in the spring months, sowing in April; bringing the livestock to the outlying pastures, puffin fowling, and peat cutting in May; lambing, wool gathering, and weeding in June; fowling, sealing, and haymaking in July and August. The fall months were taken up with storing and preserving. During the winter activities turned inside, where men and women shared the work of carding, spinning, dying, and knitting the year's wool. These collective efforts, called *kvøldsetur,* were often accompanied by the singing or recitation of legends, folktales, or ballads. The population of the islands was just over 3,000 at the end of the sixteenth century and slightly more than 5,000 in 1800.

The islands were heavily dependent on trade to provide many of life's essentials, and from 1535 this traffic was a government-controlled monopoly awarded to a variety of operators including German, Bergen, and Copenhagen merchants or trade companies, individuals, and royal agents. Under the terms of the monopoly the Faeroes were to be adequately supplied with good quality imports (grains, salt, beer, and wine, etc.) at fair prices. They were also to be paid fair prices for their exports (wool stockings, tallow, skins, fish, and meat). Obviously, there was plenty of room for abuses in this supply system, and assessments of the monopoly vary. The worst period appears to have been between 1662 and 1708, when Christoffer Gabel (1617–73) and then his son, Frederik (c. 1645–1708), held the monopoly concession. Overall, the monopoly appears to have worked fairly well until it was abolished in 1856—perhaps because smuggling was also common and profitable.

The main center for trade and administration was the islands' only real town, Torshavn, a tiny cluster of buildings and warehouses protected by two small forts on the southeast coast of the main island of Streymoy. By the close of the eighteenth century it was home to about three hundred people.

Although spared most of the ravages of Norden's early modern wars, the Faeroes were subject to pirate raids and occasional harassment by the navies of belligerents. In 1629, for example, Algerian pirates kidnapped thirty people to be sold as slaves.

Iceland

Iceland lay at the edge of the European world at the outset of the early modern period, and although that "world" became vastly larger over the next two centuries, Iceland's distance from the center remained an important factor shaping its history. So, too, did the island's harsh environment. Iceland's climate, short growing season, and volcanoes made it a difficult place for European cultures to survive. Natural disasters time and again reduced the population. The Black Death wiped out about a third in the early fifteenth century. Some 9,000 died of famine following volcanic eruptions in the early seventeenth century. A hundred

Jón Arason

Jón Arason occupies an important place in modern Icelandic history, but one must be careful in assessing his importance. Nineteenth-century historians made him a national folk hero, a champion of Iceland's religious and legal rights. To some degree this is accurate. But he was also a man driven to enhance his personal power and that of his family. His many children by his concubine, Helga Sigurdardóttir, were married into influential families or became priests of important parishes. During the Count's War he was virtual ruler of Iceland, and his actions in the 1540s indicate he hoped to continue as such. The importance of religion and rights in Arason's actions is unclear.

---

years later a smallpox epidemic reduced the population from just over 50,000 to around 34,000. In 1783 a major eruption covered parts of the island with lava and ash. A fifth of the population died of subsequent disease and starvation. As if these disasters were not enough, raids by pirates and foreign "fishermen" took their toll, too. In 1627 Algerian pirates carried off 380 Icelanders, who were sold as slaves. Twenty-seven eventually returned.

Politically, the island belonged to Denmark throughout this period, and the general trend of development was toward more centralized control from Copenhagen, at the expense of Icelandic law, traditions, and institutions. Until the Reformation, however, Iceland was left largely on its own. This changed when Christian III's new Church ordinance was brought to the island in 1538. Church leadership was divided. The new faith was accepted by Bishop Gizur Einarsson (1515–48) of Skálholt, but not by Jón Arason (c. 1484–1550), the Catholic bishop of Hólar. For over a decade a state of near civil war existed. In 1549 Bishop Gizur died, and a crisis ensued over the choice of his successor. A Lutheran, Marteinn Einarsson (?–1570), was appointed in Denmark. Arason, however, wanted to add the Skáholt diocese to his own. Supported by his sons and a small army of followers he imprisoned Marteinn Einarsson and took over the Skáholt church. Luck turned against him in late fall 1550, however. He was captured by his enemies and "illegally" executed on 7 November.

Royal authority was asserted, the Reformation imposed, and Church lands confiscated.

From the mid–sixteenth century Denmark's power in Iceland centered on a governor (until 1688 a *hovedmand,* thereafter a *stiftamtmand*), appointed by the crown. Local administrative and legal authority was exercised through about two dozen district officials (*sysselmænd*). Legal cases were handled through four levels: the district, Althing, appeals (*hovretten*), and the crown. The introduction of absolutism, reluctantly approved by the Althing in 1662, had relatively little importance. Some governmental titles changed, officials were now salaried, and a Danish-appointed bailiff was sent to Iceland as the central agent for tax collection.

One way to chart the decline of Iceland's autonomy is to follow the history of the Althing. Founded in the late ninth century, this legislative and judicial body gradually lost its functions. The last law it approved was the change to the new calendar in 1700. Its size and judicial prerogatives shrank, and in 1800 it was abolished.

Danish government interest in Iceland ran hot and cold, and it never appears to have occupied a central place in the government's priorities. This lack of consistent interest helps explain the country's poverty. In the eighteenth century, however, several efforts were initiated or supported to improve conditions there.

The economy was the most marginal in all of Norden. Agriculture was based on livestock (sheep, pigs, and horses) and fodder raising. Very little land was actually cultivated. The growing of grains virtually ceased in the period because of climate changes, which shortened the growing season. Many essentials, including foods and beverages, timber, and metal products, had to be imported through small coastal harbors and could only be paid for with fish, meats, woolen goods, and hides. There was no capital, no native merchant middle class, and no towns. Trade was a Danish monopoly, granted as a fief from 1602 to 1786 to a variety of holders, including the cities of Copenhagen, Malmö, and Helsingør, several trading companies, and individuals. Although there were regulations governing supply, prices, and quality, they were rarely followed. Poor goods irregularly supplied at high prices characterize what one historian calls a period of "economic oppression . . . and misery." For almost fifty years (1662–1708) the island was a personal fief of Frederik III's favorite, Christoffer Gabel, and then Gabel's son, Frederik, and this period is considered one of the darkest in Iceland's history.

From the mid–eighteenth century some efforts were made or supported by Copenhagen to improve the Icelandic economy. In the 1750s Skuli Magnússon (1711–94), the first Icelander to be appointed bailiff (*landsfoged*), tried to establish Reykjavík as a manufacturing and trade center. With some support from the government, he founded the Icelandic Company to foster economic development. New fishing techniques were adopted, several workshops were built to produce wool cloth using new methods and technologies, and immigration was encouraged. Although Magnússon's efforts had few immediate results, they did introduce Icelanders to many new ideas and methods, and Reykjavík became a kind of Icelandic capital—with three hundred people in 1800. During the Struensee period (1770–71) a special government commission was created to investigate conditions, study public complaints, and recommend reforms. Little came of this, but during the Høegh-Guldberg era the government took over the trade monopoly in 1774, and the medieval regulations on trade were brought up to date.

More change came in the last two decades of the eighteenth century, paralleling developments in Denmark. Another commission was appointed to study the island's problems, and several fundamental reforms followed. In 1785 the ancient Skálholt bishopric was moved to Reykjavík and consolidated with Hólar in 1801. The trade monopoly was abolished in 1786. A new high court was created, and the Althing eliminated in 1800.

As was the case throughout Scandinavia, the intellectual basis for a national consciousness developed in Iceland from the late seventeenth century. Many of the bishops and Icelanders educated in Copenhagen played important roles in this development. In the second half of the seventeenth century Skálholt bishop Brynjólfur Sveinsson (1605–75) developed an extensive collection of manuscripts, many of which were sent to the king. Arni Magnússon spent many years in the early eighteenth century gathering handwritten manuscripts of Iceland's poetry and sagas. Shipped to Copenhagen in 1720, they became the focus for the work of an ongoing circle of Icelandic scholars at the university.

During the eighteenth century a vast body of basic information about Iceland was created. Two Icelanders, Arni Magnússon (1663–1730) and Páll Vídalín (1667–1727), as members of a royal commission appointed in 1702 to study conditions in Iceland and recommend reforms, produced a general population census and an agricultural survey. Improved maps appeared in the 1730s. The Royal Danish Scientific Society sponsored a thorough study of the island's geography and nature by Eggert Olafsson (1726–68) and Bjarni Pálsson (1750–57). The results of this study were published in 1766 in Olafsson's *Reise igiennem Island* (Travels through Iceland). Perhaps the most important history from the period was Finnur Jónsson's (1704–89) four-volume history of the Icelandic church (*Historie ecclesiastica Islandiae*), published in the 1770s.

The new knowledge was accessible to a society made increasingly literate by the crown's ordinance on confirmation (1746). In addition, societies developed in Copenhagen and Iceland to spread new information, and Iceland's first newspaper, *Islandske Maanedstidender*, appeared in 1773.

Part II

The Long Nineteenth Century, 1800–1914

8

~~~~~~

The Era of the Napoleonic Wars

In 1800 there were still only two Nordic states. The Kingdom of Sweden included Finland, which constituted about one-third of the realm, Swedish Pomerania, and the Caribbean island of St. Bartholomew, purchased from the French in 1784 and sold back to them in 1878. The Kingdom of Denmark included, in addition to Denmark proper, the duchies of Slesvig and Holstein, which were tied dynastically to the crown; Norway; the Faeroe Islands; Iceland; Greenland; the Danish West Indies; several African Gold Coast forts; and the enclave at Trankebar in India. Overall, the population of these states was about 5.3 million—about 3.4 million lived in the Swedish kingdom, about 1.9 million in the Danish.

Although there were striking constitutional differences between these two states, in effect each was a monarchy in which the crown and court favorites held most of the power. (Denmark's system was absolutist in a constitutional sense; Sweden's was not, at least in theory.) Neither Nordic country was blessed with a well-qualified ruler. Denmark's Christian VII (r. 1749–1808) was mentally ill, and power actually rested with his son, Crown Prince Frederik, a bright, hardworking, but not wholly consistent young man who had assumed leadership in a coup in 1784. Sweden's Gustav IV Adolf (1778–1837) may have believed himself to be well intentioned, but he was ungifted, narrowminded, and stubborn. In late-twentieth-century historical terms, Frederik and Gustav were enlightened absolutists who, in the spirit of Voltaire, believed the monarch was to be the servant of the people, charged with promoting the welfare of his subjects. In fact, both were paternalistic and conservative in the context of the revolutionary changes of the period—interested in some social or economic reforms, but not in significant political transformations.

Beneath the crown the apparatus of the state was controlled by the nobilities of each country. Constituting social-political elites, they enjoyed near-monopolies on the highest governmental and military appointments. The structures of government were seventeenth and eighteenth century in origin. Policies flowed from the king and his court to colleges or departments in the capital. From there authority flowed to districts or counties and on to local units. Actual administration of many policies was handled at the county and local levels. For the average person, the government meant the local sheriff, regiment officer, tax collector, and pastor. Only Sweden had a representative body, the Riksdag, and this had lost most of its power with the reforms of Gustav III in the early 1790s (see chapter 5).

The Danish-Norwegian monarch ruled over two socially dissimilar societies, each with its separate identity, and without the benefit of an assembly of estates. No native high nobility existed in the king's Norwegian domain, as it did in both Denmark and Sweden. The upper level of Norwegian society instead consisted of the crown officials appointed by the king. Most of those who served in Norway, contrary to what one may be led to believe, were indeed Norwegian-born, though they were not infrequently descended from prominent Danish families. They represented the many ties that had developed over the generations between Denmark and Norway. The crown officials, Danish and Norwegian, had in fact more in common with each other than with the peasants that surrounded them on a daily basis; they had spent their student years at the University of Copenhagen, communicated in the written Danish language, owed their position to the absolute monarch, and formed a distant ruling elite with strong collegial and familial bonds.

The people of these Scandinavian monarchies lived in highly stratified societies. Everyone knew his or her station in life, and although not impossible, there were few opportunities to move beyond it. Sweden's parliament provides at least a partial picture (and until 1866 a constant reminder) of the structure of these societies. It was based on the four estates of the late Middle Ages (clergy, nobles, burghers, and freehold farmers). Others fell into a variety of recognized landless agricultural or urban groups that enjoyed no political representation. Women's social standing was defined by that of their fathers, husbands, or some other male guardian. Only widows enjoyed a measure of independent status.

In economic terms, both kingdoms were overwhelmingly agricultural. Methods of cultivation and crops had changed little since the Middle Ages except for the introduction of a few new crops such as the potato, some improvements in yield through better crop rotations, improvements in livestock through more careful breeding practices, and the gradual consolidation of smallholdings into single family farms or tenancies. All of these were largely the results of late-eighteenth-century reform efforts. Although the Nordic populations varied from region to region, 85 percent or more of the people made all or a significant part of their livings from agriculture. Both kingdoms could boast thriving internal and international commercial systems, dominated by merchant elites and providing necessities and luxuries. Most goods were produced by artisans. Manufacturing (in the preindustrial revolution sense) was limited largely to textiles, iron, copper, and armaments. Raw material industries including forest products, mining, and fishing were highly developed and important. Cities were few in number and small. Copenhagen, the largest, boasted a population of just over 100,000. Stockholm held about 65,000. Åbo/Turku was Finland's largest town with about 10,000 residents; in Norway, Bergen remained the largest city with about 18,000 residents. Christiania/Oslo held about 10,000.

During the nineteenth century, here defined as 1800–1914, dramatic, complex, and interrelated changes occurred in all aspects of Scandinavian life. At several junctures, the map of the region was redrawn. This process involved several factors including the development of increasingly articulate, politically active, and nationally conscious populations and the influence of the great powers on events in Norden. At the same time, and largely peacefully, the absolutist political institutions were replaced with slightly more democratic ones. Gradually, the birth-based social systems became based on economic class, women achieved significant gains in legal status and autonomy, and industrialization, with all its accompanying impacts, began. Linked to many of these developments were an unprecedented level of population growth and mobility. In addition to untold numbers of internal migrations, over 2 million people from the region emigrated to North America and other destinations across the globe. Contributing to these developments and being shaped by them, the Nordic countries experienced a folk and high culture renaissance.

Nineteenth-Century Nordic Monarchs

Denmark	Sweden-Norway	Grand Duchy of Finland
Christian VII: 1766–1808	Gustav IV Adolf: 1792–1809	Alexander I: 1801–25
Frederik VI: 1808–39	Karl XIII: 1809–18	
	Karl XIV Johan (Bernadotte): 1818–44	
	Oscar I: 1844–59	
Christian VIII: 1839–48		Nicholas I: 1825–55
Frederik VII: 1848–63	Karl XV: 1859–72	Alexander II: 1855–81
Christian IX: 1863–1906	Oscar II: 1872–1907	Alexander III: 1881–94
		Nicholas II: 1894–1917
Frederik VIII: 1906–12	Gustav V: 1907–50	
Christian X: 1912–47		

Norway
Haakon VII: 1905–57

Dates are of reigns.

International Relations in the Early Nineteenth Century

The wars of the French Revolution and Napoleon, 1792–1815, tested the capacities of the two Scandinavian kingdoms for survival. Their entanglement in the policies and actions of the European great powers had far-reaching consequences. They led to territorial losses; precipitated great economic problems, domestic suffering, and internal unrest; altered the constitutional order; and demonstrated the extent to which small nations—a status to which the Nordic states were now clearly relegated—are at the mercy of larger ones.

The most fateful choices made by the Nordic leaders came in the

Scandinavia in the nineteenth century.

early 1800s, when they opted to ensure what they saw to be national interests first by protecting what they believed were their neutral trading rights through the use of force and then by abandoning neutrality and entering into shifting alliances with the warring parties. In the late eighteenth century, Nordic diplomats generally had sought to defend freedom of trade in war and peace as an international principle. Trading with both sides in a conflict obviously gave considerable profit. Until 1807 commerce in the North prospered greatly under this approach. In Copenhagen, Stockholm, and Christiania small groups of merchants enjoyed the fruits of these profits, building elaborate new houses and flaunting their wealth. They also hounded their governments for protection of their lucrative business ventures, which, in part, explains the subsequent departure from neutrality.

Nordic policies were initially intended to ensure their rights as neutrals and to protect cargoes and the national merchant fleets. The latter concern in 1800 moved both Denmark-Norway and Sweden to enter into an alliance with Russia and Prussia as active members of an "armed neutrality league" whose motto was "free ship, free cargo." It came into existence as Napoleon worked to defend the principles of the French Revolution against the Second Coalition of monarchical powers and was a direct response to an intensified British blockade of the European continent and the seizure of even neutral ships calling at French ports. Britain countered in early 1801 by sending a fleet commanded by Hyde Parker and Horatio Nelson into Danish territorial waters. Copenhagen was attacked on April 2. Although Nelson's forces were clearly superior, the Danes put up a fierce fight. Many of the Danish naval vessels had been partially dismantled, but they were still able to operate as floating gun platforms. The guns of the fortified islands guarding the city's approaches were also called into action. The Battle of Copenhagen cost the British dearly and holds an important place in the national mythology of Denmark. News of the assassination of the Russian tsar, Paul, during the ensuing negotiations and the pro-English stance of the new tsar, Alexander I, convinced Crown Prince Frederik to accept the defeat. Furthermore, the Swedish government failed to send its promised fleet from Karlskrona to relieve the Danes and instead negotiated a peaceful settlement with the British. Unfortunately, Frederik and his countrymen appear to have learned little from the attack. Some concessions were made to British demands, and the profitable trade resumed. Six years later Denmark was not so lucky.

The weather and the murder of the anti-British Paul saved Sweden from Denmark's fate in 1801. But the attack did not go unnoticed, and the government moved toward a more British-oriented policy of neutrality, which had the added advantage of countervailing the historic pressures from the Russians on the eastern frontier. In 1805 Gustav IV Adolf, however, whose dislike for Napoleon bordered on the obsessive, took the fateful step of joining Britain, Russia, and Austria in the Third Coalition, formed that year against Napoleonic France. It was a high-risk decision that soon brought Sweden into direct hostilities with Napoleon in Germany.

The war against France waged in Swedish Pomerania in 1806 with subsidies from Britain was brief and resulted in Swedish defeat. Importantly, it stimulated the latent opposition to the king in the army and nobility and led to plots to depose the king. The war also introduced Swedes to their future king, though no one would have imagined it at the time. The commander of the French forces in Germany was Jean Baptiste Bernadotte (1763–1844), the future Karl XIV Johan. At the same time, external circumstances beyond Gustav's control were at work to decide the country's fate. Napoleon's victories at Jena and Auerstädt in October 1806 established his primacy in Germany, and his defeat of Russia at Friedland in June 1807 left Sweden isolated. By early fall Swedish forces had been driven from Germany.

In July 1807 Tsar Alexander I allied Russia with Napoleon against Britain in the Peace of Tilsit. Gustav IV knew nothing of the secret agreements it contained, which gave Alexander a go-ahead to annex Finland. Publicly, the treaty only stipulated the task given Alexander when he and Napoleon met at Tilsit, which was to force Swedish compliance with the Continental System—designed by Napoleon and announced in Berlin in November 1806—which was intended to deprive Britain of a positive balance of trade by closing all European ports to British ships and goods. The goals of the policy were to bankrupt Britain while unifying all of Europe under the French emperor.

Against the advice of his ministers, Gustav IV denounced the armistice Sweden had accepted following the disaster in Pomerania, ignored the implications of the Peace of Tilsit, concluded a new subsidy treaty with Britain, and prepared to continue the war, which now, in all likelihood, would become a war on two fronts.

If Gustav's foreign policy was reckless, Frederik's was no less so. The lessons of 1801 seemed forgotten. Blinded by the profits of wartime trading, the merchants of Denmark urged their king to resist British efforts to close off trade of any kind with France, and Danish protests led to growing mistrust in London. Of particular concern was the fear that Denmark's fleets (merchant and naval) would fall into French hands. Misunderstandings and misinformation amplified English worries. On 2 September 1807 Copenhagen was attacked

Bombardment of Copenhagen on the Night of 3–4 September 1807, by C. V. Eckersberg. Courtesy of Det Nationalhistoriske Museum på Frederiksborg, Denmark.

again. The city was set afire with incendiary shells. Damage and loss of life in the capital were extensive, and it would not be until 1914 that a European city would suffer such destruction again. Six weeks later the British withdrew, taking with them at least 160 ships of the Danish navy. The Danes had another event to add to their historical mythology.

Crown Prince Frederik was incensed at the unprovoked onslaught and plundering. He had initially favored joining Britain if neutrality became unworkable, despite the attack in 1801, both because warfare against the world's main maritime power would be catastrophic and because, as an Oldenburger and thus a member of one of Europe's oldest royal houses, he disliked the upstart who called himself emperor. After the British attack, however, he joined the Continental System, leaving Sweden as Britain's sole European ally in the North. Obstinacy and a certain sense of honor once his word had been given, characteristics criticized by some historians since they deprived him of political flexibility, made Frederik one of Napoleon's most enduring allies. Ultimately, he and his kingdom went down to defeat with Napoleon and suffered the consequences.

The impacts of Frederik's decision were enormous. Denmark now fell within the sphere of Britain's blockade. Although some privateers enjoyed great commercial success, and the Danes' coastal defense forces occasionally captured a convoyed British merchant vessel or bloodied a passing warship, the overall economic impacts were disastrous. International trade virtually ceased. Many of the newly rich merchants were ruined. The once bustling Copenhagen became much quieter. Shortages drove up prices. Government defense expenditures soared. The paper currency became valueless as the government printed more and more money to meet its bills. By 1813 the state was bankrupt. Norway, the Faeroes, and Iceland suffered terribly from the interruptions of trade in grain. The overseas colonies came under British control.

Gustav IV's foreign policy, up to this point risky but not disastrous, now made war with France, Russia, and Denmark inevitable. Using as justification Gustav's stubborn allegiance with Britain, Alexander I sent his troops into Finland in February 1808. His intent was to incorporate Finland into Russia and drive Sweden out of its alliance with Britain. Gross mismanagement, not entirely Gustav's fault, afflicted the Swedish campaign in Finland. The Swedish forces were not much smaller in number than those of the invading Russians. However, disease took a terrible toll, morale was low, and leadership was at best timid and at worst treasonous, as some officers chose to conspire with the Russians. Carl Olof Cronstedt (1756–1820), the commander of Sveaborg, the fortress guarding Helsinki, surrendered his troops virtually without a fight. By the end of the year Russia had conquered Finland and was harrying the Swedish coast.

At the same time, Frederik became party to plans to use French-Spanish forces under Bernadotte's command to invade Skåne. Troops were brought to Holstein for this campaign in early 1808. Sweden was saved, however, when news that Napoleon had replaced the legitimate Bourbon king of Spain with his brother Joseph reached the Spanish units and triggered their mutiny. (Ultimately, these forces were evacuated by the British and returned to Spain.) The threat to Sweden from the west and south quickly evaporated.

General dissatisfaction in Sweden over the failed campaign and the cost of the war, coupled with a fear among the peasantry of new taxes and generally bad conditions in Sweden, eventually galvanized the army leadership and a group of nobles in the capital to take decisive action to remove Gustav IV from power. The king's nearly pathological stubbornness and unwillingness to hear the opinion of even his closest advisers was not compensated for by any semblance of personal grandeur. His continued rule became intolerable. On 13 March 1809 General Carl Johan Adlercreutz (1757–1815) entered the king's apartments in the palace in Stockholm with six officers and arrested him before he could escape to Skåne, where he assumed his troops remained loyal. Gustav's intention to leave Stockholm was an act of desperation and an effort to avoid being taken prisoner by Georg Adlersparre (1760–1835), an officer on the Norwegian front who was marching with his troops to dethrone him. No leader made any effort to protect the king or to restore him to power, and less than a week after Adlersparre entered Stockholm, Gustav IV Adolf abdicated. After a period of detention he and his family left Sweden for a life of exile in Germany and Switzerland. He died in 1837.

Peace was now a primary concern of the conspirators who had deposed the king, especially since Sweden proper was under attack by Russian forces. The conflict was resolved on Russian terms in the Treaty of Fredrikshamn/Hamina in September 1809. One-third of the kingdom was lost, including Finland, the Åland Islands, and a small region in the north of Sweden. Finland became a grand duchy and thus a separate and semi-autonomous unit within the Russian Empire, the tsar assuming the additional title of Grand Duke of Finland. Peace with Denmark-Norway, reached in December, entailed no loss of territory. On 10 January 1810 the new government agreed to join the Continental System as a condition of peace with France. For a short time Scandinavia was again united in its foreign policy.

But the diplomatic drama was far from over. Neither of the Nordic governments was satisfied with the settlements of 1809–10. Many Swedish leaders hoped to recover Finland; others thought of compensation elsewhere, for example, Norway. Frederik dreamed of gains at Sweden's expense and of a new Nordic union under his leadership. More realistically, the alliance between France and Russia was considered by most to be temporary and ultimately doomed to fail. In spring 1812 the tensions between the two nations opened into an irreparable breach, and the rift presented Sweden's new crown prince, Karl Johan (formerly Jean Baptiste Bernadotte and a marshal of the French empire), with an opportunity to pursue an independent foreign policy. His sense for strategy as well as his liberation from historical and nationalistic considerations let him view the situation dispassionately and from purely military and strategic perspectives. He realized that a union of Sweden and Norway was geopolitically and strategically more reasonable than the old Sweden-Finland. This was obviously not an entirely new idea. But Karl Johan went one step further and abandoned the goal of regaining Finland. He subsequently joined Russia, Britain, and Austria in a new coalition against Napoleonic France while Denmark's Frederik VI loyally remained in alliance with Napoleon. For his support Karl Johan was promised Norway. Alexander would keep Finland unchallenged.

After the decisive defeat of Napoleon at the Battle of Leipzig/Battle of Nations in October 1813, Karl Johan, who had taken part, broke ranks and marched his troops north toward Denmark, ostensibly in response to Frederik's 3 September declaration of war against Sweden. In fact, experience had taught Karl Johan to be distrustful of political promises, and he wished to present the great powers with a fait accompli by moving through Holstein and threatening to invade Jutland. Diplomatically isolated, Frederik VI dared not deploy his forces amassed on the island of Fyn. The military situation was hopeless, and he agreed to meet with the Swedish crown price on 7 January in Kiel to negotiate a peace settlement. An agreement was signed on 14 January. Under its terms, Norway was to be ceded to the king of Sweden and his successors on the Swedish throne with full possession and sovereignty. Denmark retained control of the historically Norwegian-annexed Faeroe Islands, Iceland, and Greenland as integral parts of the kingdom. The latter treaty stipulation represented a victory for the merchants in Copenhagen, who still enjoyed considerable trade with these areas. After a brief war in which the Norwegians hoped to secure their independence in August, the actual transfer of Norway occurred. More than four hundred years of Danish domination came to an end, traded now for an unknown period of Swedish control over an increasingly nationalistic Norway.

The French Revolutionary/Napoleonic periods revealed the vulnerability of the small nations of Norden and the element of gambling in their foreign policies. During the 1790s Denmark and Sweden's leaders had charted relatively safe courses through the tangle of conflicts on the Continent. The shifts of policy in the early years of the new century were a different matter. Old voices of experience and moderation, such as A. P. Bernstorff, had died, and two young sovereigns assumed control of foreign policy decisions. Gustav IV Adolf turned against Napoleon in 1805–9 with disastrous consequences. His successors supported the emperor in 1810–12 without clear gains, and went to war against him in 1812–15, this time with obviously positive results—the winning of Norway. Denmark's Frederik VI, on the other hand, remained neutral until 1807, despite compelling reasons to abandon that course, then joined Napoleon at the cost of the country's economic position and the integrity of the realm. In each twist of diplomacy the Nordic leaders believed they were acting in the best interests of their states. They also knew they were taking risks in a complex and dangerous game and were increasingly at the mercy of the whims of the great powers.

Political Order in the New Scandinavia

In Denmark and Finland little changed in the face of the geopolitical rearrangements of the early nineteenth century. Denmark was, in many respects, a model conservative (old regime) state until 1848. Frederik VI did move back to a more collegial cabinet form of absolutism and, toward the very end of his reign, allowed the development of provincial and local assemblies with purely advisory powers. His cousin, Christian Frederik (1786–1848) succeeded him in 1839 as Christian VIII (r. 1839–48). His interests in culture and involvement in the "liberal" events in Norway in 1814 did not reveal his real political sympathies, which were fundamentally conservative. His ten-year reign was marked by conflicts with increasingly outspoken liberal political activists and a stubborn resolve to preserve the existing system.

In Finland, Alexander I was content to substitute himself for the Swedish king and rule under the strongly monarchist constitutional order established by Gustav III in the 1772 Form of Government and the 1789 Act of Union and Security. A miniature Finnish version of the Swedish parliament met in Borgå/Porvoo in March 1809 to ratify the new situation and then was not called again until 1863. Day-to-day affairs in the grand duchy were handled by the Senate, a body of aristocratic Swedish-speaking Finns that developed into a government whose actions were overseen by a governor-general appointed by the tsar. (All but one of the governors-general between 1809 and 1917 were Russians.) This system allowed the Finns a considerable measure of autonomy, aroused little opposition for nearly eighty years, and provided an environment in which other aspects of Finnish life and culture developed.

The developments in Sweden beginning with the coup of 1809 and in Norway in the context of the last years of the Napoleonic Wars were far more dramatic and extensive in their outcomes.

In Sweden the fundamental questions of the nature of a new political order were resolved quickly in favor of a conservative and peaceful revolution. Following the deposition of Gustav IV in March 1809, a meeting of the Riksdag was summoned. It assembled on 1 May 1809 to establish a government, write a new constitution, and deal with the question of succession. A constitutional committee, led by its secretary, the "radical" noble Hans Järta, and composed of six nobles, three clergy, three burghers, and three farmers, produced a draft in only two weeks. This document was a blend of Swedish constitutional elements, Enlightenment political ideals, and foreign examples. The constitution was approved by the four estates of the Riksdag on June 6 —although the farmers' estate did not fully accede to it until late June because of questions over tax equity. Duke Karl (1748–1818), Gustav IV's uncle, was elected king as Karl XIII.

The new constitution, although extensively amended, remained in force until 1974. Gustavian autocracy was cast aside, and the country became a constitutional monarchy. Although the king's powers were limited, it was clear that he would govern. The king enjoyed the right to introduce and veto legislation, appoint his own ministers who made up the council of state, and direct foreign policy. The Riksdag returned to a place of importance in the system it had not enjoyed since 1772. It was to meet at least once every five years (later every three) or in special session, and had the right to initiate legislation, reject royal proposals, review the actions of the king's ministers, and control taxation. Disappointing to more liberal elements, the old four-estate structure was retained. A separate judiciary was defined. An Act of Succession, separate Parliament Act, and Press Freedom Act adopted over the next three years rounded out the fundamental documents of the Swedish political system.

This new system was far from democratic, but it was characteristic of what was possible at the time. The parliament represented about 7 percent of the population and wholly excluded many professionals, urban and rural poor, and women—who did not fit into any of the four estates. Despite a constitutional guarantee that appointment to office was to be based on merit and not social status, the old noble elite retained a place of importance in the parliament and in the bureaucracy and officer corps of the army and navy far in excess of their numbers until well into the next century.

Although the constitutional question was settled with admirable speed, the issue of a successor to the aging and childless Karl XIII, was resolved more slowly, largely as the result of accident. The urgent concern to find an acceptable heir encouraged renewed dreams of a unified Scandinavia under a single regent. Frederik VI believed that he himself was a strong candidate and advertised this by having leaflets dropped from hot-air balloons over southern Sweden. However, his insistence on a regime based on the Danish absolutist model, in obvious denial of the new constitution, prevented him from developing a significant base of support in Sweden. Instead, Prince Christian August of Augustenborg (1768–1810), the commander of the Norwegian forces, was elected heir to the Swedish crown. During the coup against Gustav IV, Christian August had allowed Georg Adlersparre to march his Värmland troops to Stockholm without fear of an attack from the rear. It was hoped that the popular prince would bring Norway with him as compensation for the loss of Finland. The idea of a Swedish-Norwegian union even found adherents in Norway, where discontent was rising because of the hardships resulting from Frederik's decision to side with Napoleon. As crown prince, Christian August changed his name to the more Swedish Karl August. In May 1810, while reviewing troops in Helsingborg, he unexpectedly died, probably of a stroke. At his funeral in Stockholm on 20 June, an incident occurred that revealed deep and largely unexpressed discontent with the social order. Middle-class antiaristocratic feelings, fear of a Gustavian restoration in influential circles, and the rumors that the crown prince had actually been poisoned, as well as the dissemination of insinuating propaganda by a small group of radicals interested in destroying the entire system, produced an outburst of mob violence directed against Count Hans Axel von Fersen the Younger (1755–1810), the marshal of the realm. Von Fersen belonged to a group that favored a Gustavian restoration, and rumors were spread that he was involved in the alleged murder of the crown prince. As the funeral procession wound its way through Stockholm, Fersen's carriage was pelted with stones. When he attempted to seek refuge in a nearby house, he was slowly beaten to death by an enraged crowd. The authorities did nothing to protect him. It has never been fully determined who was responsible for the rumors and leaflets, though the mob apparently included dissatisfied government clerks incited by higher officials. In essence, however, this was an isolated incident, and the general revulsion that followed thwarted the wishes both of the die-hard Gustavians, who looked to Gustav IV's son as an heir, and of the radicals. The question of succession remained open, and a dynastic revolution followed.

One hope of the leaders in the new government in Stockholm was to reestablish Sweden as a great Nordic power. In their view it would be prudent to secure the approval of Napoleon, then at the height of his power in Europe, before the Riksdag resolved the issue of royal succession. Some advocated Karl August's brother, and Napoleon was willing to support him. Others believed someone new, someone unconnected with the tangle of events in Sweden, ought be chosen. A complicated series of events involving two Swedish delegations to France, Napoleon, an ex-fiancée of the emperor, several possible French candidates, and an about-face by the parliamentary committee charged with electing a successor ensued over the next few months. Finally, on 16 August, the choice fell on Jean Baptiste Bernadotte, Prince of Pontecorvo and a marshal of the empire. Five days later the parliament ratified the choice—perhaps encouraged by bribes and hopes of French subsidies. The new crown prince took the name Karl Johan, converted to the Lutheran faith, and arrived in Sweden in October 1810. Handsome, charming, articulate (in French, not Swedish), politically clever, and reasonably talented as a military leader, Bernadotte quickly won popularity. Karl XIII was delighted, but soon was incapacitated by a stroke and real power quickly fell into Bernadotte's hands. He became king on Karl XIII's death in 1818.

Historians have differed on Karl Johan's true motives and place in Swedish and Scandinavian history. For some he was, like his former master, a lowborn, crass seeker of power who at times harbored dreams of succeeding Napoleon and always guarded his own interests. Others have seen him as a lucky opportunist who took his new position seriously and was central in the reestablishment of stability in Scandinavia. Because he was a person who kept his own counsel and wrote very little about his personal thoughts, all views are based on secondhand information from people who had widely ranging opinions of him.

Norway and the Union with Sweden

The events in Norway were some of the most dramatic in all of Scandinavia in this period, and their causes and course have been matters of ongoing debates among historians. According to the traditional view, which has long been part of Norway's national mythology, the national awakening of the late eighteenth century merged with frustrations arising from the hardships precipitated by the Danes' involvement in the Napoleonic Wars in the years 1807–14. These factors lay behind the spontaneous and broad-based popular uprising precipitated by the Treaty of Kiel, which exploded in early 1814 and which was dedicated to the rebirth of a free Norway after 434 years of Danish domination. Other historians, although not discounting the importance of these factors, have focused their attentions on the development of two elite "parties" interested in redefining Norway's situation, on the machinations of Frederik VI, who hoped to regain Norway, and on the actions of Christian Frederik. As with so many complex historical events, the weight any of these views receives varies with perspectives and individual biases. The central importance of one other factor in defining the events of 1814, however, is clear: that external forces intervened to determine the outcomes of the drama. The Treaty of Kiel was upheld by the British and Russians. Instead of becoming independent, Norway was ceded by Frederik VI to the king of Sweden. Where the Norwegians helped shape their own fates lay in how the new union was to be defined in fact. Karl Johan may have wished for a realm to be absorbed and exploited. What he got was a semi-autonomous Norway with its own constitution, laws, bureaucracy, and political life.

The growing importance of interest in things and institutions Norwegian in the late eighteenth and early nineteenth centuries cannot be denied. The establishment of the Society for Norway's Welfare in 1809, repeated calls for a Norwegian university and bank, and the development of articulate political factions engaged in conversations on what status Norwegians ought seek within Scandinavia illustrate this. At the same time, it is clear that many Norwegians suffered greatly when Denmark joined Napoleon in 1807. Britain's blockade obstructed the import of Danish grain to Norway and severely limited the export of fish and timber. This action caused economic hardships and famine, especially in the interior of the country. Some people had to mix ground tree bark with the available rye flour, and the period became known as "bark bread times." Attempts by Norwegian privateers to break the blockade enjoyed some success, but only on the country's south coast. In most coastal areas people fared a bit better owing to the return of the herring, which had been absent from Norwegian waters for a long time. An expansion in potato cultivation also aided the desperate food situation. Nevertheless, mortality rates rose as a result of food shortages, and economic life suffered.

The return to a partial state of peace between 1809 and 1812 brought much-improved conditions. Frederik VI, fearing that Norwegian dissatisfaction caused by the British blockade and hunger might lead to a break with Denmark, opened the door for renewed timber trade with Britain. In return, British authorities gave free passage to vessels transporting Danish grain to Norway. These developments alleviated the suffering greatly and saved the Norwegian commercial elite from total ruin.

But the so-called licensed trade (*lisenshandeln*) ended abruptly with the renewed conflict in 1812, and a new crisis situation ensued that was made worse by crop failures. Starvation and extreme need as well as distrust of the authorities caused several local peasant riots during the two years of war. In some instances hatreds and hunger drove the peasants to attack and plunder government-owned grain storage facilities.

The population's anger, however, was directed against Britain, not Frederik VI and his policies. Few calls were heard for an independent Norway. Still, Frederik might well have viewed developments with some apprehension. In May 1813, after Karl Johan had entered Germany on his way to secure compliance with promises made to him by the great powers, Frederik sent the Danish-Norwegian crown prince, his nephew Christian Frederik, to Norway to assume full power as viceregent (*stattholder*). The twenty-six-year-old Christian Frederik was intellectually gifted, ambitious, and influenced by the ideas of human rights and enlightenment. He was also handsome and eloquent. He was sent with a specific mission, to save Norway for the dynasty and for Denmark, and until late May he could count on Frederik's support. Circumstances, however, made him play a somewhat different role in the events that reestablished Norway as a largely autonomous nation.

News of the conditions of the Treaty of Kiel reached Norway in late January 1814, and Christian Frederik worked quickly to establish himself as a shaper of events. Initially, he wanted to declare Norway's independence and assume the position of absolute ruler according to the hereditary laws of succession. He was dissuaded from doing so in early February, at a meeting of prominent men gathered at Carsten Anker's estate at Eidsvoll north of Christiania. Anker (1747–1824), a wealthy entrepreneur, merchant, and proprietor of the Eidsvoll Iron Works, and Georg Sverdrup, professor of philosophy on the small faculty of the Royal Frederik's University (founded in 1811) in Christiania, were among those present. Instead, it was announced on 19 February that a constitutional assembly would be convened. In the interim, Christian was to act as regent, and in March he moved to establish a government. Knowing that without British support all political action would be futile, a delegation under Anker's leadership was dispatched to London to attempt to secure support from the British government for Norwegian independence.

The constitutional assembly of 112 men, including 37 farmers, 59 bureaucrats, and 16 burghers, convened on 4 April—again at Eidsvoll, a safe distance from interference by foreign emissaries or inflamed crowds. Even before they met, the delegates were divided into two camps. An independence party of about two-thirds of the members consisted mainly of civil, military, and ecclesiastical officials, all of them owing their positions to the absolute king in Copenhagen. Much sympathy existed in their ranks, at least early on, for political and cultural ties with Denmark. They were joined by the peasant delegates. Among their leaders were Professor Sverdrup, Christian Magnus Falsen (1782–1830), and W. F. K. Christie (1778–1849). A pro-union party of the remaining delegates, representing some members of the commercial elite and large estate owners, was led by Count Herman Wedel Jarlsberg (1779–1840). They recognized the inevitability of some accommodation with Sweden. For the moment the independence group prevailed, however.

A constitutional committee of fifteen was chosen by the assembly and worked quickly. Its members were part of an educated elite that was well versed in the enlightened ideas proclaimed by Rousseau on the philosophy of popular sovereignty and in Montesquieu's theories on the separation of power into executive, legislative, and judicial branches of government. They were also well aware of other constitutions, particularly those of the United States and France from 1791. (The latter had established a moderate constitutional monarchy.) Johan Adler (1784–1852) and Falsen came to the convention with a draft constitution in hand. Assembly debate on the committee's proposals began in early May, modifications were made, and the final draft was approved on the 16 May. The next day the delegates affixed their signatures to it and, on the same day, elected Christian Frederik as king.

The Eidsvoll Constitution was a model of brevity, flexibility, vagueness, and adaptability. Amended, it remains in force to this day. It established a "limited and hereditary monarchy." The king was to govern. He enjoyed the power to appoint his ministers, introduce legislation, impose a delaying veto on measures sent to him by the parliament, and conduct foreign policy. The parliament (Storting) was elected as a unicameral body with 150 members, but divided itself into two chambers, the Odelsting and the Lagting, on assembly. It was to meet at least once every three years. Its powers included the right of legislative initiative, control of state finances, review of actions and advice of the king's ministers, and eventual override of a royal veto. The electorate, amounting to about 12 percent of the population, was composed of government officials, rural landowners and long-term leaseholders, and the propertied bourgeoisie. One interesting aspect of the constitution was the provision that two-thirds of the representatives must be from rural districts. The constitution also established a separate judiciary and defined the rights and duties of citizens. For its time, it was one of the most liberal in Europe, but the system as defined was far from democratic in a modern sense.

The entire process, from the election of delegates to the Eidsvoll assembly to the final declaration of independence, clearly ignited nationalistic sentiments, though their strength and extent are not easily determined and are easily exaggerated. Nationalism may in any case be regarded more as a product than as a cause of the revolt and subsequent events. Anti-Swedish feelings and the impact of patriotic propaganda were most obvious in the cities, and probably had little impact in the remoter rural areas. In fact, the far north was not even represented at Eidsvoll because of the slowness of communications and travel.

Norway's bid for complete independence failed. The day after the adoption of the new constitution Christian Frederik learned that, despite British sympathy for the Norwegian cause and growing concern over a Sweden under the leadership of one of Napoleon's marshals, the government in London would not renege on its promises to

Karl Johan. Britain's leaders were, however, willing to give support to some form of Norwegian self-determination. It was also clear that no help would come from Denmark.

Karl Johan responded to the developments in Norway with a restrained show of strength. At the end of July he invaded Norway with a superior Swedish force. Neither side distinguished itself in the so-called Cat War. No real battles were fought. Karl Johan's main concerns were to end the war as soon as possible, to remove Christian Frederik, and to establish an agreement with the Norwegians quickly. Changes in any arrangement could be worked out later. He knew a campaign in Norway would be costly. The new Swedish heir was also worried about what decisions the leaders of the great powers might make at the general European peace conference, set to convene in Vienna in October 1814.

Some historians have accused Christian Frederik of timidity and incompetence in his conduct of the war and quick agreement with the Swedes, but they have probably misinterpreted his leadership. The new king knew the outcomes of the war would be an inevitable Swedish victory and his own abdication. His attentions appear to have shifted to attempts to secure the best possible situation for Norway. A constitution was in place. Norway's independence had been declared but was not assured. No resistance would have left Karl Johan holding all the cards. Some resistance was necessary.

In a sense, both rulers succeeded. At the small town of Moss, south of Christiania, a truce was signed on 14 August. Karl Johan accepted the Eidsvoll Constitution as a basis for peace negotiations, and Christian Frederik agreed to abdicate. He left Norway on 10 October 1814. In 1839 he succeeded his uncle to the Danish throne.

An extraordinary session of the Storting convened in October to negotiate the terms of union. W. F. K. Christie, the president of the Storting, proved himself equal to the task ahead. Negotiations with the Swedish emissaries and the required amendments to the constitution were completed by November 4, and Karl XIII was elected king of Norway. Early the following year the final Act of Union (Riksakten) was accepted.

The outcome of the drama of 1814 was a personal union in what became known as the twin kingdoms or dual monarchy of Sweden and Norway. Under the final terms of the union agreement, Norway retained full independence in domestic affairs, and several of the constitutional changes insisted on by Karl Johan actually enhanced the powers of the Storting—for example, it became easier to impeach a minister of the crown. In foreign affairs, however, Sweden dominated. The king was most closely associated with Sweden and could appoint a governor or viceroy to represent him in his Norwegian capital. The Norwegian government was furthermore divided into a Christiania and a Stockholm contingent. Although the final agreement described Sweden and Norway as equal partners, reality plainly relegated Norway to a place of political inferiority.

Hindsight may tell us this union was doomed to fail from the outset. However, we should be careful in drawing this conclusion. No one could have predicted the course that the development of nationalism would take in the nineteenth century or the outcomes that that development would cause.

9

Nationalism

Nationalism, variously defined, has been one of the most important forces in modern history. Its roots lie far back in the development of the West. As was noted in earlier chapters, a consciousness of specific nation- or statehood was present and was nurtured among certain social groups (elite and common) for specific, usually political, reasons from very early times in Norden. A kind of nationalism was involved in the wars of the Kalmar Union, the Dano-Swedish conflicts of the early modern period, the imperial adventures of Sweden in the seventeenth century, and the trends and events in Finland and Norway in the late eighteenth century. None of these instances, however, involved whole populations, were widespread, or depended on a literate public increasingly interconnected by improved communications and general public education. None really motivated popular political parties. When needed, "national" propaganda, often delivered from the pulpit, would frequently call for support of a monarch rather than a state. Until the modern period, the common people's identities were defined more by farm, village, or region. One theme of the nineteenth century is how those people became national.

Although nationalism remains a tool of elites, its importance in shaping events has grown, and it also has come to involve far greater numbers of people and to hold a far more important place in the shaping of people's identities than in the early nineteenth century. Nationalism helped shape the histories of every Nordic country in the nineteenth and twentieth centuries and remains important at the close of the twentieth century. In this chapter, the development of cultural nationalism in its various forms, the politicization of nationalism, and some of the central instances in which it played a leading role are considered.

Woman at the Loom, Gulsvik, by Adolph Tidemand, 1874. The painting shows the romanticization of peasant life during a period when Norwegian national consciousness was being formed. Courtesy of the National Gallery of Norway, Oslo; copyright Nasjonalgalleriet 1998.

Cultural Nationalism

One of the first forms nationalism took was cultural, and this aspect has remained important down to the present day. It was largely the domain of intellectuals—of poets, artists, historians, folklorists, and philologists. Throughout Norden (and the rest of Europe) academics and amateurs organized societies, wrote, published, and painted. Most were engaged in searching for the defining elements of national identities—for the languages, myths and legends, folk cultures, and unique histories that defined a national identity. For the most part, they succeeded. By the close of the century the people of the Nordic countries knew who they were through art, literature, history, iconography, and ritual. Public education, the mass press in its various forms, entertainments, organizations, and politics served to inform them, and they still do.

Language

Language was viewed by many early-nineteenth-century nationalists as the central defining aspect of a nation. But until the nineteenth century, with some exceptions, the official languages of the ethnically diverse Nordic kingdoms were Danish and Swedish. Although the impacts of a kind of Danish and Swedish language imperialism varied, Faeroese, Icelandic, Norwegian, Finnish, and German in Slesvig (but not Holstein) were all secondary languages: spoken but rarely used in politics, the law, the Church, or higher education. It was in the peripheral units of Norden where languages became most importance as elements of national identity—for obvious reasons.

In the Danish kingdom, written Faeroese virtually disappeared during the early modern period. Icelandic, perhaps because of the distance from Copenhagen, the relative absence of dialects, or the existence of a large and vital body of written medieval literature, was less affected by the long period of Danish dominance and continued to be used in speech and writing. A written Norwegian language existed based on a relatively small core of medieval literature and law, but after 1536 it ceased to develop. From then on virtually all printed materials were in Danish, including the basic texts of the Reformation. What actually was the spoken language is confusing because of the large number of dialects. In the Swedish kingdom, the survival of Finnish as a spoken language was not threatened, but except for religious texts from the Reformation including a translation of the Bible, very little existed in print. Important language revivals developed in the Faeroes, Iceland, Norway, and Finland during the nineteenth century.

Jens Christian Svabo (1746–1824) was the first Copenhagen-educated Faeroe islander to study his native language extensively. In the 1770s he published a Faeroese-Danish-Latin dictionary, and in the early 1780s he spent a year on the islands writing down ballads preserved in oral tradition. His manuscripts and other collections developed by Hans Christian Lyngbye and Venceslaus Hammershaimb (1819–1909) led to the development of standardized Faeroese grammar and spelling. Hammershaimb's orthography, published in 1854, became the basis for modern written Faeroese. The use of Faeroese became an increasingly politicized issue and played a role in relations with Denmark from the 1890s. It was given official parity with Danish in 1948. Today it is the first language of the islands, and Danish is taught as a compulsory second language.

Icelandic did not suffer the same extent of decline as Faeroese or Norwegian. It continued to be written, and books were printed in it, including a complete translation of the Bible in 1584. In 1816 Rasmus Rask (1787–1832), the Danish philologist, helped found the Icelandic Literary Society. Its journal, *Skírnír,* became the mouthpiece for studies of Icelandic and its literature. The poetry of Bjarni Thorarensen (1786–1841) and Jónas Hallgrimsson (1807–45) and the folktale collections of Jón Arnason (1819–88) and Magnús Grímsson, as well as renewed interest in the medieval sagas, contributed to a renaissance in writing and cultural studies.

The issue of language was important and intensely involving in Norway. To this day it remains a matter of political and personal debate. Of all the aspects of the 434 years of Danish domination, language was what touched ordinary people most immediately. After about 1525 Norwegian vanished as a written language. Danish was the language of political and religious life and became increasingly essential in trade. There was no Norwegian university where an intellectual life in Norwegian might be nurtured. The year 1814 presented the Norwegian people with a problem. What was to be the language of the new state? Would Danish continue to dominate? What influence might the Swedes have on language in Norway? If Norwegian, then what was this language? Which of the numerous dialects was most representative?

For about the first half of the nineteenth century these language questions went unanswered. Danish, the language of the bureaucratic and economic elites who controlled political life, remained the standard. After midcentury, however, discussion intensified, and aspects of the question were politicized. Important in this transition was Ivar Aasen (1813–96), a self-taught linguist, who spent four years traveling through southern Norway collecting dialect information. In 1864 he published a grammar based on his research, followed seven years later by a dictionary. The language he created was originally called *landsmål* (now *nynorsk*), and Aasen and others believed it should be adopted as the national tongue. But *nynorsk* was not the language of all Norwegians. In a pure sense, it was the language of none of them. In response, Knud Knudsen (1806–66) and others advocated the "Norwegianization" of Danish. This Dano-Norwegian hybrid was known as *riksmål* (now *bokmål*). A third option even developed: the idea of merging *nynorsk* and *bokmål* to create a *samnorsk,* or common Norwegian. No consensus was reached. The debate that developed engaged more than linguists and other intellectuals. It became a highly charged political issue in which the conservatives supported *bokmål* and the liberals supported *nynorsk*. In 1885 *nynorsk* was officially acknowledged as an equal with *bokmål*. Ten years later individuals were given the choice of which language was to be taught in elementary schools. To this day Norway remains a country of two recognized languages and five major dialect groups. About 17 percent of school children are primarily taught in *nynorsk*, about 83 percent in *bokmål*.

As in Norway, the language of officials, the Church, and education in Finland was not the language of most of the people. Although about 10 percent used Swedish as their first language, 90 percent or more spoke one or another dialect of Finnish, a language that belongs to the Fenno-Ugric family, is related to the several Sami languages, Estonian, and Magyar-Hungarian, and is wholly unlike the other Nordic languages, which derive from Germanic origins. A written form of Finnish developed during the Reformation, but only a tiny body of literature ever appeared in print. During the nineteenth century the Finnish language issue had two elements. The first was to define and standardize the language. The second was to establish its official parity with (or superiority to) Swedish. In successfully dealing with both issues, intellectuals and political figures helped create a national consciousness and a nationalist movement in Finland.

Of particular importance in the development of standardized, modern Finnish was the work of the physician and folklorist/linguist Elias Lönnrot (1802–84). During the 1830s, while serving as a doctor in eastern Finland, Lönnrot made a series of trips through the Karelian region during which he collected songs and poems from the local people. These he assembled in an extended folk epic, the *Kalevala,* first published in 1835. Although there was a great deal of Lönnrot in the *Kalevala,* which diminishes its importance as an ancient Finnish text, the epic was a remarkable work. It became an essential part of the emerging national mythology and a point of reference for much modern Finnish literature, art, and music. The accomplishments of Lönnrot and his fellow national romantics in the Saturday Society (1830) and the Finnish Literary Society (1841) helped create Finland.

From midcentury on, the language issue moved from the intellectual to the political plane. Of particular importance in this development was the philosopher-journalist-politician, J. V. Snellman (1806–81). He was an outspoken advocate of an active nationalism, a nationalism that would bring tangible gains to the Finns. His views aroused strong feelings of support and opposition, and his writings were often censored. It was Snellman who helped secure from Alexander II the Language Edict (1863), which promised the equality of Finnish with Swedish at the end of a twenty-year transition period. (The actual establishment of this parity took longer than expected, but by the late 1880s many of the language goals of Snellman and his so-called Fennoman supporters had been achieved.)

The status of Swedish and the Finnishness of the Swedish-speaking Finns were also important issues in Finland. Some of the earliest champions of Finnish consciousness wrote in Swedish. Among them were Adolf Arwidsson (1791–1858), Johan L. Runeberg (1804–77), and Zacharias Topelius (1818–98). Arwidsson used the press to argue that all the people of Finland must work to become Finns in order to avoid becoming Russians. Runeberg's *The Elkhunters* (1832) and *Tales of Ensign Stål* (1848) were tributes to the common folk and nurtured patriotic senses. Topelius's poems, historical articles, and other writings were similar in theme and purpose.

For some in the Finnish-speaking majority the view developed during the century that the country's Swedish-speaking peoples would have to be absorbed into a greater Finland. Opposed to this position were many among the Swedish-speakers who believed that they, too, were Finns. These differences contributed to the fractures that have haunted Finland since the nineteenth century.

Literature, History, and the Arts

A body of literature was viewed as important by those who wished to establish the bases of national identities. One element of this lay in the past. Iceland's sagas; the medieval law codes and histories of Denmark, Norway and Sweden; and the religious texts of the Reformation were matters of interest and pride. So, too, were more recent works, such as the plays of Ludvig Holberg and the songs of Carl Michael Bellman.

Another element was folk literature—the orally transmitted songs, stories, and poems of the common people. Throughout the region, ancient stories, legends, traditions, and songs were collected, transcribed, and published. The effect was two-tiered. The pieces themselves were put into print, and the languages (or dialects) were given an accomplished written form. Already mentioned were the efforts in the Faeroes and Finland. Similar work was done by Peter C. Asbjørnsen

(1812–85) and Jørgen Moe (1813–82) in Norway, whose first collection of Norwegian fairy tales was published in 1841.

New works in the Nordic languages were also important in defining national groups. Important writers in every genre fill the cultural landscape. Although only some of their work was self-consciously nationalistic, much of it focused on the past or the lives of ordinary people. Nationalist poets such as Johan Welhaven (1807–73) in Norway, Esaias Tegnér (1782–1846) in Sweden, and Adam Oehlenschläger (1779–1850) in Denmark established wide popular audiences for their works. Later in the century the history dramas of Henrik Ibsen (1828–1906) and August Strindberg (1849–1912) recalled important moments from their countries' pasts while they wrestled with the psychological dimensions of important protagonists such as Gustav Vasa and Gustavus Adolphus.

History, presented through several genres, was a particularly vital element in the development of national consciousness. On the one hand, a kind of popular nostalgia patriotism was nurtured through stories and images of the past. This can be seen in Esaias Tegnér's *Frithiofs saga* (1820–25); the paintings of the "national school" in Norwegian art represented by Adolph Tidemand (1814–76) and I. C. Dahl (1788–1857); the revival of interest in runic writing or Viking ships; the growth of organizations dedicated to the preservation of folk cultures such as the Swedish Handcraft Association, founded by Nils Månsson Mandelgren (1813–90) in 1845, or Artur Hazelius's (1833–1901) Nordic Museum (founded in 1880 and based on earlier collection efforts); or the very popular historical fiction of writers such as B. S. Ingemann (1789–1862) or C. G. Verner von Heidenstam (1859–1940).

History as a discipline took two apparently contradictory paths during the nineteenth century. First, it developed a more thoroughly rigorous methodology involving careful criticism of primary source materials and underwent a process of increased fragmentation into fields of specialization. Second, it was turned to the service of nationalism through teaching, scholarship, and publications—not because of any conspiracies hatched by elites to make history the handmaiden of some political ideals but because the context of the times shaped the questions asked and the answers found. The German historian Leopold von Ranke, who believed that the nation and the folk who defined the nation stood at the center of history, had a major influence on the thinking of nineteenth-century Nordic historians. The focus of much of the history from the period was on the origins of states in the middle ages, periods of greatness, hero kings, and the people and their uniquenesses; and these concentrations were intended to nurture national identities.

National historical schools developed after 1814 at each of the Nordic universities. This was particularly the case at the new university in Christiania/Oslo. According to its adherents, such as Rudolf Keyser (1803–64), P. A. Munch (1810–63), and Christian Lange (1810–61), Nordic cultural unity was a myth, Norwegians formed a unique ethnic group, Norwegians (and Icelanders) were the principal definers of medieval Nordic culture, and Denmark had exploited Norway during the years of domination. Outside Norway the works of Erik Gustaf Geijer (1783–1847) and Harald Hjärne (1848–1922) in Sweden or Frederik Troels Troels-Lund (1840–1921) in Denmark illustrate nationalist patterns, as do the journals (the Danish *Historisk tidsskrift,* the Norwegian *Historisk tidsskrift,* and the Swedish *Historisk tidskrift*) founded by the professional historians' associations in each of the Nordic countries during this period.

Through their work, members of these schools established a body of patriotic historical literature for each Nordic country. Their versions of history were taught for the next century or more and remain important in popularly held interpretations of the past. They have shown remarkable persistence, despite efforts by later generations of historians to revise them.

Education

Without the development of systems of public education, none of the intellectual trends of the period would have had much importance in nurturing broadly held national consciousness. Schools were one of the most important transmitters of national ideas, along with the pulpit, books and newspapers, and compulsory military service systems. During the eighteenth century, literacy rates rose in much of Scandinavia, largely because candidates for compulsory confirmation into the Lutheran Church were expected to be able to read the Scriptures. Educational reforms in the nineteenth century had different goals. Economic, technological, and political changes called for better-educated publics. Needs and fears drove the political elites to establish the basics of general public education systems and to design means to control the new schools, curriculum, and teacher preparation.

Some modest gains toward general public education had been made in the eighteenth century, largely in response to calls for reforms from enlightened thinkers. In Denmark the 1789 special commission recommendation that an expanded public education system be developed was gradually implemented after 1814. Beginning in 1842 in Sweden, 1848 in Norway, and 1866 in Finland, measures designed to create systems of compulsory basic schools in which curricular focus was on practical subjects and appropriate citizen preparation were enacted. Implementation of all education reforms, however, was slow, and legislation did not translate into systems overnight. It was not until late in the century that compulsory elementary schools, teachers, and curricular materials were available for most young people.

The basic schools remained separate from the small number of elite secondary schools intended to prepare students for entrance into the universities at Copenhagen, Christiania (established in 1810), Uppsala, Lund, Helsinki (established after the academy at Turku/Åbo was destroyed by fire in 1827), and Kiel.

Several other important educational options developed in the nineteenth century. One was the folk high school. These schools were based in large part on the educational ideals of the Danish theologian, poet, and nationalist N. F. S. Grundtvig (1783–1872). He advocated rural schools with practical, historical, and poetic emphases. The first of them was founded by Christen Kold (1816–70), at Rødding in Danish-speaking Slesvig in 1844 and moved to Askov after 1864. Over the next three decades they spread to the rest of Scandinavia. Although the history of these schools has varied, they have endured, and today there are over three hundred folk high schools in Norden.

Other educational options included special schools for agriculture, commerce, forestry, teaching, and technology (e.g., Chalmers in Göteborg, 1829); new or expanded research facilities such as Stockholm's Karolinska Institutet; and adult programs, many sponsored by organizations. Practical concerns, political fears, social class, nationalism, and religion were among the factors influencing education's growth in this period.

Political Nationalism

Between 1830 and 1918 nationalism became increasingly politicized and was one of the key factors affecting events in Norway, the Faeroes, Iceland, the duchies of Slesvig and Holstein, and Finland. Recognition of uniqueness, autonomy, or independence were sought and achieved. In three cases, these events were largely peaceful; in two,

Nicolai Frederik Severin Grundtvig

A pastor, theologian, poet, historian, social critic, and teacher, N. F. S. Grundtvig (1783–1872) has been called "the most influential of all nineteenth century Danes." His ideas, writings, and actions were shaped by a potent blend of often-contradictory forces including the pietism of his own home, the rationalism of the Enlightenment, early-nineteenth-century romanticism and nationalism, and personal experiences in Denmark and Britain. He came to see mythology and history as vital expressions of a people's perceptions of life and identity, and his histories and historical poems spurred the growth of a national consciousness in Denmark. At the same time he sought to shape the Church in Denmark, which he believed placed too much emphasis on Scripture and not enough on living. In the realm of education he was critical of the classical educational model, advocating instead education for life built around the nation's language, literature, and history and practical subjects. He expressed these views in *Det Danske Fiir-Klöver* (The Danish four-leafed clover) (1836).

wars erupted that involved not just the Nordic principles but one or more of the European great powers.

The Norwegian-Swedish Union Dissolved

The traditional histories of Norway present a picture that includes the inevitable demise of the union with Sweden. Formed in struggle and accepted only of necessity, the union was foredoomed. The only question was how long it would last, not if it would. But this view is inaccurate. Although there was discord in the ninety-one-year history of the union, most of the period passed peacefully and without serious points of friction or incidents. There were a number of "symbols" of Norway's inferior status in the union, which angered some. Among these were the office of viceroy/*stattholder* (abolished in 1872 on the accession of Oscar II), the order of the countries' names on coins and official documents (settled in 1844), and the inclusion of a union symbol on state and merchant marine flags (partially settled in 1898). Until driven to take an opinion by noisy political advocates of change, the majority of the Norwegian people accepted the union and probably had no strong feelings about it. In Sweden, some Swedes, including Karl XIV Johan at the beginning of the period and a small group of ultranationalists at the end, considered the agreements reached in 1814 to be temporary only in the sense that they did not accept the limitations placed on the monarchy (or Sweden) by the Norwegians' constitution. At virtually every meeting of the Storting until his death in 1844, Karl XIV presented proposals for the constitution's revision. But none were accepted, and the king, although tempted, did not push the matter. Of greater importance in the eventual dissolution of the union were differences in economic orientation, foreign-policy concerns and sentiments, political developments, and the highly charged nationalistic environment that developed throughout Europe in the late nineteenth century.

From 1884 to 1905 the union question was among the most important issues confronting Norwegian and Swedish governments, and this period is generally seen as one long crisis leading to Norwegian independence.

By the last quarter of the nineteenth century, the union question lay behind every major political discussion in Norway. First it was woven into the question of ministerial responsibility, or *parlementarism*. Norwegian governments were appointed by the king and, although limited in their freedom by the review and impeachment powers granted the Storting by the constitution, were not responsible to or drawn from the parliament. When a measure permitting participation by members of the government in Storting proceedings (Inclusion Bill) was vetoed by Karl XV in 1872, a twelve-year governmental crisis followed. The issue of ministerial responsibility had several sides, but to liberals with increasingly nationalistic views, the problem involved the advance of democracy, the question of whether or not the union crown had veto power over constitutional reform in Norway, and the assertion of Norwegian rights within the union. In 1884 the government of Christian Selmer (1816–89) was impeached and removed from office. Oscar II, faced with a clear majority in favor of change in Norway and very little support for a firm stance in Sweden, reluctantly appointed the first parliamentary government in Norwegian history, headed by Liberal (Venstre) party leader Johan Sverdrup (1816–92). The Norwegians' success was an important constitutional defeat for Oscar, and it put Norway ahead of Sweden in the development of a more representative political system. It did not, however, lead to a breach in the union.

The right to an equal voice in the conduct of foreign affairs was the issue used to end the union. From 1814 it was clear that in this area of union affairs Norway was in an inferior position. The king, his Swedish foreign minister, and the Swedish-dominated ministerial council controlled this aspect of the dual monarchy's life. At the embassy level, most (but by no means all) diplomats were upper-class Swedes. Paradoxically in the long run, it was at the level of consulates, which dealt with maritime and economic matters, that many Norwegians found a place.

In 1885 the Swedish parliament passed legislation that unilaterally changed the way in which foreign-policy decisions were reached—in ways designed to increase the role of the parliament in decisions. In Norway this move was viewed as a way to downgrade further the Norwegians' roles in the process. The Norwegian Liberals responded with a demand for an independent Norwegian foreign minister and set to work to radicalize public opinion. For the next twenty years they used this question as a basis for their campaign to bring the union to an end. In 1891 the Liberals again called for a separate and independent Norwegian foreign minister. Following their victory in that year's election, they backed away from this and instead demanded an independent consular service for Norway. Oscar II vetoed the bill sent to him in 1892. Relations with Sweden worsened over the next several years and reached war scare proportions in summer 1895. The threat passed, however, because the Norwegians found themselves diplomatically alone in their blustering and badly prepared to fight a war.

From 1895 to 1905 Norwegian and Swedish negotiators in the third and fourth union commissions attempted to reach agreement on the foreign affairs issue without success. But a negotiated settlement was not what a group of Norwegian anti-union conservatives and liberals loosely organized into the Coalition Party wanted. In early spring 1905 Christian Michelsen (1857–1925), a Bergen-born shipping magnate, seeking to create a constitutional crisis, helped precipitate the collapse of the Hagerup government. He then became head of a new government and secured passage in the Storting of a bill establishing an independent consular service. On 27 May Oscar II, as expected, vetoed the measure. Michelsen and his colleagues now could have followed the slow constitutional option of submitting the bill for passage at each of the next two meetings of the parliament following an election, but they chose a quicker solution. The government resigned, knowing that no one would accept a call from the king to replace them. It was then argued that Oscar, unable to fulfill his constitutional obligation to form a government, had ceased to rule. Therefore, the dynastic union ceased to exist.

The approach was a risky one. The Norwegians' constitutional position was dubious. Swedish reaction was uncertain. War was possible. But the gamble worked. This time the Norwegians were better prepared for war, and Sweden appeared diplomatically isolated. The Russians were in the midst of a war with the Japanese and distracted by revolutionary events at home. The British, French, and Germans were entangled in the first Moroccan Crisis. Although there was considerable sympathy for a strong stand in Stockholm, especially among ultra-nationalistic conservatives, sufficient support for a military response was not present among the public or in the parliament, where Liberals favored dissolution and questions of suffrage seemed far more important. Oscar II, seventy-six years old and ill, was saddened but unwilling to fight, and Crown Prince Gustav, who was acting as regent during the crisis, preferred a peaceful solution. The Swedes' request for a referendum on the question demonstrated the level of popular support: 368,208 for the break, 184 against.

On 23 September 1905 the Karlstad Conventions, spelling out the details of the dissolution, were signed. In mid-November, following another plebiscite on the question of whether Norway ought to be a monarchy or a republic, Danish prince Carl was elected Norway's first independent king since the late fourteenth century by the Storting. He took the name Haakon VII (1872–1957).

An issue that had influenced Norwegian political life to varying degrees for nearly a quarter century was now settled. With independence achieved, attention could be turned to domestic matters. Norway entered a period of remarkable economic, social, and political development. At a time when international relations were becoming increasingly complex and dangerous, Norwegian leaders also had to face the serious questions confronting the small states of Europe. In 1907 an international guarantee of Norway's territorial integrity was obtained from the European great powers. With the union question settled, relations with Sweden actually improved. When World War I began in August 1914, Norway joined its Nordic neighbors in an agreement to maintain peace in the area. This was followed in December by a joint declaration of neutrality.

Historians continue to argue over the inevitability of the union's collapse and to dissect the events leading to its end. The national-patriotic view is, of course, that a free and independent Norway was destined to develop, and that Christian Michelsen is the national hero who engineered its birth; the only question was when. Others see the dissolution as merely one path that might have been taken. Certainly, many Norwegians were willing to remain within a union so long as national aspirations could be met or specific concerns satisfied. Even in 1905 compromise was still possible, and Crown Prince Gustav was prepared to allow the Norwegians their independent consular service. Still others have come to see the end of the union as an event cynically orchestrated by politicians eager to gain or remain in power. The Left nurtured popular enthusiasm and then used that enthusiasm to win elections. Conservatives adopted the union issue to guarantee its settlement and thereby deprive the Left of its most powerful issue. No doubt there are elements of truth in all these views, just as there was a certain inevitability about the union's demise, given the broader context. Nationalism was not just important in Scandinavia. It was driving events in Great Britain, the Hapsburg and Russian Empires, the Ottoman Empire, and the Balkans. Within this context it is difficult to imagine Norwegian nationalists passively accepting what many believed was domination by Sweden.

The Finns Achieve Independence

Until the late nineteenth century, Finnish nationalism remained overwhelmingly cultural in its focus. After the reemergence of the parliament in 1863, however, nationalism became increasingly political because the Finns were allowed to play a more active, though still largely advisory, role in the affairs of the grand duchy. The earliest political parties, the Finnish Party and the Swedish People's Party, developed in this period and were defined by their nationality positions. As in Norway, national identity issues appeared to color every political debate and recommendation to the tsar.

After 1863 the Finns made significant gains in establishing their identity as a unique national unit within the empire. Alexander II responded to recommendations from the Finnish assembly and allowed the introduction of a separate currency and national bank (1865–66), local government reform (1865), secular control of education (1869), equal inheritance and occupation rights for women (1877–78), and the creation of a small Finnish army (1877–78). By the 1863 Language Edict, Finnish was to achieve equal status with Swedish—although this was to take place over twenty years and actually took longer.

Among the aspects of the transition were the acceptance of documents and the conduct of official proceedings in Finnish, and the enlargement of the number of secondary schools teaching in Finnish. All these changes enhanced the position of the Finns and reinforced their confidence in the relationship with Russia.

With the accession of Alexander III (in 1881), that easy relationship began to change. Alexander was conservative and autocratic. In response to growing nationality problems in the empire, he gradually moved toward a policy designed to erase them via Russification, that is, making all of the subject national groups Russian. With regard to Finland, the Russian position was based on an interpretation of the events of 1809, which denied the Finns' view that Alexander I had given them a special status. The Finns could have a separate language and culture. They could also have their own law code and institutions. None of these, however, could compromise the general law, institutions, or interests of the empire.

Nicholas II, who succeeded to the throne in 1894, was equally narrow-minded and inept. He extended this policy and in February 1899 gave it tangible form in the "February Manifesto," a document designed by Nicholas Bobrikov (1839–1904), Finland's governor-general. A small-minded military bureaucrat, Bobrikov enthusiastically set about implementing the manifesto's spirit and subsequent edicts designed to Russify the Finns. Over the next few years, the Finns were subjected to conscription in the Russian army, and the tiny Finnish army was eliminated. The voice of the parliament was curtailed. Russian, it was declared, was to become the language of government, education, and the Church.

The Finns' response to Russification was divided. By a narrow margin, the Senate agreed to implementation. This "compliance" policy was seen by its adherents as the best hope for preserving a measure of Finnish identity. Many rejected this view, and, in general, the Russians were confronted by a policy of passive resistance. Ministers, for example, refused to read draft lists in their churches, and doctors refused to certify draft candidates' readiness for service. In response the Russians used dismissal, arrest, exile, censorship, and suppression. The most extreme act of Finnish resistance occurred on 16 June 1904, when a young bureaucrat, Eugen Schauman (1875–1904), assassinated Bobrikov and then killed himself.

In 1905 Russian policy changed—temporarily. Russia's war in the Far East with Japan and revolution at home left the government in

St. Petersburg little choice. In November many of the hated Russification edicts were withdrawn. A remarkably advanced new form of government law was completed in May 1906 and approved by Nicholas in July. According to its terms Finland was to have the world's first unicameral legislative body (the Eduskunta) elected by universal suffrage. Other measures confirmed civil rights and free speech.

A new sense of optimism developed in Finland (and in Russia) as a result of the events of 1905–6. That optimism was quickly dashed. Nicholas had no intention of dismantling tsarist autocracy or of encouraging Finnish national autonomy. Although a vital multiparty system developed under the terms of the new system of government, by 1908 the Russian authorities set about withdrawing the gains nationalists and liberals had made. The Finns were expected to send an annual contribution to St. Petersburg to support defense. The Senate was clearly still a creature of the tsar. Meetings of the new parliament were dissolved, and elections ignored. Laws passed by the Russian parliament (Duma) were extended to the entire empire.

These developments heightened growing feelings of mistrust and animosity toward the Russians. World War I confirmed them. Although Finland stood outside the conflict, the indirect impacts were significant. The economy was badly disrupted. Shortages of food caused suffering. Some prices rose by as much as 400 percent. Still, there was no agreement over what ought be done. Some advocated a continued but altered relationship with Russia. Others favored independence.

The revolutions in Russia in 1917 defined the events in Finland to a considerable degree. In spring 1917, following the first revolution in St. Petersburg, the parliament elected a year earlier finally met. The Social Democrats enjoyed a small majority and ought to have been able to establish an SD-controlled government. Splits within the party and a lack of leadership, however, weakened their position, and the new cabinet represented the socialist and nonsocialist parties equally. The atmosphere was tense. Radicals on the Left wanted a full-scale social as well as political revolution. More moderate socialists were less eager. Many of the nonsocialists, having won recognition of Finland's autonomy from the provisional government in St. Petersburg, sought to consolidate that position.

In June cooperation between the Social Democrats and the government broke down, and the so-called power law, which gave the powers of the tsar to the parliament, was passed. This was nearly a declaration of independence, and the Kerensky government in Russia rejected it, dissolved the Eduskunta, and called for new elections. A revolutionary moment passed, however. Although the Social Democrats in the parliament refused to assent to its dissolution and continued to meet as a rump assembly until late September, they did not attempt a coup. Instead, they took part in the October elections and were soundly defeated.

The outcome of the election and the Bolshevik Revolution a few weeks later radically altered the situation in Finland. As long as non-Marxists had controlled Russia, their counterparts in Finland were willing to preserve some links with Russia, but the Marxists looked to a more radical solution. Now the non-Marxists wanted nothing to do with the revolution and took steps to establish Finnish independence, while the Social Democrats closed with the Bolsheviks and took to extraparliamentary actions. The Finnish parliament passed an independence measure on 6 December. Initially, however, only the Bolsheviks in Russia recognized it.

The tangle of events in late 1917 reflected the complexity of the situation in Finland. Ideological and social differences cut across any unity nationality might generate. Finland was a nation of stark differences—of bourgeois officials, freehold farmers, small cotters, landless rural laborers, and urban workers. World War I amplified social class and economic problems. Many on the socialist Left wanted a social revolution, and the non-Marxist parliament was not going to give them that. In a sense, Finland became two nations at the end of 1917, one "Red," the other "White."

War between these factions began at the end of January 1918. Kullervo Manner, a radical Socialist, established a separate government and called on the paramilitary arm of the Socialists, the Red Guard, to arrest the government and disarm their opponents on 28 January. Most of the government escaped Helsinki for Vaasa on the Bothnian coast. The bourgeois prime minister, Per Svinhufvud, had to sneak out of Helsinki on an icebreaker.

The war, which was a civil war in the sense that it pitted Finns against each other and a war of independence in that it involved getting Russian forces out of Finland, lasted four months. It exacerbated the divisions within Finnish society and left deep scars. From the outset the Reds were outnumbered. Their centers of strength were Helsinki and Tampere. The Whites, led by General C. G. Mannerheim

(1867–1951), who had served in the Russian army, were aided by Finns who had volunteered for service in the German army (so-called Jaegers) and by German units. Tampere fell in early April, Helsinki about a month later. Following the combat, Red fighters and members of their families were interned under generally horrendous conditions. Ideological differences have clouded casualty figures. One estimate is that as many as 31,000 people died, including 8,500 by execution and 10,000 in the camps. Some emigrated to the Soviet Union, and many of these returned disillusioned in the 1930s.

The end of the war established Finnish independence, but did not define the constitutional order. It was a year before that question was settled. Initially, the leaders of the country favored making Finland a monarchy and, because of the close ties with Germany, inviting a German prince to assume the throne. Seemingly blind to the course of the war in Europe, these leaders offered the crown to Friedrich of Hesse in October 1918. He waited until after the war in Europe had ended in November to decline. In March 1919 a newly elected parliament set to work on a republican constitution. This was confirmed on 17 July, and K. J. Ståhlberg (1865–1952) was elected the first president.

An independent Finland was one of the new nations to arise from the ashes of the three empires that died in World War I. In the Baltic region, it was joined by Estonia, Latvia, Lithuania, and Poland. Although Finnish national identity had established a cultural base in the developments of the nineteenth century, the nation was hardly united in the wake of the bloodletting of 1918. Still a nation of two languages, it was also nation of social and ideological divisions. These problems remained central and contributed to fundamental weaknesses in the new nation.

Nationalisms in the Danish Multinational Kingdom

Denmark had three nationality problems to face in the nineteenth century: Faeroese, Icelandic, and German. The first two of these gave rise to relatively peaceful solutions. The third proved far more difficult and was only resolved after two wars.

The Faeroe Islands and Iceland

Cultural nationalism took on political aspects in Denmark's Atlantic island territories after 1830. Least problematic were events in the Faeroes. The islands were represented in the Roskilde provincial assembly, created by Frederik VI in 1834. The revolution of 1848–49 gave the Faeroes one representative in each house of the Danish parliament. In 1852 the historic Faeroese Lagting was restored as an advisory assembly, free trade was established in 1856, and local government reforms put in place in 1872. From the late 1880s a more vocal movement for autonomy developed, fed by an emerging popular press. Around 1900 two political parties emerged; one advocated a limited autonomy, the other favored home rule. Their most heated arguments were over which language ought be official: Danish or Faeroese.

During World War II the islands were occupied by British forces, and a measure of experience in self-government was obtained. The occupation resulted in the growth of an independence movement. In 1946 a referendum on the question of the relationship with Denmark was conducted. One could vote for either independence or home rule. The turnout was relatively low, and the results inconclusive. A year later the Lagting voted in favor of home rule, and Copenhagen responded with a Home Rule Ordinance (23 March 1948). This ordinance gave the islands control over internal affairs and provided considerable flexibility for determining competency. The Faeroes also retained two representatives in the Danish parliament.

Iceland had entered into what was considered a "personal union" with Norway in 1262. In a pattern similar to that in Norwegian history, the former "republic" gradually lost more and more of its autonomy under Danish control. (See chapter 7.) Events in the early nineteenth century undermined support for the ties with Denmark. Distance and rules that permitted only Danish subjects to trade with Iceland made the island particularly vulnerable to the interruptions brought on by the Napoleonic Wars. However, privateering and the willingness of the British to carry on trade actually led to a temporary improvement of conditions. The wartime experiences, including the interesting episode involving Jörgen Jörgensen, helped trigger increased awareness of Iceland's fragile status and thinking about the links with Denmark.

Cultural nationalism developed in the decades following 1815, and a political voice was added to the national awakening in the 1830s. Of particular importance was the *Fjölnir* group, organized by young intellectuals in Copenhagen in 1835 and named after their publication. They called for a heightened national awareness, increased use of Icelandic, and revival of the Althing (abolished in 1800). However, in the conservative environment of the kingdom at the time their appeals made little progress.

Jörgen Jörgensen

Every country has its national icons; some are serious, some are not. In the development of an Icelandic national consciousness and in the formation of opinion dedicated to the nation's independence, Jörgen Jörgensen (Jürgen Jürgensen) (c. 1780–1841) belongs in the latter group. Jörgensen was the son of a Copenhagen clock smith. A dreamer, he left school at about age fourteen and went to sea. The rest of his life is one strange adventure after another. On 25 June 1809 he and a small band of supporters, perhaps with some British support, seized control of Reykjavík, arrested the local governor, and attempted to establish an "independent" Iceland. Jörgensen saw himself as king. He set up fortifications, dressed his bodyguard in colorful uniforms, proclaimed the national flag should be three codfish on a blue sea, and ventured out on a tour of the countryside designed to establish his authority. In late August the adventure ended. British officials arrested Jörgensen and took him back to England, where he was imprisoned for a short time. Eventually, he was deported to Tasmania, where he died in 1841. In fact, Jörgensen probably had very little impact on Iceland's history, but the story reinforced the recurrent idea that ties with Denmark could cost Icelanders dearly.

More tangible changes occurred in the 1840s. In 1843 Christian VIII allowed the revival of the Althing as an advisory assembly composed of twenty elected and six appointed representatives. It met for the first time in 1845. The central person in this moment and for the next thirty years was Jón Sigurdsson (1811–79). Born in Iceland and educated in Copenhagen in philology and history, he became the leader of the cause of Icelandic autonomy and remains one of the heroes of modern Icelandic history. Through his work in the Althing and his endless stream of writings, most published in his own periodical, *Ny felagsrit* (New society), Sigurdsson pressed continuously for Iceland's interests.

The pace of change in Iceland was slow, and this is hardly surprising, given the tangle of events occurring in Denmark at the same time. High hopes that autonomy would be achieved in the wake of

1848 went unfulfilled. Sigurdsson and others argued Iceland's status in the kingdom ought to revert to the autonomy defined in the 1262 agreement and called for home rule and an Althing with legislative and fiscal powers. Officials in Copenhagen disagreed. Attempts to resolve differences in a kind of constitutional convention in 1851 yielded neither agreement nor change. The only significant gains made were the establishment of completely open trade (1854) and an assurance of freedom of the press (1855).

Following the loss of Slesvig and Holstein in 1864 and in response to nearly constant appeals from Iceland, a new "constitutional law" providing for autonomy in domestic affairs was unilaterally introduced by Denmark in 1871. This was unpopular and unleashed a new round of protest. Three years later Christian IX, on the occasion of the millennium of the settlement of Iceland, gave the island a new constitution, which provided for full autonomy in domestic affairs, enlarged the Althing's legislative and fiscal powers, and assured civil rights. The king retained veto power and control over foreign affairs. The crown would be represented by a viceroy, and Icelandic interests represented by a minister in the king's cabinet. Although not the result of negotiation, the constitution was reasonably popular and served as the basis for government for the next thirty years. In 1904 the Althing was expanded to forty members and the minister for Icelandic Affairs was made responsible to it.

In the twentieth century independence rather than autonomy became the goal of most nationalists. The first step toward this was taken in 1918, when an agreement was reached making Iceland a "sovereign state in personal union with Denmark." Under its terms, the agreement was to last for twenty years, at which time it could be renegotiated. If neither party called for renewal within three years, the union would be considered dissolved. The agreement lapsed in the midst of World War II and was not renewed. On 17 June 1944 all ties with Denmark were severed, and Iceland became an independent republic for the first time since 1262.

The German Duchies Problem
Ties between the duchies of Slesvig and Holstein and the Danish monarchy date from the fifteenth century and present a tangled history often difficult to unravel. In the early nineteenth century the two duchies, along with Lauenburg, were parts of the kingdom but not integral parts of the state. Holstein was also a member of the

Denmark and Slesvig-Holstein in the nineteenth century.

German Confederation, created in 1815. Ethnically, Holstein and Lauenburg were German. Slesvig was mixed, becoming increasingly Danish as one moved north. Until the 1830s there were no national movements in any of these, and, beyond old problems of conflicting dynastic claims and power politics, the duchies presented no special problem to the government in Copenhagen. This changed abruptly, however, in the 1830s. Cultural nationalism was being nurtured throughout the disunified German states, especially in the growing universities. The University of Kiel was no exception. In response, a Danish nationalism was fostered, especially among the farmers of north Slesvig. The nationality conflicts took on political form when the advisory assemblies established by Frederik VI first met in 1836. Over the next twelve years tensions rose. Status within the kingdom,

Scandinavianism

Paralleling the development of Nordic nationalisms was the emergence in the 1840s of Scandinavianism. This was principally a student movement, and its most enthusiastic followers were at the universities in Copenhagen, Lund, and Uppsala. Student associations hosted celebrations in 1839, 1842, and 1845 in which speeches, poems, and songs celebrated the common elements in Nordic history and culture. The movement had political aspects. In Sweden it was linked to desires to recover Finland; in Denmark it was tied to efforts to counter the problems of German nationalism in the duchies. Sweden's Oscar I and Karl XV and Denmark's Frederik VII and Christian IX were sympathetic. Oscar's limited support of the Danes in 1848–49 and his interests in Swedish involvement in the Crimean War, as well as Karl's unfulfilled promises of aid to Denmark in 1864, were influenced by these sympathies. Scandinavianism reflects the persistence of the unity theme in Nordic history—a theme with significant historical and cultural foundations, and one often lost in the shadow of national-focused histories.

form of government, royal succession, language, and culture were at issue.

These same issues became matters along which political factions in Denmark defined themselves. Conservatives advocated a unitary state (*helstat*), in which the duchies were bound more closely. The National Liberals, in alliance with freehold farmers, were willing to concede independence to Holstein and Lauenburg, but wanted to bring Slesvig into a closer union. They saw the Eider River as the appropriate southern boundary of the kingdom.

In 1848 much of Europe was caught up in a new wave of revolutions, revolutions with political, social, and often national elements. Although there were politically motivated disturbances in Stockholm, it was in Denmark and the duchies that revolutions occurred. In a largely peaceful but impassioned environment fed by liberal political speeches and public gatherings, absolutism was dismantled. Frederik VII, king only since January 1848, was persuaded to dismiss his con-

Storming the Fortress at Rendsborg, depicting the bloodless fall of the fort during the tumultuous days of March 1848, unknown artist/lithographer. Courtesy of Det Nationalhistoriske Museum på Frederiksborg, Denmark.

servative advisers, appoint a government that included a majority of National Liberals, and call for the election of a constitutional assembly. Similar events took place in the duchies, and in mid-March a delegation representing German interests in Slesvig and Holstein came to Copenhagen to negotiate a new constitutional arrangement for the duchies. Although the duchies' representatives were willing to compromise on Slesvig, they were met with intransigence by the new government and sent home in frustration. The response of the German nationalists was to declare the duchies independent and establish a new government in Kiel. Unwilling to accept the loss of Slesvig, the government leadership in Copenhagen opted for war.

The "Three Years' War" that followed reflected many of the complexities of mid-nineteenth-century European history. Power balance, constitutional, and nationality issues were involved at one time or another. What should have been a war between Denmark and the German nationalists in Slesvig and Holstein became a war between Denmark and "the German nation"—supported by Prussian troops. The influence of Tsar Nicholas I, a change of view by Prussia's Frederick William IV, and diplomatic intervention by Austria, France, and Great Britain ended the conflict in 1851–52.

Initially, Danish troops had a relatively easy time of it. They outnumbered the duchies' forces and were better trained, equipped, and led. There was enthusiasm on both sides. The Danes scored an impressive victory at Bov in early April and occupied all of Slesvig—stopping at the Eider. But then Prussia entered the conflict. The numbers and quality factors turned. The Danes were forced to retreat, and Jutland was invaded. But the Prussian successes alarmed the Swedish and Russian leaders, neither of whom wanted a Prussian-dominated Denmark. Oscar I agreed to send 15,000 troops—though they were not to be used in combat—and the Russians applied diplomatic pressure. Frederick IV conceded, and Prussian troops were withdrawn from Jutland.

The war should have ended at this point, but did not. No settlement of the issues was reached, and the fighting resumed in April 1849 with mixed results. A treaty was finally concluded with the Prussians and the German Confederation in July 1850. Left alone, the army of the duchies fought on until January 1851 when, largely because of mounting international pressure, all parties were forced to accept a status quo situation. The London Protocol, designed by the great powers and signed in 1852, stipulated that Holstein and Lauenburg were to remain parts of the German Confederation. Slesvig could not be incorporated into the Danish state because of its historic ties to Holstein. Each duchy was to be autonomous in managing its internal affairs. A state council with representatives for the duchies was to handle foreign affairs and defense. Finally, the agreement recognized the right of inheritance to the Danish throne through female lines, designated Christian of Glücksburg as Frederik VII's heir, and denied the succession claims of the Duke of Augustenburg. All appeared settled.

In fact, no one was really satisfied with the final agreements. Status, constitutions, administration, education, language, and succession remained at issue. A series of Copenhagen governments struggled to avoid a new conflict, and, depending on their political party ties, refused to abandon either the unitary state or Eider border solution. In 1863, believing the international situation was favorable, C. C. Hall's (1812–88) National Liberal ministry chose to act. Russia appeared distracted with a revolt in Poland. Prussia seemed weakened by an internal conflict over defense reform appropriations. Support from Sweden, Great Britain, and France seemed likely in a crisis. In March the government issued the March Patent, by which Holstein and Lauenberg were to be separated from the kingdom and promised a separate constitution, and a new constitution for Denmark and Slesvig would be written. A crisis soon developed, however. Copenhagen ignored demands from the German Confederation to withdraw the March Patent. In November Frederik VII suddenly died. He was succeeded by Christian of Glücksburg, who, bolstered by promises of assistance from the Swedes, reluctantly signed the new constitution. In response, both the Slesvig and Holstein estates declared their independence, and the Duke of Augustenburg's son, Frederik, declared himself king "Frederik VIII."

If there was a favorable moment for decisions that clearly violated the London Protocol, it had vanished. Russian, French, and British diplomats tried to get the Danes to back down. Although Karl XV promised 20,000 troops, there were strings attached, and his government was less than enthusiastic about delivering on the promise. Prussia was not paralyzed by the struggle between the king (and his chancellor) and the parliament over defense reform funding. The new chancellor, Otto von Bismarck, relished the moment. He could assert his leadership, play to German nationalists, and make gains for Prussia. But it was not only their flawed reading of the international situation that drove Danish leaders on. They were also pushed by a public eager for a nationalist resolution to the question of the duchies and by their own enthusiasm. The Danish Government refused to comply with a Prussian ultimatum and on 1 February 1864 faced an attack by Prussian-Austrian forces acting under authority of the German Confederation.

The second Slesvig-Holstein war lasted eight months and cost the Danes dearly. Two governments were forced to resign. Danish weapons were no match for the modern artillery and breech-loading rifles of the Germans, and able leadership was sadly lacking. Combat casualties were high, especially at the siege of Dybböl. Under the terms of the Treaty of Vienna (30 October 1864) Holstein and Slesvig were taken from Denmark and placed under Austrian and Prussian administration respectively. One-third of the kingdom's territory and one-third of its population were lost, and 200,000 Danish-speakers came under German rule. In 1866 both duchies were taken over by Prussia and restructured as a single province. (Lauenburg was sold to Prussia in 1876.)

As one historian has put it, in 1864 Denmark became a "dwarf" in the European state system. Twice in less than twenty years, the Danes had been shown their vulnerability when the interests of the great

Slesvig Danes in Germany

The treatment of the Danes in Slesvig after 1866 illustrates how divisive nationalism can be when uniformity is demanded in a pluralistic situation. Although the treaty that ended the Austro-Prussian War (1866) included an article that provided for the return of the Danish parts of Slesvig to the kingdom via a referendum procedure, this did not happen. From the late 1870s the Germans worked to Germanize the Danes in the region. Use of Danish was discouraged, and the teaching of Danish virtually banned in 1889. Young men were subject to conscription, and a loyalty oath was demanded of them. Danish-speaking officials were fired. Lands belonging to those who did not cooperate were confiscated. Some 60,000 emigrated or were expelled. In the 1890s the senior German official for the area, Ernst M. von Köller, was particularly enthusiastic in his efforts. But Danishness was not erased, and many of the Germans' actions merely strengthened the ethnic Danes' resolve and nurtured deep bitterness. In 1920 the boundary between Denmark and Germany was redrawn based on lines determined by the results of referenda in north and central Slesvig that were preceded by intense and highly emotional campaigns by both nationalities.

powers were or were not focused on them. Seen in a positive light, however, the relative weakness of the country was impressed on its leaders and its most divisive nationalities problem settled. Foreign policy could be and was adjusted to match realities, and attentions could be now be turned elsewhere.

During the nineteenth century, nationalism clearly played important roles. In the major kingdoms and the peripheral units identities were developed based on various cultural elements including language, literature, and history. National consciousness was fostered through the growth of compulsory schooling, organizations, and publications. Politicized nationalism was a central element in both domestic politics and international relations, and contributed to all the territorial changes of the period.

10

〜〜〜〜〜〜〜〜〜〜〜〜〜〜〜〜〜〜〜〜〜〜〜〜〜〜〜〜〜〜〜〜〜〜〜〜

The Road to Political Democracy

B uilding on the constitutional foundations established in 1809 in
Sweden, 1814 in Norway, 1849 in Denmark, and 1905 in Finland, political democracies were slowly established throughout
Norden by about 1920. In Denmark, Norway, and Sweden this meant
democratic constitutional monarchies replaced crown-dominated
oligarchies; in Finland it meant a republican form of government
replaced Russian autocracy. In specific terms, sovereignty moved from
the crown to the people, executive power moved from the crown to
governments responsible to parliaments elected by universal suffrage,
legislative power came to reside almost entirely with parliaments, and
aristocratic or bureaucratic elites were replaced by new ones based
mainly on wealth. At the same time, political participation by an increasingly literate public grew, political parties based on social class
lines and ideologies developed, and a popular press emerged as a central element in political life.

None of these changes came quickly, and very little "progress"
was made in the first half of the century. Often change came in bursts,
as in 1814 in Norway, 1848–49 in Denmark, 1863–66 in Sweden, or
1905–6 in Finland. The first two decades of the twentieth century
was a period of particularly rapid change.

For the most part, the transitions were peaceful, although emotions often ran high. There was no lack of public demonstrations for
political change in Norden during this period, and troops were occasionally on hand, as in Sweden in December 1865, in case violence
erupted. Events in Finland in 1918 are the exception to this general-
ization, where, as has been seen, a complex war erupted.

Many factors caused these developments. They include the presence of new political ideologies, profound social and economic
changes, inspired leadership, persistence, external developments, and

the willingness of established elites to accept change because they no longer feared it or believed it was better to control the forces of change than to risk revolution.

Denmark

Denmark began the nineteenth century as a constitutional absolutist state. There was no national parliament, or provincial or local assemblies. The king made law, and his appointed officials administered it. Although significant social, economic, and legal reforms were carried out in the last decades of the eighteenth and early nineteenth century, there was no political revolution (see chapter 5).

Crown Prince Frederik (from 1808, Frederik VI) showed no interest in altering the constitutional order. Not until 1834 did he see fit even to open the door a crack to the clamor from liberals demanding change. Then he created four advisory assemblies to meet at Roskilde, Viborg, Slesvig, and Itzehoe. They were chosen by a tiny electorate amounting to about one-fortieth of the population, and their recommendations imposed no obligations on the king. Frederik believed they were "schools" where an ignorant public could begin to learn about sharing political power.

Danish liberals' hopes for change were high on the accession of Christian VIII in 1839. After all, as Christian Frederik he had presided over the birth of Norway's constitution in 1814. These hopes were quickly dashed. Christian was no liberal. Although intellectually gifted and highly cultured, the fifty-three-year-old monarch was a conservative who believed in the appropriateness of aristocracies and absolutism. (How one explains his apparent sympathies for liberalism in 1814 is uncertain. One possibility is that those sympathies were false. Christian was a captive of the moment. If his hopes for a restoration of the Dano-Norwegian union had been fulfilled, there is no telling what might have happened to Norway's constitution.) Only modest gains were made during the 1840s. Local or parish councils were created to give a voice in local affairs to small landowners, and city and county self-government was extended. Still, the decade of the 1840s was lively in terms of the political conversation carried on by Conservatives and National Liberals in the press and public gatherings. The lines of conflict for ensuing decades were largely drawn in this period —against the backdrop of growing German nationalism—and they even drove Christian to begin considering constitutional reform.

The task of carrying out actual change, however, was suddenly dropped on his son, Frederik VII (1808–63) in January 1848, just as Europe erupted in a wave of revolutionary turmoil. Frederik was a complex figure; obese, fond of the good life, on his third marriage (this time a morganatic one to Louise Rasmussen/Danner (1815–74), a former dancer), and apparently not interested in politics. Little was expected of him. But there was a serious side to Frederik, and he played the role of reformer king very well. Copenhagen became a hothouse of political debate. On 21 March leaders of the city government marched on the royal palace accompanied by a large crowd. They wanted a new government and a new constitution. Frederik agreed to all their demands. Absolutism vanished virtually overnight. A National Liberal–controlled government was appointed. A constitutional assembly was elected and produced a new constitution, which the king approved on 5 June 1849.

Denmark was now a constitutional monarchy. The king continued to govern with a government appointed by him. A two-chamber parliament (Rigsdag) was to have legislative and fiscal powers, as well as the right to review the actions of ministers in the government. The king retained an absolute veto. Suffrage was given to males over thirty meeting certain property qualifications. About 15 percent of the population received the vote. Differences in age and property qualification requirements for candidates to the two houses of the parliament and mode of election defined their differences. About 1 in 7 were eligible to hold seats in the Folketing, and only 1 in 333 for the Landsting. These requirements ensured that the Landsting would be a conservative chamber acting as a brake on any Folketing radicalism. The constitution also ensured an independent judiciary and civil rights.

Following the defeat in 1864, Denmark had two constitutions in effect, one from June 1849 and the other from November 1863. Two years of debate resulted in a compromise merger of these that ensured the conservative nature of the Landsting and left unresolved questions of parlementarism and which of the two chambers was the more powerful. For most of the next thirty-five years Denmark was governed by the king, his ministers, and the conservative landowners who dominated the Landsting.

The most important person during this period of "Landsting parlementarism" was J. B. S. Estrup (1825–1913), a conservative Jutland landowner who abhorred the notion of popular democracy. He served as prime minister from 1875 to 1894 and during that time blocked every attempt at further democratic reforms. His tactics were similar to many of his contemporaries (e.g., Bismarck and Disraeli). To quiet lower-class unrest, he used social legislation, such as measures to supplement the resources of sickness benefit societies and economic development schemes; to quell demonstrations, he employed the police, including a special force; and to silence the press, he relied on the publisher liability aspects of the freedom of the press law.

The issue on which political debate turned during much of the Estrup period was national defense. The prime minister realistically understood Denmark's vulnerability, and he believed the best way to ensure the country's safety was to provide Copenhagen with strong defenses against a land attack. The liberals preferred the idea of a strong defense through a national militia. Time and again disagreement over defense triggered what amounted to constitutional crises. The parliament would be paralyzed as one house checked the other. When this happened, Estrup would keep the government running by invoking the emergency powers clause of the constitution that allowed the government to stay in business through provisional finance measures. Finally, in 1894, a compromise was reached by which the Left agreed to support Estrup's defense plan and the Right conceded on more democratic procedures for appropriation bills. A 100-kilometer arc of defensive installations became one of the most costly public works projects in Danish history.

But the time for Estrup's and the conservatives' control was drawing to a close. By the 1890s Denmark was a far different country than even twenty years earlier. Economic changes gave rise to an expanded middle class and an industrial working class. Labor gained a political voice in 1876 with the founding of a Social Democratic Party. (The first Social Democratic representatives to the Folketing were elected in 1884.) The diverse interests of the Left were indicated by the party's split in 1894. The dominance of a tiny landowning elite and the monarch ran counter to these developments, and the calls for Folketing parlementarism grew louder. Even the crown prince, Frederik, realized change had to come.

In 1894 Estrup was forced to resign, and for the next seven years attempts were made to preserve the conservatives' hold on power through a series of ministries. Finally, in 1901, following a Folketing election in which the Right won only eight seats, Christian IX agreed to appoint a government that would have the Folketing's confidence.

It was headed by Johan Henrik Deuntzer (1845–1918), but the real leader was Jens Christian Christensen (1856–1930), a Jutland schoolmaster and head of the Left Reform Party. In 1905 a more genuine parliamentary government was founded when Christensen became prime minister.

The events of 1901 and 1905 are called "the system change" in Danish political history. Power passed peacefully from a handful of large landowners to a larger, but still rural-based, elite of small holders. Folketing parlementarism appeared to have won the day. These changes and several "liberal" measures including broadened suffrage, abolition of the old land tax system, and a more democratic education system were supported by Frederik VIII (1843–1912) during his short reign, 1906–12.

In 1915, after several years of debate and taking advantage of a political truce brought on by World War I, a second "June Constitution" was enacted that erased the conservative elements of the 1866 constitutional compromise. The new constitution introduced universal suffrage, proportional representation, and plebiscites. It also reduced the differences between the two chambers of the parliament. The 140-member Folketing was to be elected directly every four years. The Landsting was to have seventy-two members. Gone were the royal appointees. Eighteen members would be chosen by the assembly before an election, the remainder by electors. Representatives served for eight years, and half of the house was elected at each four-year election. Candidates had to be at least thirty-five years old. The Landsting was considered now to be the chamber of continuity rather than a bastion of conservatism. Gradually, the Landsting came to mirror the Folketing, and it was abolished in 1953. In addition, the new constitution eliminated the possibility of a government ruling through provisional finance measures.

The new constitution moved Denmark closer to genuine political democracy, but there was still a ways to go. In fact, a subtle two-level political system prevailed. On the one hand, there was the king-cabinet-parliament; on the other, Christian X (1870–1947) and a clique of powerful friends including merchants, bankers, bureaucrats, and military officers. The latter was what the crown preferred. One more crisis was needed to push Denmark into genuine political democracy, and it came in 1920.

The so-called Easter Crisis was actually a set of problems that coalesced in spring 1920. One was constitutional. This involved continued

Landsting conservatism, the political conservatism of Christian X, the desire within C. T. Zahle's (1866–1946) government to democratize further the electoral sections of the constitution, and the calls by Social Democrats for even more far-reaching changes. These issues contributed to a tense political atmosphere made more volatile by European revolutionary and counterrevolutionary developments. Another problem was the continuation of wartime economic restrictions, including price controls. A third entailed growing social class tensions arising from the failure of three months of wage talks between the Trade Union Federation and the Employers' Federation, strikes, and lockouts. Finally, there was disagreement about where the Treaty of Versailles–mandated change of border between Denmark and Germany ought to lie. The new border was supposed to be founded on the results of referenda in two zones of northern Slesvig. Moderates (and the Zahle government) favored what is the present border. Some argued for a slightly more southerly line and the inclusion of Flensburg. The most radical argued for the so-called Dannevirke border.

Unhappy with Zahle's positions, Christian X called the prime minister to the Amalienborg palace on 29 March. The king wanted Zahle to resign and elections to be held, even though the government enjoyed a majority in the Folketing and had not lost a vote of confidence. The exchange that took place was heated, and in the end Zahle was dismissed and the parliament dissolved. The situation was made worse because Christian failed to ask his prime minister to stay on until a caretaker cabinet could be appointed. As a result, Denmark was without a government.

Many believed the king had exceeded his constitutional rights. Much of the political Left thought he had gone too far, and the socialists had a field day with these developments. The king was accused of orchestrating a coup. Large demonstrations were held outside the Amalienborg palace, and calls of "down with Christian" were heard. Denmark may have been on the verge of revolution.

Seven hours of intense negotiations on the night of 3–4 April 1920 (the fourth was Easter) resolved the crisis. The king agreed to form a new caretaker government, talks were to begin on electoral reforms, the employers' lockout was to end, and new elections were to be held as soon as possible. Over the next few months a new political peace was established.

In the April 1920 elections the Radical Left lost half their seats—

largely to the Conservative Peoples' Party and the Left. The Social Democrats barely held their own, and the party soon after split down communist and revisionist lines. It appeared clear the majority of those who voted were prepared to support political democracy, but they were not prepared to carry through any sort of full-scale social revolution.

The new parliament then passed a package of constitutional reforms by which the voting age was dropped to twenty-five, the size of the Folketing was fixed at 149, the size of the Landsting was set at 76 (19 chosen by the chamber), and foreign policy brought under parliament's control. These changes firmly established the bases of political democracy, and a period in Danish political history begun in 1848 ended. At the same time, a new era dominated by the development of social and economic democracy began.

Finland

The triumph of democracy in Finland was inseparably linked with the country's relationship with Russia, internal ethnic and social issues, and external events. Six periods help define the process. During the first, 1809–63, there was very little political life per se. Government was by bureaucracy, directed by the Senate and under varying degrees of Russia control. The second, 1863–c. 1890, saw the emergence of an active political culture bolstered by the revival of the parliament. Two periods, c.1890–1905 and 1908–17, followed. These were dominated by Russification efforts. A brief, but important, interlude, 1905–7, separated these, and it was then that a new parliament structure and suffrage laws were put in place. The final period, 1917–19, was defined by the achievement of independence, civil war, and the development of a new constitutional order.

The Finns established some of the necessary bases for an active political culture during the period of "frozen constitutionalism." From 1809 to 1863 the parliament did not meet. The tsar was under no constitutional obligation to call it, and neither Alexander I nor Nicholas I saw reason to do so. Nonetheless, interest in political ideas grew, especially among intellectuals and students in Helsinki and Turku, and was fed by news of events outside the country. After midcentury political factions representing liberals, Swedish-speaking Finns, and Finnish-speakers developed. In addition, newspapers such as *Suometar, Helsingfors Dagbladet,* and *Helsingin Uutiset* were established to foster the various political and nationalist views of these groups.

An active parliamentary life returned to Finland in September 1863, when the old four-estate parliament met for the first time since 1809. This was the result of pressure from the Finns, led by J. V. Snellman, and the reforming interests of Alexander II. For the next seventeen years it appeared as if Finland was on a track that promised continued autonomy and liberal political development. In 1869 Alexander issued an edict promising a meeting of the Diet every five years. This interval was shortened to every three years in 1882. Three years later, the Diet was given the right to initiate legislation—until then it could only petition the tsar. These changes were complemented by language, currency, banking, press, and defense measures that reinforced Finnish autonomy and faith in the relationship with Russia.

The liberal honeymoon ended in the early 1890s. Alexander III and Nicholas II were autocrats seemingly incapable of bringing their country into the modern era. Repression was their response to the political and nationality problems in the empire. In Finland this meant curbing the parliament's activities and enforcing measures designed to turn Finns into Russians. But the Russo-Japanese War and the Revolution of 1905 in Russia forced Nicholas to edge toward reforms, and the Finns were caught up in these events. Demands for changes varied depending on political outlook. The beginnings of modern political parties appeared during the last four decades of the century, and these groups carried their ideals into the turmoil of 1905–6. The moderate nationalist party, the Finnish Party, established after 1863 to champion the use of the Finnish language and the development of an educated Finnish-speaking elite, split during the 1890s. Its more conservative element, labeled the "Old Finns," favored a cautious and conciliatory policy toward Russia. The more radical element, labeled the "Young Finns," and Swedish People's Party advocated democratic political reforms. The Social Democrats, who organized a general strike, argued for far-reaching political and social reforms.

Nicholas responded with the November Manifesto (1905), in which he agreed to suspend various Russification measures and authorized the Senate to prepare new laws covering the parliament and fundamental civil rights. Under the leadership of Leo Mechelin these were readied and approved by the tsar in July 1906. Finland took a leap into the twentieth century under the terms of these measures.

The old four-estate Diet was replaced by a two-hundred-seat, unicameral body, the Eduskunta. It was to be elected by universal suffrage. Traditional civil rights, such as freedom of speech, assembly, and association, were guaranteed. Only parlementarism was not assured. Six political parties took part in the first elections under the new system in March 1907, setting a pattern for the future.

The democratic interlude was short-lived in both Finland and Russia. By 1908 Nicholas was dissolving the parliament when it suited him, asserting his authority to enforce legal uniformity in the empire, and demanding financial contributions from Finland for the empire's defense. He even went so far as to appoint Russians to the Senate in 1912. A new parliament, elected in July 1916, did not meet until April 1917 — after the beginning of revolution in Russia.

The final chapter in the emergence of democratic institutions in Finland came following the 1918 war. A yearlong struggle over what form of government to establish was resolved in early 1919. The pressure of internal and external events hastened the process and forced compromises. In the end, Finland's constitution, which is really a set of fundamental laws passed over the next several years and revised many times since, provided for a republic. Sovereign power resides with the people and is exercised through the parliament, a cabinet responsible to the parliament, and the president. For the most part, the parliament's structure, size, and election procedures were carried over from 1906. Elections were to be held every three years (now four). Suffrage was universal, representation proportional. The president was to be chosen indirectly by three hundred electors every six years. Among the president's powers were legislative initiative, a delaying veto, and direction of foreign policy and the armed forces. The design of the presidency reflected the interests of the conservatives, who feared an all-powerful parliament. Although the system appears to have built into it a recipe for paralysis, it has in fact worked quite well. Conflicts between president and parliament have been resolved, and the presence of two focal points of power have allowed for flexibility in responses to situations.

Norway

The system established by the men of 1814, although relatively liberal in the context of the times, was far from democratic. For a real breakthrough to be achieved, the powers of the crown would have to be curtailed, the primacy of the Storting established, and the near-monopoly in political affairs of the officials' class (*embetsmenn*) eliminated. At the same time, the timidity of the farmers in public affairs would have to be overcome and a new political culture nurtured.

For most of the first thirty years following 1814, the Norwegians had to struggle with the attempts by Karl XIV to circumvent and revise the union settlement and the constitution. Karl was by disposition an autocrat and regarded the 1814 agreements with Norway as temporary. In 1821 he appears to have been giving serious thought to a coup to eliminate a system he found far too liberal. He backed away from this approach, however, when the acquiescence he expected from the European powers and support from pro-unionists in Norway was not forthcoming. In 1824 he submitted a package of thirteen constitutional amendments including an absolute veto, the right to dismiss officials and to nominate the Storting's president, and measures to restrict the parliament's legislative initiative powers. None were accepted then or at any other session of the parliament down to Karl's death in 1844. Paradoxically, a tendency to draw away from involvement in Norwegian affairs developed in Karl's later years, and this was shared by his successors.

The decline of crown interest in Norway led to an increase in the powers of the council, or cabinet. Dominated by members of the officials' class, the government jealously guarded its position and developed a growing mistrust of the parliament, although some supported closer ties with the Storting in order to control it. At the same time, the parliament was unable to counter this trend. The assembly was not a particularly effective leader of the country. Its members represented various interests and social groups, there was little formal organization of factions, and it was difficult to reach consensus on matters. The farmers, the most powerful single group, were concerned more with issues of taxation and trade than with constitutional matters. A divided parliament could make little headway against the position of the educated, experienced, and relatively uniform officials.

The economic, social, and demographic developments of the century, coupled with educational reforms and the rise of a popular press, contributed to the gradual emergence of a new political culture opposed to the bureaucracy of the official class. This was manifested in the Thrane Movement around midcentury and the founding of a Liberal (Venstre) Party by Johan Sverdrup in 1869.

The first step in the democratic breakthrough came in 1884, when

Marcus Thrane

In the late 1840s Marcus Thrane (1817–90) began to agitate for liberal political and social reforms as editor of the *Drammens Adresse*. He also established over four hundred craft-worker-farm laborer associations with over 30,000 members, mostly in the central and eastern parts of the country. In some areas, these groups dominated local affairs. Their calls for universal suffrage, free trade, and improved working conditions, along with disturbances organized by more radical members, frightened the authorities. Thrane was arrested in 1851, held in prison for three years without trial, and eventually sentenced to another four years of confinement. In 1862 he emigrated to America, where he worked among Norwegian Americans as a photographer, journalist, playwright, and dramatist. He never abandoned his liberal ideals, and they eventually made him a national hero in the fight for democracy. In 1949 his remains were returned to Norway for reburial.

Oscar II was compelled to appoint a genuinely parliamentary government headed by Liberal leader Johan Sverdrup. This moment marked the culmination of a twelve-year constitutional battle over parlementarism and the question of royal veto power in constitutional matters (see chapter 9). The outcome, which preceded similar developments in Denmark and Sweden by twenty years or more, laid the groundwork for the evolution of a multiparty parliamentary system.

Universal suffrage came to Norway in a series of steps. By 1884 the restrictive income requirements had been lowered, and they were eliminated entirely in 1898, when the vote was given to all males over twenty-five. Three years later women were given the vote in local elections, and full women's suffrage was introduced in 1913. The indirect voting procedures adopted in 1814 were finally replaced by direct election in 1905, when new single-member constituencies were apportioned and the so-called French System of holding a second election in a district if no candidate secured a real majority in the first polling was adopted. This complicated procedure was replaced in 1919 by proportional representation and multimember constituencies based on the Norwegian counties.

In the context created by these reforms and social and economic developments, a multiparty system also evolved. Prior to 1914 this included the Liberals (Venstre) and its several offshoots (Moderate, Workers Democrats, and Radicals), the Conservatives (Høyre), and Labor. The roots of these parties lay far back in the nineteenth century —in the pro-unionists of 1814, the Thranites of midcentury, and the Liberal Reform Society of 1859. However, it was not until the breakthrough of parlementarism, the extension of the electorate, and greater participation in elections made national organization necessary, that they moved from the stage of being loose and often short-lived parliamentary factions to truly "modern" political parties.

Sweden

Sweden's conservative revolution in 1809 established the constitutional bases for the country's political history down to 1974, when changes made over the preceding 165 years were consolidated in a new set of fundamental laws. The years 1809–10 defined Sweden as a limited constitutional monarchy in which the king ruled with the advice of his council of state and shared legislative power with a four-house parliament based on essentially medieval social groups. The system represented less than 10 percent of the country's 2.5 million people. Despite legislation legally ending many of the nobility's privileges and the voices assured to representatives of the clergy, burghers, and farmers in the parliament, the nobles retained their influence, appointments, and power. Sweden was, in many respects, an aristocracy.

To establish political democracy, the Swedes needed to replace the estates parliament with one founded on universal suffrage and move executive power from the crown to a government responsible to the parliament. It took over a century to accomplish these changes.

Structural reform of the ancient Swedish parliament was suggested in 1809. At that time such an idea received only passing attention because the framers of the new constitution were pressed by a fear of radicalization and the four estates still represented fundamental realities of the country's society. Over the ensuing decades, however, social position based mainly on birth lost importance while social position based on economic realities became more common. The growth of the middle class was especially important, but so too were gains made by landowners, the expansion of professional classes, and the birth of an industrial working class. Sweden's society became increasingly diverse and complex. By the middle of the century it was clear that reform had to come.

Calls for restructuring were frequently vented in the emerging liberal press of the 1830s and 1840s, and formal proposals were introduced often in sessions of the parliament. The Riksdag's constitutional committee presented one in 1845. Three years later, Riksdag liberals founded the Friends of Reform Society to press for change. At the same time, Oscar I, who was believed to have genuine liberal sympathies, asked the parliament's constitutional committee to prepare a reform legislation package for consideration and added a few liberals to his council. Noisy demonstrations on 18–19 March 1848 and events on the Continent helped change the king's mind, however. By the end of the year he and parliament had moved to more conservative positions. Although reform ideas were discussed over the next six years, none were enacted. The 1840s proved it was relatively easy to suggest a new format for the parliament. It was quite another to settle on who would be represented. Conservatives, especially in the House of the Nobility, were not about to agree to any reform that would remove them from their positions of power.

Eventually, social changes, growing awareness of political issues and involvement in them, and external political change compelled the forces of order to concede. In 1863 Karl XV's first minister, the forty-year-old Louis De Geer, introduced a measure designed to replace the old parliament with a two-chamber one. His plan was conservative and had Karl's support because it made no change in the executive position of the king. Discussed and amended, the proposal came up for final vote in early December 1865. It was quickly passed by the burghers and farmers. The clergy waited to see what the nobles would do. For four days the nearly seven hundred members of the estate debated. Speeches were passionate, nostalgic, and angry. Outside the chamber hundreds gathered, anxious to hear the outcome. Additional troops were on hand to maintain order. Many believed a no-vote would mean a revolution. Finally, on 7 December, the vote was taken: 361 nobles voted yes, 294 no. The four-estate parliament, with its roots in the 1400s, peacefully passed out of existence, and a nobility voted itself from the center of the political stage. The changes became law in 1866, and the first elections for the new parliament were held the same year. The new Riksdag, which in ways was more conservative than the last four-estates parliament, met for the first time in January 1867.

Sweden's new parliament had two chambers of equal competency. The so-called First Chamber had 125 (150 by 1894) seats. Its members were chosen by county assemblies and town councils, which were themselves elected by a very small electorate limited to those who were at least thirty-five years old and who owned property valued at 80,000 riksdaler or had an annual income of 4,000 riksdaler. (If women met these qualifications, they could vote.) The term of office was nine years, and one-third of the house was elected every three years. This was a plutocratic house, representing wealth and property: only about 6,000 men in all of Sweden were eligible to run for seats in it. The Second Chamber's 190 (230 after 1894) members were elected directly by men over twenty-one who owned 1,000 riksdaler in taxable property, leased property worth at least 6,000 riksdaler, or earned 800 riksdaler per year—about 5 percent of the total population, or about 20 percent of all adult males. This was to be a house of the urban middle class and the well-to-do farmers. Parliament was to meet annually.

Obviously, the reform was not a democratic breakthrough. But then democracy had not really yet been established elsewhere in Norden or Europe either. Sweden came, more or less, into line with Denmark, Norway, and Great Britain. The reform did set the stage for the development of a new political environment and culture, and for subsequent reforms—either enacted or accomplished in practice.

The first two decades of the new parliament's history were largely conservative. Taxes, tariffs, and defense dominated discussions. Participation by the newly enfranchised was very low. Gradually, however, the issues of suffrage and parlementarism came to the fore. These issues were driven by rapid economic and social change in the late nineteenth century, the development of political "parties" and organizations with interests in political issues such as the Verdandi Society (1882), and the active involvement of reform-minded individuals such as (Sven) Adolf Hedin (1834–1905) and Karl Staaff (1860–1915).

Suffrage was the central political issue around the turn of the century. Proposals for extending male suffrage were introduced in the Second Chamber at virtually every session of the parliament. Every one of them was defeated, however, in a labyrinth of parliamentary games usually controlled by conservative forces in the First Chamber. Finally, in 1909, conservative first minister Arvid Lindman secured the passage in both houses of a compromise suffrage reform that gave the vote to most males over twenty-four, introduced proportional representation in Second Chamber elections, and enlarged the First Chamber electorate. About 20 percent of the population was enfranchised.

Although Liberal Coalition leader Karl Staaff attempted to put through further suffrage reform in 1914, World War I intervened, and the final steps in the process were taken in 1917–18. Then the atmosphere was charged by the revolutionary events in Russia and elsewhere in Europe, and there was widespread labor unrest in Sweden. High prices, low wages, rationing, and shortages contributed to working-class anger. There were food riots and lootings. The socialist movement was split in two with the founding of a revolutionary Left Socialist party that called for the end of the monarchy. In December 1918 the parliament passed legislation guaranteeing virtually universal and equal suffrage in elections for both chambers. In effect, the two houses became identical, except that turnover was much slower in the First Chamber.

A second aspect of "the revolution of 1917–18" in Sweden was another step toward parlementarism. Since 1866 two changes had been slowly taking place in terms of the council of state. One involved a shift in the power balance between king and council. Although Karl XV, Oscar II, and Gustav V were conservatives and not inclined to give up the powers of the crown, in fact they did. The council became the government—the shaper and executor of policies. The second shift involved the drift toward parlementarism. Increasingly, the council was expected to have the confidence of the Second Chamber. Gustav's appointment of Uppsala University history professor Nils Eden (1871–1945) as prime minister following the Second Chamber election in 1917 and his acceptance of the coalition government Eden built, which included four Social Democrats, were important steps in this process. Although, as in Denmark, the king could still appoint a government that did not have the parliament's confidence and express himself on matters of state—as Gustav not only had done in the so-called Palace Yard Speech in 1914, when he repudiated the government's defense policies and brought down the Staaff government, but also would do in World War II when confronted with German demands that would compromise the country's neutrality.

11

~~~~~~

New Economies and New Societies

As in the rest of Europe, Norden underwent profound demographic, economic, and social changes during the nineteenth century. Often these changes are categorized as revolutions, but the use of this term is coming under increasing question. If revolution implies extensive change, it is appropriate. If, however, it implies rapid change, then it is less so. These particular changes had roots reaching far back into the early modern period, developed over half a century or more, and are ongoing in certain respects today.

Regardless of the arguments over terminology, however, it is clear that important and extensive changes occurred. The populations of the Nordic countries, in general, tripled between 1800 and 1914. The people of Scandinavia became more urban and less rural. Over 3 million found new homes in Europe, North and South America, the Pacific, and elsewhere across the globe. In many production sectors machines replaced hand labor, and new energy sources replaced animate, wind, or water power. The organization of companies changed, as did the nature of delivering products to consumers and modes of transportation. Trade contacts became more complex. Accompanying these economic changes were the growth of the middle class, the white-collar sector, and the working class, and the decline of the agricultural and artisan sectors. There were also important changes in the roles and rights of women in these "modernizing" societies.

The developments, which fundamentally altered the nature and quality of life in ways unimaginable to a person in 1800, were inseparably linked with political developments and problems, international affairs, and intellectual and cultural movements covered in the preceding chapters.

Until the mid–eighteenth century, the population of the Nordic countries grew only very slowly, and any gains were often wiped out by wars, famines, or epidemics. Beginning about 1720, however, gradual growth gave way to more and more rapid expansion, which reached unprecedented proportions in the nineteenth century. What were the causes of this growth?

In a response that has become virtually a cliché, Swedish poet Esaias Tegnér attributed it to "peace, vaccines, and potatoes." This glib answer to an enormously complex question is useful and even quite accurate. Peace was a factor. With the exception of the two Slesvig-Holstein wars around midcentury, Norden avoided involvement in Europe's conflicts after 1814. This meant that young men were not lost from the reproductive-age population. Medical advances are more difficult to define. Only a vaccine against smallpox was commonly used in the nineteenth century—smallpox vaccination was made compulsory in the Danish kingdom in 1810. But Tegnér's use of the word implies other modest advances in medical and health-related practices, including better training for doctors, better personal and environmental hygiene, improved urban water and sewage facilities, cleaner and safer hospitals, use of anesthetics, and an emerging understanding of the causes of some diseases. The potato is symbolic for improvements in diet. Although there were crop failures, famine was far less the scourge it had once been. Agricultural improvements including field consolidations, crop rotations, more fertilizer, new crops, and better livestock made more food available. Diets also became more diverse as a result of improved transportation (steamships and railroads) and the invention of refrigeration. Overall, medical and dietary changes made people healthier, and they lived longer.

However, in most areas the growth was not because birthrates rose; they tended to remain constant or even fall. It was common for women in their late twenties to postpone marriage, which meant fewer babies. But women had longer reproductive periods and bore healthier babies, and more children survived to reach reproductive age. Statistically, it is the drop in death rates that explains population growth.

Obviously, the increases in population had important social, economic, and geographic impacts. They placed impossible pressures on the largely agricultural economies of Norden, which soon reached saturation points in terms of employment opportunities. Agricultural expansion was limited and usually involved less fertile lands. In some areas farms were divided among the increasing number of surviving heirs until they became so small they could not support a family. The

The Demographic Revolution

Nordic Population

	Denmark	Faeroes
1800	.93 million	5,000
1850	1.4 million	8,000
1900	2.45 million	15,000
1914	2.8 million	—

Nordic Council of Ministers, *Yearbook of Nordic Statistics, 1996.*

Swedish government made the practice of farm division below a minimum size illegal in the 1840s. The pool of available labor swelled and could only be partially absorbed. The landless classes suffered the worst degradations. Social polarization among the rural populations worsened, and tensions grew. For a half century or more, the safety valve of emigration helped alleviate pressure, and by about 1900 growth in other primary sectors and industrial development provided relief as well. At the same time, this growth contributed to the redistribution of population within the Nordic countries. Movement from the countryside to other rural areas with employment opportunities and to towns and cities was widespread.

Emigration and Scandinavians Overseas

The people of Norden became more mobile than ever before in the nineteenth century, and this mobility was reflected in several ways. On the one hand, extensive internal migration occurred, involving both rural and rural-to-urban movement. Although difficult to measure, it is probably safe to say that most young people, unless they stood to inherit a viable family farm, moved once or more before they "settled down." These moves may have been linked to internal agricultural "colonization," life as a permanently itinerant laborer, or migration into developing new economic sectors. There was also some intra-Scandinavian migration, as, for example, when Finns moved to northern Norway. Out-migration, or emigration, was another important aspect of nineteenth-century population mobility. Between about

Finland	Iceland	Norway	Sweden
.83 million	47,000	.88 million	2.35 million
1.64 million	59,000	1.49 million	3.5 million
2.66 million	78,000	2.24 million	5.14 million
3.2 million	—	2.4 million	5.5 million

1830 and 1930 almost 3 million Scandinavians left their homelands to settle in other parts of Europe and overseas, including about 200,000 Danes and a similar number of Finns, 20,000 Icelanders, 800,000 Norwegians, and 1.3 million Swedes. Although the most important recipient of these emigrants was the United States, they also settled in Canada, parts of South America and South Africa, and even as far away as Australia.

They left for a variety of reasons that are often categorized into those that "pushed" them from their homelands and those that "pulled" them to the recipient countries. Foremost among the push factors were the economic and social problems related to the rural population growth outlined above. In simple terms, opportunities

Urbanization

City	Population in 1800	Population in 1900
Bergen	18,000	80,000
Christiania/Oslo	10,000	250,000
Copenhagen	104,000	370,000
Esbjerg	c. 30	13,000
Göteborg	12,800	130,600
Malmö	4,000	61,000
Stockholm	75,000	300,000

were limited and social and economic degradation common. For many, their situations seemed hopeless. Religious push factors included discontent with the existing state-controlled Lutheran churches and an internally based Pietist revival. Sectarian missionary activities by Methodists, Baptists, and Mormons were important, especially in the early phases of the migration. In addition, the hierarchic social systems, with their rigidity and the demeaning behavioral expectations they imposed on the lower classes, as well as the undemocratic political systems that excluded most commoners, growing military service demands on young men, and a host of personal reasons influenced the decisions of the emigrants. To a degree, the pull factors were the opposites of the above: economic opportunities (cheap land or better-paying jobs), religious freedom, more genuine democracy, more open societies, and the chance to start over. In addition, once early settlements were established, they acted as magnets on prospective emigrants. Several facilitating factors also contributed. One was the flow of information carried by the newspapers, books, and pamphlets circulated in the Nordic countries; emigration agents; and letters from emigrants. Another was the availability of transportation. The mass migration was big business, and by the late nineteenth century, steamship and railroad companies competed intensely for the emigrants' traffic. One estimate is that 55 million people left Europe as emigrants or labor migrants between 1830 and World War II. It is easy, however, to overanalyze and remove the human aspect from emigration. Every decision was a personal one. In the early stages, before regular steamship traffic across the Atlantic was established in the 1870s, it meant probably never returning to one's home, never again seeing those who stayed behind. Although the decision became less permanent over time, it must have remained a difficult one for many.

This "great exodus" began with the departure of relatively small groups. For the Norwegians it was the fifty-two "sloopers" who left Stavanger in 1825 and settled first in Kendall, New York. Within a few years, however, most had moved on to an area along the Fox River in Illinois, about seventy-miles southwest of Chicago. Although there were earlier settlers, some see a starting point for Swedish emigration in the departure of revivalist Erik Jansson and his followers, who founded the communal settlement of Bishop Hill in western Illinois in 1846. Danes, Finns, and Icelanders came somewhat later. Following these and many other pioneer beginnings around the mid–nineteenth century the rate of emigration varied and depended on conditions at home and in the receiving countries. Peaks in the flow came in the late 1860s, the early 1880s, the early 1900s, and just after World War I.

In the early stages, the emigrants tended to leave as male-led groups of families, and their goal was to make new lives as farmers on the frontier. By the 1880s more and more of the emigrants left alone or in small groups of unrelated individuals. Their destinations were increasingly urban, and their goals were employment centered. Some of these later migrants crisscrossed the Atlantic several times during their working lives as members of an international labor market. Throughout the emigration period women were involved, and their motives and experiences make up an important chapter in the history of emigration.

In their new homelands some of these immigrants quickly took on the prevailing language and customs and vanished into the mainstream society. For many others, however, this highly varied and individualistic process took a generation or two—sometimes even longer—and might involve a changing degree of assimilation depending on age or circumstances. All the Scandinavians, in patterns repeated by other immigrant groups and in other times and places, established complex and constantly evolving immigrant or "hyphenated" cultures (Danish American, Finnish American, etc.). These cultures evolved out of the personal encounters of the immigrants with the new culture, but they also were, and continue to be, consciously shaped by leaders of the respective ethnic groups—some of whom, like the Norwegian immigrant author Ole Rølvaag, firmly believed that links with the homeland had to be maintained. The defining aspects of the Scandinavian-immigrant cultures were many.

For decades and sometimes longer, the immigrants maintained spatially definable rural and urban communities. Usually, each one was made up of immigrants from one of the Nordic countries—but from many different localities in that country. This was particularly true of most urban communities. Some rural settlements, however, were very homogeneous and were based on immigrants from a few parishes or a small region in the homeland.

The immigrants quickly established their own churches, and their clergy, many of whom were staunch advocates of holding on to the homeland cultures, provided group leadership for several generations. Lutherans predominated, and for almost a century the Danes, Finns, Icelanders, Norwegians, and Swedes had their own synods in America. Nordic immigrants also founded other ethnic-specific churches or congregations within larger denominations. There were several variants of mainstream Lutheranism, as well as Nordic-based Baptist, Methodist, Presbyterian congregations and Salvation Army corps. These churches provided their services in the native language for a generation or more. In the United States the language use came under attack during World War I, declined in the 1920s and 1930s, and then gradually vanished following World War II. They also were vitally important in providing schools, colleges, hospitals, homes for the elderly, orphanages, and other service institutions. Many of these institutions survived into the late twentieth century and continued to preserve and celebrate some measure of their ethnic identities. Among them were over a dozen colleges.

Secular organizations were also important parts of the ethnic communities, and their range is remarkable. Some were built around common interests, such as singing, dramatics, gymnastics, marching, or cycling. Others were based on occupation and included ethnic-based trade unions and professional organizations. There were also fraternal aid societies, which offered members sickness or death benefits as well as comradeship, and clubs based on the provincial origins of members. Important in the creation and preservation of ethnic identities were historical societies such as the Norwegian-American Historical Association (1925) and the Swedish-American Historical Society (1948).

Serious and popular entertainment media also helped define and sustain the ethnic populations. Theater groups staged productions of plays by Ibsen or Strindberg. There were also immigrant playwrights who wrote specifically about and for immigrant audiences. The less serious theater involved an ethnic vaudeville, and each Nordic group had its popular entertainers whose tours brought comedy, song, and melodrama to enclaves across North America until the mid–twentieth century. At the same time, a calendar of celebrations of identity evolved. Some of these were specifically homeland based, such as the Swedes' Lucia festivals in December or the Norwegians' seventeenth of May fests. Others were created within the ethnic communities and often merged with American or other host country celebrations.

Another important definer and preserver of ethnic identity was the press, dominated by an articulate elite whose members often had specific outlooks to present and foster. Hundreds of newspapers, usually weeklies, were published, and all of them had a political or religious viewpoint as well as an ethnic character. Most appeared in the native language, at least until the 1920s. Only a few survived into the last decade of the twentieth century. The magazines were equally biased. Most appeared monthly or quarterly and also were targeted at a specific sector of the immigrant population. Some were designed for women. Books were often reprints of works first published in Scandinavia; histories, editions of national romantic poetry, and religious tracts were particularly common. At the same time, a large and important body of ethnic literature developed. Immigrant authors addressed their experiences in novels, short stories, poems, and plays. Some of them, such as Ole Rølvaag or the Dane Sophus Winther, established a canon of the immigrant experience that has been difficult to move beyond.

Late-twentieth-century Scandinavian immigrant identities contained some of these early elements. There were still some rural and urban ethnic communities. Individuals and a few organizations continued to use the languages, and younger generations showed some interest in learning them. Most of the press was gone, and only a few newspapers remained. Although congregations continued to nurture their ethnic roots, the synods had, for the most part, merged into larger national units. There were fewer organizations, but this side of Nordic ethnic life continued to be vital and appeared to have a future. These groups played important parts in preserving the heritages of the immigrants and continuing the celebrations and cultural customs.

Important in fostering continued ethnic identity in America was a late-twentieth-century revival among early immigrant groups including the Scandinavians. This began in the 1960s, perhaps in response to the rise of the civil rights movement. It was sustained by the arrival of new immigrants to America and the continued importance of nationalism globally. The new ethnicity was and is a complex phenomenon with many forms. For some it meant a naive attachment to a romanticized, uncritical, and often error-ridden view of the past. National heroes like Gustavus Adolphus, long debunked in the Nordic countries, remained heroes, and dubious evidence of Viking presence in the middle of the country was accepted without question. Myths abounded. Foods no longer popular in Scandinavia and celebrations oddly modified persisted. The descendants of emigrants who had fled the political oppression of kings and nobles scrambled to be parts of royal visits. Organizations on the edge of extinction revived and numerous new ones developed.

On the other hand, there was a more serious and critical side to the revival. A whole new generation of professional historians in Scandinavia and America, many trained since the 1970s, contributed new perspectives on the Nordic immigrant experiences. Popular interest in family history and genealogy was extensive. Interest in the study of the Nordic languages, literatures, histories, and contemporary societies sustained several college and university programs as well as the educational programs of organizations and institutions. For many, then, identity was with contemporary Scandinavia, not with the past.

The great migration had many impacts on the Nordic countries. Obviously, it siphoned off what was for a time surplus population that could not be absorbed by the existing economic base. One estimate, for example, is that emigration offset half of Norway's population growth. More than sheer numbers were involved. One "positive" aspect was the use of emigration to get rid of political radicals or other undesirable persons—as in the case of Danish officials sending Louis Pio, the founder of the Socialist movement, off to America, or in the case of Marcus Thrane, who emigrated after spending several years in prison. As emigration increasingly involved returns to the homeland and became for many an avenue of temporary employment or education, it also served as a two-way avenue of capital, intellectual, cultural, religious, and political transfer. Scandinavian migrants invested in their homelands, and they brought back to them many new ideas, technologies, and organizational models. The exodus also had its negative sides, including the loss of labor resources, customers, talent, and potential soldiers. Although these negatives aroused heated opposition to emigration, opponents were never able to put a stop to it.

Economic Transformations

Between about 1850 and World War I, all the Nordic countries underwent profound economic changes including a decline in the importance of agriculture (except in Denmark) and an offsetting increase in the importance of primary sectors (raw materials) and an industrial sector based on one or a few fundamental core industries. Accompanying these changes were other developments that are often used to define the term *industrial revolution*. These included changes in business organization and management systems, enterprise finance bases, banking, production techniques, machinery, power sources, communications, locational patterns, social classes, gender roles, political and interest groups, and political agenda. Among the key symbols of the industrial revolution were the steam engine, the railroad, the joint-stock company, the entrepreneur, the factory, the time clock, the industrial working class, the trade union, and the slum. All these applied to the countries of Norden—in varying degrees. The region was fundamentally changed in the span of about seventy-five years. Although not fully "modern, urban, and industrial," the Nordic countries were certainly becoming so by World War I.

Denmark

Denmark's nineteenth-century economic transformation was unique among the Nordic countries because of the central importance played by agriculture. It was agriculture that became industrial in the last third of the century, and the changes stimulated many other essential economic and social developments including urbanization and the growth of an industrial manufacturing sector producing for the home market.

The transformation of Danish agriculture was, to a degree, prepared for by the reforms of the late eighteenth century (see chapter 6), which had helped develop a class of farmers with small- and medium-sized holdings. This process was furthered by the decline of commodity prices following the Napoleonic Wars, which encouraged some large holders to sell portions of their estates to leaseholders. Strong prices, chiefly for grain exports, and free trade sustained small and large farmers from the 1840s to the 1870s. At the same time, state educational reforms and the growth of the folk high school movement helped make rural Danes better informed, less parochial, and more willing to risk change.

Grain prices collapsed in the 1870s in the face of falling transportation costs and North American and Russian competition. In response, Danish farmers shifted to dairy, cattle, hog, and livestock feed production. The principal exports became butter, cheese, and bacon. To accomplish this change, Danish farmers adopted the concept of cooperation. The first dairy cooperative was founded in Hjedding in Jutland in 1882. Within a decade there were some 700; by World War I, there were about 1,200. The earliest cooperative slaughter operation came in 1887 at Horsens. These agricultural factories involved shared resources (and risks), product standardization, quality control, and management centralization. In addition, farmers established cooperative purchasing societies and retail stores. According to some, the specialization and cooperativization of Danish farming also contributed to a return to new variants of village-based agricultural communities. Technological innovations were also important in this overall transformation, including the cream separator, refrigeration, new agricultural machines, and the constant expansion of international markets—especially England, which absorbed well over half of Denmark's growing production.

The direct results of these changes were remarkable. Between 1874 and 1914, milk production rose from 1.15 million tons to 3.34 million tons, butter from 38,000 tons to 110,000, and pork from 50,000 tons to 210,000. The value of agricultural exports rose by almost five times in the same period. This increase translated into a period of prosperity for some sectors of Denmark's rural population, especially the medium and large landowners. Few got rich, but many did very well.

Indirectly, the changes in agriculture helped precipitate changes elsewhere in the economy and society. Agriculture's development involved greater efficiency and use of new technology. Labor demands fell, and the output increases were actually accomplished by a diminishing rural population. Some of that surplus population moved into towns and cities, some emigrated. Rural prosperity increased the demand for consumer goods, which triggered the growth of craft and industrial production and the expansion of the retail sector. Transportation needs stimulated the building of railroads and port development. Although the country's first rail line from Copenhagen to Roskilde opened in 1847, the first real boom in construction came in the 1870s when the principal east-west and north-south lines were laid—in all about 900 kilometers. The system was largely complete by World War I. At the west terminus of the system linking Copenhagen with Jutland was Esbjerg, a town of thirty people in 1870. It became the principal port for trade with England, and in 1901 had a population of over 13,000.

The core sectors of a broader and relatively complex industrial economy were also established in this period. Although never a dominant factor in this process, the production of textiles, especially cotton, and clothing increased. Drawing on the country's limestone resources, quarrying expanded and a cement industry developed. The sugar industry, based largely on imports from the West Indies, also grew. The changes in the production of beer in Copenhagen provide an interesting story—one that illustrates a pattern common to many

Carl Frederik Tietgen

One of the people most responsible for Denmark's economic transformation was Carl Frederik Tietgen (1829–1901). Born in Odense, he spent almost seven years in Manchester, England, where he was strongly influenced by the ideas of economic liberalism and the pace of economic development. Back in Copenhagen in 1855, he became an export agent and quickly made an impression on several powerful city merchants. In 1857 he was appointed director of the newly founded Privatbanken (The private bank), an institution that played a leading role in enterprise formation. Under Tietgen's leadership for the next forty years, the bank supported the growth of all of the central sectors of the country's early industrialization including railroads, telecommunications, shipping, international commerce, brewing and distilling, sugar refining, banking, and the establishment of a new "free harbor" in Copenhagen. One source calls him Denmark's first modern capitalist.

of these sectors. Down to midcentury, brewing was in the hands of many small producers. It was decentralized, tradition-bound, and unscientific. Jacob Christian Jacobsen (1811–87) changed all this. In the 1870s the founder of Carlsberg introduced German lager to the Danes, concentrated production in a few large breweries, and made brewing a scientific enterprise. A small high-technology sector also developed, specializing in ship engines and other maritime products. Burmeister and Wain was the most important company in this field.

Finland
Finland was, to a considerable degree, the Nordic country that did not go through an industrial transformation in this period, although important foundations were laid for later developments. In 1870, 80 percent of the Finns were engaged in agriculture; forty years later 66 percent were. If one takes into account population growth, there were actually more people in the agricultural sector in 1910 than in 1870. Only about 350,000 were employed in industries. Nonetheless, there were important economic changes, many of which were forced on the country first by the virtual free trade that existed with Russia from

1859 to 1885 and then by the closure of that market. After 1885 Finns had to find new markets, develop new products, and improve the quality of their goods in order to compete.

The country's grain-based agriculture underwent a production specialization shift in the 1870s similar to that in Denmark. Unable to compete with foreign grains in the export markets, Finnish farmers turned to dairy products, especially butter, which became the single-most important agricultural export. At the same time, the importance of Finland's forest resources grew and soon became the predominant export sector. Steam engine–driven saws were introduced around 1860, and the output of lumber increased by a factor of five over the next two decades. A boom in the 1870s led to further growth. Britain was the principal market. At the same time, a paper pulp industry selling chiefly to the Russians developed. In 1914 forest products accounted for 70 percent of all of Finland's exports. Of less importance were the textile, mining, and engineering sectors. The last was largely limited to machines for the forest products industry. Railroad building began in earnest in the 1870s. The first line opened in 1862, and six years later the link between Helsinki and St. Petersburg was finished. By World War I, Finland had about 2,600 miles of lines. The country's internal communications system also benefited from the building of new roads, an extensive canal system, and steam-powered boats. The earliest commercial bank dates from 1862.

Despite these changes, the country remained overwhelmingly rural and agrarian until well into the twentieth century. External developments were the principal agents of change, not internal ones. The middle class remained tiny. Capital resources were limited.

Norway

Until the mid–nineteenth century Norway's economy was overwhelmingly agrarian and, because of geography and poor communications, highly localized. The country's economic transformation down to World War I rested more on an expanded service sector and especially shipping than on industry, although significant growth in several areas including forest products, fishing, and electro-chemicals did occur in the late 1880s, the late 1890s, and around World War I.

At midcentury the agrarian sector was inefficient and principally subsistence based. Its most important export was emigrants. As happened elsewhere in Norden, Norwegian farmers were forced to shift from grain growing to dairy and livestock production and to raising oats and other fodder crops. Increasingly, horses were used for farm work, as machines dependent on them became available. Norway also witnessed the development of agricultural cooperatives. As was the case in earlier times, most farmers in Norway had two occupations: farmer-fisherman, farmer-forester, farmer-timber cutter, etc.

A small textile sector developed after about 1840 but was badly hurt by the ending of the "common market" between Sweden and Norway in 1897. The growth of more concentrated production of clothing, tobacco products, and alcoholic beverages was also important. Shipbuilding witnessed both growth and the consolidation of smaller firms. Forest products were Norway's most important exports. As in Finland and Sweden, production centered on sawed lumber products until the 1870s. Thereafter, the paper and pulp divisions expanded rapidly and replaced lumber as the primary export shortly after 1900.

Throughout this period fish remained Norway's second most important export, and the industry entered into a period of significant modernization. Although small sailboat fishing predominated, some larger steam-driven vessels came into use. More important was the development of gasoline engines, which were added to the small-boat fleets after 1900 and vastly increased the range of operations and their safety. Fishing became a year-round activity, and the variety of catches and products increased to include fish meal, various types of herring, and tinned sardines.

Some progress was made in improving communications and knitting the country together as a unit. Norway's first railroad line, between Eidsvoll and Christiania, opened in 1854 and was used to carry timber down to the capital. Thereafter, however, building slowed. A link between the capital and central Sweden was completed in 1879, and the Christiania-Trondheim line opened a year later. The line between Bergen and Christiania was not finished until 1909. The development of regular, year-round steamship service along the coast was also important and was initiated in 1893, when regular traffic between Trondheim and Hammerfest was begun by the Vesteraalen Steamship Company, led by Richard With. Gradually, service on the "Coastal Express" (Hurtigruten) was extended south to Bergen and north to Kirkenes, and it continues to play important roles in the economy carrying goods, mail, passengers, and tourists.

Toward the close of the century important growth occurred in hydroelectrical power generation and in several industries that drew on this power, especially electrochemicals and electrometals. Kristian Birkeland and Sam Eyde developed a process for producing potassium nitrate using electricity and established the basis for Norway's fertilizer industry. Imported technologies were used to refine aluminum. Norsk Hydro, established in 1905, became the core of this sector. Output increased eight times between 1900 and 1905 alone, and by 1909 there were seventeen hydroelectric-based factories.

Shipping was the most important single element in the Norway's economy. It accounted for one-third or more of annual export earnings. Several crucial developments occurred during this period. First, the overall size of the fleet grew from about 320,000 tons in 1852 to over 1.8 million tons in 1914. Second, there was a gradual transition from sail to steam, which began in the mid-1880s and continued into the 1920s. Third, as capital costs increased, a growing number of joint-stock companies were established. Related to these changes were the conversion of the Norwegian shipbuilding industry to steamship production and extensive consolidation.

Most of Norway's development was driven by external factors: demand for products and transportation, technologies, and capital. Original inventions were few, the banking system highly localized, and expertise lacking. Great Britain was Norway's most important customer. Capital flowed into Norway from Britain, France, Germany, and Canada. The extent of this reached alarming proportions in the early 1900s. Nearly 80 percent of the mining sector was foreign-owned, for example. This situation resulted in the passage of legislation before World War I designed to curb foreign ownership, and the trend was significantly reversed during the war.

Sweden

In the mid–nineteenth century, Sweden was also an overwhelmingly rural and agrarian country. In 1870 nearly three-quarters of all Swedes still earned their livings in farming. Forty years later, this figure was just under half. By World War I, almost a third of all workers were employed in industry. A quarter of all Swedes lived in towns and cities. Industrial products accounted for 35 percent of all exports. The gross national product was three times what it had been in 1860. Per capita income had risen 2.3 times. In three periods of accelerated development, the 1850s, the 1870s, and the 1890s, Sweden underwent some of the most remarkable changes in its history and was well on its way to becoming one of the industrial nations of the West.

Six patterns define the development of Sweden's agricultural sector during the nineteenth century. First, the amount of land under cultivation increased from about 344,000 acres in 1800 to about 1.3 million in 1900, as common woodlands, pastures, and forests owned by farmers were converted, lowlands were drained, and new areas in the north were developed. Second, farming became more scientific, with developments leading to better seeds, improved animal breeding, and more intensive soil management practices. Third, farming became more dependent on technology and less labor intensive. New horse-drawn machines including plows, reapers, and mowers meant that fewer farmers could produce more food. These developments amplified the rural population problems and helped sustain high levels of emigration. Fourth, farmers had to be well informed if they were to succeed. To meet these needs, an agricultural college was founded in 1811. In addition, rural associations were set up throughout the country to provide education, information, and expert services. Fifth, adaptation and specialization occurred as Swedish farmers worked to meet changing market realities. As elsewhere in Norden, the flood of American grain that reached world markets in the 1870s created a crisis, and many Swedish farmers reoriented their operations. The familiar shift from grain growing to livestock raising and dairy production was one option. Other farmers turned to raising sugar beets. However, grain production continued to be important, and efforts were made in the 1880s to protect farmers with tariffs on imported grains. In the long run, the tariffs and later quota programs only served to postpone finding real solutions to the problems of grain-raising farmers. Finally, farming became less a subsistence enterprise and more a profit-oriented one that demanded capital as well as know-how. A winnowing out of the inefficient was a by-product of this trend and contributed to further decline in the size of the rural population.

Sweden's iron industry, historically so important, went through several important changes driven by market demands and technological developments. New iron production techniques were gradually adopted. The Bessemer process came into use at the end of the 1850s, introduced into Sweden by G. F. Göransson, founder of Sandviken. More important were the Martin-Gilchrist and Thomas processes. The latter was particularly vital to Sweden, because it specifically allowed for the use of the country's high phosphorous ore in the production of steel. The new processes also called for significant capital outlays and other rationalization steps. For centuries steel was made using charcoal. This was costly, slow, and made Swedish steel less competitive despite any qualitative edge. In addition, using charcoal became less feasible as new demands were placed on the country's forests. Coal, coke, and electricity gradually replaced charcoal in most foundries. Another important trend was concentration. The number of foundries fell from around four hundred at midcentury to just over two hundred in 1900 and to seventy-four in 1933, and most of the industry was dominated by a few large concerns including Finspång, Sandviken, Bofors, and Domnarvet. Finally, iron ore became an increasingly important sector of the industry. Export was prohibited until the 1850s and grew slowly until the closing years of the century. By World War I iron ore accounted for about 10 percent of Sweden's export trade.

The development in Sweden's forest products sector resembles that in Finland and Norway. Sawed lumber became increasingly important after 1850, when steam engine–driven saws allowed the location of mills near port facilities. Logs were now floated to the mills. The depletion of Norwegian forest reserves provided added impetus to the development of this industry. The pulp and paper industries emerged in the last third of the century in response to world demand and technological advances including C. D. Ekman's work on the sulfite process for producing high quality paper for printing. By World War I this industry accounted for almost 18 percent of the country's exports.

One of the most unique aspects of Sweden's development in this period was the growth of production sectors for the domestic industrial and consumer markets. Sweden's economy became the most diverse in Norden. On the one hand, this diversity involved the growth of an important engineering/machine tool sector. Machines (locomotives, rail cars, steam engines, and the like) were imported in the early stages of the economic transformation. Quickly, however, the Swedes came to produce their own—often copied—industrial machines. Another important industrial sector that expanded in the 1890s concentrated on the manufacture of domestic products including textiles, clothing, shoes, housewares, etc. Only in Denmark did a similar sector emerge in this period. At the same time, the output of consumer goods by craftspeople or artisans also increased.

Several factors helped bring about these changes. The growth of a multifaceted education system that included general compulsory schools from 1842 and specialized technical institutions contributed to an essential adaptability and level of creativity. During the periods of greatest growth, export market demands were high and Swedish products enjoyed high prices, while import prices were relatively low. Foreign capital was available, and venture-oriented banks with sufficient capital, such as A. O. Wallenberg's Stockholms Enskilda Bank (founded in 1856), were established, which encouraged and sustained economic development. Export earnings allowed for capital investment and for improved incomes, which contributed to the growth of a manufacturing sector aimed at the internal market. In addition, Sweden's infrastructure boasted the most extensive railroad system in Norden—almost 11,000 kilometers by 1900—which connected principal population centers like Stockholm and Göteborg and opened up remote parts of the country like the far north. Planning for this system began in the late 1840s, and the first line opened in 1856. Its construction reflected another aspect of Sweden's economic development: state involvement. In this case, the main lines were financed by the government; loans to private developers helped pay for the branch system. Another aspect of state involvement was the introduction of import tariffs on a wide range of agricultural and industrial products after 1888. Finally, Sweden was fortunate to have many extraordinarily talented inventors and entrepreneurs.

Social Classes/New Societies

Inseparably linked to the demographic and economic developments of this period was the emergence of a more complex and mobile society in which classes based on incomes and occupations were superimposed on the old estates based on birth or status. Unquestionably, the noble, church, bureaucratic, agricultural, and other estate-based elites remained important in this period (and they continue to be important down to the present). However, as the economies changed, so too did the groupings within the Nordic societies, and with these transformations came new hierarchies with their own haves and have-nots. Among these developments were a number of themes. First, for much of the century many rural areas were in states of almost unending crisis because of the unprecedented growth of population and the strains it imposed on a limited agricultural base. Second, the working population became larger, more diverse, and more mobile. Third, only gradually did an industrial

Inventors and Entrepreneurs

Carl Daniel Ekman (1845–1904). Developed a sulfite papermaking process in 1872 and revolutionized the Swedish forest products sector.

John Ericsson (1803–89). Active for many years in England and America, invented a locomotive, the screw propeller, the "Monitor" class of naval ships, turbines, and many other machines.

Lars Magnus Ericsson (1846–1926). Invented a telephone and other communications equipment and founded L. M. Ericsson AB.

Göran Fredrik Göransson (1819–1920). Introduced the Bessemer process to Sweden in 1857, founded Sandviken AB in 1866, and was a major figure in the rationalization and modernization of iron and steel production.

Alexander Lagerman (1836–1904). Developed machines dedicated to the manufacture of safety matches.

Gustaf De Laval (1845–1913). Invented a centrifugal cream separator, other dairy production devices, and a steam turbine. Founder of Separator AB.

Alfred Nobel (1833–96). Held thirty-three patents on products including dynamite and smokeless gunpowder. Founder of Nobel Industries. His will established the Nobel Prizes.

André Oscar Wallenberg (1816–82). Founded Stockholms Enskilda Bank and was a dedicated advocate of venture financing.

Sven Winquist (1876–1953). Developed a process to manufacture ball bearings and founded Svenska Kullagerfabriken/SKF in 1907.

working class emerge to absorb the rural population surpluses. Fourth, traditional economic groups, such as artisans and itinerant merchants, saw their places in the economic order threatened. Fifth, the formerly small middle class became larger and more complex. Sixth, professional and service segments of the societies grew. Finally, traditional

roles, attitudes, legal situations, and opportunities for women were radically altered.

The rapid growth of Norden's population, limited expansion pos-
sibilities, and the gradual decline in human labor needs in the agricultural sector led to a polarization of the rural society. On the one hand,
many landowners witnessed improvements in their situations, especially if they were among those who adapted to the changing market
conditions of the period. Sharing in this prosperity were many renters
who were able to purchase their leaseholds, often from nobles wishing to reduce the size of their estates as part of rationalization efforts.
A farming bourgeoisie in each of the Nordic countries enjoyed relative economic affluence, social prestige, and political influence.

This heyday of the middle-sized farm owner was not shared across
rural society. Owners of smaller, less viable farms or farms in less
productive regions were certainly left out. So, too, was the ever-
growing rural proletariat: the cottagers who exchanged their labor
for leases on tiny plots on the fringes of farms, the young men and
women who worked in the homes and fields of landowners on contracts, and the landless itinerant workers—a group virtually nonexistent a century earlier. These groups were made up of the sons and
daughters of every rural social group. In Sweden this agricultural proletariat grew from just over half a million in 1775 to 1.29 million in
1870—about one-quarter of the population. It was from this pool of
rural poor that many of the workers (men and women) in the developing urban and rural industries, as well as tens of thousands of emigrants, came.

An industrial working class emerged in this period, but its size varied widely across Norden. By World War I it accounted for about a
third of Sweden's workforce (over a million people), versus about 28
percent in Norway and less in Denmark, Finland, and Iceland. As
was so typical across Europe in the industrial revolution, this group
suffered from low wages and poor working conditions. Its growth
contributed to the explosion of urban populations, and most workers lived in slums. Industry-based trade unions were established,
mostly from the 1880s, and national union federations were organized around the turn of the century. Counterpart employers' federations developed at the same time. In Denmark a basic agreement was
reached between these two cornerstones in 1899, which guaranteed
certain rights to workers and employers and established a foundation

for negotiations. Workers' political parties, ideologically rooted in the socialist movement of the period, were founded in 1876 in Denmark, 1899 in Finland, 1916 in Iceland, 1885 in Norway, and 1889 in Sweden. Together the trade unions and socialist parties contributed to some gains for the working class in terms of wages, working conditions, the right to organize and strike, and political representation down to World War I, but much remained to be accomplished.

Less fraught with confrontation, but no less important, was the growth and diversification of the middle class. Spread across a hierarchy of status, this involved increases in the number of entrepreneurs, industrialists, managers, professionals, retailers, secretaries, clerks, and bureaucrats. They, too, soon had their own interest organizations and political parties.

Women and Women's Rights

The demographic revolution was not gender selective, and although the impacts varied widely in geographic distribution and in how the various social classes were affected, the economic, social, intellectual, and political developments of this period brought important changes in the roles, behavioral norms, status, educational and career opportunities, and legal and political rights of women. The first real women's movement(s) also took shape during this period. They were led, on the one hand, by articulate bourgeois women through a group of organizations and defined by its activities and publications, and, on the other, by working-class women working mostly through trade unions and the new socialist parties. Their achievements included winning important legal and political rights.

In the economic sphere, the complementarity that had characterized the relationships between men and women on the farm and in the production and delivery of goods for centuries was eroded. Rationalized and mechanized farming depended less and less on the work of women. Goods production shifted from the craft shop to the factory, delivery from the shop to the retail store. The family unit, which had been central to these two sectors, was often broken up and roles redefined, and in both women became less economically essential, more homebound, and less important. At the same time, women lost part of their importance in the education of children, as public schools took over. Adult, married women, regardless of social class, were to keep house and tend to the emotional well-being of the family.

An extreme illustration of this situation, coupled with a male-dominated system that denied women legal equality, can be seen in Henrik Ibsen's play *A Doll's House* (1879), which concerned women's issues, social norms, expectations, personal development, and late-nineteenth-century (Norwegian) bourgeois society.

What options were there in the changing economic sphere for women? Unmarried, usually young working-class women joined in the complex regional, rural to urban, internal European, and overseas employment and migration processes. Within this mobile world, choices for women were limited. Thousands found work as urban domestics—an option sustained by the urban and middle-class growth and by a bourgeois society in which one measure of success was the number of domestic servants employed. (For middle-class women, this last trend removed them further from traditional functions in the home, as housework, child care, cooking, and the like were parceled out to domestic help. Compensating for this were increased expectations vis-à-vis household management and greater free time.) Also important were growing employment opportunities in certain industries including textiles, clothing, tobacco, confections, food processing, and safety matches. Only gradually, as the economic, technological, educational, and retailing infrastructures changed, did new opportunities develop in retail (as clerks), in telecommunications (as operators), in business (as secretaries), in medicine (as nurses), and in education (as teachers). In all these areas, women constantly encountered wage inequalities, exploitation, and limits on advancement. The professional woman was rare indeed, and until the close of this period most professions and government jobs were closed to women. If not always the reality, certainly the expectation was that employment should occupy only a brief period in a woman's life between childhood and marriage.

Hampering any progress for women was the slow development of educational opportunities. Compulsory elementary school laws excluded girls until late in the century (1886 in Denmark, for example). In rural areas the home was the school for girls. In urban areas, private schools provided some educational opportunities. In general, women simply were not expected to get an education, and this attitude changed only very slowly.

Change did come in the last few decades of the century. After about 1860, teaching seminaries were founded, and gradually the universities opened their doors to women. Sweden's parliament made it legal for women to pursue degrees in the arts and medicine in 1865, but university authorities remained opposed. In 1870 women were to be allowed to take the entrance exam in medicine and, if they passed, to study for a degree. In 1873 all fields were opened to them except theology and law. The first woman student enrolled that year. The first doctorate was awarded to Ellen Fries ten years later. By 1910, 8 percent of the 2,000 students at Uppsala were women. In Copenhagen similar events occurred. Twenty-four-year-old Nielsine Nielsen (1850–1916) applied to the Ministry of Religion and Education for permission to study medicine in 1874. Her request went through a labyrinth of reviews before being granted by the medical faculty. Even then it was another three years before she and Johanne Marie Gleerup passed the entrance exam and were admitted. Nielsen graduated in 1885, later obtained specialist training in gynecology in Switzerland, and remained active in the women's movement for the rest of her life. Typically, the vociferous opponents of women's admittance to the universities saw them as denying their nature, rejecting their expected roles as mothers and wives, and as morally indecent. The critics believed women had no place in the universities.

As important as the developments in employment opportunities and education were the advances women made on the legal and political fronts. When the century began, women were not considered the legal equals of men, were rarely protected by legal guarantees, and had no direct political influence. They were almost always under the domination of a male, whether father, husband, or legal guardian. Women never reached an age of legal independence. Their inheritance shares were smaller than men's; their rights to own property were restricted. Their incomes, material possessions, and children belonged to men. These legal realities defined their lives, their options, and the predominant attitudes toward them. It was believed they were intellectually and physically inferior, licentious, ruled by their emotions, and unable to understand financial matters. A women's place was in the home—a world of the kitchen, the children, and the church.

Of course, as we have already seen, realities often contradicted the world of women as it was legally and societally defined. What was different about the nineteenth century, however, was that the number of voices of protest increased, and thoughts and laws changed. The status of women and their lack of legal rights became issues of discussion. The new voices defined a body of literature and the development of organizations that attacked the situation and helped bring about reform.

From the 1830s on writers across Scandinavia addressed aspects of the growing "woman's question" in their work. Swedish author Carl Jonas Almqvist (1793–1866) attacked the oppressive nature of the male-dominated marriage of the period in *Det går an* (It can be done) in 1838. He advocated marriage as a union of equals, and his work unleashed an acrimonious debate and scathing criticism from the establishment. Another Swede, Frederika Bremer (1801–65), argued for greater equality in marriage in *Hemmet* (The home) in 1839, but supported the idea of the family as the critical unit in society. In a later novel, *Hertha* (1856), she attacked men's oppression of women and the patriarchy and called for equality. Bremer is generally regarded as the founder of the women's movement in Sweden, and she is seen as the first in a continuing series of important Swedish women writers. In Norway, Camilla (Wergeland) Collett (1813–95) played a similar role. Her novel, *Amtmandens Døtre* (The governor's daughters) (1855) also attacked the patriarchy and its ideals for women. She advocated women's rights to love, to their own lives, to legal equality, and to work, and helped set the women's rights movement in motion in Norway. In Denmark, Mathilde Fibiger (1830–72) opened the assault on traditional norms and expectations in 1850 in *Tolv Breve* (Twelve letters), written under the pseudonym Clara Raphael. She argued for women's inner freedom—for women's right to personal lives of their own. Taken by many as an attack on marriage, her work unleashed another storm of controversy. It also stimulated a response from Pauline Worm (1825–83), another of Denmark's early feminists, who argued in *Fire Breve om Clara Raphael til en ung Pige fra hendes Söster* (Four letters on Clara Raphael to a young girl from her sister) that material gains would have to be achieved before any personal emancipation occurred.

As interesting and important as the works of these early Scandinavian feminists are their biographies, which reflect clearly the strength of their characters and the limitations women faced in this period. Bremer was born in Finland and grew up in Stockholm, one of seven children in an upper-middle-class family. During her life she traveled widely in Scandinavia, Europe, and America and was the author of novels, travelogues, and articles. Collett grew up in a hothouse of intellectual activity, punctuated by cultural feuding and romantic disappointment. Her marriage to Peter Collett was based on cooperation,

Nordic Women's Organizations

Danish Women's Society, 1871
Norwegian Feminist Society, 1884
(Norwegian) Women's Suffrage Union, 1898
(Norwegian) National Women's Suffrage Union, 1898
Finnish Women's Association, 1884
Icelandic Women's Association, 1894
(Swedish) Society for Married Women's Property Rights, 1873
Frederika Bremer Society, 1884
(Swedish) National Association for Women's Suffrage, 1902

not love. Her writing career blossomed after her husband's death in 1851. Fibiger, the daughter of an army officer, spent most of her life in poverty. Her writing career was brief and earned her little besides a small annual allowance from the dowager queen, Caroline Amalie (Christian VIII's widow). To earn a living she taught school for a short time and worked as a seamstress. She also became Denmark's first woman telegraph operator in 1863. Worm's writing career spanned over two decades and was linked to a life as a teacher and supporter of education for girls.

From the last quarter of the century each of the Nordic countries witnessed the founding of organizations that focused on women's rights issues. These were primarily controlled by middle-class women —who had the free time to become involved in the issues. Working-class women tended to give their time to labor union and socialist political party activities and to be more concerned with work-related issues including wages and working conditions. Both types of organizations contributed to the important gains made by women during this period, which redefined their legal positions, brought women into the political processes as voters and potential candidates, expanded their educational and career opportunities, and contributed to the development of new societal attitudes about women.

Throughout the struggle to achieve these gains women met resistance from men and from other women. The success of their work rests on at least two bases. First, because of the losses women experienced in their own importance within the family, as their contributions to the economy of the household and their roles in education

Legal Gains for Women in Sweden

1845	Equal inheritance
1846	End of guild privileges
1852	Improved women's and children's working conditions
1853	Right to teach in elementary schools
1858	Single women's right to declare legal independence at age twenty-five
1861	Founding of women's teacher training seminaries
1862	Suffrage in communal elections
1864	Equal rights to work in artisan crafts
1870	Right to take university admissions exams
1884	Legal age lowered to twenty-one
1909	Women could serve on municipal councils
1919	Equal pay for women in state jobs
1920	Right of married women to seek employment without their husbands' approval
1927	Equal rights to royal government appointments
1928	Equal access to all branches of higher education

and child raising declined, the place of women in society had to be redefined. Legal rights and the vote became goals in women's struggle to affirm their importance and secure a voice in decisions important to them. Second, these gains, and especially the vote, were also part of the larger process of political democratization (see chapter 9).

Women Gain the Vote

1862	In communal Swedish elections
1906	In all Finnish elections
1907	Limited women's suffrage in Norway
1913	Unlimited women's suffrage in Norway
1915	Women's suffrage in Denmark
1921	Women's suffrage in Sweden

Part III

The Twentieth Century

12

~~~~~~

World War I and the Interwar Years

The three decades between 1914 and 1945, encompassing the two world wars (which can also be seen as a single conflict, the Thirty-one Years' War, interrupted by a twenty-year truce) and the troubled, dynamic, and exciting 1920s and 1930s, help define another period of profound economic, social, political, and cultural turmoil and creativity.

The world wars are two of the most important events of modern history. All the clichés historians are so apt to use apply: turning point, watershed, pivotal moment. Each was enormously important in its immediate history and in its impacts. Europe, the West, the world were forever changed by each. Over 15 million people, combatants and civilians, died in World War I. Estimates run as high as 50 million dead in World War II. The material destruction in the first round of conflict was limited mostly to specific areas such as northern France. New weapons made the second round much more destructive. After World War I, the German, Hapsburg, Russian, and Ottoman Empires disappeared, and a host of new states were born. After World War II, the map was again redrawn, this time along bipolar ideological lines. Both wars affected political, economic, and social systems, altered gender roles and relationships, deeply influenced the arts and literature, and undermined faith in liberal, bourgeois, capitalist, Christian Western civilization.

The years between the wars witnessed dramatic swings in economic conditions, currency fluctuations, high unemployment, chronic problems in some economic sectors, continued social tensions, and disillusionment. A major focus of political debate in the interwar years was how government ought to respond to these and other problems, problems that contributed to social polarization and the rise of radical movements on the Left and the Right.

The 1920s and 1930s also had more positive aspects. The dispersion of technological developments for entertainment, the home, and transport (symbolized by the motion picture, the radio, electrical appliances for the home, and the automobile) dramatically changed everyday life. The arts flourished. Societies became, in some ways, less conflict oriented. Building on experiences gained in the war, governments in several Western states assumed increased roles in regulating economies and ensuring at least a minimum standard of living for the people, and this development was the founding era of the modern welfare states.

Norden and World War I

The first decade and a half of the twentieth century was marred by a series of diplomatic and military crises that brought the Continent closer and closer to the brink of a general war. In this highly charged atmosphere, the leaders of Denmark, Norway, and Sweden, realizing Norden's security weaknesses and dependence on trade for survival, resolved to avoid involvement in any general European war. In 1912 they issued a joint declaration of their intent to remain neutral in the event of a great power conflict. They followed through on that resolve. When the struggle began in August 1914, each Nordic government declared its neutrality.

In theory, at least, the Nordic governments adhered to that policy throughout the conflict. None became directly involved. Although subject to some of the war's impacts, including shortages, rationing, inflation, disruption of normal trade relations and economic life, and increased government control, the Nordic countries escaped the worst of the war. Finland came the closest to direct involvement. Russian authorities imposed taxes and rigid controls on the Finns. Although they were not made to fight for the Russians, many young men joined volunteer units including special "Jaeger" battalions trained by the Germans. Social class, ethnic background, and political ideologies continued to divide the Finns during the war, and the problems of the period heightened these differences, as has already been seen. Losses of life and property fell almost entirely on the crews and ships of the merchants fleets. Norway's losses were the greatest: as many as 2,000 sailors and half its tonnage, over eight hundred vessels, were lost.

Neutrality is easy to declare; it is quite another matter to be neutral

—especially in a conflict as extensive and long as World War I. The viability of the policy depends on the willingness and the capacity of the neutral to defend its position and on the willingness of the belligerents to have neutrals in a war. During World War I both sides of this equation were more or less present. However, genuine, or "impartial," neutrality was rare. For varying reasons the actual policies, actions, and attitudes of each of the Nordic countries tilted toward one side or the other or were steered toward partiality by external and internal realities.

Opinion of monarchs, politicians, elites, and the general public was an important factor in policy formulation and decision making. The Danes' sentiments toward the belligerents were mixed. One might have expected Christian X to favor the Germans, given his preference for monarchy and government by personal favorites and his marriage to Alexandrine of Mecklenburg-Schwerin. On the other hand, the fact that England's George V and Russia's Nicholas II were his cousins seems to have worked in the Entente's favor. (Christian was related to much of Europe's royalty. In addition to the English and Russian connections, his brother was Haakon VII of Norway, and another cousin, Konstantin, was the king of Greece.) In general, Christian's personal preference was for Britain. Conservatives and some farming interests were inclined to side with Germany. Liberals, Radical Liberals, and Social Democrats found greater affinity with England's more "liberal" political system and tilted toward the Entente. Despite these preferences, the Radical Left government, headed by Carl Theodor Zahle (1866–1946) and supported by the Social Democrats, sought to maintain favorable relationships with both the Allied and Entente Powers throughout the war.

Others factors that influenced policies and actions were history, geography, and economic realities. Bordered by Germany to the south, Denmark was in the most dangerous strategic position, and few believed the Germans could be stopped should they decide to protect their northwest flank by invading Denmark across Jutland or from the sea. Danish defenses, which were concentrated on the Jutland-Slesvig border and around Copenhagen, reflected two aspects of the country's history: the British attacks on the capital in the early nineteenth century, and the Slesvig-Holstein wars. History made either great power a natural enemy. The conflicts with Prussia were more powerfully imprinted on the Danes, either through memory or propaganda, and the lingering bitterness of defeat was aggravated by Prussian/

German policies in the lost Slesvig territories. However, animosities were offset by profitable and essential trade relations. Germany and Great Britain were Denmark's primary trade partners, taking 60 percent and 30 percent of exports and providing 17 percent and 33 percent of imports, respectively. Denmark's agricultural, manufacturing, raw material, and energy sectors were heavily dependent on foreign trade, and these economic realities did much to shape its policies and actions.

For Norway, its geographic location and recent history for the most part placed the country outside the threat of direct attack, and sentiments toward one side or the other were less complex. Still, Norway may have been the least neutral of the Nordic states, and historian Olav Riste has called Norway "the neutral ally" with good reason. Haakon VII (1872–1957) was married to George V's sister, Maud. Official and popular opinion were mostly with the Entente Powers, especially Britain, and these feelings were reinforced by powerful economic interests. England was a primary market for Norwegian exports and a primary provider of essential imports including fuels and industrial goods. The Norwegian merchant marine was the most important carrier of this trade. Gunnar Knudsen's (1848–1928) Liberal government served through the war and successfully guided the country through the labyrinth created by the demands and counterdemands of the British and German governments for favorable trade and shipping deals.

Sweden's opinions and policies were more complex, and the country's neutrality went through major shifts of direction. For two years, 1914-16, behind the guise of neutrality, Sweden's Conservative government, headed by Hjalmar Hammarskjöld (1862–1953), showed a consistent favoritism toward Germany, and Swedish businesses carried on a lucrative trade with their Baltic neighbor. This alignment was hardly surprising. To a large degree Sweden was a Baltic state historically and geographically. Germany was its most important trading partner, and its access to the West through Göteborg could be easily controlled. The country had strong intellectual, cultural, and commercial ties with Germany. Gustav V's mother was Sofia of Nassau, and his wife was Victoria of Baden, a cousin of the Kaiser. Beyond these affinities, Germany was seen as the bulwark against Russian expansion, still feared by many in Sweden, and even as a possible ally who would help Sweden recover the Åland Islands—a temptation held out to the Swedes in 1917. For many in Sweden, the war between

Germany and Russia was the most important element in the conflict, and the war in the West was simply unfortunate. Initially, few in Sweden saw the struggle as ideological—pitting the forces of democracy against those of autocracy. That outlook came later.

For two years, 1914–16, the war provided the basis for an economic boom in Norden. The belligerents were prepared to purchase almost every major export of the region and even to enter into new trade. Danish meats, dairy products and livestock; Norwegian fish, pyrite ores, and nitrates; Swedish iron ore, forest products, and ball bearings were among the goods for which the Allied and Entente Powers competed. They also wanted to acquire or control Nordic merchant carrying capacities. Although both sides engaged in economic warfare from the early stages of the war, deals could be struck, and the diplomatic history of Norden in this period involves a maze of negotiations and agreements on trade and merchant traffic through the surface and submarine blockades and mine fields. The relative balance on the battlefield in the West worked in the Nordic states' favor. Working against them was their extreme dependence on international trade for fuels (especially coal), raw materials, and certain foodstuffs. The longer the war dragged on, moreover, the more intense the economic aspects of the conflict became and the less flexible Germany, Great Britain, and from 1917 the United States were with the neutrals.

The relatively comfortable situations for the Nordic neutrals ended in summer 1916. As the conflict continued, the belligerents turned more seriously to economic warfare to break the stalemate on the battlefield. This change involved increasingly uncompromising trade talks, blacklisting, ship and cargo confiscation, withholding of deliveries, and intensified surface and submarine naval actions. On 1 February 1917 the Germans resumed unrestricted submarine warfare. The entry of the United States into the war in April 1917 made matters worse, because the former champion of neutral rights now took a wholly uncompromising position. If the neutrals would not cease all trade with Germany and its allies, they would be completely cut off from supplies, and their ships would be confiscated. Critical situations developed for the Danes, Norwegians, and Swedes in late summer 1916 and continued virtually to the end of the war. Interestingly, this new situation fostered Nordic cooperation. For example, Danish dairy and meat products were exchanged for Swedish industrial goods, and Danish grain for Norwegian chemicals.

The situation became critical for the Danes in early 1917. With the resumption of unrestricted submarine warfare by the Germans, shipping came to a virtual standstill for several months, and when sailings resumed, sinkings soared. To some degree, British and American inflexibility pushed the Danes into the arms of the Germans for critical materials like coal, iron, chemicals, and salt; and the Germans took every advantage of the situation by demanding payment in gold.

British demands on the Norwegian government for reduced deliveries to Germany increased in summer 1916. The Germans responded with their own demands and increased attacks on Norwegian shipping. The leverage advantage was with England. In December a coal embargo was imposed on Norway that lasted through the winter. Intense negotiations led to three agreements: an arrangement to sell almost all of Norway's pyrite ores to England, another to reduce fish exports to Germany, and a third to provide merchant vessels to Britain and its allies. In return, essential deliveries were promised, and Norwegian vessels joined British convoys. In effect, these deals made Norway a "neutral ally."

The more difficult phase of the war for Sweden also began in mid-1916 and became critical in summer 1917. Hammarskjöld's government came under growing public criticism and fell in part because of policy disagreements between the prime minister and the foreign minister, Knut Wallenberg. The Conservative caretaker government under Carl Swartz (1858–1926) and then the new Liberal–Social Democratic coalition under Nils Edén (1871–1945) were subjected to increased demands from Germany and Great Britain. The Germans tried to bring Sweden into the war as an ally with promises of supplies and the return of the Åland Islands. The British and Americans tried (probably successfully) to affect the outcome of the September 1917 elections by releasing information about the long-known-about use of Swedish diplomatic-cable communication channels by the Germans. (This use became the so-called Luxburg Affair, because focus fell on the shipping information being sent to Berlin by Count K. L. von Luxburg from the German legation in Argentina via Sweden.) From fall 1917, Sweden's neutrality became more balanced, and then, in the last few months of the war, increasingly pro-Entente. This final swing can be most clearly seen in the May 1918 trade agreement with Britain whereby iron ore trade to German was cut by about 30 percent, the Allies agreed to provide essential supplies, and Swedish ships were to be turned over for use by the Allies.

For many people in Norden, including farmers, fishermen, forest and industrial workers, and merchant sailors, the first years of the war meant good economic times. Unemployment was almost nonexistent. Wages were high. At the same time, a few people became very rich very quickly as a result of wartime production, trade, shipping, commodity and share speculation, or market brokering. The Nordic governments' efforts to control the development of this group through high taxes on profits and capital gains, restrictions, and regulatory agencies were unsuccessful. In all three countries these people were derogatorily referred to as the "goulash barons" because, despite their new wealth, many were essentially tasteless and uncultured. They built gaudy homes and furnished them with ugly things, spent their money wildly and foolishly, showed no social responsibility, and helped heighten social tensions as the war went on. The worst of the new rich were often seen to have been those in the shipping trade, who had no regard for the lives of the seamen they sent out on vessels that stood good chances of being sunk, because they won either way: if a shipment went through, they profited; if it was lost, they collected on insurance. An insightful but highly politicized play about these profiteers is Nordahl Grieg's (1902–43) *Our Honor, Our Glory* (1935).

Although the war may have been good for most Scandinavians in the first years, it imposed greater and greater hardships as time went on. Supplies of essential imports became increasingly difficult to obtain. Despite controls, prices rose—about 250 percent in Denmark and Sweden, 300 percent in Norway, and as much as 400 percent in Finland between 1914 and 1918. Eventually, most daily necessities were rationed including sugar, bread, flour, dairy products, meat, tobacco, coffee, and even potatoes. The consumption of alcohol, especially distilled products (*akvakit* or *brännvin*), was discouraged by high taxes and outright prohibitions because the liquor was produced from necessary food grains. (Interestingly, the war forced on Scandinavia what the temperance movements had advocated for decades.) Although industrial and primary sector workers enjoyed some of the benefits of the booms of the early years, the quality of their lives declined overall. In the last years of the war most manufacturing sectors faced production declines. Unemployment rose. Real wages declined. Retailers were hurt by supply problems and high prices. Merchants witnessed the disappearance of long-established domestic and international market connections. People on salaries and other types of fixed incomes were hit especially hard by rising living costs.

Farmers had governments telling them what to raise and setting the prices of their products, and for many small farmers profitability declined.

The war may also have had a negative impact on women. In the belligerent countries, women were drawn into the workforce in ever-increasing numbers to replace men sent to the front. But in Norden employment opportunities did not increase significantly or become more varied for women. At the same time, their domestic lives were often complicated by supply problems and having to manage households on declining resources.

One of the most striking developments of the war throughout the West was the increased influence and sheer size of governments. This development was especially evident in the growth of governmental regulation of economies. Some argue that, although tentative steps were taken earlier, it was during the war that the roots of the economic aspects of the modern welfare state first developed. Certainly, most notions of laissez faire disappeared during the war. In Denmark special legislation was passed in early August 1914 empowering the government to regulate prices and supplies of essential goods. Interior Minister Ove Rode (1867–1933) was the central figure behind the development of economic regulations, many of which were designed and implemented in cooperation with special commissions that directly involved affected interest groups. These controls eventually affected imports, exports, production, pricing, distribution, currency, banking, taxation, and wages. A similar pattern of economic management emerged in Norway. A Provisioning Commission with local branches was established in 1914 and replaced in 1916 by the Ministries of Food and Industrial Supply and a price board. Compulsory arbitration was imposed on the labor market. Rent controls were introduced in the principal cities in 1916. The government also created a grain and flour monopoly. The sale of most alcoholic beverages was banned in December 1916. In Sweden Hammarskjöld's Conservative government was less inclined to formalize the planning processes. Still, regulations on import and export of food products were imposed in December 1914, a special trade commission was set up in June 1915, and rationing came in 1916. The more ad hoc approach, which may have been no better nor worse than Denmark and Norway's formal approaches, earned the prime minister the nickname "Hungerskjöld." Edén's Liberal–Social Democratic coalition (1917–20), in which Social Democratic leader Hjalmar Branting was finance minister, may have been inclined to plan the economy, but it put more energy into reaching a new trade agreement with Great Britain to alleviate the worst supply shortages and confronting growing constitutional issues.

As much of the above indicates, the first few years of the war saw the suspension of internal political and social rivalries in what has been called a "political truce," or *borgfreden*. The Zahle, Knudsen, and Hammarskjöld governments enjoyed almost unanimous support from their parliaments. However, the domestic debates did not completely vanish, and the bleakness of the later years of the war and anger over profiteering, black markets, declining real wages, rising unemployment (which, for example, went from 5 percent in 1916 to 18 percent in 1918 in Denmark), and government regulations that did not seem to work amplified tensions. Old issues like constitutional reform, genuine political democracy, the realities of social inequalities, and worker exploitation resurfaced. Demands for reforms increased and were embodied in campaigns for universal suffrage and the eighthour work day.

In the last year of the war and the first year or so of peace, the tenor of discontent and protest reached very serious levels. Finland descended into civil war, and the specter of revolution was taken very seriously in Denmark, Norway, and Sweden. Demands for change primarily came from the industrial working class and its leaders, although there was extensive discontent within almost every social group. The moderate groups representing the working class wanted suffrage reform, the eight-hour day, and social reforms that would further ensure their members' well-being. These included the major trade unions and the Social Democratic parties. But the Left became increasingly fragmented in the last years of the war. In Denmark and Sweden, Social Democratic leaders such as Thorvald Stauning and Hjalmar Branting became revisionists in their outlook and believed change should come through existing political institutions. They managed to retain control of a majority of their members, but Communist-inspired splinter groups developed. Complicating this picture were the Syndicalists, the "labor opposition," who had their own trade unions in Denmark and Sweden. In Norway, however, the Left was united for a time in the Labor Party, which became more and more radical. By the close of the war its leaders, including the Syndicalist, Martin Tranmæl, and Kyrre Grepp, had aligned the party with the Bolsheviks in Russia and were committed to revolution. They advocated the overthrow of the existing order and believed in the general strike as a fundamental tool of revolution.

All of Norden was subject to various expressions of public discontent and revolutionary sentiments. Frustration over the economic problems led to strikes, looting of shops, intimidation of farmers suspected of hoarding food supplies, and even insubordination in military units (where social class and rank were usually very closely tied). More serious and better organized actions also occurred. In Copenhagen, Syndicalist-led demonstrations took place in February and again in November 1918. The first of these focused on the stock exchange (Borsen), which was seen as the symbol of capitalism at its worst. The second developed out of a Syndicalist call for a one-day general strike to protest the imprisonment of radical leader Christian Christensen (1882–1960). Although the strike call failed, large numbers of workers gathered in Grönttorv on 13 November. They stopped traffic and commandeered trolleys, which the leaders used as platforms from which to address the crowd. Both demonstrations were finally broken up by the police. In Norway, the Labor Party issued a call for a revolution on 12 November 1918 and organized a march in support of the Soviet government in July 1919. In Sweden mounted police were used to disperse a large public demonstration for democratic reforms on 5 June 1917, and nearly 600,000 turned out for meetings across the country on May Day 1918.

The level of discontent was high in Norden, and the threat of revolution very real at this time. There were well-organized groups with articulate and popular leaders who favored revolution over evolution and were willing to use force. They were buoyed up by events in Russia, Germany, the former Hapsburg Empire, and even in France and Great Britain. These groups were taken very seriously by the forces of order, and paramilitary groups on the Right committed to the maintenance of order were formed.

The threat of revolution passed fairly quickly. Why? First, the political reforms demanded by moderates were achieved. In Denmark, the prewar discussions of constitutional reform continued during the war, and a package of changes was enacted with broad support in May 1915 and took effect that June. The changes included universal suffrage, lowering the voting age, proportional representation constituencies, and new procedures for electing the seventy-two members of the Landsting, including the end to royal appointment and special wealth-based requirements for voting or serving. The Landsting now was to elect one-fourth of its members and the rest would be chosen indirectly, half every four years for eight-year terms. Although conservative forces continued to control the Landsting for a time, it gradually came to mirror the Folketing.

In Sweden parlementarism became firmly established in practice and government more fully democratic through electoral reforms. With regard to the first of these changes, the Hammarskjöld government resigned in March 1917 because of the defeat of its defense proposal in the parliament and growing dissension over foreign policy within the government and was replaced by a caretaker ministry under Carl Swartz. In the September 1917 elections the Conservatives fell from eighty-six to fifty-seven seats in the Second Chamber, the Liberals moved up to sixty-two, the Social Democrats dropped to eighty-six, the new Farmers Party won fourteen, and the Left Socialists secured eleven. King Gustav resisted, but finally appointed a Liberal–Social Democrat coalition under Nils Edén. This was a victory for parlementarism.

The constitutional reform struggle in Sweden was fought out in 1918 and 1919. At issue were universal suffrage and the continued domination of municipal/local council and the First Chamber elections by conservative forces through the old system of multiple votes and stricter voter and candidate requirements. One proposal for reform was defeated in early 1918, but the Conservatives, fearing revolution, showed greater willingness to compromise in the fall. A new municipal/local voting code was passed. Reform of the Riksdag election rules came in 1919 and 1921. Together these reforms brought almost universal suffrage in all elections, and 54 percent now had the vote. Most important, they democratized municipal and local government and the First Chamber of the parliament by making the requirements for voting the same as those for the Second Chamber.

A second factor in calming the revolutionary spirit was the adoption of the eight-hour day as the norm for industrial workers (as well as government employees and others) throughout Norden by mid-1919. In addition, although supply and economic dislocation problems continued, some improvements occurred. Government willingness to use force to quell disorder was probably another factor. Finally, there is the matter of traditions of political behavior. Violence, revolution, coup d'états, and the like were generally not part of modern Scandinavian political history, whereas public demonstrations, widespread discussion in the press and in public meetings, and peaceful change of and within the constitutional frameworks were. The importance of histories of successful adaptation cannot be over-estimated here or in other instances. The histories of peaceful demo-cratic development in Denmark, Norway, and Sweden may be of pri-mary importance in explaining the absence of revolution at the close of World War I.

The Interwar Years

Crises and Politics

The first few years following the Great War were deeply troubled ones throughout Europe. Despite wishes for a rapid return to normalcy, stability came slowly—and in some aspects was never recovered. The people of Norden, their economies disrupted by shortages and dis-torted by wartime demands and markets, now fell victim to problems that demonstrated repeatedly throughout the interwar years just how dependent the region was on the health of an increasingly global economy. If certain sectors of their economies are focused on, such as agriculture or forest products, the entire interwar period may be seen as one of prolonged crisis. From other perspectives, one sees an era of slow but important economic growth, marred by two great crises: the immediate postwar recession (c. 1921–22) and the worst years of the Great Depression (1930–34).

Regardless of perspective, it is clear that after a brief postwar boom, serious difficulties returned, and most Scandinavians were faced with falling currency values, sluggish trade, low domestic purchasing power, overstocked inventories, excessive productive capacities, and rising unemployment. One of the largest banks in all of Scandinavia, Den-mark's Landmansbanken, failed because of careless loan policies, tak-ing others with it. Employers tried to meet sluggish or falling demand with layoffs, shortened working hours, or wage reductions to make prices more competitive. The economic woes contributed to contin-ued social and political tensions. Although the threat of revolution seemed to have passed by early 1920, the specter remained, and Nor-dic societies continued to be divided along class lines. There was every justification for seeing class warfare as a basic element of the period's history. Strikes were frequent, and much of the socialist Left revolu-tionary. The Norwegian Labor Party joined the Communist Interna-tional and was committed to revolution for much of the 1920s, at least in its programs and rhetoric. Communist parties also broke off from the increasingly revisionist Social Democratic parties in Denmark and Sweden. In Finland, the Social Democrats were deeply mistrusted and the Communists, aided by the Soviets, remained active under a variety of new labels.

Stability returned after about 1922, and the late 1920s are generally to be seen as years of recovery. These trends were brought on by gradual improvement in global economic conditions and, perhaps, by government policies, which were largely deflationary and involved holding on to some wartime controls, carefully controlling state expenditures, and currency devaluations. Markets were restored and new ones found. Confidence returned and investment, some of it highly reckless, increased. Still, recovery was not universal, and the experiences of working classes were very mixed. Norwegian and Swedish forest industry workers, for example, faced virtually chronic unemployment and constant threats to their security from employers. On the other hand, merchant sailors enjoyed a temporary rise in opportunities when Norwegian shipping interests turned to carrying more specialized cargoes, such as fruits and oil, and experienced a 500 percent growth in trade between 1925 and 1930.

The bottom began to fall out of the world economy again in late 1929. The collapse in America spread to Europe and reached Scandinavia in 1930. Demand for raw materials, manufactured goods, and services fell. Businesses failed. Private, corporate, and agricultural borrowers defaulted on their loans, and customers rushed to banks to withdraw their savings. Banks collapsed. The ruin of the Swedish industrialist Ivar Kreuger's (1880–1932) financial empire illustrates what amounted to a kind of economic implosion. During the 1920s Kreuger built a financial empire based on some four hundred businesses and control of a major share of the world's safety match market. From this base, he borrowed hundreds of millions of dollars that he then lent to private concerns and governments, believing he was helping stimulate global economic development. When his borrowers defaulted on their loans and Kreuger's creditors demanded repayment, his house of cards collapsed. Facing ruin, he committed suicide in March 1932. In Sweden the stock market had to be closed for a week to prevent its collapse. Large and small investors were ruined, and many of his companies were sold off to meet debts. Prime Minister C. G. Ekman was forced to resign when he was implicated in Kreuger's shady dealings. Confidence in the economic system and the government was shaken.

Again the working class was hard hit. Although varying widely by sector, unemployment soared. In January 1933 nearly 43 percent of union workers in Denmark were without jobs, and similar rates could be found throughout Scandinavia. Typically, employers responded to the problems with layoffs or demands for more output for less pay. The workers, whose unions enjoyed a renaissance after the moderate versus communist crises of the early 1920s, responded with strikes, and the employers countered by bringing in strikebreakers. Violence often followed. At Mensted, a Norsk Hydro docks facility near Skien in the southeast, one of the most serious disputes erupted in June 1931, and troops had to be called in to restore order. A similar situation at Ådalen in northern Sweden developed in spring 1931, in which strikebreakers were brought in to replace striking workers. On 14 May, for reasons still unclear, troops opened fire on a large group of marchers protesting the hiring of scabs and government policies. Four workers and a young woman looking on were killed. Both of these events were shocking to publics with largely peaceful histories. In the long run, the intensity of the labor disputes of the early 1930s probably contributed to extensive shifts in attitudes and voter behavior and influenced election outcomes. It also contributed to the efforts to establish lasting and stable arrangements between the principal groups in the labor market such as the "basic agreement" reached in Norway in 1935, and the Saltsjöbaden Agreement concluded between Sweden's central trade union federation (Landsorganisationen i Sverige/LO) and the national employers association (Sveriges Arbetsgivareföreningen) in 1938.

Overall, government responses to the problems of the Depression varied, and whatever they did may have been less important than the passage of time and developments outside Norden. By 1935 recovery was general, and the last years before World War II were generally good ones for the region.

Politically, the history of this period divides in two periods— although the dates for each vary across Norden. The first was characterized by short-lived, weak governments, either minorities or coalitions formed along socialist/nonsocialist lines, frequent elections, and a lack of legislative productivity on the major issues. These traits were the result of several factors. First, no single party or stable grouping of parties in the typical Nordic five-party system (Communist and Social Democrat versus Farmer, Liberal, and Conservative) developed. Second, the socialist versus nonsocialist division was viewed by many on each side as black and white, good versus bad, and irreconcilable, which made cooperation or compromise nearly impossible on issues like unemployment insurance, defense, or government's role in cushioning society during economic downturns. The second was a period of ministerial stability defined by socialist-dominated coalitions or socialist minority governments (in Denmark, Norway, and Sweden) working in cooperation with one or more nonsocialist party (usually the Farmers), elections at normal intervals, and exceptional legislative productivity. The change was the result of increased socialist electoral and parliamentary strength, greater willingness on the part of socialist and nonsocialist parties to reach working compromises, very able leadership across the political spectrum, the development by the moderate socialist parties of programs that emphasized the unity of the nation in the face of problems and deemphasized class and economic system differences, and external developments including the success of antidemocratic forces in Germany.

Although no less troubled by economic and social problems during the 1920s and 1930s than its Nordic neighbors, Denmark was least subject to the governmental merry-go-round. Four governments span the entire interwar decades. These were headed by Niels Neergaard (Liberal, 1920–24), Thorvald Stauning (Social Democratic, 1924–26), Thomas Madsen-Mygdal (Liberal, 1926–29), and Stauning (Social Democrat–Radical Left, 1929–40). However, the first three of these were not strong enough to carry legislative programs that departed from a narrow "center," and their accomplishments were modest. The eleven years under Stauning before World War II were another story entirely. Following the 1929 election, Stauning was able to form a coalition with the Radical Left, led by Peder Munch, which enjoyed a two-vote majority in the Folketing. The government's position was strengthened in January 1933 through the Kanslergade Agreement, an understanding with the Agrarians only reached, according to one account, after failing negotiations were resumed in the wee hours of the morning over what were supposed to be parting cocktails. This was one of the so-called red-green deals concluded during this period in Norden, and it assured Left support of government proposals to deal with unemployment, labor market problems, and social programs in exchange for government support of legislation to help farmers hard-hit by the Depression through price supports. In the 1935 election the Social Democrats ran on the campaign slogan "Stauning or Chaos" and won over 46 percent of the vote; the Radicals received just over 9 percent. The coalition secured a Landsting majority the following year. Between 1932 and 1940 Stauning's "people's home" was built through legislation that increased the state's role in economic planning, provided unemployment relief in public works projects, further democratized and extended public education, and guaranteed social protection for the unemployed, the sick or injured, and the old. Although many of these reforms were extensions of earlier programs, as a whole they exceeded everything that had come before. They also embodied a fundamental change of attitude about society's responsibility. The one disappointment of this era was the failure to pass a constitutional reform package that would have eliminated the Landsting and lowered the voting age to twenty-one. Although the package received the necessary parliament approval, it failed because too few people voted in the required popular referendum in 1939 (45 percent of the electorate were required to cast votes, 44.46 percent did).

Finland was the Nordic country most subject to political instability between the wars. The antipathies between socialists and nonsocialists were amplified by the civil war and carried into the interwar years. The moderate Social Democrats were mistrusted, and cooperation with them was avoided by the nonsocialists. The ongoing and very disruptive revolutionary activities of the Communists, who worked through the trade union movement they controlled and various front parties, reinforced the Right's perceptions of the threat from the Left, and encouraged the development of radical right-wing groups such as the Lapuan Movement and the Patriotic National Movement. In addition, there was always the language question and the concerns of the Swede-Finns. Twenty coalition governments came and went between 1919 and 1940, sixteen of them before 1932. Of these, eight were headed by Progressives (Liberal), six by Agrarians, five by Conservatives, and one by the Social Democrats.

Underlying the tumultuous nature of elections and turnover of governments was considerable stability and consistency of direction. The four presidents of the period contributed to this. At the same time, coalition changes, which often involved only minor restructuring, did not mean a break in political order, and the red-green cooperation between Social Democrats and Agrarians increased throughout the 1930s. The composition of the parliament also changed relatively little through the period. The Social Democrats were the largest party. They held eighty seats in 1919, fell to fifty-nine in 1929, and rebounded to eighty-five in 1939. The Agrarians increased their numbers from forty-two to fifty-six. The Conservatives (National Union) cycled from twenty-eight in 1919 to forty-two in 1930 to twenty-five in 1939. As was so typical across Europe in these years, the liberal Progressives faced an almost steady decline, falling from twenty-six to six seats, and the Swede-Finns dropped from twenty-two to eighteen. The Communists held seats only between 1922 and 1929, twenty-seven and twenty-three, respectively. During the 1930s the disruptive, right-wing Patriotic National Movement (Isänmaallinen Kansanliike/IKL) won between eight and fourteen places. The bureaucracy, which administered policy and program, was not reshuffled with every election or coalition change.

The Finns were notably successful in dealing with the ethnic, social, economic, and political problems of the interwar years. Immediate postwar economic recovery was aided by fiscally conservative currency reform, state debt management, and tax policies. Although subject to the same cyclical fluctuations as the rest of Norden, the economy grew overall. Industry, dominated by forest products, advanced. New international markets were developed, and a favorable balance of foreign trade maintained. Major social and economic problems in agriculture were aggressively addressed by governments, especially in the 1920s. Here the basic problems were that Finland had too few landowners, too many farmers who held their land on short-term leases, and too many landless agricultural workers. State-sponsored programs to alleviate these problems were developed, most notably a comprehensive 1922 measure designed by Minister of Agriculture Kallio to provide land and the means to buy it. An application and review process allowed state, corporate, or privately owned land to be expropriated and then sold to persons wanting either small plots to work for supplemental income or larger pieces for full-time farming. State financing provided the means. Overall, a landownership revolution of sorts occurred, which, coupled with improved methods, specialization toward dairy production, and cooperatives, resulted in significant social and economic improvements. In the 1930s, especially, legislation following the same pattern as elsewhere in Norden addressed nagging social reform questions including working conditions, accident and health insurance, old-age pension, family matters, housing, and women's rights and opportunities.

Norway's political history in this period is very similar to that of Finland. There were twelve minority governments between the wars: four Liberal, four Conservative, two Agrarian, and two Labor. Eleven of them held office between 1920 and 1935. Until 1935, virtually all were based on parliamentary minorities. Narrowly perceived issues or interests defined conflicts. Programmatic vision was lacking. Legislation was conservative.

From 1920 to 1927 the Liberals and Conservatives cycled in and out of power, as they sought to deal with the two great problems of the period: the economy and prohibition. In many respects, solution of the former was beyond their control, and neither party was willing to pursue anything but conservative measures. The early postwar bubble burst in 1920. Unemployment soared, the krone lost value, and real incomes fell. These developments, coupled with the typical responses of employers to cut expenses by uncompensated increases in work schedules or pay cuts, led to an explosion of labor disputes. In 1921 some 3.6 million worker-days were lost to strikes or lockouts, and in 1924 this figure was over 5 million worker-days. At the same time, the real costs of the war were revealed in the form of a national debt that made state responses to labor or agricultural problems all the less likely. Tax income in real value also fell, and many local governmental units were on the verge of bankruptcy. This situation contributed to a crisis for commercial banking.

The problem of prohibition, the pet of the Liberals, was socially damaging and no less easily solved. The wartime controls on hard liquor were continued, and in October 1919 a majority of Norwegians voted in favor of prohibition except on certain wines and beer, and measures designed to enforce this followed. What then happened amounted to an eight-year farce. Trade relations with wine-producing countries such as France and Spain degenerated into a series of diplomatic crises, threats, and reprisals against Norwegian industries, including fishing. Actual enforcement was lax. Sales of wine and beer rose. Many people got around the ban on hard liquor by obtaining "prescriptions" from willing physicians. Home-distilled products were easily obtained. A second referendum in 1926 led to an end to the temperance experiment. It also left the Liberals discredited and contributed to their decline from fifty-four seats in the Storting in 1918 to twenty-three in 1926.

Until 1935 the nonsocialist parties dominated Norwegian political life. The radicalization of the Labor Party (and the union movement) had begun before the war, especially as a result of the agitation work of Martin Tranmæl. For a time, he led the Syndicalist opposition within both the party and the unions. During and after the war, however, he and his followers moved toward Bolshevism, became committed to revolution, won control of the party, and took it into the Communist International in 1921, a move that led to the founding of a moderate Social Democratic Party. When Labor rejected Moscow's control demands and left the Comintern in 1923, a new Communist Party was also born.

This fragmentation rendered the socialists virtually powerless in parliament until the reunification of the Social Democrats and Labor in 1927 and the gradual abandonment of international and revolutionary ideals for reformist and nationalist ones. Exactly when this shift occurred is a matter of debate, but it is clear that by 1933–35 the transformation was in place. The Labor Party's "Three-Year Plan" for economic recovery, its 1933 election campaign slogan, "Work for All," and the conclusion of a "basic agreement" between the trade union federation and the employers, which in large measure brought peace to the labor market in 1935, bore witness to this. In the 1933 election, Labor won sixty-nine seats in the Storting. Two years later, following lengthy behind-the-scenes negotiations, a red-green agreement was reached with the Farmers Party (founded in 1920) on parliamentary cooperation, which lasted until 1937, when the Liberals became the primary partners of the government. These developments allowed Johan Nygaardsvold to form a government in 1935, which lasted, with some changes, until 1945.

The emergency programs for labor and agriculture and the social legislation enacted over the next five years did not constitute so much a change of approach as a change of degree. By this time all parties in the system accepted the need for governmental action. How much and at what costs were yet to be determined. State involvement in the economy and social programs included greater support for small farmers, public works projects to reduce unemployment, unemployment insurance, broadened health insurance programs, the extension of the eight-hour day to agriculture, old-age pensions, education reform, and increased taxes.

Sweden was subject to the same ministerial instability as Finland and Norway. The parties on the Left included the Communists, Left Socialists, and Social Democrats. On the Right were the Liberals (who were divided between 1922 and 1934 into the free church, prohibition, antidefense Liberal People's Party and the antiprohibition and prodefense Liberal Party, both of which then merged as the People's Party Folkpartiet), the Farmers, and Conservatives or Right. Of the fifteen interwar governments, four were led by the Liberals, two by the Conservatives, six by the Social Democrats, and one by the Agrarians. Two were without party identification. Most of the instability came between 1920 and 1932, when no party commanded a majority in either house of the Riksdag, coalitions were fragile, the political environment was badly polarized between socialist and nonsocialists and these blocs were fragment by dissension, and cooperation in the parliament usually amounted to short-lived voting agreements on single issues. Stability was built in the early 1930s in another of those Nordic cooperative red-green relationships between Farmers and Social Democrats.

The issues that dominated Swedish politics in the 1920s included prohibition, defense, education, the economy, and the labor market. There was no consensus across the party spectrum on any of these. With the achievement of political democracy, prohibition became an obsession of a faction of the Liberal Party. In a 1922 referendum the voters returned a slight majority against extended liquor regulation. Without a decisive vote, Hjalmar Branting's Social Democratic government did not proceed and opted instead for continued controls (rationing) based on the so-called Bratt System adopted gradually between 1913 and 1917. This regulated consumption through a state liquor monopoly, high taxes, and ration cards. Given the Norwegians' experiences (or the Americans'), the decision seems almost prophetic.

Defense emerged repeatedly as an issue throughout the 1920s. The Social Democrats and Liberal People's Party favored reductions because they believed international cooperation and collective security through the League of Nations made costly defense systems unnecessary. In addition, there was only so much money available, and social programs were more important. The Conservatives, Liberals, and Agrarians favored growth or at least maintaining the status quo. In 1924 Ernst Trygger's Conservative ministry fell on the defeat of a relatively modest defense proposal. Hjalmar Branting formed his third government, but he died in early 1925. A new generation, including Rickard Sandler, Ernst Wigforss, Gustav Möller, and Östen Undén, now emerged as the leaders of the party. A deal was struck with Liberal People's Party leader Carl Gustaf Ekman, and a new defense bill accepted that involved cutting the recruit training period to 140 days, reducing the size of active forces, allowing for conscientious objectors, and creation of an air force. This measure set the tone for Swedish defense policy until 1936, when the changing international scene made a reassessment essential.

Economic and labor market issues were linked. Swedes faced the same problems as their Nordic neighbors, and the political environment made aggressive policies impossible to pursue. Extent and not fundamental approach separated Social Democratic measures from those of the bourgeois bloc, which included government economies, minimal and regulated unemployment compensation, and attempts to pacify the labor market. A particularly contentious issue was whether or not striking workers should receive unemployment benefits. Rickard Sandler's Social Democratic government fell over this question in 1926.

One of the most successful personalities in this period was C. G. Ekman, who was called the "weighmaster" and "the government killer" for his ability and willingness to put together or destroy voting majorities on specific issues. He headed two minority governments, 1926–28 and 1930–32. The first enjoyed some successes. A school reform measure aimed at democratizing a complicated system of education divided along class and gender lines was adopted with Social Democrat support. All students were now expected to spend four years in a compulsory elementary school (*folkskolan*). Moreover, girls were now admitted to state secondary schools. Ekman also put through, with Conservative support, legislation that weakened labor's right to strike and introduced a labor court to settle disputes. His second ministry became increasingly preoccupied with the growing economic crisis. Ekman's deflationary, probusiness, and antilabor policies amplified social tensions. He was weakened politically by the killings at Ådalen and was forced to resign when it was revealed that Ivar Kreuger had made contributions to Ekman's political coffers at a time when he was seeking loans from the central state bank.

The economic crisis, the shock of the killings at Ådalen, the Kreuger scandal, the Ekman-Kreuger connection, the ineffectiveness of the bourgeois parties' policies, the increasingly moderate and national programs of the Social Democrats, and the growing willingness of the Farmers to cooperate with the Social Democrats contributed to a kind of peaceful revolution in 1932–33. In the September 1932 election, the Social Democrats, who campaigned for an aggressive anti-Depression program designed by Ernst Wigforss, raised their Second Chamber strength from 90 to 104 seats; the Farmers moved from 27 to 36. In contrast, the two liberal parties' strength dropped from 32 to 24 seats, and the Right's from 73 to 58. Per Albin Hansson formed another minority cabinet. What made this situation different was the "crisis agreement," or the "cow deal" (*kohandeln*), worked out in May 1933 with a new generation of leaders in the Farmers Party. In exchange for import restrictions, a margarine tax, and other farm supports, Hansson was assured a majority in both chambers of the parliament and could set about passing emergency economic measures and social reforms aimed at creating "the people's home" (*folkhemmet*). The elections of September 1936 strengthened the Social Democrats in both chambers, and this time Hansson formed a coalition that included Farmer Party leader Axel Pehrsson i Bramstorp. The government's direction was also supported by the reunited liberals in the late 1930s.

Although Hansson stood as the great proponent of change for the good of the whole, credit for the design of programs and the economics behind them belongs to Gustaf Möller (social minister), Ernst Wigforss (finance minister), and many other very capable leaders within the party and the trade union movement. The government abandoned the notion of balanced budgets and government economies in favor of deficits and increased government spending in times of trouble—which in theory would be offset during good periods. It also adopted fully the concept that the welfare of a society is a social responsibility. The whole works for the good of all. The poor, the unemployed, the sick, the old, the young . . . belong to the whole. Their well-being is essential to the health of the society. In concrete terms this meant an unemployment insurance system paying market wages (1934), improved old-age pensions (1935, 1937), the eight-hour day for farm workers (1936), state support for new mothers (1937), housing loans (1937), guaranteed two-week vacations (1938), protection of workers from strikebreakers (1938), help for small farmers (1938), and many other measures. Much of this was paid for with the profits of the liquor monopoly and taxes, which by late-twentieth-century standards were remarkably low, on income, property, and inheritance.

Although all of Norden passed through the interwar years with its democratic institutions intact and proven effective, this does not mean they went unchallenged. That the Communists and Syndicalists contributed to the unrest and instability of the 1920s and early 1930s is undeniable. So, too, is the fact that radical right-wing groups appeared throughout Norden, paralleling similar developments throughout

Europe. In general, these groups were nationalistic, held romanticized views of the past, saw society as polarized between Left and Right, considered socialism in all its variants as evil, were antidemocratic, and believed they were destined to save their countries from the decadence of modernity. The importance of racism, anti-Semitism, and religion varied, and these issues tended to be the causes of dissension and divisiveness within organizations.

There were literally hundreds of such groups and organizations in Scandinavia, but only a few stand out. One authority claims there were twenty-nine "Nazi" parties in Denmark during this period. Of these, however, only the Danish National Socialist Workers' Party (Danmarks National Socialistiske Arbejder Parti), founded in 1930 and headed by Cai Lembcke until 1933 and then by Fritz Clausen (1893–1947), was significant. The party had about 4,900 members in 1939 and managed to elect three members to parliament just before the war. More important was the Farmers' Union (Landbrugernes Sammenslutning) and its political arm, the Farmers' Party (1934). These groups, however, were mainly concerned with issues facing the agricultural population. They were not dedicated to the overthrow of the political system.

Finland, as already mentioned, had the most tumultuous political history of this era, and several radical right-wing groups played central roles in making this the case. The National Defense (Suojeluskunta/ SK), founded in the 1920s, was a paramilitary organization that supported the activities of several other groups. More important was the Lapuan Movement, an organization that emerged in 1928 in the wake of red-white clashes in Lapua, a small town in western Finland. Although not a political party, the group formed ties with leaders of the Conservatives. Their activities, which included kidnapping, beating, and dumping their opponents across the Soviet border, influenced elections, the choice of governments, and policies for several years. In 1929–30, for example, they were important in securing the passage of laws designed to increase the powers of the president in "emergencies" and make the Communists illegal. The year 1932 was crucial. The Lapuan leaders became increasingly radical and bold, and plans were laid for a coup that was to grow out of clashes between Left and Right at Mäntsälä in late February. Their plottings failed, however. The government stood firm, other radical groups did not rally to the revolt, and the moderates, alienated by the drift toward extremism, abandoned the Lapuans. The organization was banned and its leaders arrested. (The court proceedings that followed were almost comical, and the sentences minor.) This was not the end of the radical Right in Finland, however. In the place of the Lapuans appeared the Patriotic National Movement (IKL), a political party dedicated to crushing socialism, ending the era of party politics, and expanding to the east. The group was more a nuisance than a real factor in Finnish political life. In 1933 and 1936 elections they captured fourteen seats in the parliament. Their black-shirt uniforms and obnoxious behavior in the Eduskunta alienated almost everyone and led to the passage of antiuniform legislation in 1934. Legal action against the IKL was initiated in 1938, but was still in court when war came in 1939. The organization was banned under the terms of the armistice with the Soviet Union in 1944.

The Right in Norway also had many bases. One of earliest and largest was the League of the Fatherland (Fŏdrelandslaget), founded in 1925 by Christian Michelsen and others who advocated higher defense spending, anticommunism, nationalism, and stronger leadership. In 1930 the group had some 100,000 members. Most important, at least in historical terms, were the organizations founded and led by Vidkun Quisling (1887–1945). The son of a pastor, he served as an army officer, a diplomat, and the minister of defense in 1931–33. During his tenure in office he was important in the development of the Leidangen, a state police force designed to deal with domestic unrest. In 1930 he established the Nordic People's Resurgence (Nordisk Folkereisning), a group that emphasized Nordic racial superiority. More important was the founding of National Union (Nasjonal Samling) in 1933. This became Norway's version of Nazism, and Quisling assumed the role of a self-styled clone of Hitler. Although Quisling and his group, which may have had as many as 15,000 members, were relatively insignificant in the 1930s, never managing to elect a member to the Storting, they would play a part in World War II.

In Sweden there were two Nazi-inspired political parties: the National Socialist People's Party (Sveriges nationalsocialistiska parti), which evolved from a group founded by Birger Furugård in 1924, and the National Socialist Workers' Party (Nationalsocialistiska arbetarpartiet), established by Sven Olof Lindholm as the result of a coup in Furugård's organization in 1933. Both were highly localized in their support, may have had about 1,000 members, and never won seats in the parliament. Slightly more influential was the Conservative Party's independent youth organization, the National Youth League (Sveriges

Nationella Ungdomsförbund). Among other issues, this group opposed defense cuts and idolized a skewed version of Bismarck. It established the National Party in 1934 and worked to influence members of the Conservatives' parliamentary delegation.

Overall, one should not, however, underestimate the importance of these groups. That they existed at all points to the presence of disillusionment, discontent with the existing systems, and deep social cleavages. They were noisy and disruptive. During World War II several acquired new importance. They also appear to have played a positive role in Norden's political development, because their threats to the system increased the willingness of the mainstream parties to compromise and helped effect the workings of democracy rather than hasten its downfall.

Underlying the political history of Norden during the interwar years is the successful transition each country experienced from near or actual revolution to minority parlementarism to majority parlementarism operating with a high regard for consensus, compromise, and moderation. During a period when so much of Europe was plagued by the polarization of politics between radical Left and radical Right, the erosion of the Center, the paralysis of democratic institutions, and the rise of the Nazis and other authoritarian regimes, the Nordic countries proved that modern societies could come together, democracy could work, and the serious problems of the period could be ameliorated.

How does one explain these successes? There is no simple answer to this question, and one must be careful not to overemphasize what might have been largely a matter of luck. Factors that were certainly important include political histories of success in meeting crises effectively, the general absence of revolution, acceptance by an overwhelming majority of the democratic systems that had evolved in Norden, the absence of festering animosities or legacies from World War I, histories that included long-term regard for the less fortunate, largely homogeneous societies, and the presence of capable leaders across the political spectrum willing to compromise.

Social and Economic Developments

When this period began, Norden was still a world of hierarchical class societies, although it could be argued it was really a world of two hierarchical societies: an older, more traditional one with its nobilities and peasants, and merchant elites; and a new, modern, and increasingly urban one with new social groups, tastes, and norms. Certainly, an old nobility continued to exist, especially in Denmark and Sweden, as did long-established urban elites. The rural populations continued to be divided into owners, renters, and workers, each group with its own internal differentiations. The newer rural and urban industrial sectors were divided along worker-employer lines, which were clearly reflected by the organizations that represented them, the unions and employer federations. Small-scale artisan producers survived, but faced constant threats to their viability from industry. The increasingly complex urban societies had their own hierarchies. This social organization influenced all aspects of life including economic opportunity, culture, social behavior, and education. Generally, the lower classes resented and increasingly resisted many of these realities while the upper classes sought to preserve them. The validity of the idea of class warfare was widely accepted.

By the close of this period important gains had been made to reduce at least some of the differences in Nordic societies in terms of income, education, opportunity, welfare, and the quality of everyday life. Despite the economic difficulties of the period, there were improvements in incomes, housing, diets, dress, and social services for people at the lower end of the social spectrum. Leisure moved from the domain of the upper classes to become an aspect of working-class life. These tangible changes were accompanied by the lessening of social tensions and the growing sense of social unity. This shift may be clearly seen in the differences between election campaign slogans of the 1920s, which emphasized class differences and conflict, and those of the 1930s, which emphasized social cohesion and cooperation. The concepts of social and economic democracy were at the center of this progress.

In terms of economic development, it is too easy to focus only on the negative aspects of this period, as serious as they were. Progress was made in almost every economic sector. On average, the output of goods and services rose throughout Norden. For the 1920s annual growth rates in the gross national product (GDP) averaged around 2.5 percent for Norway and Sweden, 3.9 percent for Denmark, and 5.3 percent for Finland. During the 1930s these figures were 2.6 percent for Sweden, 2.7 percent for Norway, 3.8 percent for Finland, and 2 percent for Denmark. The worst years were between 1928 and 1935, when the GDP actually fell. Although agriculture was in some respects chronically depressed and the human costs of failures and foreclosures enormous in this period, rationalization, government assistance, and mechanization resulted in higher efficiency and productivity. The output of primary products such as ores, fish, and forest products rose. The extent and complexity of manufacturing grew, aided by foreign and internal investment, electrification, new production techniques, and new technologies. Domestic and foreign demand for goods and services increased. Export volume rose. Among the key "industries" were Danish agriculture; Norwegian fishing and electrochemicals; Swedish iron, steel, ore, and engineering; and Finnish agriculture and forest products. Denmark supplied nearly 40 percent of the world's bacon and 29 percent of its butter. The Norwegian merchant fleet was modernized, as more and more ships were built or converted to diesel power. Also, new specialized vessels were added to the fleet. Sweden exported nearly 14 million tons of iron ore annually, principally to Germany and Great Britain. Its leading companies, including SKF, L. M. Ericsson, and Electrolux served worldwide markets and established global subsidiary networks. At home, domestic demand, supported by the general rise in real wages, fostered the growth of consumer product industries and the retail sector. Communication construction, sometimes linked with crisis unemployment projects, resulted in better rail, road, and telephone networks.

An important contributor to the economic growth of the region was the ongoing development of cooperatives, especially in Finland and Sweden. In contrast to elsewhere in Norden, the Finnish cooperative movement grew from a core, the Pellervo Society, founded in 1899 by Hannes Gebhard, a university professor, and other middle-class individuals who believed such a movement would benefit the lower classes. The society provided information, management advice, and assistance to actual cooperatives that grew up mainly in dairy, retail, and credit. There were about 65 such groups in 1902. By 1918 there were over 500 dairy and almost 600 retail and credit cooperatives, and on the eve of World War II these figures were 676, 539, and 1,168, respectively. Membership in 1937 was nearly 800,000. Nine-tenths of the country's butter was produced by VALIO co-ops. Other cooperatives accounted for half of all grain production and one-third of all retail trade. Finnish cooperatives were also involved in match, candy, tools, farm machinery, fertilizer, clothing, and margarine production.

In Sweden the individual cooperatives developed before a central organization. Hundreds of small groups with varying activity emphases came and went between 1850 and 1900. In 1899 the Cooperative Union (Kooperativ Förbundet/KF) was founded as a center for information and education. Gradually, it evolved into a central administrative body for most of the country's producer and consumer cooperatives. In 1904 KF began to act as a wholesaler. Four years later it established its own banking facilities. From around 1910 the movement became involved in a series of struggles with cartels that produced and fixed the prices on essential products. Two of these involved margarine. Just prior to World War I and again shortly after the war, KF undertook to manufacture its own margarine. Doing so brought down the price and broke the cartel. An even better market position was established in 1932, when KF opened a vegetable oil production facility, thereby ending dependence on monopolistic foreign sources. In what may seem to be a somewhat comical conflict, the co-ops also broke a monopoly controlling the manufacture of rubber boots, the "galoshes cartel" in the mid-1920s. In the process they halved the price of a necessity for most Swedes. Similar successes were reached in the production of light bulbs (LUMA), automobile tires, toilet fixtures, wood and paper products, soaps, flour, and candies. At the same time, cooperatives also became involved in insurance (Folksam) and housing construction and mortgage credit (Hyresgästernas Sparkasse och Bygnadsförening/HSB and Svenska Riksbyggen/SR).

Women

For women the interwar years brought new behaviors, styles, and opportunities, as well as continued subordination and exploitation. Many women questioned long-accepted manners and morals, including their submissiveness and the double standard for sexual behavior in their relationships with men. Although resisted by authorities throughout Scandinavia, sex education programs, linked with information about and distribution of condoms, contributed to liberalized sexual behavior and population control efforts. Women's fashions, underclothing, hairstyles, and makeup habits changed. A few women even dared to smoke in public. The vote and access to careers in government service and legislatures brought women into politics. However, their voting participation tended to be lower than men's except when particular issues, such as prohibition, were involved. Very few sought or were elected to national parliaments. A few were appointed to cabinet positions including Nina Bang, minister of education in Denmark (1924–26), and Miina Sillanpää, assistant minister of social affairs in Finland (1926–27). In the professions, women continued to make gains, especially in medicine and education. Although women continued to find work in white-collar jobs as secretaries, clerks, and the like, they remained almost entirely closed out of management. Industrial jobs tended to be closed to them during periods of high unemployment—times when the pressures on women to follow traditional domestic expectations also increased.

An important aspect of women's history in this period, especially among the rising working and middle class, was the development of the concept of the ideal housewife and the emergence of an outlook that being a housewife was like having a career. In this context, it has been argued that a unique and brief moment in women's history opened during the interwar years when most women did not and did not have to work outside the home. Science, technology, economic conditions, demographics, and government policies were important in creating this moment. The spread of electrification from cities into rural areas and a host of new machines for the home (vacuum cleaners, washing machines, small kitchen appliances, etc.) reduced the need for domestic help, decreased some of the drudgery in household work, but also increased the demands on wives. Housework became a subject for study, and so too did cooking and nutrition, and an ideal of the perfect home evolved. Women were expected to cook healthy meals and raise perfect children. Educational programs, organizations, and publications were devoted to the new demands on women in the home. At the same time, general increases in incomes by men made it less necessary for wives to work, and social concerns and worries over level or declining populations resulted in government policies that encouraged women to stay home and have children. Sigrid Undset's 1936 novel, *Den trofaste hustru* (The faithful wife), addresses many aspects of women's lives in this period, including the home, affairs, divorce, children born out of wedlock, employment, and traditions versus new ideals and behaviors.

Cultural and Intellectual Trends
For literature, in which words like *restlessness, nihilism, criticism,* and *pessimism* help define this era, the interwar decades were dynamic and fruitful times. All the Nordic countries produced writers of poetry,

fiction, and drama of lasting importance. Some authors focused on finding meaning in a world whose values, they believed, had been shattered by the Great War; others focused on deeply personal psychological questions. Among them were Jacob Paludan, Kjell Abell, Kaj Munk, and Jörgen Stein in Denmark; Sigrid Hoel and Tarjei Vesaas in Norway; and Pär Lagerkvist, Karin Boye, and Agnes von Krusenstjerna in Sweden. Others, including so-called social realists and proletarian authors, addressed what they saw as the class warfare or other social issues of the period through a variety of genre. Among these writers were the Norwegians Sigrid Undset and Nordahl Grieg, and Sweden's Ivar Lo-Johansson and Vilhelm Moberg. Painting also followed these patterns, as seen in the abstractions of Otto Carlsund or the social realism of Reidar Aulie or Albin Amelin.

This was also the era in which Scandinavian architecture and interior design became internationally famous. In architecture, three trends spanned the interwar years. One was a continued interest in historical or national romantic themes, reflected, for example, in the new Stockholm city hall, designed by Ragnar Östberg and completed several years after World War I, or in P. V. Jensen-Klint's Grundtvig Church in Copenhagen. Another carryover was neoclassicism, exemplified in Gudolf Blakstad and Herman Munthe-Kaas's town hall in Haugesund (Norway) or Johan Sirén's Finnish parliament building. Most important, however, were the Functionalist town halls, medical facilities, libraries, university complexes, and apartment buildings of Denmark's Arne Jacobsen, Vilhelm Lauritzen, Kay Fisker, C. F. Möller, and Povl Stegmann; Finland's Alvar Aalto; Norway's Lars Backer, Finn Bryn, Ove Bang, Arnstein Arneberg, and Magnus Poulsson; and Sweden's Gunnar Asplund. These buildings displayed a mastery of setting, form, and function.

Similar patterns of style and significance appeared in the design of domestic and industrial products and interiors. A new period of design creativity developed in the 1880s that has lasted to the present day. Although highly varied both regionally and stylistically over time, this period has been characterized by a concern for purity of form, functionality, tradition, utilization of natural materials, restrained aesthetic expression, and the links between design and social values. These concerns formed the basis, especially in the 1930s, for the development of the "Scandinavian modern" style in furniture, ceramics, glasswares, metals, housewares, lighting, and textiles. Among the outstanding persons of this era were Alvar Aalto, Carl Malmsten, Kaare

Workers Café (1936), by Albin Amelin (1902–75). Courtesy of Statens Konstmuseer, Stockholm, Sweden.

Klint, and Herman Munthe-Kaas in furniture; Georg Jensen in silver; Märta Måås-Fjetterström in textiles; Nora Gulbrandsen, Wilhelm Kåge, and Edward Hald in ceramics; and Simon Gate in glasswork. Companies such as Porsgrunds, Gustafsberg, Rörstrand, Orrefors, and Bing and Gröndahl became internationally recognized and were vital in supporting the designers of this period.

The interwar period was also a time when localized folk cultures were eroded and mass popular cultures developed in Norden to a degree never before seen—and in which the working class played important roles. Despite the economic difficulties, the eight-hour day and guaranteed vacations became the norm for most people in towns and cities, which created more and more leisure time. Filling that time was seen by some as socially and politically important and an important sphere of economic development. Political parties, trade unions, volunteer organizations, the state, and businesses became increasingly involved in leisure. The technologies of the period, including the motion picture, radio, phonograph, telephone, bus, and automobile,

The Seventeenth of May, by Norwegian artist Johan Berner Jakobsen. Courtesy of Oslo Kommunes Kunstsamlinger, Stenersenmuseet, Oslo, Norway.

contributed to the erosion of localism and the shaping and spread of these cultures. In turn, the mass cultures contributed to the growth of reactions to the countercultures of many of the right-wing organizations that looked back to a romanticized past or emphasized similarly romanticized views of folk life.

The popular cultures of this period had many aspects. They were defined by entertainment media and personalities, fashions, fads, sports, dance steps, public behaviors, and literature. The cinema was especially popular and important. One estimate puts daily Danish film attendance at 60,000 during these decades. During the 1920s Nordic silent films, often loaded with heavy doses of rural nostalgia and the melodramatic, competed successfully with imports. The Danish comic team "Fyrtårnet og Bivognen" (known to English audiences as "The Long and the Short") was as popular as Charlie Chaplin, and the serious works of directors, such as the Dane Carl Dreyer and the Swedes Mauritz Stiller and Victor Sjöström, enjoyed international reputations. In the 1930s the development of color and sound technologies drove up the price of filmmaking and changed the nature of the people who acted in them, and these changes hurt the small national film industries. American films often appeared in the hundreds of movie houses throughout Scandinavia in the 1930s, and they helped set off fears of "Americanization" long before the post–World War II blue jeans and Coca-Cola invasion. Still, the 1930s witnessed the production of many important films in Norden, films that focused on the plight of the workers, bourgeois values, and social realism. Overall, both the light and the serious Nordic films of this period have their place in film history and established the bases for important developments of this genre following World War II.

The phonograph and radio also were powerful media for cultural development. The former carried national and international music into the home. The latter, largely under the control of the state, grew in popularity from the mid-1920s. Radio clubs were formed. By the mid-1930s it has been estimated there were half a million radios in Denmark alone. The radio and the spread of telephone systems throughout Norden broke down distance barriers and opened the region to instant communication and news. They also contributed to the erosion of localisms and dialect differences, developments that continued after World War II.

Improved transportation also worked to bring down barriers, spread culture, build nations, and foster tourism. The bicycle, automobile, bus, and airplane were added to the train and the steamship as facilitators of mobility. Road systems throughout Norden were expanded, and hundreds of bridges built. By 1939 Norway had some 119,000 registered motor vehicles. The rail links across Norway's mountains were also completed. Airports, like Kastrup near Copenhagen and Fornebu near Oslo, were built in the 1930s, and international and inter-Nordic air service companies including Det Norske Luftfartselskap and the predecessor of today's Finnair were created. Quite simply, people were now able to and did move about more than ever before.

Also important in the development of popular culture were the activities of ancillary groups based on the political parties, trade unions, cooperatives, and other voluntary organizations. Youth groups, women's auxiliaries, athletic clubs, and the like sponsored hiking, camping, and cycling outings. Swimming, boxing, gymnastics, and dancing enjoyed great popularity, as did new activities such as motor racing and flying. The folk high school movement enjoyed renewed growth, and adult education, study and reading circles, and a variety of cultural activity groups such as singing and dramatic societies flourished. In addition to fostering their organizations' idealogies and national ideals, many of these groups were dedicated to nurturing values such as good health and love of nature in an industrial society.

13

Norden and World War II

The Nordic countries' experiences in the World War II were varied and, at the same time, highly similar. Each sought to remain outside the maelstrom, but only Sweden succeeded in doing so — and then only in certain ways. The Faeroe Islands and Iceland were occupied by the Allies, Denmark and Norway fell to the Nazis in April and June 1940, respectively, and Finland actually fought three wars in the context of the wider struggle. The war brought vast human suffering, interrupted highly promising patterns of political, economic, social, and cultural development throughout the region, and triggered reassessments of past domestic, foreign, and security policies during and immediately after the war. The conflict both divided and united the Nordic peoples. Some have seen the war as one of the most important factors in shaping contemporary Scandinavia (and Europe). Others have seen it as an accelerator of patterns of change already in place or as merely an interrupting interlude in a longer period of great change. Whichever the case, the years between 1939 and 1945 certainly were among the most eventful and important in recent Nordic history.

Paradoxically, the Nordic countries' World War I experiences both created the widely held impression that neutrality could be maintained during global conflicts and shook the consensus about the viability of neutrality as a foreign policy. In the immediate postwar years, whether or not to continue that line was an issue linked with the question of joining the League of Nations, which was set up in 1919 to provide collective security and to act as a medium for the peaceful settlement of international disputes. Despite opposition from the socialist Left, which saw the league as a tool of capitalist imperialism, and the Right, which was reluctant to compromise national sovereignty, all the Nordic countries became members and supported

Norden's Nobel Peace Prize Winners

In all, eight Scandinavians have been awarded the Nobel peace prize.

1908: Fredrik Bajer (1837–1922). Proponent of Nordic neutrality, opponent of exorbitant military appropriations to defend Copenhagen, founder of the Danish Peace Society, and advocate of an international organization dedicated to the maintenance of peace.

1908: Klas Pontus Arnoldson (1844–1916). Riksdag representative, a founder of the Swedish Peace and Arbitration Society, editor, influential in shaping public opinion in Sweden in 1905 for the peaceful settlement of the union question.

1921: Hjalmar Branting (1860–1925). Early leader of the Swedish Social Democratic Party, journalist, Riksdag representative, three times Swedish prime minister in the early 1920s, critic of the Versailles Treaty, advocate of small-state interests in the League of Nations.

1921: Christian L. Lange (1869–1938). Secretary of the Norwegian Nobel Commission, delegate to the League of Nations, secretary general of the Interparliamentary Union from 1909 to 1933, social theorist who believed in the "unity of humanity."

1922: Fridtjof Nansen (1861–1930). Naturalist, Arctic explorer, supporter of a peaceful solution to the union crisis in 1905, Norwegian delegate to the League of Nations, instrumental in the repatriation

the league's activities until it began to unravel in the early 1930s. The rise to power of the Nazis in Germany, the failure of the league to deal with Japanese aggression in China and the Italian attack on Ethiopia, and the breakdown of any pretense of arms limitation efforts pushed Norden's leaders to reassess their policies.

Linked with Norden's involvement in the league was the commitment of the region's leaders and important interest groups to international humanitarian efforts and to other international organizations such as the World Court in the Hague, the International Red Cross, and the International Federation of Trade Unions. Four Scandinavians received Nobel peace prizes during the interwar years. Sweden's of hundreds of thousands of POWs and refugees following World War I and in organizing relief efforts in the 1921 Russian famine. Created the "Nansen passports," which were crucial in the resettlement of refugees and were copied in later times by, among others, Raoul Wallenberg.

1930: Nathan Söderblom (1866–1931). Pastor, theologian, archbishop of Sweden, and advocate of Christian ecumenicalism. Organized the 1925 Stockholm Conference on Christian unity and believed the churches were an essential medium for promoting peace.

1961: Dag Hammarskjöld (1905–61). Economist, public servant, two-term secretary general of the United Nations (1953–61). Believed the UN should play an independent role in world diplomacy and took an active role in negotiating settlements in China and Egypt. Died in a plane crash in the Congo while on a peacekeeping mission. The prize was awarded posthumously.

1982: Alva Myrdal (1902–86). Social reformer, advocate of women's equality, director of the UN's Department of Social Affairs, Swedish ambassador to India. Became involved in disarmament in 1961. Minister of Church Affairs and Minister of Disarmament in Sweden for twelve years; served as Sweden's representative at UN disarmament conferences. In her acceptance speech she severely criticized the great powers for nuclear proliferation.

Social Democratic leader Hjalmar Branting (1860–1925) and the Norwegian pacifist Christian L. Lange (1869–1938) shared the prize in 1921 for their work as peace advocates. Norway's Fridtjof Nansen (1861–1930), who worked tirelessly through the 1920s to assist relief and refugee repatriation efforts, was the 1922 recipient. Sweden's Nathan Söderblom (1866–1931), church leader and spokesperson of ecumenicalism, received the price in 1930.

For more than a decade, the League of Nations was a moderating medium for several issues affecting the Nordic countries. For example, an international commission made up of representatives from Great Britain, France, Norway, and Sweden presided over the February and

March 1920 plebiscites in north and central Slesvig and adjudicated the readjustment of the Slesvig border, which went into effect in July 1920.

The league was also important in settling the ongoing question of control over the Åland Islands—an issue that aroused strong opinions in Finland and Sweden. The islands had been included with the mainland as part of the Grand Duchy of Finland in 1809. In response to Swedish security concerns, they were demilitarized in 1856, following the Crimean War, and they were a pawn in German attempts to draw Sweden into World War I. Amid the political turmoil in Finland in 1918, Swedish troops occupied the islands. If the principle of national self-determination contained in Woodrow Wilson's fourteen points and carried over to the league was followed, the islands would go to Sweden. Over 90 percent of the population was Swedish-speaking and in a postwar plebiscite expressed a preference for a link with Sweden. The league worked out a settlement in 1921 that awarded sovereignty to Finland under the conditions that Åland be allowed to develop as a self-governing province, that the Swedishness of the islands be protected, and that they remain demilitarized.

Although Norway generally took an active part in trying to make the league effective, and two of its political leaders, J. L. Mowinckel and C. J. Hambro, served as presidents of the assembly, a few Norwegians pursued a line of policy some have called "Arctic Imperialism," which was intended to serve Norwegian interests and enhance international prestige. This curiously paradoxical aggressiveness was fed by scientific and commercial interests, the exploration adventures of Nansen, Roald Amundsen, and Lars Christensen (in the Antarctic), and some enthusiastic nationalists including Fredrik Wedel Jarlsberg. In its most serious form, it involved attempts to assert land claims in eastern Greenland and to establish sovereignty over Spitsbergen/Svalbard.

The first of these developed into a simmering conflict with Denmark in 1921, when the Copenhagen government announced that it was extending its claim to sovereignty over Greenland from the western coast to the east. This move, it was believed, would hurt Norwegian economic interests, and it aroused old resentments propped up by an interpretation of the Treaty of Kiel (1814), which some Norwegians argued did not include the transfer of Norway's medieval claims to Greenland (and Iceland and the Faeroes) to Denmark. A gradual increase in fishing and whaling activities during the 1920s by

Norwegians heightened tensions, as did an organization in Norway dedicated to Greenland expansion led by Gustav Smedal and several highly vocal newspapers including *Dagbladet* and *Tidens Tegn.* A crisis came in June 1931, when a small group of Norwegians "occupied" a stretch of coast in eastern Greenland and named it "Erik the Red's Land." The dispute was settled by the International Court in 1933, when Denmark's sovereignty over all of Greenland was acknowledged.

The coal resources (and later the uranium) of Spitsbergen, the riches of its surrounding waters, and the scientific aspects of the area attracted commercial interests and Arctic researchers from Norway, Sweden, and Russia. Before World War I, the island was owned by no one and remained open to multinational exploitation. After the war, pressure grew in Norway for annexation of the island. Norwegian sovereignty was recognized at Versailles in 1920—along with the understanding that the resources of the island would remain accessible to other nations, and it continue to be demilitarized. Norwegian political presence was established in 1925, and the island's name changed to the medieval Svalbard. In fact, the island was shared with the Soviet Union.

The Finns' main diplomatic preoccupation during the interwar years lay to the east, with the Soviet Union. The Treaty of Tartu/Dorpat (in Estonia), signed in October 1920, ended over two years of on-and-off negotiations. Under the terms of the agreement the state of war between the two countries ended and Finnish independence was affirmed; questions of fortifications, neutralization of territories, and transit and waterway traffic were addressed; and borders were established. Finland was awarded Petsamo in the northeast and agreed to leave two parishes in East Karelia between the White Sea and the frontier. By all appearances the treaty established a stable situation. However, a legacy of mistrust remained in Finland, which was perpetuated throughout the period, first by the ongoing subversive activities of the Communists in Finland, which clearly had Soviet support and encouragement, and then by the Soviet demands for territorial concessions in 1938–39.

Norden and World War II

The gradual collapse of peace in Europe, punctuated by one crisis after another from 1931 on, gave the Nordic governments reason to reassess their policies and adjust to the changing situation. The failure

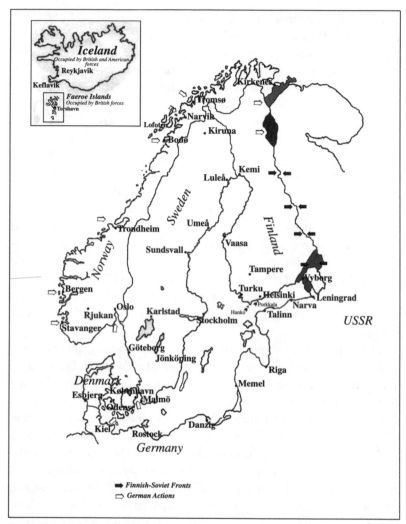

Scandinavia during World War II.

of the league to deal effectively with the Japanese attack on China and the Italian invasion of Ethiopia, the mockery Hitler and Mussolini made of the nonintervention policy in the Spanish Civil War, and the rise of Hitler and his campaign of rearmament and negation of the Treaty of Versailles combined to redirect Nordic foreign and security policies. Never fully abandoned, neutrality was reemphasized. From 1932 on, a series of Nordic foreign ministers meetings were held. Generally, these meetings were devoted to discussions of issues and ended with joint communiqués of common ideals, such as the May 1938 joint declaration of neutrality in the event of a European war. More tangible suggestions for cooperation met with resistance. Of course, the leaders in each country were working from different historical contexts and had different perceptions of the darkening situation in Europe. For example, they perceived no common enemy. Germany was the primary danger to the Danes; for the Finns it was the Soviet Union. Norwegians believed everyone would leave them alone in the event of a war, and that the British would save them if need be. Swedes generally preferred not to alienate any of the great powers. In general, the Nordic governments found it easy to share neutrality as a policy, but were uniformly unwilling to compromise independence of action in the defense of that policy.

Several specific examples illustrate this breakdown in common effort. In 1936 the idea of a Nordic defensive pact to defend neutrality was raised but received little support, largely because there was no agreement on who "the enemy" was, because of fears that a pact would arouse great power concerns and create less security instead of more, and because of the absence of the military strength to make it effective.

Another illustration of this lack of real unity in Norden may be seen in the responses of the various governments to Hitler's offer of nonaggression pacts in April 1939. The Finnish, Norwegian, and Swedish governments politely declined. In communiqués each argued that relations between their countries and Germany were good and would remain so and that a nonaggression pact was unnecessary and potentially alarming to the other powers. Thorvald Stauning's government in Denmark accepted and signed an agreement in May 1939. The decision was explained for two reasons. The pact was seen as a tacit acceptance by the Nazis of the 1920 Slesvig border settlement, and it offered a reasonable assurance of security. For the following eleven months the pact, combined with neutrality and trade agreements, was the basis of Denmark's foreign policy until April 1940—perhaps until August 1943.

Finally, there is the case of a joint Finnish-Swedish attempt to refortify the Åland Islands. Talks between government officials began in the fall of 1938, and in January 1939 the so-called Stockholm Plan was ready. It was circulated to the signers of a 1922 agreement that reiterated the islands' demilitarized status. The Soviets were also informed, although only slowly. For a time it looked as if the plan would receive the desired approval and could proceed. However, the Soviets began to raise objections, which led to Sweden's withdrawal in early June. A joint effort that Sweden's foreign minister Rickard Sandler described as "putting a padlock on a neutralized area" collapsed. The Finns went ahead independently to install fortifications.

Despite what amounted to diplomatic insularity by each Nordic country in the last years before World War II, remarkably little was done throughout the region to prepare to defend neutrality. During the 1920s the issue of military appropriations was one cause over which the nonsocialist and socialist parties were bitterly divided. In general, expenditures in Denmark, Norway, and Sweden remained steady or declined into the mid-1930s. The Danes enacted small increases in 1937. The short-lived caretaker government of Axel Pehrsson-Bramstorp successfully passed a measure to increase expenditures in Sweden in summer 1936. Norway's leaders stood by a very limited defense plan adopted in 1937 right down to April 1940. Because of the lingering fear of the Soviet Union, internal unrest, and the stronger position of non-Marxist parties, the Finns spent proportionally the most on defense (about 25 percent of budget) throughout the period. Still, none of the Nordic countries was prepared to defend itself against an attack by a major power. Troop numbers were small, and equipment was outmoded and in short supply. No Nordic country had a modern air force, and naval forces were deficient. In general, Norden was unprepared to deal with the crises that came with the outbreak of war in September 1939, especially when one considers how the second phase of the twentieth century's great war far exceeded the first in scope and destructiveness.

Finland's Three Wars

Finland was the first to be drawn into the maelstrom. Triggered by growing security concerns vis-à-vis Nazi Germany and coupled with pressure on Estonia, Latvia, and Lithuania, in the spring of 1939 the Soviets mounted an ongoing campaign to force Finland to turn over control of island groups in the Gulf of Finland, accede to border adjustments in the Karelian Isthmus, and grant them a lease on the Hangö/Hanko Peninsula west of Helsinki for a naval base in exchange for compensating territories.

From the Soviet perspective these demands were reasonable. For Finnish leaders they were threatening and confirmed old fears of Soviet/Russian designs on Finland. They were consistently refused.

The conclusion of the Nazi-Soviet Non-Aggression Pact in August 1939 did nothing to remove Soviet fears of Germany or to cancel the requests coming from Moscow. In fact, given a free hand in the eastern Baltic, Stalin renewed the pressures. Repeated efforts to reach an agreement in October failed, despite the fact that the Soviets offered substantial territorial concessions in exchange for an agreement. In early November negotiations were replaced with serious military planning in Moscow. Using a case of mistaken or staged artillery fire on Soviet positions on 26 November as an excuse, the Soviets broke off relations with Finland two days later and began military operations on the thirtieth. The so-called Winter War had begun.

Initially, the war was a stalemate. Soviet advances were met with fierce resistance and stopped. Although outnumbered and inferior in supplies, the Finns enjoyed a few advantages. Their very successful defensive tactics were based on hit-and-run skirmishes using camouflage, terrain, and climate. Moreover, the fight was on their own familiar territory, and the Finnish forces fought with patriotic fervor against a long-mistrusted enemy probably weakened by Stalin's purges. Working against the Finns in the long run were the lack of international support, save for volunteers including approximately 8,000 from Sweden and "humanitarian assistance," and the overwhelming advantages the Soviets held in numbers and matériel.

Although stalled in December and January, the Soviet advance resumed with a major assault in early February, and Finnish forces were rolled back under the pressure of overwhelming odds. In early March army commander C. G. Mannerheim admitted the situation was hopeless, and the Ryti government accepted Soviet peace terms. The Treaty of Moscow was signed on 12 March 1940. Under its terms Finland lost far more than the Soviets had demanded six months earlier. All the Karelian Isthmus, the city of Viipuri, several islands in the Gulf of Finland, and territory on the western shore of Lake Ladoga were ceded. The Soviets also secured a thirty-year lease to the Hanko Peninsula west of Helsinki for a naval base. In addition to the human, economic, and political costs of the war, which included over 23,000 killed and more than 47,000 wounded, the Finns had to absorb over 300,000 refugees from the southeast. Finding housing, land, and jobs for these people was an incredible national achievement.

It is hardly surprising that many Finns were deeply disappointed, felt betrayed by the Western powers and their Nordic neighbors, were resentful of the treaty, and hoped for an opportunity to take revenge.

The Soviets fed these feelings with new demands for more concessions from the Finns and even meddled in domestic affairs. Few
doubted that Finland would not be absorbed into the Soviet Union
like its Baltic neighbors. (This intent had been expressed to German
leaders and was received negatively in late 1940.)

It is also not surprising that Finland was an easy target for Nazi
Germany's overtures and offers of assistance in 1940 and 1941. At
first these led to the granting of transit rights across the far north
and purchases of military equipment. They culminated in Finland
fighting alongside Germany. The exact nature of the Nazi-Finnish
cooperation was murky, and it can be argued the Finns entered their
second war (the Continuation War) with the Soviets independently.
Only after the Germans had launched Operation Barbarossa against
the Soviet Union (22 June 1941) and the Finns had, according to
their perspective, initiated countermeasures in response to Soviet
assaults made against them in late June 1941 did Finland enter into
understandings that made the country a cobelligerent with Nazi
Germany. For the most part, the Finns fought their own war, despite
the presence of German advisers and troops in some sectors, especially the far north. They repeatedly rebuffed German requests for
a formal alliance and ignored German calls for help in the assault on
Leningrad. Although a few Finns advocated a far more extensive
war to recover the lost territories and then advance east to create a
"greater Finland," once the territories lost in 1940 were recovered
the advance stopped, and a "sitting war" followed. This was a bloody
war of trenches, sniping, and small-scale incursions by both sides
that took a terrible toll.

Efforts to end the Finnish-Soviet conflict began as early as February 1943, but were unsuccessful. In March 1944 the Soviets revealed
their conditions for peace, which included territorial annexations,
reparations, and reductions in Finnish arms. Helsinki found itself
caught in a very difficult situation. Thousands of German troops were
stationed in Finland. The country was dependent on Germany for
arms and domestic supplies. But the Nazis were clearly losing the war,
and the Finns hoped to save their freedom in the postwar world. The
risks of every policy decision were high, and summer 1944 brought a
confusing sequence of events.

On 9 June the Soviets launched a major counteroffensive that
rolled back the Finnish forces and issued a demand for unconditional
surrender, and the Germans renewed their call for a formal alliance

The Soviet Perspective

Soviet history presents these two conflicts very differently. Each was purely defensive. The Soviet Union was only protecting its northwest flank from an anticipated German attack that was sure to come. Its requests for territorial concessions were reasonable and always involved compensation. In 1939 the Soviet Union was attacked by Finnish forces numbering 600,000 men and aided by Britain, France, Sweden, and Germany. The 1941–44 conflict is not presented as a separate war, but rather is treated as a part of the Great Patriotic War. Finland is viewed simply as an ally of Germany—along with Italy, Hungary, and Romania. The 1944 summer offensive in Finland is broken into a set of attacks, the most important being the Svir'-Petrozavodsk Operation (or Viborg Operation). Virtually nothing is said about the treaty (1944 armistice agreement and 1947 Paris Peace Treaty) that ended the struggle.

and assurances that there would be no separate peace with the Soviet Union. The Soviet demands stiffened the Finnish resistance, and the front was stabilized. However, President Risto Ryti, in what may have been a clever ploy, sent a personal letter of assurance to Hitler that was regarded as an alliance commitment. On 1 August, with the Finnish forces stretched to their maximum, Ryti resigned in a move designed to abrogate his deal with Germany. C. G. Mannerheim succeeded him, a new coalition government was created, and serious peace talks opened with Moscow. Fighting stopped on 4 September, and the preliminary peace was signed on the nineteenth. The 1944 treaty, which was affirmed in slightly modified form at Paris in 1947, involved the recognition of the 1940 borders, a fifty-year lease on the Porkkala Peninsula, access and transit rights to Porkkala, the loss of Petsamo, removal of all restrictions on the Communists in Finland, punishment of war criminals, reduction of armed forces to minimal levels, and payment in kind of reparations amounting to $300,000,000. In addition, the Finns were expected to drive the remaining German troops from their country within a few months. This last campaign amounted to Finland's third war, and it proved particularly costly, especially because as the Germans retreated, they destroyed roads, bridges, rail lines, villages, and farms, and took revenge on the local populations.

The Continuation War was more costly than the first. About 54,000 men lost their lives; slightly more were wounded. Many of the refugees who had returned to Karelia after June 1941 now chose to leave again. Nearly 1,000 died driving out the Germans. Overall, these conflicts cost nearly 80,000 lives. One-twelfth of the country was turned over to the Soviets. When the direct and indirect costs are tallied up, they come to the equivalent of nearly $10 billion in late 1990s terms.

The "Phony War" and Invasion

For the people and governments of Denmark, Iceland, Norway, and Sweden, the first six months of the war seemed, by comparison with events in Finland, relatively quiet. The Poles capitulated following the fall of Warsaw on 28 September 1939, no major campaign by either side followed, and there were even hopes peace could be negotiated. During this lull, the so-called phony war, or sitting war, there appeared to be every reason to expect that neutrality would again prove to be a viable policy for the small states of the North. Although volunteers, especially from Sweden, went to fight in Finland, the Nordic governments maintained a strictly formal detachment from that conflict, fearing any actions would involve them in the struggle. Trade agreements appeared to point toward a measure of economic security.

The phony war was, however, an illusion behind which intense planning by both sides to gain control over parts of Norden took place. In late 1939 and early 1940 the French and British developed plans to assist the Finns by sending troops and equipment through northern Norway and Sweden. In fact, the plans were mostly a ruse to establish control of the crucial Norwegian port of Narvik and the iron mines of northern Sweden, which were vitally important to the German war efforts. Refusal by both the Norwegian and Swedish governments to allow the transit of Allied forces and the end to the fighting in Finland forced the Allies to shift their focus.

At the same time, Hitler became increasingly concerned about the importance of Scandinavia to German military and economic interests and was convinced that none of the Nordic countries could actually defend their neutrality. Preliminary planning for an invasion began in December 1939, and a month later Hitler ordered formal preparations be laid for an attack on Denmark and Norway (Weserübung/Operation West). The final decision was taken following the so-called *Altmark* Affair in mid-February. This incident, which involved the pursuit and boarding of the *Altmark,* a support ship for the German battle cruiser *Graf Spee,* by British naval vessels operating inside Norwegian territorial waters, was little more than a rationalization. Hitler wished to protect his northwest flank, seal the Baltic, and ensure deliveries of Swedish iron ore via Norwegian territorial waters. However, he was not alone in laying plans to invade Norden. The British began to lay mines in Norwegian waters on 8 April 1940, the day before the German attack, and troops had embarked to counter any German response. The Allied moves, however, were too little, too late, and they reflected the problems inherent in conducting war by committee that plagued the Allies through the war.

Operation West was another matter. At dawn on the morning of 9 April 1940, German forces launched simultaneous attacks on Denmark and Norway. Land forces swept up through Jutland, Danish port authorities were met by Nazi troops on the morning ferries from Germany, and Luftwaffe planes flew over Copenhagen and dropped leaflets. Given the country's geography and lack of preparedness (Denmark had about 15,000 troops in combat readiness), and although several of the country's military leaders advised that a token resistance be mounted, Stauning's government and Christian X recognized that to fight would be foolhardy, and the country surrendered almost immediately. In the few hours before an agreement was reached with the Nazis, some fighting occurred and sixteen Danes lost their lives. The costs, human and material, over the next five years would be considerably greater.

Although no better prepared, the Norwegians took a different course. Johan Nygaardsvold's government called for resistance. The ancient guns of Oskarsborg successfully sunk the German battle cruiser *Blücher* at the mouth of Oslo harbor, thereby delaying German troop landings and giving the king and government time to escape to Hamar. The small Norwegian forces fought on and were joined by French and British units in mid-April. The Allies' assistance suffered from lack of planning and support, especially around Trondheim. Only in the north, at Narvik, were they successful. There the British navy destroyed a German force, and British, French, and Polish troops actually recaptured the port. Ultimately, however, the fight proved futile. Allied troops were withdrawn at the end of May, following the German attack on the Low Countries and France. Without Allied support, the situation was hopeless. The king and government went into exile in England, and the Norwegian forces capitulated on 9 June 1940.

The Years of Occupation and Resistance

Denmark

The Danes' surrender on the morning of 9 April involved the end of hostilities and the government's acceptance of a set of German demands that, on paper, seemed very moderate. Denmark would continue to exist as a sovereign state. Its constitution, government, administration, justice system, and military would remain. In return, Denmark was expected to accede to German requests. For most Danes the next three years was a period of relatively relaxed occupation of a model protectorate of the Reich. On the surface things appeared normal. A series of coalition governments, headed by Thorvald Stauning until his death in May 1942, Vilhelm Buhl until November 1942, and Erik Scavenius until August 1943, directed the country's affairs. The parliament continued to meet. Even the regular parliamentary elections were held in March and April 1943—in which nearly 95 percent of the eligible voters participated, casting ballots overwhelming in favor of the coalition parties. Business went on as usual. Of course, much of this "independence" was pure fiction. Nearly 40,000 German troops were stationed in the country. The shadow of German control hung over everything, and there was little doubt about who was in charge. Economically, Denmark became "Germany's larder." Although Nazi demands were submitted to the Danes for consideration and minor concessions were made, the government's "policy of negotiation" was little more than an illusion. Still, there was no overt campaign to turn Danes into Nazis or to absorb the country into the Reich, and so long as the Danes behaved and the war went well for Germany, this situation remained stable.

Several factors worked in Denmark's favor, including the personal conflicts inside Nazi Germany for power and the way in which the same "fiefdom" might be fought over by several individuals—leaving Hitler to act as the great resolver of differences. Industrial interests, the army, the foreign office, and the Nazi police organizations competed over Denmark. Until the fall of 1942, the most important German in the country was the diplomat Cecil von Renthe-Fink. He advocated a soft-gloved approach, which he believed would yield the most for Germany, and he enjoyed the support of Foreign Minister

Joachim von Ribbentrop in Berlin. Then Hitler's growing anger with the Danes' failure to fall into line and the "telegram crisis" that developed over his feeling that Christian X had intentionally snubbed him in a message thanking the German leader for his birthday wishes led to the appointment of a new military commander, Hermann von Hanneken, the installation of a new political officer, Dr. Werner Best, and the creation of new cabinet in Denmark more acceptable to the Germans and headed by Erik Scavenius. Von Hanneken represented Hitler's preferred line of thinking; crush any resistance and bring Denmark into the Nazi sphere. Best believed in the old policy of negotiation. Scavenius, who was apparently almost insufferably arrogant, was a realist willing to make concessions to preserve Denmark's special place in the New Europe. For almost a year the locus of German power shifted back and forth, dependent on events in Denmark, the course of the war, and how the winds of politics were blowing in Berlin; and Scavenius tap-danced through a growing thicket of German discontent with resistance activities.

The sham of an independent Denmark was ended on 29 August 1943. Resistance to the Nazis had been slowly growing, especially since the surrender at Stalingrad in February. In response, the Germans attempted to impose curfews in several Danish towns, and this was met with street fighting and strikes that started in Esbjerg and spread east to Odense and on to the capital. The unrest led to several visits by Best and von Hanneken to Berlin, a series of talks with the Danish government, and an ultimatum that clearly spelled out a new German course. Among the demands Scavenius and his colleagues were asked to approve were the declaration of a state of emergency, the end of most civil liberties, the reinstatement of the death penalty, and the handing over of the Danish fleet. Upon their refusal, the government was removed. Best oversaw the state's affairs, but only with the help of the heads of governmental departments. Order was to be maintained by von Hanneken and, after mid-September, German police agencies including the Gestapo, headed by Günther Pancke. The terms of the ultimatum were imposed. Terror replaced law. Censorship was to be strictly enforced. Civil liberties were erased. The Danish army was disarmed. The navy scuttled twenty-nine of its vessels rather than have them fall into German hands. This situation prevailed until the Germans' surrender in Denmark on 8 May 1945.

Throughout the occupation the Danes resisted, but the nature and extent of their actions depended on the course of the war. So long as

Germany was winning, and this appeared to be the case at least until early 1943, most accepted the government's policy of negotiation and saw organized, violence-based resistance as futile. Instead, many Danes showed their feelings about the occupation by ignoring the Germans, treating them as if they were not there, or ridiculing the Danish Nazis. Patriotic nationalism became more intense as well, and the high voter participation in the 1943 elections and their outcome indicated a commitment to Denmark's democratic system and a rejection of Nazism.

More active resistance efforts developed gradually. Among the first was a small spy network based on a group of army intelligence officers and the journalist, Ebbe Munch. It began to gather information on German troop movements throughout Norden and to relay that information to Britain via Munch in Stockholm in fall 1940. Following the Nazi invasion of the Soviet Union in June 1941, a campaign aimed at rounding up the Communists in Denmark and closing down party activities was forced on the government—a campaign that also involved Denmark's joining the Anti-Comintern Pact in November 1941. This triggered the growth of an organized Communist resistance. The year 1941 also saw the expansion of a resistance press, usually in the form of small local newspapers with limited circulations. Several, including *Frit Danmark, De Frie Danske,* and *Frihedsstøtten,* were national. Another important voice of resistance was the Conservative Party leader John Christmas Møller. An outspoken critic of the negotiation policy and the Nazis, he was forced to resign his post as minister of commerce in October 1940 and from the Folketing in January 1941. The same year he helped establish *Frit Danmark.* In May 1942 he escaped to England, from where he literally served as the voice of a free Denmark on the BBC. (Møller subsequently became the foreign minister in the first postwar government.)

The development of paramilitary resistance operations aimed at the Germans grew slowly. Most involved amateurs and tended to be based on localities or political parties. Efforts were highly balkanized. Until 1943 they were ill equipped, received little help from Britain's Special Operations Executive (SOE), and had no central coordinating body. Illustrative of this early phase in the resistance was the "Churchill Club," made up of schoolboys from Ålborg, and Communist cell groups. Both set the pattern for subsequent activities through their attacks on German barracks, transport facilities and equipment, and military storage depots in spring 1942. Gradually, however, a more cohesive movement developed, culminating in the founding of the Freedom Council (Frihedsrådet) in September 1943. This group of about ten resistance leaders acted as a coordinating body and, increasingly, as a countergovernment.

The resistance, of course, infuriated the Germans and led to recurrent crises between the Nazis and the Danish government, which proved unable to stop the resistance activities. The installation of von Hanneken and Best in fall 1942 and the German takeover of 29 August 1943 were largely the result of Nazi anger, and in September 1943 a concentrated campaign of counterterror was initiated, directed largely by SS Colonel Otto Bovensiepen. Acts of sabotage or Allied raids against the Germans were met with attacks against the Danes. The resistance blew up factories, and the British bombed the Gestapo headquarters in several Danish cities. In response, restaurants, theaters, and even Copenhagen's beloved Tivoli amusement park (25 June 1944) were damaged or destroyed. Innocent citizens were randomly rounded up. Killings were met with more killings. In the so-called clearing murders, the Germans singled out notable people for assassination, including the pastor-poet-playwright Kaj Munk in January 1944.

Another important episode in the history of the resistance was the "people's strike" in Copenhagen (26 June–5 July 1944). This spontaneous action came in reaction to a rising campaign of German terror and restrictions including the imposition of an 8 P.M. to 5 A.M. curfew in spring 1944. It was initiated by the workers at Burmeister and Wain, who left work early on 26 June to "tend their gardens." Other workers followed suit, and by Friday, 30 June, a virtual general strike brought most production to a halt. The Germans responded with more terror, declared an emergency situation and brought in additional military forces, and cut off the public utilities. Economic life came to a standstill, and the Nazis regarded the city to be under siege. Paradoxically, in what must have been an utterly chaotic situation, the Danes also continued to enjoy the pleasures of summer: barricades and shooting contrasted by lovers' trysts and sunbathing.

It was obvious to both the Germans and the Danes that the situation could not go on indefinitely. Life in the city, cut off from supplies and services, would quickly become impossible. Every day it continued meant lost production for the German war effort. But neither side was willing to concede. The Freedom Council established the bases for a settlement, and several civilian politicians and Georg Duckwitz, the German shipping attaché in Copenhagen, played key roles in moving negotiations along. The strike ended on Wednesday, 5 July, in a victory for the Danes. Best agreed to end martial law and remove some of the worst of the counterterror groups and restore services. The people of Copenhagen agreed to return to work.

The outcome was a moral victory for the Danes. The strike, however, came at a time when the Germans were faced with both Soviet gains in the east and the Allied invasion in France. They were not in a position to invest much to stop the strike or to risk losing what little they still were extracting from Denmark.

One of the most remarkable acts of Danish resistance was the rescue of almost all the country's approximately 7,500 Jews. Woven into the changes of August and September 1943 was the decision to round up and deport Denmark's Jews to Germany for extermination. In contrast to what some might expect, there appears to have been little enthusiasm among the Nazi leaders in Denmark for this campaign. Although Best stood at the center of the decision, he also allowed news of it to be leaked to Jewish leaders through Georg Duckwitz. In what is often described as a spontaneous act of national resistance, the people of Denmark took part in warning, locating, concealing, and transporting the Jews to Sweden. In all, only about two hundred were captured. Why did the operation succeed? First, the success depended on the unselfish aid given by the non-Jewish Danes, who saw their country's Jews as Danes, not as Jews. Second, it lay in the fact that the Jewish community in Denmark was historically very old. Some Jews could trace their Danish roots to the sixteenth century. Third, Denmark was relatively far less anti-Semitic than most of Europe. Fourth, the success came partly from greed. There was money to be made. Fifth, the willingness of the Swedes to accept the Danish Jews was essential, and this condition was the result of the turning of Germany's fortunes in the war. Finally, there was the aforementioned lack of enthusiasm on the part of the Germans in carrying out the roundup. Whatever the reasons, however, the rescue involved countless heroic acts and stands as one of the great exceptions in the history of the Holocaust.

Although there were nearly 200,000 German troops in Denmark by the end of the war, their capitulation came relatively quietly on 5 May 1945. The transition to peace was aided by resistance forces and the "Danish Brigade," a force of about 5,000 men trained in Sweden.

Iceland's Independence

World War II created the context in which Iceland achieved its independence. The Nazi occupation of Denmark severed ties with Copenhagen. The British occupation of the island on 10 May 1940, followed by the American takeover in the summer of 1941, brought an economic boom but left the Icelanders on their own politically. Gradually, careful steps were taken to reach full independence. In 1941 the Althing chose Sveinn Björnsson to assume the powers of the crown. It also passed a resolution in May 1941 that declared Iceland's right to dissolve the union and its intent not to renew the tie with Denmark, which was sent to Copenhagen. The war and the decision to honor the three-year clause on renewal in the 1918 union act delayed the actual break. In February 1944 the Althing voted not to renew the union and approved a republican constitution a month later. Both were ratified in a referendum. Independence was declared on 17 June 1944 at Thingvellir. Denmark's Christian X sent his best wishes. Iceland was now the fifth independent state in Norden.

They did have to do some mopping up of SS units and collaborators. The exception was on Bornholm, where the German commander refused to surrender to the Soviets. In response the towns of Rønne and Neksø were badly damaged in air raids. The Germans finally surrendered to Soviet forces on 9 May. Vilhelm Buhl returned as prime minister of the first postwar government, and a semblance of normalcy returned fairly quickly.

The end of a war that had cost, by some estimates, 1,300 lives did not bring real peace at home, however. As was true elsewhere in Europe, the Danes had to deal with the collaborators—with the men and women who had supported, aided, and fought for the Nazis; with the men and women who had betrayed their fellow Danes as spies and informers. Even before the war ended lists of approximately 40,000 suspects were prepared, including members of the Danish Nazi Party and those who had served the Germans in special Danish military or police units. As many as 34,000 were arrested and interned in 1945. A special national treason law (*landsforræderiloven*) was passed to cover the actions of collaborators, and the legal proceedings went on for years. Some 20,000 people were investigated, about 13,000 were convicted, and 46 were executed. Werner Best and Otto Bovensiepen were condemned, but their sentences were commuted to five years and life in prison, respectively. General von Hanneken was sentenced to serve eight years in prison, but was later released.

Norway

The history of the political, administrative, and military aspects of Germany's occupation of Norway during the war is markedly different from Denmark's; the history of resistance and everyday life is similar. The military and political resistance to the invasion resulted in a different attitude and a stronger military presence on the part of the Germans, which eventually reached over 350,000 men, and less willingness to pursue a "soft" approach. In addition, the departure of King Haakon and the Nygaardsvold government for exile in England created a power vacuum, which was initially filled by Vidkun Quisling. Believing he had Hitler's support, Quisling stepped forward and formed a new civilian government packed with his Nasjonal Samling cronies on 9 April 1940. Not surprisingly, he was ineffective and unable to secure any popular support. Within a few days he was replaced by a nonpolitical "administrative council." On 24 April Reichskommissar Josef Terboven, cold, efficient, hardworking, and completely committed to the Nazi ideals, became the real center of power in Norway. He tried throughout the summer to establish a cooperative relationship with existing political and administrative units that would be accepted as legitimate by the Norwegians. After this attempt failed, a new system was installed on 25 September 1940. Terboven now headed a reconstructed council of thirteen members, ten of whom were Nasjonal Samling collaborators. At the same time normal political life came to an end. All political parties except Nasjonal Samling were banned. In January 1941, elections for local government positions were abolished. A final system change occurred on 1 February 1942, when Quisling became "minister president." The title was almost entirely honorific because Terboven remained the real head of state. However, Quisling and Nasjonal Samling were given a relatively free hand in efforts to nazify Norway and create a corporate state based on Quisling, the party, and a host of party-controlled organizations—efforts that fit neatly with German intentions to bring Norway into the New Europe as a well-ordered puppet state.

Vidkun Quisling

Vidkun Quisling (1887–1945) has been described as shy, well mannered, frugal, scrupulous to a fault in his private life, intelligent, and obsessive. A graduate of Norway's military academy, he served for a decade in the army. During the 1920s he worked with Nansen and tried to make a career in the diplomatic service. In the late 1920s he turned to politics, and his fiercely anticommunist ideas quickly won him favor on the Right. From 1931 to 1932 he served as minister of defense. In 1933 he founded Nasjonal Samling, an organization patterned after the Nazis. Over time he developed a virtually religious conviction that he was destined to be the savior of his country. He also believed he had the support of Hitler. From April 1940 to May 1945 he collaborated with the Germans. From February 1942 to May 1945, he was "minister president" of Norway. His movement grew from about 7,000 in 1940 to over 43,000 in 1943, and many of its members served in political or administrative positions or fought in special units for the Germans. Quisling was tried for a variety of war crimes and executed in October 1945.

Until mid-1943, most Norwegians accepted (or seemed to accept) these developments. Disappointed by what seemed like little more than token assistance from the British and French, and pessimistic about the course of the war, it seemed like the only thing to do at the time. The reorganization of the political and administrative systems went ahead largely unopposed. The economy was turned to serving the German war effort. Nasjonal Samling party membership grew to more than 40,000, and between 5,000 and 6,000 Norwegians joined special corps to fight with the Germans.

However, there was resistance from April 1940. It took many forms, changed over time, and enjoyed varying degrees of success. The government-in-exile retained the allegiance of Norwegians outside the country and was able to direct important national resources to the Allied war efforts, including 85 percent of the merchant fleet. Special Norwegian military units were established that contributed in several theaters of the conflict. It was hardly surprising that virtually all military resistance in Norway stopped after the capitulation of the country's armed forces on 10 June. Civilian resistance, however, to many of the Nazis' efforts did develop. Shunning and ostracizing the enemy and acts of civil disobedience were common. In December 1940 the entire Supreme Court resigned rather than accept making a mockery of the legal system. Teachers and clergy refused to turn their classrooms or pulpits into agencies of propaganda. In February 1942 the bishops of the Church and many parish clergy resigned their posts in protest against the nazification policies of the new Quisling government. Organizations protested their dissolution and replacement by Nasjonal Samling–dominated groups. Strikes by the unions of the Norwegian Trade Union Federation in 1941, which cost two leaders their lives, came in response to attempts to nazify the labor movement. Attempts to organize national youth labor programs were boycotted. Civilian resistance also extended to hiding individuals and organizing escapes. Coordination of these activities developed slowly. The Circle (Kretsen) had its roots among the bourgeoisie of Oslo; the "Coordination Committee" (KK) was based on several large national interest organizations. These two came to work together more closely, and in early 1944 the "Homefront's Command" (Hjemmefrontens Ledelse) emerged and eventually directed all noncommunist civil and military resistance.

Because "Fortress Norway" was a key in Hitler's overall strategic thinking, a bastion against British naval and Soviet land incursions, coordinated and effective armed resistance developed slowly and faced German forces that were considerably larger and more combat ready than in Denmark. From mid-1941, the Communists established their own network of organizations and carried out sabotage attacks independently for the rest of the war. Although many small, local armed resistance cells existed after June 1940, a leadership council for the military arm of the resistance, MILORG, evolved only gradually. It took direction from London, and Norwegian units tended to supply support for sabotage attacks planned by Britain's Special Operations Executive, often against port or economic targets. Among the most remembered sabotage efforts were the three assaults on the German heavy-water facilities at the Norsk Hydro facility at the Vemork power station near Rjukan in Telemark. Heavy water was a byproduct of the plant and was to be shipped to Germany to be used in the Nazis' atomic bomb project. An SOE attack planned for November 1942 failed entirely, when one of the tow-planes and the two gliders carrying the British special forces crashed, and all the men were either killed or captured and executed. A second assault at the end of February 1943 succeeded in destroying supplies of heavy water and stopping production for several months. In November 1943 the Allies staged a bombing raid on the plant that did little real damage. A fourth operation involved sinking the ferry *Hydro* on Lake Tinnsjö in February 1944, which sent 600 kilos of heavy water to the bottom of the lake, but at the cost of twenty-six Norwegian lives. According to Jörgen Hæstrup, the success of these operations put an end to the German bomb project, and is one of the few cases during the war when acts of sabotage had such far-reaching results.

As in Denmark, all resistance, civilian and military, was met with threats, Gestapo counterterror, torture, arrests, reprisals, and deportations. The former women's prison at Grini near Oslo became an internment camp, and an estimated 20,000 Norwegians spent varying periods of time there. In one of the worst acts of counterterror against the Norwegians, the coastal town of Televaag, near Bergen, was razed in April 1942. Its fishing boats were sunk, most of its men deported, and most of the women and children interned. This act came in reprisal for the killing of two Germans and the involvement of some people in the town in the resistance. In March 1942 some 1,300 teachers were arrested and about 500 were transported to Kirkenes in the far north. In November 1943 over 1,000 students and about 20 faculty at the University of Oslo were arrested for undermining the fundamental views of the Nazis. A storm of protest, which included demonstrations by students in Sweden and a formal complaint from the Swedish government, ensued. For whatever reason, the Germans released most of those arrested. Some of the worst acts of reprisal occurred in the far north of Norway. The Germans regarded northern Norway and northern Finland as a single military zone, and as they retreated from Finland in the campaign of late 1944, they practiced a scorched-earth policy. Bridges, roads, and port facilities were destroyed and local populations uprooted. Kirkenes, Tromsö, and Narvik suffered heavy damage. Hammerfest was virtually leveled in November 1944.

The war had other costs for the Norwegians, too. Allied bombing operations destroyed port and manufacturing facilities, and 706 ships of the merchant fleet were sunk. One estimate puts casualties at 4,000 sailors of the merchant fleet, 2,000 armed forces personnel, 2,100 members of the resistance, and 1,340 in concentration camps. Included in this last figure are the 734 Jews who were rounded up under Nasjonal Samling direction and sent to Auschwitz between October 1942 and February 1943. (The remainder of the Norwegian Jews, about 900, escaped to Sweden either earlier or during the roundup.) In addition, Norway suffered from the reorientation of its economy to the service of the Germans and the loss of export markets and established economic patterns.

As in Denmark, the war ended relatively quietly in Norway. German forces surrendered on 7 May 1945, and order was kept by resistance forces and almost 13,000 police trained in Sweden. Terboven committed suicide. The government returned from England on 30 May; Haakon came home on 7 June—exactly five years after his escape. Then came the problems of making peace at home. The psychological division of the country into resistors and collaborators had taken its toll. In the denazification that took place following the war, some 90,000 Norwegians were investigated, 46,000 were tried and found guilty, 18,000 were imprisoned for varying periods, and 28,000 were fined, many of them losing their rights as citizens. Quisling and 29 others were condemned; 25 were executed. There were also less official forms of trial, judgment, and punishment. Hundreds of women were publicly disgraced for fraternizing with enemy soldiers, and the children that came from some of these liaisons were often branded outcasts. Aside from Quisling, one of the most notable victims in this purification process was the author Knut Hamsun. Accused of treason for the support he gave to the Nasjonal Samling and the Germans, he was investigated, subjected to a demeaning psychological exam, tried in a civil court, and found guilty. Although spared a prison sentence, he was fined and deprived of nearly 80 percent of his personal worth.

Although this process was probably inevitable in both Denmark and Norway, it was hardly healing. In many cases, the German defeat turned acts of survival or accommodation during a time when a Nazi victory appeared to be inevitable into collaboration. The cleansing led to suffering, exile, and social scars that only time will erase. At the same time, the resistance side of the history of the war has come to occupy a place of exaggerated importance. It is a popular topic and an important part of the national record. Monuments to the resistance can be found throughout the country. As appears to be the case with resistance movements across Europe, the Norwegian resistance was more important as a keeper of hopes than as a factor determining the outcome of the war. Time is making the picture of resistance more balanced, as can be seen in the museum dedicated to the resistance on the grounds of Akershus fortress in Oslo.

Sweden

Sweden was neither invaded nor occupied during the war, but this does not mean the country escaped many of its costs. Throughout the conflict, Sweden's government attempted to maintain at least a semblance of neutrality while it bent to the demands of the prevailing side in the struggle. Although effective in preserving the country's sovereignty, this approach generated criticism at home from many who believed the threat to Sweden was less serious than the government claimed, problems with the warring powers, ill feelings among its neighbors, and frequent criticism in the postwar period. In the late 1990s renewed attention was turned to Sweden's policies and actions during the war, which focused on the possible receipt of confiscated Jewish property from the Germans in trade deals. The Swedish ambassador to the United States was called to testify before a Senate committee, and a special commission was established in Stockholm to study the issues. For the most part, past and present critics are guilty of taking events out of context. Morality did not dictate the decisions of the Swedish government during World War II.

Charting a path that might ensure the survival of the state was the government's primary goal. Per Albin Hansson and his colleagues were confronted with at least three undeniable realities. First, from 1939 to summer 1943, Nazi Germany was winning the war, and its resources were overwhelming. Although not invaded in April 1940, Sweden was virtually encircled, and the threat of German action was perceived to be ever present until well into 1944. Second, although Swedish armed forces strength rose to over 400,000, it was recognized that they could not prevent an invasion or defeat one—though they could exact a high price. Third, given the economic disruptions brought on by the war, Sweden's economy was thrown into chaos. Most export markets were closed. Even in the best of times, Sweden was heavily dependent on imports of raw materials, fuels, certain foodstuffs, and industrial products. For almost four years Germany had Sweden in an economic stranglehold. By mid-1941 the Baltic was essentially a German lake. Göteborg's access to the Atlantic and world trade centers was literally rationed, principally by the Germans.

In many respects, Sweden's position was only slightly better than

Denmark's. German requests had to be weighed carefully against the risk that denial would mean military or economic reprisals, and this balancing act became more complicated in 1944, by which time it was clear that the Allies were going to win the war. Then a Soviet victory in the Continuation War between the Soviets and the Finns increased Allied pressures on Sweden to cut off trade with Germany, and post-war economic and security concerns became factors in Swedish deci-sion making.

When the war began, Hansson's Social Democrat–Agrarian co-alition was in office, and the principled, idealistic, and intellectual Rickard Sandler was foreign minister. In December 1939 the govern-ment was rebuilt as a national coalition, still under Hansson, but with members from the Conservatives, Liberals and Agrarians. (The Com-munists were excluded.) Christian Günther, a more realistic career diplomat, replaced Sandler at the Foreign Office, and he played a cen-tral role throughout the war fielding and responding to German and Allied demands.

The story of Sweden's neutrality during the war falls roughly into four periods. In the first, from September 1939 to April 1940, neutral-ity appeared to be viable. The government avoided any official in-volvement in the Winter War and tried to steer a middle course be-tween Germany and the western Allies. During the second, from April 1940 to summer 1943, neutrality was a sham. In fact, Sweden was a virtual ally of Nazi Germany. Repeatedly, the Swedes conceded on German demands. On 6 July 1940 they accepted a transit agree-ment that for the next three years provided daily trains between Trelleborg and Kornsjö and weekly trains between Storlien and Narvik (the "horseshoe line") for German military personnel and equipment. In the same period, access routes through Swedish terri-torial waters for German shipping and courier flights between Nor-way and Finland over Swedish territory were permitted. In late June 1941 the Swedish government allowed the passage of the German "Engelbrecht division" from Norway through northern Sweden to Finland.

During this period Swedish trade policies and the commercial agreements the government negotiated with both sides from Decem-ber 1939 were dictated by military and economic realities. Trade almost ceased with Britain and the world at large and was regulated through the so-called Göteborg Traffic. Under a series of deals ap-proved by Britain and Germany, approximately four ships per month

Raoul Wallenberg

In the last year of the war, Sweden became a factor in humanitarian efforts and attempts to end the war. It also became a haven for refugees from Norden and the Baltic states, and Swedes were involved in rescuing Scandinavian victims of internment camps. In the context of these actions, the work of Raoul Wallenberg (1912–?) stands out. In June 1944 Wallenberg was apparently recruited by Iver Olsen, an American security services operative in Stockholm, to go to Budapest, where he would play a dual role: as a representative of the War Refugee Board (WRB) attempting to save the lives of Hungarian Jews and as an agent of the OSS (Office of Strategic Studies and precursor of the CIA) serving as a contact with the anti-Nazi resistance. The Swedish government bowed to American pressure and made the assignment. Reaching Budapest in July 1944, Wallenberg dove into the maelstrom of the Holocaust. He confronted the German Nazis, including Adolf Eichmann, and their Hungarian allies. By issuing special Swedish passports, he is credited with saving the lives of at least 20,000 people. At the same time he apparently fulfilled his mission with the resistance.

Wallenberg's position was a very dangerous one—with the Nazis and the Soviets. In mid-January 1945 he went to meet the commander of the Soviet forces taking the city and never returned. The Soviets believed he was a spy operating in their sphere of interest—a charge proved by his links with the WRB, which they knew was a front for American espionage work. What was probably Wallenberg's humanitarian zeal cost him his freedom and his life. He vanished into the Soviet court and prison system. His presence was denied. His file closed. In 1957 the Soviets claimed he had died in 1947, but accounts filtered out from the gulags and fed hopes that he was still alive. Even with the end of the Cold War, the Soviets remained mostly silent. They returned his personal belongings to his family in 1989. Russian President Yeltsin initiated an inquiry in 1991 that yielded little. Raoul Wallenberg remained a prisoner of the Cold War: the new Russia, the United States, and Sweden were all unwilling to let the truth be discovered.

in and out of Göteborg were permitted. Simultaneously, commerce with Germany and its allies or satellite states flourished. (In 1941 all but 6.2 percent of Sweden's international trade was with Axis-controlled Europe.) Deliveries of iron ore, ball bearings, and other commodities useful to the German war effort were maintained at or above prewar levels.

It was also during this period that information and opinion were most energetically suppressed. The government's information agency attempted to shape public views. At the same time, anti-Nazi/anti-German views were controlled through the confiscation of editions of publications and court actions. Torgny Segerstedt, the outspoken anti-Nazi editor of *Göteborgs Handels-och Sjöfartstidning,* believed neutrality was impossible in a war that pitted force against right. Several issues of the paper were confiscated under the security provisions of the 1812 Press Freedom Ordinance. Ture Nerman, editor of the weekly *Trots Allt!* spent several months in prison for his criticisms of the Nazis and government policies. In March 1943 seventeen newspapers were subjected to confiscation in order to avoid irritating the Germans while papers expressing pro-German sentiments went untouched.

Serious literature and popular culture also served as media through which to express anti-Nazi opinions and to criticize government policies. Vilhelm Moberg's *Rid i natt* (Ride by night) (1941) was widely read and became a popular play and film as well. Songs, musical reviews, and absurd comedy served as ways to ridicule as well. Pro-Allies war films such as Alfred Hitchcock's *The Foreign Correspondent* (1940) were also very popular.

At least a measure of balanced neutrality was possible during the third period, from summer 1943 to mid-1944. Only from the perspective of 1945 and after was it clear that the course of the war had turned by mid-1943, but this was not entirely evident in the context of the times. Still, the defeats at Stalingrad, Kursk, and in North Africa, along with the collapse of Mussolini's regime in Italy, bolstered the willingness to resist German demands and even renege on earlier concessions. The government canceled the transit agreement in August 1943, and in June 1944 courier overflights between Norway and Finland were terminated. By late 1943 Sweden was a haven for some 11,000 refugees from Denmark, including over 7,000 Danish Jews, and about 30,000 Norwegians. Officials also sanctioned the development of facilities and programs to train Danish and Norwegian police, under the direction of Harry Söderman. These forces helped maintain order in their home countries when the war ended. Press restraints were eased as well, and some Swedes became more openly concerned with what they had known about for a long time, the treatment of the Jews in Nazi-occupied Europe.

In the final period, from mid-1944 to the end of the war, the government moved Sweden toward becoming a "neutral ally" of the West. This shift was most evident in trade policies, which turned against Germany, but it could also be seen in the increased humanitarian efforts organized by Swedes. The Allies became more and more insistent that Sweden end its trade with Germany. For leverage they threatened to withhold deliveries of needed goods and blacklist firms that continued to deal with Germany. In June the ball-bearing giant, Svenska Kullagerfabriken (SKF), reached an agreement to reduce deliveries to the Germans. Shipping insurance on cargoes to Germany became impossible to obtain in late summer, and in September the government closed Sweden's Baltic ports to trade with Germany. Virtually all trade with Germany ended in January 1945.

Life in Norden during the War

Although there were striking differences across Norden in terms of everyday life dictated by the specific situations the people of each country faced, there were also similarities that can be discussed collectively.

The Nordic economies were subjected to enormous pressures during the war. Occupied Denmark and Norway became suppliers of goods and services to the Nazis. Denmark provided agricultural products and engineering goods such as ship engines; Norway supplied fish, ores, and nitrates and provided naval facilities. In general, everything that could be was sent to Germany, and the Danes and Norwegians had to make do—oftentimes quite cleverly. For a time virtually all of Sweden's production of industrial goods and raw materials went to Germany in exchange for necessary fuels, food stuffs, and manufactured goods. Trade with the Allies was severely restricted by Germany. From March 1940 to September 1944 Finland's economy was almost entirely dependent on Germany. These developments also affected prices, wages, job opportunities, and gender roles. Almost every aspect of economic life was subjected to control by governments or Nazis officials. When the war ended all of Norden's economies were skewed by the wartime developments.

Whether occupied, belligerent, or neutral, each Nordic country experienced shortages of almost all everyday commodities. Rationing began as early as fall 1939, and by late 1940 coffee, tea, tobacco, sugar, meat, milk, cheese, bread, shoes, clothing, coal, and gasoline were unavailable or rationed through special coupon books. Hot-water use was regulated. Private cars virtually disappeared. Gasoline was available only for emergency vehicles. Trucks, buses, and some cars were converted to run on methane, generated in odd-looking wood-fired cookers. Fundamental aspects of everyday life changed, including diet, dress, personal cleanliness, and transportation.

Several general developmental patterns were amplified either by the war or its aftermath. Respect for the monarchies of Denmark, Norway, and Sweden and commitment to democratic institutions was strengthened. At the same time, the roles played by interest organizations in the development and implementation of programs were enhanced. Experience in controlling many aspects of life and especially the economy by central authority was gained and became more acceptable. The war created new and expanded opportunities for women in industry, administration, the military, and resistance movements. Another trend was the social leveling that came with the war. There were, of course, profiteers who made fortunes during this war, just as there had been twenty years before, and social class did not disappear. However, social rank did not determine one's place in the lines for rationed necessities, and the suffering and shortages cut across class lines. In addition, the shared wartime experiences reinforced the sense of social responsibility for alleviating common problems, a sense with very old roots in Norden and that certainly was given more concrete forms in the welfare programs of the 1930s. The war triggered new efforts to define the good society and the steps necessary to achieve it. Finally, the war led to reevaluations of foreign and security policy directions.

14

~~~~~~

The Contemporary Era:
Norden since 1945

Traditionally, the half century following the end of the Thirty-one Years' War has been divided into three periods: recovery and reconstruction from 1945 to the early 1950s, growth and prosperity from the early 1950s to about 1973, and problems and transitions from 1973 to the close of the century. It is also possible to construct two periods. The first, from the 1930s to the 1970s, was dominated by a set of political parties based on social classes and defined by such developments as full industrialization, democratization, and the building of the welfare state. (In this World War II was merely an interruption.) The second, beginning in the early 1970s, was defined by new dominant groups and far-reaching political, economic, social, and cultural changes—many of which appeared to presage the closing of a unique window in Nordic history during which the achievements of the previous forty or fifty years had been possible.

Whichever periodization one prefers, it is clear that from many perspectives the second half of the twentieth century was one of the most positive and dynamic periods in modern Western and Nordic history. Denmark, Finland, and Norway rebuilt rapidly, and the region's economic recovery fed into the longest uninterrupted period of growth in the century. Affluence spread through the North, and a quality of life second to almost nowhere else in the world became the norm. In the context of the economic developments, politics were strikingly stable, and the systems were effective in designing and implementing change and directing and exploiting the favorable economic conditions. Extensive and expensive social welfare systems were developed. Having achieved political democracy before 1939, Norden's governments set about extending economic, social, and gender democracy with what appeared to be great success. This environment of affluence and stability also encouraged cultural activities and a wide-spread expansion of educational opportunities. Taken together, these and other developments have been called "the Nordic Model," an alternative held up to much of the world until the last two decades of the century as a "middle way" in a world polarized by political-economic ideologies.

Of course, all was not perfect. There were disagreements and problems among and within the Nordic countries. The Cold War created a context of fear and tension that resulted in significantly differing foreign and security policy directions by the five Nordic states. The economic prosperity was not solely Nordic but, in many respects, worldwide. Fluctuations in one part of the global economy could and did have impacts in Norden. The region (except for Norway after about 1980) was highly dependent on foreign sources of energy, particularly oil. The social welfare programs were dependent on affluence, the willingness of the people to pay for them, and a sense of social responsibility. The economic shocks and uncertainties of the late twentieth century undermined all these foundations. Another problem related to the welfare systems was that they seemed to have created some serious difficulties of their own beyond cost, including their impacts on initiative and behaviors. The whole cast of modern societal problems including crime, drugs, gangs, soaring divorce rates, and the decline of the family took root in Norden. Finally, there was the problem of the disappearance of homogeneity. Although in-migration had repeatedly brought new peoples into the region, the last fifty years of the century saw more people from more diverse homelands settle in Scandinavia than at any other time in modern history. This immigration fundamentally altered the ethnic composition of the societies and created both a new richness and serious problems.

Political Development

The years between 1945 and the end of the century were largely stable and productive in the political arena. The democratic systems that evolved in the interwar years were quickly restored in the months following the end of the war and proved their effectiveness in meeting the varied challenges of the postwar period. Several general trends help define the political history of Norden during these years. Royal political power continued to decline, most notably in Sweden, where

Twentieth-Century Nordic Monarchs

Denmark
Christian IX: 1863–1906
Frederik VIII: 1906–12
Christian X: 1912–47
Frederik IX: 1947–72
Margrethe II: 1972–

Norway
Haakon VII: 1905–57
Olav V: 1957–91
Harald V: 1991–

Sweden
Oscar II: 1872–1907
Gustav V: 1907–50
Gustav VI Adolf: 1950–73
Carl XVI Gustaf: 1973–

Postwar Finnish Presidents
Carl G. Mannerheim: 1944–46
Juho Paasikivi: 1946–56
Urho Kekkonen: 1956–82
Mauno Koivisto: 1982–94
Martti Ahtisaari: 1994–2000
Tarja Halonen: 2000–

the king became little more than a public relations figure and symbol of continuity, and where talk of abolishing the monarchy was most often heard. At the other end of the spectrum was Norway, where the king's signature was still required on legislation, governments were still formed by the monarch, and the crown enjoyed considerable respect and popularity. Largely because of the role the president played in foreign relations, presidential power and prestige grew in Finland. In the 1990s, however, the Finns changed the way they chose their presidents, moving from an electoral college to a two-round, direct popular election system. They also set a two-term limit. New constitutions in Denmark (1953) and Sweden (1974) brought form into line with practice. Unicameralism became the norm throughout the region when Denmark abolished the Landsting in 1953, and Sweden moved to a single-chamber Riksdag in 1970. (Initially, the new Swedish parliament had 350 seats, but this number was dropped to 349 in 1973, after a period when the socialist and nonsocialist blocks each had 175 seats.)

Another characteristic of the period was a remarkable degree of stability, despite the relatively high frequency of minority or coalition governments, and, in the case of Finland, the frequent turnover of

Nordic Social Democratic Leaders

Denmark
Hans Hedtoft
H. C. Hansen
Viggo Kampmann
J. O. Krag
Anker Jörgensen
Poul Nyrup Rasmussen

Finland
Karl A. Fagerholm
Mauno Koivisto
Kalevi Sorsa
Paavo Lipponen

Norway
Einar Gerhardsen
Torvald Bratteli
Odvar Nordli
Gro Harlem Brundtland
Thorbjörn Jagland
Jens Stoltenberg

Sweden
Tage Erlander
Olof Palme
Yngve Carlsson
Göran Persson

governments—thirty-seven between April 1945 and June 2000. This stability was based in part on the development and maintenance of broadly based consensuses on important issues until late in the period. Differences tended to be over degree and not over fundamental policies or institutions. The stability also rested on the powerful position held by the social democratic parties, especially in Denmark, Norway, and Sweden. They led Denmark for seventeen of the years between 1945 and 1973. In Norway Labor was in office except for a few months until 1965 and then returned to power in 1973 for another eight years. In Sweden the Social Democrats governed from 1945 until 1976. They were out of office until 1982. A corollary of the leadership role played by the social democratic parties was the talented people who led them or served as prime ministers.

Political stability was also the result of the survival of the prewar constellation of political parties in each country down to the 1970s. Typically these were divided into two blocs: Communists and Social Democrats on the Left; Liberals, Agrarians (Center), and Conservatives on the Right. Except for Norway, where Labor enjoyed an absolute majority between 1945 and 1961, the Social Democrats had to reach working arrangements with either the Communists or one of the nonsocialist parties, usually the Agrarians. Red-Green coalitions were common, but so too were seemingly contradictory socialist/nonsocialist governments, especially in Finland (where stability was provided more by the president) and Iceland. Also important in regard to stability were nonvolatile electorates that did not change party affiliation from one election to the next or, if they did, tended to move from party to party within the blocs. Social Democrats might lose votes to Communists or Liberals to the Center Party, but bloc strengths remained fairly constant. Finally, stability often rested on the ability of Nordic leaders like Denmark's Poul Hartling to put together majority voting blocs on individual issues and on the willingness of parties to join such blocs. Both of these aspects reflected the lack of doctrinaire inflexibility within the Nordic systems.

The importance of organizations, including the trade, white-collar, and professional unions, employers' federations, and economic sector groups (or their leaders) in the political process continued. The standard pattern of program or reform development involved the appointment of a commission composed of parliamentary, bureaucratic, and organization representatives, followed by an extended period of study and the submission of reports or recommendations. Dissenting views were expressed in minority statements. Proposals were usually based on consensus. Parliaments tended to act as ratifiers. In some cases organizations were also called on to implement programs. Although this approach was seen by many as a good example of participatory democracy, critics argued there were flaws in the system. The number of individuals who took part in the planning process was small, and they tended to be the leaders of organizations and not the members. Trade-union federation leaders, for example, did not necessarily speak for rank-and-file locals. The parliaments also were marginalized in the policy-making processes according to some analysts.

Another important aspect of the political history of this period was the reform of local (county and municipal) government. Principally, this process involved grouping rural communities into larger political and administrative entities. During the 1960s and 1970s the number of such units in Norway dropped from 744 to 454; in Sweden they fell from 2,498 to 288. The reforms were important because of the roles these units played in the delivering policies and programs.

A new political environment developed in the last two decades or so of the century characterized by challenges to social democratic predominance and some erosion of their electoral strength, the apparent decline of the old "consensus," the importance of "populist" leaders critical of the status quo, the growth of single-issue and new more broadly based parties, the decline of the older parties (especially the Liberals), and greater voter and party allegiance volatility. None of these developments was surprising in light of the social, economic, and demographic developments within Norden and global and Western events.

The Social Democrats' apparently firm hold on power was least continuous in Denmark. Although nonleftist coalitions governed the country from 1945 to 1947 and then from 1950 to 1953, the Social Democrats held power for the next eighteen years. Beginning in 1968, however, cabinet stability disappeared, and bloc shifts came with almost every regular election. In Finland, where coalitions were the rule, the Social Democrats led thirteen of the thirty-seven governments that held office between 1945 and 1997—accounting for about twenty-six years—and participated in many more. One unique development was the so-called Blue-Red coalition created by Harri Holkeri in 1987. This united the conservative National Coalition Party with the Social Democrats, the Swedish People's Party, and the Ruralists. The Norwegian Labor Party governed from 1945 to 1965, with only a brief interruption in 1963. Power then oscillated between Labor and nonsocialist coalitions until 1986. Labor governments held office from 1986 to 1989, from 1990 to 1997, and returned to lead in 2000. The Swedish Social Democrats governed for all but nine years of the period 1945–2000—but never had an absolute majority. Minority governments were the rule, except from 1951 to 1957, when they formed coalitions with the Agrarian/Center Party. Between 1976 and 1982 a sequence of coalition and minority governments involving the Center, Conservative/Moderate, and Liberal/Folk Parties led the country, and a nonsocialist coalition led by Moderate Carl Bildt was in office between 1991 and 1994.

From the late 1960s a group of critics of the status quo, sometimes referred to as populists, achieved popularity and political success throughout Norden. This group included Mogens Glistrup in Denmark, Veikko Vennamo in Finland, and Anders Lange in Norway. They formed what some have called "the unholy trinity." Although they stood more in the mainstream, Hannibal Valdimarsson and Thorbjörn Fälldin played similar roles in Iceland and Sweden, respectively. The targets of their attacks included the welfare state's impacts on individual initiative, high taxes, and ballooning bureaucracies; political systems dominated by insiders who no longer listened to their publics; security policies that did not appear to provide security; and disregard for environmental issues. Glistrup emerged as a public figure in 1971, when he revealed that he had never paid any income tax, despite his considerable wealth and income. He called for a complete revision of the Danish tax system, cuts in welfare, and the elimination of the country's defense establishment. (In place of the last he suggested the media simply be prepared to broadcast "we surrender" in Russian in the event of an attack.) Glistrup clearly struck a chord with the electorate, and he was one of twenty-eight members of his Progress Party who won a seat in the 1973 election. Although support for these views declined, the party still held eleven seats following the 1994 election and in the context of Denmark's multiparty system remained important. Vennamo broke with the established Agrarians to form his own Rural Smallholders' Party in 1959. Initially, he was most critical of President Uhro Kekkonen for being too compliant with Moscow, but he was more successful with his attacks on government elitism and the Agrarian/Center Party's shift away from its rural roots and its support of agricultural rationalization programs. Party strength peaked in 1970, when it won about 11 percent of the vote, and it split in 1975. Anders Lange's attacks on the Norwegian tax system evolved into another Progress Party that had a mixed history. Under Lange's leadership it never secured more than four seats in the Storting. However, in the confusing 1989 election, it captured twenty-two seats. Four years later it lost all but six. Valdimarsson was on the left of the spectrum, in contrast to the others. He broke away from the Communist-led People's Alliance in 1970 to form a new left-liberal group highly critical of the Independence Party–Social Democrat coalition that had governed since 1963. Fälldin, leader of the Center Party, was an outsider in the Stockholm establishment and a man who projected an image of being more at home on a tractor than in politics. He was critical of the political status quo and called for sweeping tax and bureaucratic reforms. He also was concerned with the dangers of nuclear power—an issue that will haunt Sweden well into the twenty-first century. After the 1976 election the nonsocialist parties formed a coalition government with Fälldin as prime minister. It lasted two years and then was rebuilt in 1979. Dogged by economic problems, labor unrest, and energy questions, Fälldin was forced to compromise on many issues.

To varying degrees across Norden, the intrusion of new political parties also destabilized Nordic political life in the last three decades of the twentieth century. In Denmark, Norway, and Sweden the traditional number was five (communist, moderate socialist, agrarian, liberal, and conservative). Finland usually had seven, with two additional parties being added because of the Swedish question and the presence of a separate party for small landholders. During the 1970s and 1980s the number of political parties grew. Thirteen parties took part in the 1990 Danish election, nineteen in the 1995 Finnish election, and thirteen in the 1993 Norwegian election. In contrast, only eight ran in the 1994 Swedish election and six in the 1995 Icelandic balloting.

Generally, the creation of new parties involved the formation of either splinter factions from the traditional parties or entirely new groups that usually occupied the edges of the political spectrum. It was caused by discontent within the older parties, frequently running along generational lines, over specific policies or the general movement by those parties toward the center, by frustrations over the failure of the traditional parties to deal effectively with economic problems, and by the development of specific new issues. The splintering was illustrated by the formation of the Left Socialists and then the Socialist People's Party in Denmark, the Socialist People's Party in Norway (1961), or Vennamo's Rural Smallholders' Party. The New Democrats in Sweden, Lange's party, the development of Christian Democratic parties, and even Glistrup's Progress Party illustrate the trends toward new parties on the Right. Single issues such as the environment, energy, immigration, and women's rights served as the basis for several groups. Many of the new parties were short-lived, and some eventually merged with older groups. Although most received little voter support and few won seats in parliament, they did have important impacts. By taking votes away from traditional parties, they affected the distribution of power within parliaments, altered the composition of coalitions, and imposed new agendas on governments.

Another factor that temporarily affected the traditional party situations in Norden was the collapse of the communist regimes in the Soviet Union and its former satellite states in the early 1990s, which discredited both independent and Soviet-aligned parties in Norden and cut the latter off from their Moscow support. Hardest hit were the Finnish communists. The old party went bankrupt and dissolved into the Left Wing Alliance and a small Communist Workers' Party. Elsewhere the parties had long since shed any slavish attachment to

Moscow and usually stood for policies only slightly more radical than those of the Social Democrats. Overall, the results of mid-1990s elections, in which their share was 7 percent in Denmark, 11 percent in Finland, 14 percent in Iceland, 9 percent in Norway, and 6 percent in Sweden, showed that the parties were able to recover from the events of 1989–91 and adapt to the new situation—albeit often with new names.

Finally, it was in the context of all these developments that voters became less loyal to political parties and tended increasingly to shift their votes from one election to the next. This volatility, sometimes referred to as "protest and polarization," produced some remarkable elections. In Denmark in 1973, 40 percent of the electorate changed party allegiance. All the traditional parties except the Communists lost ground, as 36 percent of the voters opted for new parties. When the Norwegian voters went to the polls in 1989, frustrated with the lack of progress in dealing with economic issues, one-fourth of them voted for the Progress Party or the communist Socialist Left Party at the expense of the center; between 1985 and 1989 39 percent changed party vote. The environmentalist Greens, New Democrats, and Christian Democrats complicated elections from 1988 in Sweden. In 1991 the two right-wing parties won sufficient votes to cross the 4 percent minimum vote threshold and gain seats in the Riksdag while the Left lost ground and the Social Democrats left office. Three years later, the Social Democrats and Left Socialists together won 51.5 percent, the New Democrats vanished, and the Greens gained.

Taken together, these developments reflected either the breakdown of or a change in the nature of the "Nordic consensus." There was a shift in the widely accepted faith in existing political institutions and the commitment to building the welfare model and all that it entailed. For some, cynicism and mistrust of individuals, institutions, and processes replaced acceptance, optimism, and a sense of shared responsibility. For others the focus changed from altering the status quo to maintaining it. The old consensus politics were based on national communities committed to improving the quality of life for all, to building "the people's home." Shared sacrifice was accepted. This attitude was now subsumed by selfishness and fears of threats to the good life or by a sense that the welfare models had gone too far or were too expensive.

It would, of course, be naive to think that politics would not change, given all the economic, social, demographic, and international developments of this period, and these developments paralleled those elsewhere in Western Europe and the United States. Norden in 1975 or 1995 was far different from the Norden of 1945. The old party system had its roots in the nineteenth century, and the many workings of that system were forged in the 1930s. The postwar "consensus" belonged to a generation that came of age between 1930 and 1945. Just as the liberal parties of Europe declined in the interwar years when their goals had been achieved, the parties of the postwar period, and especially the Social Democrats, saw many of their dreams fulfilled. They were then confronted with the question of where to go next. The historical have-nots had been eliminated. Norden became a region of haves eager to hang on to their affluence in the face of serious challenges, and many voters gravitated toward the political right. The apparent social and economic radicalism of the previous four decades gave way to a new conservatism.

The Nordic "Welfare States"

During the half century following World War II, Scandinavia earned a new place of importance in Western history. Whether seen positively or negatively, the Nordic countries were where the "welfare state" became most firmly rooted and most extensive, where a viable "middle way" between unfettered capitalism and communism evolved. Just what the term *welfare state* meant was (and remains) widely debated, and each country developed its own forms within its own unique historical context. There were, however, certain shared aspects, which may be summed up in the words *solidarity, equality, democracy, participation,* and the *planned economy.* As a concept, *solidarity* focused on the belief that a society was an entity in which individuals were entitled to benefits but were also responsible for contributing to the good of the whole. *Equality* had several aspects, including social, gender, and age. The objective of the builders of the welfare states was to create societies free from the older distinctions. The full range of benefits within the society, including all aspects of the social safety net as well as economic, educational, and cultural opportunities, were to be available for all equally. One of the best statements of this concept was Alva Myrdal's *On Equality,* prepared for the Swedish Social Democratic Party Congress in 1968. In the postwar period *democracy* was extended beyond the political realm to reach into all aspects of the societies including the workplace and schools. *Participation* in the development

The Welfare State: Why in Norden?

Why and how did the welfare states develop in Norden? One argument is that there are deeply rooted traditions of state-sponsored "welfare" (and taxation) in these societies that were simply given new forms in the late twentieth century. For example, the state has been closely involved in education, health, and poor relief at least since the Reformation, and there is nothing new about state roles in economic matters. In the same vein, but more critical, is the argument that the welfare states are merely the latest version in a long history of docility toward and exploitation by central government. Although there is some truth in both arguments, a more complete explanation lies in the convergence of the historical context, ideas, leadership, and favorable opportunities. Social democracy provided the ideology. A group of exceptionally able individuals provided the leadership. The political dominance of the social democratic parties provided the political opportunity. The affluence of the postwar years provided the economic base.

and implementation of the welfare state by its members was viewed as an essential corollary of democracy. In practice, it took the form of commissions designed to study problems and prepare programs, organizational participation in legislation development and implementation, and active involvement in the political processes. All these aspects required a commitment to education and the extensive dissemination of information. Finally, none of these ideals or the specific programs that reflected them could be achieved without economic resources. Capitalism was by no means abandoned, but it was to be turned to the service of the common good.

The specific programmatic aspects of the Nordic welfare states developed far beyond the groundbreaking legislation of the late nineteenth and early twentieth centuries or the modest expansion of programs in the 1930s. The growth occurred in two stages. In the 1950s basic elements were defined and special commission studies conducted; in the 1960s and early 1970s legislation enlarged the range, scope, and costs of programs. During this period the cradle to the grave "safety net" was established. Comprehensive health care, sickness and accident insurance, and disability payment programs served to protect individuals throughout their lives. A host of payment programs including child and family allowances and housing subsidies tended to even out income differences and standards of living. Child allowances, day care, and parental leave programs gave women more freedom and opportunities. The basic education reforms of the late 1950s and 1960s were designed to democratize education—to provide nine- or ten-year compulsory systems that were social class and gender blind and that opened opportunity doors by reducing the early tracking of students into academic, professional, trade, or labor career lines. At the same time, the range of educational opportunities was expanded across Norden. New universities including those at Ålborg, Odense, and Roskilde in Denmark; Vaasa in Finland; Bergen, Trondheim, and Tromsö in Norway; and Umeå and Linköping in Sweden were opened. An ongoing commitment to the idea of lifelong learning led to the expansion of evening, community, and organization educational programs. Guaranteed paid vacations, regulation of work conditions, unemployment insurance, and retraining and relocation programs ensured lifelong employment in quality environments while long-standing "basic agreements" ensured peaceful labor-management relations. Pensions rose from subsistence levels to become sufficient to maintain a relatively high standard of living—largely through the introduction of the hotly debated "supplemental pensions" introduced in the 1960s. In addition, these systems sought to provide a high-quality infrastructure including extensive public transportation networks, up-to-date telecommunication and energy systems, and efficiency in the delivery of programs. They also supported recreational and cultural resources including parks and museums, the theater arts, film, music, literature, and both contemporary and traditional crafts.

All this was paid for through direct and indirect taxes on individuals and companies, and through worker and employer contributions. The average Nordic citizen saw 50 percent or more of her or his earnings eaten up by taxes. For a brief time, the tax code in Sweden actually demanded over 100 percent of income on some self-employed individuals—a situation that received wide media attention when it affected popular author Astrid Lindgren. Sales or value-added taxes reached levels over 20 percent, and high taxes on commodities like alcoholic beverages, tobacco products, or gasoline were designed both to raise revenues and control consumption—with a variety of social motives and outcome expectations. The high tax burden was made palatable by the returns individuals, families, and businesses received in terms of payments, services, and infrastructure.

Economic growth and full employment were essential to these systems, and the Nordic governments employed a variety of methods to maintain both, including tax reductions, subsidies, investment incentives, loan programs, private-public ownership schemes, extensive regional development programs, international trade policies, and membership in international trade and monetary organizations. Related to these goals were a variety of private and public attempts to enhance worker democracy and, thereby, improve productivity. Throughout Norden during the 1970s labor gained a greater voice in management (*codetermination*) through schemes designed to place worker representatives on factory or business councils and boards of directors. At the same time, legislation was passed that was designed to improve job satisfaction and performance by enhancing the work experience. Employees were supposed to feel they were valued and that their jobs were learning experiences. Corporate experiments with the job environment and work routines, such as Volvo and Saab's team assembly systems, were also common. Finally, and most notably in Sweden, so-called worker funds were created. An idea with its roots in the 1930s, these funds were to be based on business profits and were to be used by labor to purchase shares in corporations. In theory they would give workers ownership in the private sector, which could end in majority control by labor while providing a pool of investment capital to encourage growth. Hotly debated, Sweden established five such funds in 1983. They served the last purpose, but did not transfer ownership or control to labor and were soon abandoned.

The ongoing debate about the success, value, impacts, and future of the welfare states has been as interesting as the Nordic model itself. A vast literature developed representing advocates and critics. For some the Nordic states presented ideals of the good society, in which capitalism was tamed, and individuals could develop to their fullest potential. They were examples of the best that Western society had to offer. Others saw quite the opposite. The safety net destroyed individual initiative and the will to work. The governments' so-called economic planning stifled growth, preserved dying industries, and skewed natural economic development. The public sectors became bloated, self-serving, and inefficient; they were enormous drains on limited economic resources that could be better used else-where. The tax systems turned honest citizens into tax evaders or, worse, drove them to emigrate; suffocated entrepreneurial initiative; and pushed established companies from the countries. In addition, the welfare states were seen as authoritarian and oppressively conformist.

Foreign and Security Policies

In the optimism of the immediate postwar years, there were hopes that the wartime great power coalition would survive and that the United Nations would serve as an effective agent for the peaceful settlement of disputes. Few imagined the East-West polarization that evolved between 1945 and 1950, and several of Norden's leaders sought to act as "bridge builders" between the Soviets and Americans in hopes of preserving the wartime cooperation. Relatively little atten-tion was given to security issues before 1947–48. The Nordic coun-tries joined the United Nations. As occupied states, Denmark and Norway were charter members of the league's successor. Iceland and Sweden entered in 1946; Finland followed in 1955. Norway's Trygve Lie became the first secretary general of the organization and served until 1953, when he was succeeded by Dag Hammarskjöld of Sweden.

The gradual development of the Cold War in the late 1940s forced each of the Nordic countries to adjust its security and for-eign policies to the realities of a bipolar world. Denmark became increasingly concerned over the proximity of the East-West border in north Germany and the country's importance as a potential gate-keeper of the Baltic. Finnish leaders confronted the realities of two lost wars with the Soviets, the immense military power of its neigh-bor, and the fates of the eastern European border states. Icelanders were torn by the strategic realities of their position in the north Atlantic, their own military weakness, and strong desires to avoid having Icelandic culture and independence undermined by joining a Western power bloc. The Norwegians, ever mindful of the Ger-man invasion and occupation, were particularly sensitive to their common border with the Soviets in the far north and the growing importance of the Arctic region in submarine warfare. Sweden's leaders, confident in the security they believed neutrality could pro-vide, were less concerned about any direct threat from either power bloc, but realized there was a new security environment in the North. In general they wanted to do nothing that would infringe on their own freedom of action or make Norden a focal point of East-West tensions.

Developments in 1948—including the coup in Czechoslovakia in February; Soviet pressures on Finland that led to a security agreement; the conclusion of a mutual defensive agreement by Great Britain, France, Belgium, the Netherlands, and Luxembourg; the gradual emergence of a West German state through the consolidation of occupation zones; and the initiation of the Berlin blockade—created considerable anxiety in Norden. Concern was, for example, expressed by Norwegian foreign minister Halvard Lange in April. Fears were aroused in Sweden that the apparent postwar Nordic consensus on nonalignment was unraveling, and this led Tage Erlander's government to put out feelers in Copenhagen and Oslo for a Nordic defensive pact in May 1948. Although there were clear differences, the responses were generally positive, and a series of preparatory talks led to serious negotiations in January 1949 in Karlstad, Copenhagen, and Oslo. Despite a good deal of common ground, the negotiations broke down principally over questions of weapons' sourcing and U.S. reluctance to provide arms to nonaligned states, doubts that the alliance would actually provide security, and Denmark and Sweden's insistence on the neutrality of the bloc versus Norway's belief it should be linked with the emerging NATO group. Danish and Norwegian leaders then opted to abandon their attachment to neutrality, a policy no doubt called into question by the experiences of World War II, and took their countries into NATO in 1949. (Iceland, excluded from the defensive pact discussions, turned to NATO first, a decision that generated heated public outcries.) As NATO members Denmark and Norway developed modest-scale modern military services and spent about 2–3 percent of GDP on defense through the Cold War period. However, all three countries placed limits on their participation in NATO. Denmark and Norway refused to allow foreign bases (except in Greenland) or nuclear weapons on their territory. Iceland, which maintained only a coast guard, reached a basing agreement in 1951 that gave the United States use of the airbase at Keflavík. This limited participation in NATO dovetailed with the security policies of Finland and Sweden, and was intended to minimize East-West friction in the Nordic region.

Sweden's government was left to pursue an independent course based on a foreign policy defined as nonalignment in times of peace so that neutrality would be possible in the event of war. Sweden's leaders, and especially Foreign Minister Östen Undén, who was the principal architect of the country's postwar foreign policy, believed this would give Sweden the greatest range of options. As a corollary, a security policy based on strong national defenses designed to discourage, but not prevent, attack was pursued. For the next several decades, the Swedes poured an annual average of about 5 percent of GDP into making their defenses credible. They designed and built their own small arms, artillery, military vehicles, warships, and aircraft. Although many of their weapons systems were dependent on U.S. technologies and components, they were state-of-the-art and also highly competitive in the international arms market, for example, Saab aircraft and Bofors antiaircraft cannon. The Swedes also pursued an active atomic weapons development program until about 1970. It was abandoned for several reasons, including cost, the conclusion that possessing atomic weapons would not ensure Sweden's security or, more likely, might ensure the country's destruction, and the belief that the United States would protect Sweden in the event of an attack. (Sweden also signed the Nuclear Nonproliferation Treaty in 1970.)

The Finns followed a very different course. Their foreign and security policies were defined by the 1944 armistice agreement, the 1947 Paris treaty, and the April 1948 Treaty of Friendship, Cooperation, and Mutual Assistance (FCMA)—all signed with the Soviets. The first two defined borders, territorial changes, reparations, and the size of Finnish military forces. They also assured the presence of a Soviet naval base on the Porkkala Peninsula west of Helsinki. The 1948 treaty stipulated that the Finns would resist any attack by "Germany or any state allied with the latter" and, if it was deemed necessary and mutually agreed upon, accept Soviet assistance in repelling an attack. It was also agreed that the two countries would work for closer cultural and economic relations and would respect each other's sovereignty. The initiative for the treaty came from Stalin, but the final form was the product of a lengthy process of stalling and negotiation led by Finnish president Juho Paasikivi. It was a deal that held out gains for each side. In the context of the developing Cold War, which was evident in the Soviet takeover of Czechoslovakia in late February 1948, worsening East-West relations in Germany, and U.S. attempts to undercut communist influence in Western Europe through the Marshall Plan, the Soviets believed they had assured themselves a compliant Finland as a piece of their northwest flank security puzzle. The Finns, on the other hand, believed they had secured their independence in a very dangerous context and created a key element in a policy designed to avoid confrontation and build trust with the Soviet Union—a policy referred to as "the Paasikivi Line." Under the umbrella provided by these agreements, Finnish leaders subsequently pursued a course of flexible nonalignment in international affairs while maintaining a modest defense establishment whose limits were set by the 1947 treaty and cost about 1.5 percent of GDP annually.

Given the Cold War context and the differing interpretations the Soviets and the Finns placed on these agreements, it is not surprising that there were several crises between 1948 and 1991. In 1949 Soviet opposition forced the government of Karl A. Fagerholm, a Social Democrat, to resign. In 1958 Moscow's lack of faith in the five-party coalition government installed following that summer's elections developed into the so-called Nightfrost Crisis. The new cabinet, headed by Fagerholm, included two members of a strongly anti-Soviet faction within the Social Democratic Party and three Conservatives. Khrushchev and his colleagues in the Kremlin considered this government "unfriendly" and made their position known through economic and diplomatic means, which included a delay in replacing the Soviet ambassador to Finland. These pressures led to the collapse of the government, and direct talks between Uhro Kekkonen, who had succeed Paasikivi as president in 1956, and Khrushchev took place that were intended to restore Soviet confidence. The so-called Note Crisis occurred in late 1961, amid another round of worsening East-West relations over Germany and the breakdown of disarmament negotiations. Unilaterally invoking the 1948 treaty agreement, Moscow called for defense talks. But exactly what the Soviets' intentions were remains unclear. One factor seems to have been genuine concern over the changing security situation arising from German rearmament. Another factor was concern about the upcoming January 1962 presidential election, in which Kekkonen faced a challenge from a multi-party coalition supporting Olavi Honka, whom the Soviets regarded as unfriendly. Security, Finland's continued adherence to the Paasikivi Line, and Finnish politics were all aspects of the crisis that was again settled through direct talks between Kekkonen and Khrushchev. A similar but less extensive incident occurred in 1978, when the Soviet minister of defense suggested joint military exercises. Other examples of Soviet meddling in domestic Finnish politics occurred in 1972, when Moscow sent negative signals concerning a Finnish trade agreement with the European Community, probably to encourage Kekkonen to run for another term as president, and in 1982 when they conspired to block Mauno Koivisto's election as president.

From one perspective the Finnish policies were both clever and successful. So long as it was necessary, Finland's presidents (Paasikivi to 1956, Kekkonen from 1956 to 1982, and Koivisto from 1982 to 1991) followed this policy "line." The 1948 treaty was renewed early in 1955 for twenty years, and it was renewed again in 1975. In exchange for the 1955 renewal, the Soviets gave up their Porkkala base. They also made no objections to Finland joining the United Nations and did not pressure the Finns to join the Warsaw Pact, which was established that year. Within this context of carefully maintained trust, the Finns were able to follow an independent course that included active membership in the UN, entry into the European Free Trade Association in 1961, and hosting the 1975 Helsinki meetings of the Conference on Security and Cooperation in Europe (CSCE)—an organization intended to foster East-West detente. They were also increasingly willing to take an independent, critical stance on issues such as the Soviet intervention in Afghanistan in December 1979.

The alternative perspectives on the Finns' policies and actions are less positive. Some go so far as to argue that by the end of the 1940s Finland was a virtual satellite of Moscow, albeit one controlled with a "silk glove" rather than a mailed fist. To protect the country's "independence," its leaders gave up their sovereignty in international affairs, and this surrender spilled over into other aspects of Finnish life including domestic politics, economics, trade policies, and even expressions of opinion. The term *Finlandization* was based on a negative assessment of this policy line and the history that went with it. Coined in the 1970s, the term developed in a context of fear that Europe was being lulled into a malaise that would end in a silent, creeping Soviet takeover.

As more balanced analysts have pointed out, however, the situation was never one-sided or simple. The FCMA treaty was not a dictated agreement and contained basic points of Paasikivi's design. After 1948 the Finns did not accede to every Soviet demand. A measure of foreign policy autonomy was always maintained, although it tended to fluctuate widely depending on who was in power in the Soviet Union and Cold War conditions. From 1955 on the Finns explicitly referred to their country as neutral, and the Soviets accepted this. Domestic politics were largely free of Soviet influence. From 1960 on only about one-fifth of Finland's international trade was with the Soviet bloc. Public policy, culture, and opinion developed independently. The special relations between the two countries also served Soviet interests. Finland could be held up to prove that Moscow was not driven by a policy of unbridled expansionism. At the same time economic interests were served, and Finland acted as a window and a bridge into the West.

Economic Developments

Recovery from the material damage and economic shocks of the war was more rapid than many expected. It was helped along in all of Norden except Finland by U.S. support through the Marshall Plan and participation in the Organization for European Cooperation and Development (OECD). The constraints on the Finns' foreign and security policies kept them outside the West European programs, and their recovery was spurred instead by the Soviet reparations demands, which were met by the delivery of goods including wood products, ships, and industrial machinery. The rapidity of this process, which concentrated on the restoration of infrastructure, markets, and fiscal stability, came at the expense of the public, which faced five to ten years of austerity characterized by continued government controls on wages, prices, and consumption.

Sustained economic expansion, which transformed the Nordic states into affluent consumer societies and provided the bases for the welfare states, came in the 1950s and 1960s. By almost all measures these were good times. Annual growth rates averaged around 4 percent. Real incomes rose in an atmosphere of labor-management peace. There was virtually no unemployment. Consumer goods were available, and people bought them. The welfare safety net was built with steadily increasing tax revenues.

Initially, much of this growth came in the primary sectors of the Nordic economies and in a few historically important industries including forest products, shipping and shipbuilding, mining, metal manufacturing, and agriculture. Gradually, however, fundamental changes occurred throughout the region. In an increasingly global economy, these elements in the Nordic economies faced more and more competition and lost importance relative to new sectors and enterprises. Technology-intensive industries took their place. The private and public service sectors became the largest contributors to

GDP, as Norden moved from industrial economies to ones termed postindustrial, service, or informational.

The erosion of the importance of primary sector activities, relative to others, was remarkable. Agriculture, a chronic economic problem in every Nordic country, was plagued by high production costs, debt, competition from abroad, and declining interest in farming as a career. The decline of farming was evidenced by the drop in the number of farms and a flight from the land. This pattern was most pronounced in Denmark, where the number of farms fell from 185,000 in 1950 to 69,000 in 1994. (The figures for Finland were 262,000 to 164,000; Norway, 143,000 to 78,000; Sweden, 282,000 to 90,102.) At the same time, the percentage of people employed in farming dropped to between 3.4 percent (in Sweden) and 8.6 percent (in Iceland). In part this decline involved the abandonment of small, unprofitable farms and consolidation of holdings, which can be seen in the growth in the numbers of farms of 20 or more hectares (50 acres). The decline also involved the return of some agricultural land to its natural state. On the positive side, consolidation, more machines, new chemicals, improved techniques, and more specialization actually increased productivity. Sweden claimed self-sufficiency. Unfortunately, high production costs—often aggravated by heavy debt loads—and low commodity prices continued to plague agriculture. Without government price supports, subsidies, crop insurance, and loan programs, farmers would have even greater problems. Government commitments to support agriculture were enormously expensive and skewed both domestic and international economic policies. Agricultural concerns also played in the Nordic countries' decisions on membership in the European Union—with some voting yes because of the expanded market and others voting no because of competition from imports. (In the 1990s the largest single element in the EU budget was support for member states' agriculture. This matter was of great concern, especially in light of the possible membership of new states in eastern Europe with large agricultural sectors.)

Although the forest product resources of Finland, Norway, and Sweden remained important, especially as exports, far-reaching changes occurred in this area as well. The demand for wood and charcoal as fuels declined. Global competition took a toll on the pulp industry. One response was extensive rationalization and mechanization in order to keep costs down, and Sweden demonstrated its effectiveness by retaining its position as the world's third largest exporter of paper and pulp products. Finnish producers turned very successfully to making high-grade bond papers. Complicating the situation for the forest products industries were pressures from environmentalists concerned about deforestation, ecosystem losses, and very serious air and water pollution problems. These environmental concerns led to improved forest management and pollution control programs.

Mining faced problems as well. Dwindling resources, rising extraction costs, and international competition translated into mine closings and consolidation and are illustrated by developments in Sweden. By 1993 there were only nineteen ore-producing mining operations in the entire country. Almost all iron mining was in the hands of the state-owned LKAB (Luossavaara-Kiirunavaara Aktiebolaget) and took place in the far north around Kiruna. The great copper mine at Falun shut down extraction operations in 1992, but the company, Stora AB, continued to produce the paint pigment from mine tailings that is the base for the red so common in rural Sweden. The sector employed only about 9,000 people. At the same time, steel production became more specialized and increasingly concentrated in a few companies, the largest of which was Svenskt Stål (SSAB). Iceland and Norway exploited their hydroelectric potential to make aluminum production profitable.

Fishing remained important, especially in the Faeroes, Iceland, and northern Norway; however, as with the other primary industries, it tended to employ fewer people and captured a proportionally smaller share of GDP in the face of competition, declining resources, and the new directions in economic development. In the early 1990s, for example, fishing employed about 5.5 percent of Iceland's workforce and accounted for about 10 percent of GDP. The crucial role of fishing in the country's economy for much of this period, however, was reflected in the risks Iceland took by extending its territorial waters from three miles to two hundred miles between 1952 and 1975 in moves intended to ensure Icelandic fishermen adequate resources. The 1952 step was from three to four miles, and aroused little attention except from Great Britain. The move to twelve miles in 1958 initiated the first "Cod War," a three-year crisis that pitted Iceland against Great Britain. The situation was repeated in 1972 and again in 1975, and each time encroaching boats were intimidated and confiscated, nets were cut, and the Royal Navy was sent in to protect British fishermen. In the last instance the British even broke off diplomatic relations. Treaties ended the first two conflicts, and the third was resolved in 1977, when the EU accepted Iceland's position. In decisions that proved deeply troubling to environmental groups such as Greenpeace and violated an international moratorium, the Norwegians resumed whaling operations in the mid-1990s on a very limited basis. Their actions were difficult to defend in economic terms. Cultural and regional factors were certainly involved, but they may have been motivated more by nationalism than anything else.

Shipping and shipbuilding were hard hit by the swings in global business cycles, and the late 1970s and early 1980s were especially difficult times. Although Norway continued to have one of the largest merchant fleets in the world, it faced growing competition from carriers with vessels registered in developing counties. The precipitous collapse of shipbuilding in the 1970s led to yard closings and soaring unemployment. What was really needed was fundamental restructuring and adaptation to changing market conditions. Heavy government subsidy programs in Norway and Sweden designed to keep yards open and employment up failed. The successful specialization of the Finnish shipbuilding industry illustrated how the situation could be met. By shifting production to deep-sea oil rigs (many for the Norwegian North Sea fields), container vessels, and icebreakers, the industry was sustained without huge and ultimately nonprofitable government investments. In general Norden experienced an upswing in a much-changed shipbuilding sector in the late 1980s.

Late in the period similar problems hit some industries in the Nordic consumer product sector as well. Textiles, clothing, and shoe manufacturing fell off drastically, unable to compete with producers in the developing world because of high costs.

The rationalization and expansion of older industries, diversification, and capitalizing on new technologies and markets more than offset these declines. Alongside Danish butter and pork products came Lego toys, Bang and Olufsen audio equipment, and beautifully designed housewares. The Finns turned to the production of high-quality bond papers, papermaking machinery, and specialized ships and oil rigs. They also capitalized on the demand for electronic communication devices like cell phones—a sector dominated by Nokia. Icelanders moved to rationalize their agriculture and protect their fishing industry and expanded hydroelectric capacity and metal production. Norway also built on its hydroelectric potential to expand its chemical and metallurgical sectors. Sweden, whose economy was the most diverse in Norden, experienced the greatest growth in the engineering, high-grade specialty metals, and pharmaceutical industries. In addition, Sweden's security policies fed the growth of the armaments divisions of several major corporations including Bofors, Nobel Industries, and Saab. Tourism also became an increasingly important contributor to the Nordic economies.

Prosperity was highly dependent on the growth of exports. Government policies throughout the period were designed to encourage international trade and ensure product competitiveness. Norden took part in international tariff development through GATT from 1947. In 1959–60 Denmark, Norway, and Sweden joined with Great Britain, Austria, Switzerland, and Liechtenstein to form the European Free Trade Area (EFTA). Finland became an associate member of the group in 1961, and Iceland joined in 1970. A purely trade-centered organization, EFTA was designed to provide an open trade community without the potential compromises of national sovereignty or great power bloc alignment of the emerging European Union (the Common Market, the European Economic Community). Continuous efforts were made to develop open-market arrangements with what became the European Union. Danish and Norwegian governments favored EU membership from the late 1960s, and Denmark joined in 1973, following a referendum in which 63 percent voted yes. Norway took the opposite course. A deeply divisive campaign led up to the September 1972 referendum. Almost 80 percent of the electorate turned out, with 53.5 percent voting no. Twelve years later the question came up again, this time with Finland and Sweden also considering membership in a far more extensive European community. Opinion was divided between and within political parties as well as along class and age lines. Regions were pitted against regions, such as the far north of Norway versus the urban east. It was the most troublesome issue to face Norden since the war, according to some observers. The results of all three referenda were close. The Finns voted yes with the strongest percentage, 57 percent; 52.3 percent said yes in Sweden; and the Norwegians again said no, 52.2 percent to 47.8 percent. Finland and Sweden became members of the EU in January 1995. Norway, along with Iceland, remained outside the organization, but both countries continued to have access to the market through the European Economic Area agreement of 1994. In addition to trade agreements and community participation, the Nordic governments devalued their currencies several times during the period in order to maintain competitiveness. In some cases these policies were negated by government efforts to shore up uncompetitive industries, but, overall, they were effective in growing the export sectors.

One of the most important aspects of economic development was the growth of the private and public service sectors—the "third leg" of the Nordic economies after domestic manufacturing and trade. Buying, selling, financing, moving, and marketing goods and services defined the private sector. Design, management, and delivery of the social services of the welfare states defined the public sector. Spectacular growth occurred in both. By the close of the century nearly two-thirds of all employed people were in these fields, and they accounted for a similar proportion of GDP. In Sweden the public services share of GDP rose from about 13 percent in 1950 to almost 30 percent in 1980.

During the last twenty-five years of the century a host of problems plagued the economies of Norden and the West. Although many were present before, the 1973 and 1980 global oil crises acted as catalysts in bringing them to the fore. Energy prices increased eight to ten times, which drove up the costs of everything. Stagflation set in, characterized by falling demand, production cuts, large inventories, and a new round of inflation. Price increases created wage pressures, and the previously harmonious labor-management situations began to unravel. Nordic products became less competitive in the world markets and exports declined while import needs remained constant, which led to adverse trade balances. Political commitments to growth and full-employment forced some Nordic governments to spend and borrow, and national debts grew.

Norway and Sweden responded to the crises in certain industries first by throwing money at them. Loans, subsidies, tax breaks, and government takeovers were aimed at maintaining the all-important goal of full employment. Seriously troubled industries such as shipbuilding and forest products were artificially sustained. Paradoxically, Sweden's nonsocialist governments of the late 1970s poured enormous amounts of capital into the collapsing shipbuilding industry and acquired virtual control through the state-owned holding company, Svenska Varv. Only gradually did the state shift toward rationalization policies that included facility closings, worker retraining and relocation, and the end of subsidies. Denmark and Finland's governments were less able and, therefore, less inclined to bolster failing economic sectors. Another successful course was followed by Sweden's two automobile builders, Saab and Volvo. Each secured new partners in

Europe in order to share development technologies, remain competitive, and preserve autonomy. Saab joined with Fiat and Volvo with Renault in arrangements to spread the costs of new car development. A later proposal to merge Volvo and Renault failed, but the company succeeded in stabilizing its position through internal reform, product development, and careful attention to matching products to markets. For example, in the United States, where fewer models were offered, Volvo moved up-market and competed successfully with the entry-level cars from BMW and Mercedes. Perhaps a victim of its own successes, the rejuvenated company's automotive division was taken over by Ford in a $6.45 billion merger deal in 1999. Always the smaller of the two Swedish automobile builders, Saab's car division struggled. In 1990 General Motors acquired controlling interest and completed the takeover in early 2000. Together these changes marked the end of three quarters of a century of independent car development in Sweden. This development echoed a global trend toward internationalization through mergers and buyouts. Many of Norden's largest corporations either expanded to become multinationals or were absorbed. Electrolux grew to become the largest producer of household appliances in the world. Nobel Industries were acquired by Dutch Akzo. ASEA merged with Brown Boveri, a Swiss firm. Denmark's Burmeister & Wain was bought out by MAN of Germany.

Energy sources, resources, and policies caused various problems in Norden, especially after the 1973 and 1980 OPEC oil price increases. Until the development of the North Sea petroleum discoveries in the 1980s, Denmark had to import virtually all its fuels. The exploitation of offshore oil and natural gas resources benefited the country to some degree, but not as extensively as Norway. Finland imported all its coal, oil, and natural gas—much of it from Russia—and built several nuclear generating plants. Iceland imported some coal and petroleum, but its dependence on these sources was lessened by its hydroelectric generating capacity and the development of geothermal sources—by which the entire city of Reykjavík was heated. Like Finland, Sweden was heavily dependent on imported fuels. Its hydroelectrical capacity was maximized. Half of the country's electricity came from nuclear generating stations in 1994. Government policy aimed to fulfill the wishes of the public to phase out the country's nuclear power stations, as expressed in a 1980 referendum. Two of these were scheduled for shutdown by 2001. What would replace them was unclear. Confronted by limited resources and high costs, all

Population

	1900	1950
Denmark	2.5 million	4.3 million
Faeroes	15,000	32,000
Finland	2.7 million	4.0 million
Iceland	78,000	144,000
Norway	2.2 million	3.3 million
Sweden	5.1 million	7.0 million

Nordic Council of Ministers, *Yearbook of Nordic Statistics, 1996*, 39–40, 49. All figures have been rounded off to the nearest 1,000.

of Norden sought to exploit alternative or renewable energy sources including wind, biomass, and peat.

Norway became the exception to this energy picture. Until the 1970s it was as dependent on foreign energy sources as the rest of Scandinavia. Its one great natural resource was in hydroelectric potential. Then came the discovery and exploitation of the North Sea oil and gas finds. Although enormously expensive to explore and then bring into production, they became "the goose that lay the golden eggs" for Norway. They attracted investment, generated industrial development and jobs, and fed the coffers of the state. Almost overnight, it seemed, Norway became the energy giant and growth leader of the region.

Social Developments

Norden's societies underwent many changes in the postwar period. Overall, the regions' populations grew slowly. Among the important trends were falling birthrates, increased life expectancies in the region (to around seventy-five years for men and eighty years for women), the gradual aging of the population, and continued urbanization. Other important changes occurred in employment distribution patterns, marriage and divorces rates, the composition of families, crime rates, immigration, and the ethnic composition of populations.

In terms of employment distribution, the primary industries

1994	2000 (projected)
5.2 million	5.3 million
44,000	42,000
5.1 million	5.2 million
267,000	280,000
4.3 million	4.5 million
8.8 million	9 million

(agriculture, forestry, farming, fishing, and mining) and manufacturing employed fewer people. This decline was offset by the rapid growth in the private and public service areas. The Nordic countries became nations of white-collar workers, salespeople, social workers, clerks, teachers, financial agents, and bureaucrats. At the same time, marriage rates fell and divorce rates soared. More and more people chose to live together without marrying, and many of them chose to have children. Norden became a region in which half of all marriages ended in divorce, and about two-fifths of all children either lived with a single parent (overwhelmingly their mothers) or in nontraditional families based on unwed parents.

One of the most serious social problems facing Norden at the close of the twentieth century was crime. For many it symbolized the decay of formerly peaceful and harmonious societies or the decadence of the welfare state. The increases were clear in the statistics and played up in the media. The growing frequency of violent crimes was particularly distressing to publics that had long believed that Norden was immune to the kind of violence that plagued America and other Western societies. The 28 February 1986 murder of Sweden's Prime Minister Olof Palme near Sergelstorget in the middle of Stockholm's downtown shocked the nation and the region. Political assassinations were virtually unheard-of in Scandinavia. (Equally disturbing were the investigations that followed and the botched trial that may have let the assassin go free.) As much as anything, this act

Crime in Norden: 1960 versus 1994

	Recorded Offenses
Denmark	126,367 vs. 546,926
Finland	65,201 vs. 360,289
Norway	38,584 vs. 218,821
Sweden	276,314 vs. 975,690

Nordic Council of Ministers, *Yearbook of Nordic Statistics, 1996*, 330–32.

symbolized a loss of innocence. Since then numerous other violent crimes have attracted public attention, including a shooting spree in a Stockholm disco that claimed several lives and racially motivated attacks on immigrants. Drugs and gangs were also elements in the rising crime rates. One of the most troubling illustrations of this problem were the so-called biker wars between rival motorcycle gangs in Denmark and Sweden, which involved escalating acts of violence including street fights, murders, and even antitank rocket attacks on rival gang headquarters.

After 1945 Norden became a region of net in-migration. Initially, the migration was fed by peoples displaced by the war and postwar events. Small numbers of Germans fled to Denmark before the Russians (few remained), and Baltic peoples sought (but did not always receive) refuge in Sweden. In the 1950s the open labor market contributed to the migration of almost half a million Finns to Sweden. In addition, labor migrants from the former Yugoslavia, Turkey, and other less developed countries moved to Norden, especially in the 1960s and early 1970s, to take jobs—often at the bottom of the employment ladder. Political turmoil around the globe and generous immigration and asylum regulations encouraged settlement in Norden, especially Denmark and Sweden, by refugees from Southeast Asia, Latin America, and the Middle East.

Government policies were usually quite generous toward the newcomers. The welfare safety net was available. New programs were introduced to facilitate adjustment to the Nordic societies and to help the immigrants preserve their homeland cultures through organizations, activities, and education. In the public schools, time was set

Murders	Rapes	Robberies
18 vs. 79	189 vs. 481	344 vs. 2,046
109 vs. 147	222 vs. 387	294 vs. 2,122
14 vs. 46	66 vs. 349	65 vs. 891
46 vs. 159	512 vs. 1,812	469 vs. 5,331

aside for instruction in the native languages of immigrant children. On the downside, policies and legislation could not force either assimilation or toleration. Often the immigrants lived in densely populated ethnic communities—by choice and by official design. Some of these communities became virtual ghettos. Religious and cultural differences, to say nothing of the differing physical characteristics of many of the immigrants, set them apart. Many faced isolation, discrimination, and even physical attacks. Racist youth gangs, sometimes called "skin heads," preyed on immigrants. When economic conditions worsened, the newcomers faced additional problems and criticism from noisy neo-Nazi organizations. Political opposition developed within some established parties and new groups on the Right, such as Norway's White Electoral Alliance. The open immigration policies, especially for those seeking work in Norden, vanished in the mid-1970s, asylum seekers found the doors closing in the 1980s and 1990s, and many of the cultural maintenance programs fell victim to government cutbacks.

The infusions of new peoples had many impacts on Norden's homogeneous societies, especially when they were coupled with the relatively low birthrates of the native populations. The impacts were most noticeable in Sweden, where nearly one in five Swedes was either foreign-born or the child of foreign-born parents in the 1990s. Ethnic diversity made Scandinavians more aware of the world as a global community. It forced homogeneous societies to see and to try to accept differences. It tested the generosity of the Nordic model, and in most instances that model met the challenges. Norden was richer in talent and culture because of this migration. Film, music, the

Foreign-born Population in 1994

Denmark	264,055
Finland	100,415
Iceland	10,585
Norway	233,375
Sweden	922,055

Nordic Council of Ministers, *Yearbook of Nordic Statistics, 1996*, 43–44

Principal Foreign-born Groups in 1995

Denmark

Other Nordic countries	55,668
Turkey	34,967
Africa	13,481
United Kingdom	11,860
Germany	10,102
Iran	7,678
Pakistan	6,401
Poland	5,216
United States	4,815

Finland

Other Nordic countries	35,535
Former USSR	22,762
Africa	6,215
Vietnam	1,812

arts, language, and literature were affected. One of Sweden's leading authors in the 1980s and 1990s was Theodor Kallifatides, a Greek immigrant. Another interesting example of the cultural impacts was the immigrants' influence on food tastes and options. In 1965 Stockholm had one pizza restaurant. Twenty years later it had dozens, along with restaurants and shops offering the foods of the new, multiethnic Swedes.

United States	1,775
Turkey	1,178
Iran	1,125
Norway	
Other Nordic countries	88,020
United Kingdom	11,234
Africa	11,603
Pakistan	10,311
United States	9,181
Vietnam	6,371
Iran	5,916
Turkey	4,995
Sweden	
Other Nordic countries	174,750
Former Yugoslavia	40,368
Iran	32,670
Africa	29,151
Turkey	21,995
Poland	16,070
Chile	14,097
Germany	13,092
United States	9,101

Nordic Council of Ministers, *Yearbook of Nordic Statistics, 1996,* 46–47

Women

The postwar years, and especially those since 1970, brought important progress for women throughout Nordic society. The legal and political gains achieved in the late nineteenth and early twentieth centuries were, in many respects, superficial and had not brought true gender democracy to the Nordic societies. Parliaments and governments contained few women. They remained disadvantaged in the educational systems. Career options were still largely limited to traditional areas such as health care and teaching. Pay differences remained, and almost no women could be found in corporate management positions. Although these and other problems were recognized by organizations such as the Red Stockings in Denmark and by influential individuals like Alva Myrdal, progress was painfully slow. Icelandic women sought to increase awareness of these issues through their Women's Strike on 24 October 1975. On this day women stopped work—both at and outside the home. The action demonstrated the importance of all aspects of women's work, and it was repeated on the same day in 1985 and again in 1995. The country's Women's Alliance captured nearly 5 percent of the vote and three seats in the Althing in the 1995 election.

Serious attempts to build greater gender equality were made. Day care and parental leave programs alleviated some of the problems of working women—half or more of all women in Norden worked outside the home. Educational reforms improved basic opportunities and options. In the late twentieth century a higher percentage of women were likely to get a university education than men. Women made significant gains in local and national politics. In 1997, 39 percent of the members of the Finnish parliament were women, and the corresponding figure was 36 percent in Norway, 33 percent in Sweden and Denmark, and 24 percent in Iceland. Eleven ministers of Sweden's twenty-one-member cabinet were women the same year, a figure approached in Denmark and Finland. Vigdís Finnbogadóttir served as Iceland's president from 1980 to 1996, and Gro Harlem Brundtland was Norway's prime minister in 1981, from 1986 to 1989, and again from 1990 until her retirement in 1995. In February 2000 the Finns elected Tarja Halonen as their new president. Ms. Halonen had been the minister of foreign affairs. A minor financial scandal prevented Mona Sahlin from succeeding Yngve Carlsson as Sweden's prime minister in 1996.

Yet, as a 1989 Swedish report showed, much remained to be won. Women continued to be underrepresented in many areas of society. Only a small percentage of the people working in the research sciences and a mere 1 percent of the business "elite" were women. Occupation distributions continued to follow traditional lines. An exception to this was in the growing importance of women in Nordic governments. Although they were often appointed to head ministries that echoed traditional occupation or activity areas such as social services or health, a pattern of change was clear in, for example, the selection of women to hold posts as minister of justice, foreign affairs, and finance in the Swedish government formed in 1994. It also was clear that many women continued to have two jobs—one outside the home and the other at home. True equality and breaking down entrenched social attitudes clearly were going to take far longer than a generation or two to achieve.

At the Close of the Century

Although the generalizations made by historians about the late twentieth century will certainly change over time, from the perspective of 2000 several trends or patterns of development helped organize this overview. Some of them were curiously contradictory, such as the increased global and regional involvement of Norden versus strong national and local perspectives, affluence amid ongoing economic problems, and continued concern for social welfare versus an increased self-centeredness. Other aspects of this period were the flux and uncertainties in political developments, a changed and uncertain security environment, and the expansion within Norden of many of the West's worst societal problems.

During the five hundred years surveyed here, Norden gradually became more and more a part of Europe and then the world. At no time was this more apparent than in the last half of the twentieth century. Then, as before, the region was both a giver and a receiver in the process of globalization. The Nordic welfare model; Scandinavian design, film, art, architecture, management and production techniques; and unique industrial products and technologies were shared with the world. At the same time products, enterprises, ideologies, and cultures flowed into Norden—symbolized by the presence of multinational corporations like IBM, ideologies like Thatcherism and Reaganomics, and cultural icons such as Levi's and Coca-Cola, and delivered via the Internet, satellite TV, and cellular phones.

At the same time, formal and informal regional combinations grew. As has been seen, Norden participated in postwar recovery programs and a host of economic cooperation organizations. In the fifty years after World War II, the Nordic states developed greater regional cooperation through wider informal contacts and through structures such as the very successful Nordic Council, founded in 1953 to deal with economic, social, and cultural matters, and the Nordic Council of

Scandinavia and the Baltic at the end of the twentieth century.

Ministers, founded in 1971. By 1995 Denmark, Finland, and Sweden were members of the European Union, and Iceland and Norway were linked to it through the European Economic Area agreements. At the close of the century, following the collapse of the Soviet Union, cooperation among the Nordic States, especially Finland and Sweden, and the new Baltic states grew. This trend was seen by some as evidence to support the idea of the growth of a new "superregion" based on the Baltic, and reminiscent of the Hanse.

Conversely, however, national and even regional or local identities remained strong and in some contexts even grew in importance. This development was particularly clear in the EU membership debates. The Norwegians' second rejection of EU membership in 1994 and the close votes in Finland and Sweden, as well as the Danes' initial rejection of the Maastricht Treaty in 1992, were, in part, anti-internationalist or regionalist statements. Similarly, the importance of nationalism was reflected in the continued concerns of Icelanders with the purity of their language and foreign influences. Norway's oil-based economic prosperity, set against the economic problems in the rest of Norden, also gave rise to a new round of nationalistic sparring, especially between Sweden and Norway. Although some saw this competition as just expressions of a friendly rivalry between Nordic neighbors, others viewed it as a form of revenge: finally, it was Norway's turn to be the richest nation in the region.

As in much of the rest of the West, the Nordic economies gradually adapted to the realities of the period and seemed to share in the cautious economic optimism of the late 1990s. Although the exceptional prosperity of the 1960s did not return, growth rates recovered as specialization and rationalization trends continued and were bolstered by foreign investments. Although the primary sectors continued to lose ground, Norden became increasingly a region producing competitive, high-quality, design-intensive products including automobiles, aircraft, computers and other electronic equipment, industrial machinery, and chemicals. Conversely, all but the Norwegian economy were still plagued by unemployment rates that ranged from around 4 percent in Iceland to 15 percent in Finland, unfavorable trade balances, and high state deficits. The several decades of prosperity had raised the expectations of most people. At the same time, social problems—including the changing nature of the family, the aging of the populations, drug and alcohol abuse, crime, and ethnic and racial discrimination—placed added burdens on the already strained welfare states. It was in this context that a new self-centeredness appeared. Many in Scandinavia jealously sought to keep what they had gained and were increasingly unwilling to share during troubled times. The welfare state consensus bred in the Depression and World War II appeared to be breaking down.

This erosion of consensus partially explains the continued flux and uncertainty in Nordic politics, which was illustrated by the popularity of new parties on the Right and voter volatility. Although some mid-1990s elections in Norden seemed to presage a return to stability, such was far from certain, and the results of the September 1997 Norwegian election reflected this: "Nobody won." On the Left, both Labor and the Socialist Left dropped about two percentage points to 35 percent and 6 percent of the vote, respectively. The Center Party's strength was cut in half to 8 percent, the Conservatives fell to 14.3 percent, the Liberals gained slightly with 4.4 percent, and the Christian Democrats made the strongest showing with 14 percent. The far-right Progress Party was the "winner," securing 15.3 percent of the vote and moving up from ten to twenty-five seats in the parliament. The ruling Labor minority government of Thorbjörn Jagland resigned, and several weeks of politicking ensued before a minority coalition led by Christian Democrat Kjell Magne Bondevik and joined by Center and Liberal members took office. Although the new government's position in the Storting was weak, it survived until March 2000 because the Norwegian constitution does not provide for elections in the event of a cabinet's collapse. A year later, in September 1998, the Swedes went to the polls in record low numbers, and here too the real winners were difficult to identify. The Social Democrats, led by Göran Persson, captured just over 36 percent of the vote, down from 45 percent in 1994. Other losers included the Center and Folk parties. The Moderates and their popular leader, Carl Bildt, just matched their 1994 tally with slightly over 22 percent. The greatest gains were made by the Left Party (the old Communist Party), which doubled its share to 12 percent, and the Christian Democrats, whose share rose from 4 percent to nearly 12 percent. Although Persson remained as prime minister, he was faced with the necessity of negotiating working arrangements with a much-strengthened Left and the smaller parties in the Center. Clearly, the future directions of Nordic politics were anything but predictable.

In the sphere of international relations and security, the end of the Cold War completely changed the environment, but did not remove the importance of Norden in almost any conceivable European security picture. What was the purpose of NATO now that there was no enemy? What was Sweden to do now that there was no real nonalignment issue in Europe? What was Finland's policy to be, following the collapse of the Soviet Union? Because of the uncertainties in the new situation, little changed in Nordic foreign and security policies. All of

Norden remained committed to the UN and other international organizations. NATO did not dissolve, and Denmark, Iceland, and Norway continued as members. What was the purpose of the organization now that there was no great enemy to the east, and why should one belong? These questions were not clearly answered, but one Danish defense official was convinced NATO's purposes were to foster communications and understanding among its members and thereby to avoid conflict within Europe, and these were reasons enough to remain in the organization. Finland and Sweden held to their nonalignment policies, a commitment reflected in the limits they placed on their membership in the European Union.

The last half of the twentieth century was a period of remarkable change and achievement in Norden. From the troubles of the Depression and the second round of the century's great war, the countries of the region rose to become five of the most economically, politically, socially, and technically advanced nations in the world. From many perspectives the quality of life in Norden was exceptional. The unique merging of democracy, social responsibility, the good of the community, the freedom of the individual, and economic planning that developed in each of the Nordic countries set them apart and made them models for the rest of the world. There was much to praise about these small countries on the fringes of Europe.

All was not perfect, however, and these exceptional times were destined to be short-lived. Neither removed from their pasts nor immune from the problems facing all modern societies, the welfare states of Norden did not erase chemical abuse and addiction, crime, class or racial discrimination, gender biases, violence, or loneliness. The people of Norden consumed the fruits, public and private, of the postwar prosperity with little regard for the future or for the limits of resources, the exploitation of developing world labor, or environmental issues. The 1973 oil crisis ended thirty years of unprecedented growth. This history ends amid what appears to be a new period in Nordic history: one fraught with promise and with questions and problems.

Bibliography

~~~~~~

The literature in Scandinavian history is extensive and diverse, provided one reads the Nordic languages. In contrast, the literature in English, although quite extensive, tends to be rather idiosyncratic. Some topics are covered exceptionally well; others have never been touched. At least two factors have contributed to this situation. First, the community of scholars in the field has always been relatively small, and the literature has largely reflected their interests. Second, the market for translations of Nordic materials is also small and limits what finds its way into English-language editions.

The bibliography below lists some of what is available. With a few exceptions, I have limited citations to English-language materials. I have not attempted to include journal articles, but I have listed the principal scholarly journals in the field. In this regard, readers should note that the Nordic countries' history journals often contain articles in English or with English summaries. Also, I have not attempted to list the ever-increasing number of cites on the Internet pertaining to Scandinavian history. The few cited provide superb starting points, however.

Abrams, Irwin. *The Nobel Peace Prize and the Laureates: An Illustrated Biographical History, 1901–1987*. Boston: G. K. Hall, 1988.

Allardt, Erik, et al. *Nordic Democracy: Ideas, Issues, and Institutions in Politics, Economy, Education, Social and Cultural Affairs of Denmark, Finland, Iceland, Norway, and Sweden*. Copenhagen: Det Danske Selskab, 1981.

Andrén, Nils B. *Government and Politics in the Nordic Counties: Denmark, Finland, Iceland, Norway, and Sweden*. Stockholm: Almqvist and Wiksell, 1964.

Arter, David. *The Nordic Parliaments: A Comparative Analysis*. New York: St. Martin's Press, 1984.

———. *Scandinavian Politics Today*. Manchester: Manchester University Press, 1999.

Barton, H. A. *Scandinavia in the Revolutionary Era*. Minneapolis: University of Minnesota Press, 1986.

Beer, Eileene H. *Scandinavian Design: Objects of a Life Style.* New York: Farrar, Straus and Giroux, 1975.

Brown, Berit I., ed. *Nordic Experiences: Exploration of Scandinavian Cultures.* Westport, Conn.: Greenwood Press, 1997.

Cerny, Karl H., ed. *Scandinavia at the Polls: Recent Political Trends in Denmark, Norway, and Sweden.* Washington, D.C.: American Enterprise Institute for Public Policy Research, 1977.

Connery, Donald S. *The Scandinavians.* New York: Simon and Schuster, 1966.

Derry, Thomas K. *A History of Scandinavia: Norway, Sweden, Denmark, Finland, and Iceland.* Minneapolis: University of Minnesota Press, 1979. Updated edition, 2000.

Donnelly, Marian C. *Architecture in the Scandinavian Countries.* Cambridge: MIT Press, 1992.

Einhorn, Eric, and John Logue. *Modern Welfare States: Politics and Policies in Social Democratic Scandinavia.* New York: Praeger, 1989.

Elder, Neil, Alastair H. Thomas, and David Arter. *The Consensual Democracies? The Government and Politics of the Scandinavian States.* Oxford: Martin Robertson, 1983.

Frederiksen, Inge, and Hilda Römer, eds. *Kvinder, mentalitet, arbjede: Kvindehistorisk forskning i Norden.* Aarhus, Denmark: Aarhus Universitetsforlag, 1986.

Grell, Ole Peter. "Scandinavia." In *The Reformation in National Context,* edited by Bob Scribner, Roy Porter, and Mikulás Teich. Cambridge: Cambridge University Press, 1994.

Griffiths, Tony. *Scandinavia.* Kent Town, Australia: Wakefield, 1991.

Haetta, Odd Mathis. *The Sami: An Indigenous People of the Arctic.* Translated by Ole Petter Gurholt. Vaasa: Davvi Girji o.s., 1996.

Holst, Johan J., ed. *Five Roads to Nordic Security.* Oslo: Universitetsforlaget, 1973.

Ingebritsen, Christine. *The Nordic States and European Unity.* Ithaca, N.Y.: Cornell University Press, 1998.

Jörberg, Lennart. "The Nordic Countries, 1850–1914," trans. Paul Britten Austin. In *The Emergence of Industrial Societies.* Part 2, edited by Carlo M. Cipolla. New York: Harvester Press, 1976.

Karlsson, Sven Olof, ed. *The Source of Liberty: The Nordic Contribution to Europe.* Stockholm: Nordic Council, 1992.

Karvonen, Lauri, and Per Selle, eds. *Women in Nordic Politics: Closing the Gap.* Hants, U.K.: Darmouth Publishing Company, 1995.

Kirby, David. *The Baltic World, 1772–1993.* New York: Longman, 1995.

———. *Northern Europe in the Early Modern Period: The Baltic World, 1492–1772.* London: Longman, 1990.

Kuoljok, Sunna. *The Saami: People of the Sun and Wind.* Jokkmokk: Ajtee, 1993.

Lindberg, Folke. *Scandinavia in Great Power Politics, 1905–1908.* Stockholm: Almqvist and Wiksell, 1958.

Lindström, Ulf. *Fascism in Scandinavia, 1920–1940.* Stockohlm: Almqvist and Wiksell, 1985.

Lisk, Jill. *Struggle for Supremacy in the Baltic, 1600–1725.* Birmingham, U.K.: Minerva Press, 1968.

Lundholm, Kjell O., et al. *North Scandinavian History.* Luleå: I-Tryck/Grafiska Huset, 1996.

McFadden, David R., ed. *Scandinavian Modern Design: 1880–1980.* New York: Harry N. Abrams, 1982.

Mead, W. R. *An Historical Geography of Scandinavia.* London: Academic Press, 1981.

Mead, W. R., and Wendy Hall. *Scandinavia.* New York: Walker and Company, 1972.

Nissen, Henrik S. *Scandinavia during the Second World War.* Minneapolis: University of Minnesota Press, 1983.

Nordic Council/Nordic Council of Ministers. *Nordisk statistisk årsbok/Yearbook of Nordic Statistics.* Nordisk udredningsserie. Stockholm and Copenhagen: Nordic Council. This annual publication first appeared in 1962. The translated title became *Nordic Statistical Yearbook* in 1997.

Nordstrom, Byron J., ed. *Dictionary of Scandinavian History.* Westport, Conn.: Greenwood Press, 1986.

Oakley, Stewart P. *Scandinavian History, 1520–1970: A List of Books and Articles in English.* London: Historical Association, 1984.

———. *War and Peace in the Baltic, 1560–1790.* London: Routledge, 1992.

Öberg, Jan, ed. *Nordic Security in the 1990s: Options in the Changing Europe.* London: Pinter Publishers, 1992.

Rossel, Sven. *A History of Scandinavian Literature.* Translated by Anne C. Ulmer. Minneapolis: University of Minnesota Press, 1982.

Rystad, Göran, ed. *Europe and Scandinavia: Aspects of the Process of Integration in the Seventeenth Century.* Lund, Sweden: Lund Series in International History, 1983.

Sawyer, Birgit, and Peter Sawyer. *Medieval Scandinavia.* Minneapolis: University of Minnesota Press, 1993.

Scott, Franklin D. *Scandinavia.* Cambridge: Harvard University Press, 1975.

Shetelig, Haakon. *Scandinavian Archaeology.* Translated by E. V. Gordon. 1937. New York: AMS Press, 1968.

Sinding, Paul C. *History of Scandinavia, from early times . . .* Pittsburgh: W. S. Haven, 1864.

Solem, Erik. *The Nordic Council and Scandinavian Integration.* New York: Praeger, 1977.

Sömme, Axel, ed. *A Geography of Norden.* New York: Wiley and Sons, 1961.

Sundelius, Bengt, ed. *Foreign Policies of Northern Europe.* Boulder, Colo.: Westview Press, 1982.

Swanson, A., and E. Törnqvist, eds. *Europe: The Nordic Countries.* Amsterdam: Rodopi, 1998.

Tägil, Sven, ed. *Ethnicity and Nation Building in the Nordic World.* Carbondale: Southern Illinois University Press, 1995.

Toyne, S. M. *The Scandinavians in History.* 1948. New York: Barnes and Noble Books, 1996.

Turner, Barry, and Gunilla Nordquist. *The Other European Community: Integration and Cooperation in Nordic Europe.* New York: St. Martin's Press, 1982.

Valkeapää, Nils-Aslak. *Greetings from Lappland: The Sami, Europe's Forgotten People.* Translated by Beverly Wahl. London: Zed Press, 1983.

Vikör, Lars S. *The Nordic Languages: Their Status and Interrelations.* Oslo: Novus Press, 1993.

Woolf, S. J. *Fascism in Europe*. London: Methuen, 1981. Contains chapters about Denmark, Finland, and Norway.

Wuorinen, John. *Scandinavia*. Englewood Cliffs, N.J.: Prentice-Hall, 1965.

Zahle, Erik. *A Treasury of Scandinavian Design*. New York: Golden Press, 1961.

Zuck, Virpi, ed. *Dictionary of Scandinavian Literature*. Westport, Conn.: Greenwood Press, 1990.

Denmark

Andersen, Harald Westgård. *Dansk Politik i går og i dag*. Denmark: Fremad, 1982.

Anderson, Robert T. *Denmark, Success of a Developing Nation*. Cambridge, Mass.: Schenkman Publishing, 1975.

Bech, Sven Cedergreen, Erik Kjersgaard, and Jan Danielsen, eds. *Köbenhavns historie*. 6 vols. Copenhagen: Gyldendal, 1980.

Birch, John H. *Denmark in History*. 1938. Westport, Conn.: Greenwood Press, 1975.

Christianson, John R. *On Tycho's Island: Tycho Brahe and His Assistants, 1570–1601*. New York: Cambridge University Press, 1999.

Danstrup, John. *A History of Denmark*. Copenhagen: Wivels Forlag, c. 1947.

Danstrup, John, and Hal Koch, eds. *Danmarks historie*. 14 vols. Copenhagen: Politikens Forlag, 1977.

Glob, P. V. *Denmark: An Archaeological History from the Stone Age to the Vikings*. Translated by Joan Bulman. Ithaca, N.Y.: Cornell University Press, 1971.

Goldberger, Leo, ed. *The Rescue of the Danish Jews: Moral Courage under Stress*. New York: New York University Press, 1987.

Lauring, Palle. *A History of the Kingdom of Denmark*. Translated by David Hohnen. Copenhagen: Höst, 1981.

Logue, John. *Socialism and Abundance: Radical Socialism in the Danish Welfare State*. Minneapolis: University of Minnesota Press, 1982.

Miller, Kenneth E. *Friends and Rivals: Coalition Politics in Denmark, 1901–1995*. Lanham, Md.: University Press of America, 1996.

Molesworth, Robert. *An Account of Denmark As It Was in the Year 1692*. 1694. Copenhagen: Rosenkilde and Bagger, 1976.

Oakley, Stewart P. *A Short History of Denmark*. New York: Praeger, 1972.

Petersen, E. Ladewig. *Fra standssamfund til rangssamfund 1500–1700*. Vol. 3 of *Dansk social historie*. Copenhagen: Gyldendal, 1980.

Rying, Bent. *Danish in the South and the North*. Vol. 2 of *Denmark: History*. Copenhagen: Code Group DK, Royal Danish Ministry of Foreign Affairs, n.d.

Saxo Grammaticus. *The History of the Danes*. Edited by Hilda E. Davidson. Translated by Peter Fisher. Cambridge, Mass.: Rowan and Littlefield, 1979–80.

Steensberg, Axel, ed. *Dagligliv i Danmark*. 8 vols. Copenhagen: Nyt Nordisk Forlag Arnold Busck, 1982.

Strack, Viggo. *Denmark in World History* . . . Philadelphia: University of Pennsylvania Press, 1963.

Stybe, Svend Erik. *Copenhagen University: Five Hundred Years of Science and Scholarship*. Copenhagen: Royal Danish Ministry of Foreign Affairs, 1979.

Thoren, Victor E. *The Lord of Uraniborg: A Biography of Tycho Brahe*. Cambridge: Cambridge University Press, 1990.

Ulfeldt, Leonora Christina. *Memoirs of Leonora Christina* . . . Translated by F. E. Bunnett. New York: E. P. Dutton, 1929.

Faeroe Islands

West, John F. *Faroe: The Emergence of a Nation.* London: C. Hurst and Company, 1972.
———. *The History of the Faroe Islands, 1709–1816.* Vol. 1: 1709–1723. Copenhagen: C.A. Reitzels, 1985.
Wylie, Jonathan. *The Faroe Islands: Interpretations of History.* Lexington: University Press of Kentucky Press, 1987.

Finland

Alapuro, Risto. *State and Revolution in Finland.* Berkeley: University of California Press, 1988.
Chew, Allen F. *The White Death: The Epic of the Soviet-Finnish Winter War.* East Lansing: Michigan State University Press, 1971.
Engle, Eloise, and Lauri Paananen. *The Winter War: The Soviet Attack on Finland, 1939–1940.* Harrisburg, Pa.: Stackpole Books, 1973.
Hall, Wendy. *The Finns and Their Country.* London: Max Parish, 1967.
Hämalainen, Pekka. *In Time of Storm: Revolution, Civil War, and the Ethnolinguistic Issue in Finland.* Albany: State University of New York Press, 1978.
Jakobson, Max. *Diplomacy of the Winter War.* Cambridge: Harvard University Press, 1961.
———. *Finland: Myth and Reality.* Helsinki: Otava, 1987.
———. *Finland Survived: An Account of the Finnish-Soviet Winter War, 1939–1940.* Helsinki: Otava, 1984.
———. *Finnish Neutrality: A Study of Finnish Foreign Policy since the Second World War.* New York: Praeger, 1969.
Jägerskiöld, Stig A. *Mannerheim, Marshall of Finland.* Minneapolis: University of Minnesota Press, 1986.
Jutikkala, Eino, with Kauko Pirinen. *A History of Finland.* Translated by Paul Sjöblom. New York: Frederick A. Praeger, 1962.
Kekkonen, Urho. *Neutrality: The Finnish Position* . . . Translated by P. Ojansuu and L. E. Keyworth. London: Heinemann, 1970.
Kirby, David. *Finland and Russia: 1808–1920* . . . New York: Barnes and Noble Books, 1976.
———. *Finland in the Twentieth Century.* Minneapolis: University of Minnesota Press, 1979.
Klinge, Matti. *A Brief History of Finland.* Helsinki: Otava, 1990.
Koivisto, Mauno. *Witness to History: The Memoirs of Mauno Koivisto, President of Finland, 1982–1994.* Translated by Klaus Törnudd. Carbondale: Southern Illinois University Press, 1997.
Mazour, Anatole. *Finland between East and West.* Princeton, N.J.: Van Norstrand, 1956.
Penttilä, Risto. *Finland's Search for Security through Defence, 1944–89.* London: Macmillan, 1990.

Puntila, L. A. *The Political History of Finland, 1809–1966.* Translated by David Miller. Helsinki: Otava, 1974.

Rintala, Marvin. *Four Finns: Political Profiles.* Berkeley: University of California Press, 1969.

Singleton, Frederick B. *A Short History of Finland.* Cambridge: Cambridge University Press, 1989.

Tanner, Väinö. *The Winter War: Finland against Russia, 1939–1940.* Stanford: Stanford University Press, 1957.

Tillotson, H. M. *Finland at Peace and War, 1918–1993.* Norwich: M. Russell, 1993.

Trotter, William R. *A Frozen Hell: The Russo-Finnish Winter War of 1939–1940.* Chapel Hill, N.C.: Algonquin Books, 1991.

Upton, Anthony. *The Finnish Revolution, 1917–1918.* Minneapolis: University of Minnesota Press, 1980.

Vloyantes, John P. *Silk Glove Hegemony: Finnish-Soviet Relations, 1944–1974.* Kent, Ohio: Kent State University Press, 1975.

Wuorinen, John H. *A History of Finland.* New York: American-Scandinavian Foundation and Columbia University Press, 1965.

Iceland

Byock, Jesse. *Medieval Iceland: Society, Sagas, and Power.* Berkeley: University of California Press, 1988.

Einarsson, Stefan. *A History of Icelandic Literature.* New York: Johns Hopkins Press for the American Scandinavian Foundation, 1986.

Gjerset, Knut. *History of Iceland.* New York: Macmillan, 1924.

Hjálmarsson, Jón R. *History of Iceland: From the Settlement to the Present Day.* Reykjavík: Iceland Review, 1993.

Magnússon, Sigurdur A. *Northern Sphinx: Iceland and the Icelanders from the Settlement to the Present.* London: C. Hurst, 1977; Reykjavík: Snaebjörn Jonsson, 1984.

Thorsteinsson, Björn. *Island.* Translated by Preben M. Sörensen. Politikens Danmarks Historie. Copenhagen: Politikens Forlag, 1985.

Tomasson, Richard F. *Iceland: The First New Society.* Minneapolis: University of Minnesota Press, 1980.

Norway

Cohen, Maynard. *A Stand against Tyranny: Norway's Physicians and the Nazis.* Detroit: Wayne State University Press, 1997.

Dahl, Hans F. *Quisling: A Study in Treachery.* New York: Cambridge University Press, 1999.

Danielsen, Rolf, et al. *Grunntrekk i norsk historie fra vikingtid til våre dager.* Oslo: Universitetsforlaget, 1991.

———. *Norway: A History from the Vikings to Our Own Times.* Translated by Michael Drake. Oslo: Scandinavian University Press, 1995.

Derry, Thomas K. *A History of Modern Norway, 1814–1972.* Oxford: Clarendon Press, 1973.

———. *A History of Norway.* London: Allen and Unwin, 1957.

Eckstein, Harry. *Division and Cohesion in Democracy: A Study of Norway.* Princeton, N.J.: Princeton University Press, 1966.

Gjerset, Knut. *History of the Norwegian People.* New York: Macmillan, 1915.

Greve, Tim. *Haakon VII of Norway.* Translated by Thomas K. Derry. New York: Hippocrene Books, 1983.

Hauglid, Roar, ed. *Native Art of Norway.* New York: Praeger, 1967.

Helle, Knut, ed. *Aschehougs Norges Historie.* 12 vols. Oslo: Aschehoug, 1994.

Hoidal, Oddvar. *Quisling: A Study in Treason.* Oslo: Norwegian University Press, 1989.

Hubbard, William H., et al, eds. *Making a Historical Culture: Historiography in Norway.* Oslo: Scandinavian University Press, 1995.

Kiel, Anne C. *Continuity and Change: Aspects of Contemporary Norway.* Oslo: Scandinavian University Press, 1993.

Kurzman, Dan. *Blood and Water: Sabotaging Hitler's Bomb.* New York: Henry Holt, 1997.

Larsen, Karen. *A History of Norway.* Princeton, N.J.: Princeton University Press for the American-Scandinavian Foundation, 1948.

Lindgren, Raymond E. *Norway-Sweden: Union, Disunion, and Scandinavian Integration.* Princeton, N.J.: Princeton University Press, 1959.

Lovoll, Odd S. *The Promise Fulfilled: A Portrait of Norwegian Americans Today.* Minneapolis: University of Minnesota Press, 1998.

————. *The Promise of America: A History of the Norwegian-American People.* Rev. ed. Minneapolis: University of Minnesota Press, 1999.

Midgaard, John. *A Brief History of Norway.* Oslo: Tanum, 1969.

Mykland, Knut, ed. *Norges Historie.* 15 vols. Oslo: J. W. Cappelens Forlag, 1977.

Nelson, Marion, ed. *Norwegian Folk Art: The Migration of a Tradition.* New York: Museum of American Folk Art; Oslo, Norwegian Folk Museum, 1995.

Popperwell, Ronald G. *Norway.* London: Benn, 1972.

Riste, Olav. *Norway, 1940–45: The Resistance Movement.* Oslo: Tanum, 1984.

Selbyg, Arne. *Norway Today: An Introduction to Modern Norwegian Society.* Oslo: Norwegian University Press, 1986.

Stewart, Janice S. *The Folk Arts of Norway.* New York: Dover Publications, 1972.

Stokker, Kathleen. *Folklore Fights the Nazis . . .* Madison, N.J.: Fairleigh Dickinson University Press, 1995.

Storing, James A. *Norwegian Democracy.* Boston: Houghton Mifflin, 1963.

Ström, Kaare, and Lars Svåsand, eds. *Challenges to Political Parties: The Case of Norway.* Ann Arbor: University of Michigan Press, 1997.

Vigness, Paul G. *The German Occupation of Norway.* New York: Vantage Press, 1970.

Sweden

Ahlund, Nils G. *Gustav Adolf, the Great.* Translated by Michael Roberts. Princeton, N.J.: Princeton University Press, 1940.

Ahnlund, Erik, Ingrid Hammarström, and Torgny Nevéus, eds. *Historia kring Stockholm: Stockholm från förhistorisk tid till sekelskiftet.* Stockholm: Wahlström and Widstrand, 1965–67.

Åkerman, Susanna. *Queen Christina of Sweden and Her Circle: The Transformation of a Seventeenth Century Philosophical Libertine.* Leiden: E. J. Brill, 1991.

Andersson, Ingvar. *A History of Sweden.* Translated by Carolyn Hannay. New York: Praeger, 1956.

Andrén, Nils. *Power-Balance and Non-Alignment: A Perspective on Swedish Foreign Policy.* Stockholm: Almqvist and Wiksell, 1967.

Bain, Robert Nisbet. *Charles XII and the Collapse of the Swedish Empire, 1682–1719.* New York: G. P. Putnam's, 1902.

Behre, Göran, Lars-Olaf Larsson, and Eva Österberg. *Sveriges historia 1521–1809: Stormaktsdröm och småstatsrealiteter.* Stockholm: Esselte Studium AB, 1985.

Bengtsson, Frans G. *The Sword Does Not Jest: The Heroic Life of King Charles XII of Sweden.* Translated by Naomi Walford. New York: St. Martin's Press, 1960.

Board, Joseph. *The Government and Politics of Sweden.* Boston: Houghton Mifflin, 1970.

Boman, Monica, ed. *Design in Sweden.* Translated by Roger Tanner. Stockholm: Swedish Institute, 1985.

Carlgren, W. M. *Swedish Foreign Policy during the Second World War.* Translated by Arthur Spencer. New York: St. Martin's Press, 1977.

Carlsson, Sten, and Jerker Rosén. *Svenska Historia.* 2 vols. Stockholm: Esselte Studium, 1980.

Cornell, Jan, director; Sten Carlsson and Jerker Rosén, principal authors; and Gunvor Grenholm, principal editor. *Den svenska historien.* 15 vols. Stockholm: Bonniers, 1966–68. Rev. Ed. 1992–93.

Daun, Åke. *Swedish Mentality.* Translated by Jan Teeland. University Park: Pennsylvania State University Press, 1996.

Defoe, Daniel. *The History of the Wars of His Late Majesty Charles XII, King of Sweden . . .* London, 1720.

Englund, Peter. *Poltava: Berättelsen om en armés undergång.* Stockholm: Atlantis, 1988.

Freeman, Ruth. *Death of a Statesman: The Solution to the Murder of Olof Palme.* London: Hale, 1989.

Gould, D. E. *Historical Dictionary of Stockholm.* Lanham, Md.: Scarecrow Press, 1997.

Hadenius, Stig. *The Riksdag in Focus: Swedish History in a Parliamentary Perspective.* Stockholm: Swedish Parliament, 1997.

———. *Swedish Politics during the Twentieth Century.* Stockholm: Swedish Institute, 1985.

Hallendorff, Carl J., and Adolf Schück. *History of Sweden.* Translated by Lajia Yapp. 1929. New York: AMS Press, 1970.

Hancock, Donald. *Sweden: The Politics of Postindustrial Change.* Hinsdale, Ill.: Dryden Press, 1972.

Hatton, Ragnhild M. *Charles XII of Sweden.* New York: Weybright and Talley, 1969.

Hinshaw, David. *Sweden: Champion of Peace.* New York: G. P. Putnam's, 1949.

Klein, Barbro, and Mats Widbom, eds. *Swedish Folk Art: All Tradition Is Change.* New York: H. N. Abrams, 1994.

Koblik, Steven. *The Stones Cry Out: Sweden's Response to the Persecution of the Jews, 1933–1945.* Translated by David Mel Paul and Margareta Paul. New York: Holocaust Library, 1988.

———. *Sweden: The Neutral Victor: Sweden and the Western Powers, 1917–1918. A Study of Anglo-American-Swedish Relations.* Stockholm: Läromedelsförlag, 1972.

Larsson, Thomas B., and Hans Lundmark, eds. *Approaches to Swedish Prehistory: A Spectrum of Problems and Perspectives in Contemporary Research.* Oxford: B.A.R. 1989.

Levine, Paul. *From Indifference to Activism: Swedish Diplomacy and the Holocaust.* Uppsala: Ubsaliensis S. Academiae, 1996.

Lindkvist, Lennart, ed. *Design in Sweden.* Translated by Claude Stephenson. Stockholm: Svenska institutet, 1977.

Lindqvist, Herman. *Historien om Sverige.* Stockholm: Norstedts, 1994–. Multivolume project survey of Swedish history.

Lindroth, Sten. *A History of Uppsala University, 1477–1977.* Uppsala: Uppsala University, 1976.

Losman, Arne, et al. *The Age of New Sweden.* Stockholm: Livrustkammaren, 1988.

MacKenzie, Faith C. *The Sibyl of the North: The Tale of Christina, Queen of Sweden.* Boston: Houghton Mifflin, 1921.

Masson, Georgina. *Queen Christina.* New York: Farrar, Straus and Giroux, 1968–69.

Metcalf, Michael. *Russia, England, and Swedish Party Politics, 1762–1766 . . .* Stockholm: Almqvist and Wiksell, 1977.

———, ed. *The Riksdag: A History of the Swedish Parliament.* New York: St. Martin's Press, 1987. A translation of *Riksdagen genom tiderna.*

Milner, Henry. *Sweden: Social Democracy in Practice.* Oxford: Oxford University Press, 1989.

Misgeld, Klaus, Karl Molin, and Klas Åmark. *Creating Social Democracy: A Century of the Social Democratic Labor Party in Sweden.* 1988. University Park: Pennsylvania State Press, 1992.

Moberg, Vilhelm. *A History of the Swedish People.* Translated by Paul Britten Austen. 2 vols. New York: Pantheon, 1972–73.

Mosey, Chris. *Cruel Awakening: Sweden and the Killing of Olof Palme.* New York: St. Martin's Press, 1991.

Ohlmarks, Åke, and Nils Erik Baehrendtz. *Svenska krönikan.* Stockholm: Forum, 1981.

Olsson, Nils-Olof. *Stockholm: Seen by Five Centuries of Artists.* Translated by Paul Britten Austin. Stockholm: Stockholmia Förlag, 1997.

Plath, Iona. *The Decorative Arts of Sweden.* New York: Dover, 1966.

Ringmar, Erik. *Identity, Interest, and Action: A Cultural Explanation of Sweden's Intervention in the Thirty Years War.* Cambridge: Cambridge University Press, 1996.

Roberts, Michael. *The Age of Liberty: Sweden, 1719–1772.* Cambridge: Cambridge University Press, 1985.

———. *The Early Vasas: A History of Sweden, 1523–1611.* London: Cambridge University Press, 1968.

———. *Essays in Swedish History.* Minneapolis: University of Minnesota Press, 1967.

———. *From Oxenstierna to Charles XII: Four Studies.* Cambridge: Cambridge University Press, 1991.

———. *Gustavus Adolphus.* London: Longman, 1992.

———. *Gustavus Adolphus and the Rise of Sweden.* London: English University Press, 1973.

————. *Sweden as a Great Power, 1611–1697.* New York: St. Martin's Press, 1968.

————. *The Swedish Imperial Experience, 1560–1718.* Cambridge: Cambridge University Press, 1979.

————, ed. *Sweden's Age of Greatness, 1632–1718.* New York: St. Martin's Press, 1973.

Rothstein, Bo. *The Social Democratic State: The Swedish Model and the Bureaucratic Problem of Social Reforms.* Pittsburgh: University of Pittsburgh Press, 1996.

Rustow, Dankwart A. *The Politics of Compromise: A Study of Parties and Cabinet Government in Sweden.* Princeton, N.J.: Princeton University Press, 1955.

Scobbie, Irene. *Historical Dictionary of Sweden.* No. 7 of *European Historical Dictionaries.* Metuchen, N.J.: Scarecrow Press, 1995.

Scott, Franklin D., with Steven Koblik. *Sweden: The Nation's History.* Carbondale: Southern Illinois University Press, 1988.

Stolpe, Sven. *Christina of Sweden.* Edited by Alec Randall. Translated by Alec Randall and Ruth Bethell. New York: Macmillan, 1966.

Stomberg, Andrew A. *A History of Sweden.* New York: Macmillan, 1931.

Sundelius, Bengt, ed. *The Committed Neutral: Sweden's Foreign Policy.* Boulder, Colo.: Westview Press, 1989.

Tingsten, Herbert. *The Debate on the Foreign Policy of Sweden, 1918–1939.* Translated by Joan Bulman. London: Oxford University Press, 1949.

Trulsson, Sven G. *British and Swedish Politics and Strategies in the Baltic after the Peace of Tilsit in 1807 . . .* Lund: Gleerup, 1976.

Upton, Anthony F. *Charles XI and Swedish Absolutism.* Cambridge: Cambridge University Press, 1998.

Voltaire, Francois M. A. *Voltaire's History of Charles XII, King of Sweden.* Translated by Winifred Todhunter. 1908. New York: E. P. Dutton, 1912.

Wallentin, Hans. *Svenska folkets historia.* Verdandi-debatt 83. Stockholm: Prisma/Verdandi, 1978.

Periodicals

American Scandinavian Review, 1913–75
Historisk tidsskrift (Danish), 1840/1857–
Historisk tidsskrift (Norwegian), 1871–
Historisk tidskrift (Swedish), 1881–
Historisk tidskrift för Finland, 1916–
Scandia, 1928–86
Scandinavian Economic History Review, 1953–
Scandinavian Journal of History, 1976–
Scandinavian Review, 1975– (new title, replaced *American Scandinavian Review*)
Scandinavian Studies, 1911–
Scandinavica, 1961–

Electronic Sources

The Nordic Pages at http://www.markovits.com/nordic/. This is an entrance point for hundreds of other Internet sites related to Scandinavia.

Index

Byron J. Nordstrom is professor of history and Scandinavian studies at Gustavus Adolphus College, where he has taught since 1974. He has held visiting appointments at Pacific Lutheran University, the University of Washington, and the University of East Anglia. He is editor of *Dictionary of Scandinavian History,* author of numerous articles and papers on Swedish-American history, and the current editor of *The Swedish-American Historical Quarterly.*